' C0061 69184

D1582100

The Nicholas Cases

The Nicholas Cases

Casualties of Justice

Bob Woffinden

Bojangles Books

Published and printed entirely in the UK.

Published in 2016 by Bojangles Books

www.bojanglesbooks.com

Copyright © Bob Woffinden

Bob Woffinden has asserted his right under the Copyright,
Designs and patents Act 1988 to be identified as the author
of this work.

A CIP catalogue record for this book is available from
the British Library.

Design: David Eldridge of Two Associates

Typesetting: Judith Fisher at Regent Typesetting, London E8 4RT

Set in 12pt Monotype Bembo

Printed and bound by
TJ International, Padstow, Cornwall PL28 8RW

Production manager for Bojangles Books: Anne Culliford

The moral right of the author has been asserted

All rights reserved. No part of this publication may be reproduced,
stored in or introduced into a retrieval system, or transmitted, in
any form or by any means (electronic, mechanical, photocopying,
recording or otherwise) without the prior permission of both the
copyright owner and the publisher of the book.

ISBN: 978-0-9930755-0-6
eISBN: 978-0-9930755-1-3

For my parents,
Joan and Ray

Glasgow Life Glasgow Libraries	
L	
C 006169184	
Askews & Holts	25-May-2016
364.941 C	£20.00

Injustice anywhere is a threat to justice everywhere

Inscription at UK Supreme Court, Parliament Square, London

Contents

Prologue

In early Byzantine times, Myra was the capital of that part of Asia Minor known as the Lycian coast. It was there, sometime around 330AD, that a local businessman bribed the governor, Eustathius, to sentence three young men to death. The details of the dispute are not recorded, but it is clear that the three had done no wrong.

When news of their impending fate reached the local Bishop, he rushed to the site where the execution was scheduled to take place. In a rescue as dramatic as any contrived by Hollywood, he gripped the arm of the executioner just as he was about to sever the head of the first of the three men. He prevailed upon him to stop, and then went to confront Eustathius. The governor was soon admitting his shame and, thoroughly penitent, begging for forgiveness. The three men were set free. The Bishop had given them back their lives.

As it happened, the Bishop, whose name was Nicholas, had personal experience of injustice. Some years earlier, he had suffered torture and wrongful imprisonment, a victim of the persecution of Christians ordered by the Emperor Diocletian. He was only freed after Diocletian was succeeded by Constantine.

Nicholas's saving of the three condemned men was hardly a miracle – it was perhaps just a timely intervention by a man of natural authority – but a miracle soon ensued. The events at Myra had been witnessed by three officers of the imperial army who were en route to Phrygia. After completing their tour of duty, they returned to Constantinople. Unfortunately, they fell into disfavour with the Prefect Ablavius. He had them imprisoned on false charges, but then went further and obtained a warrant from Constantine for their execution.

The soldiers recalled what they had seen in Myra and prayed to Bishop Nicholas, asking him to intercede in some way. That night, he appeared in a dream to the Emperor. In the morning, Constantine sent for Ablavius, who then related that he had had exactly the same dream. So Constantine released the three men and had them brought before him. Having given them back their liberty, he asked them to return to Myra to deliver a letter to Nicholas, in which he asked the Bishop to pray for the peace of the world.

In the years before this, Nicholas had already won a reputation for benevolence and great kindliness. His parents died when he was a young man, leaving him a large inheritance which enabled him to make generous disbursements to the poor and needy. One particular example has been narrated down the centuries. A merchant in Patara, where Nicholas was born, lost all his money and could not afford dowries for his three daughters. This necessarily meant (it seems) that, unmarried, they would be forced into prostitution.

However, the family was spared this calamity. One night, a bag of gold, sufficient for the eldest girl's dowry, was lobbed into the house. A second dowry duly arrived in the same way. The merchant stayed up all night in order to discover, when it happened a third time, the identity of their benefactor; it was Nicholas.

During his lifetime, therefore, popular knowledge of Nicholas's good works and intense spirituality was widely established. He died on 6 December 343 and was buried, as was his wish, in Myra. A church was built over his tomb. The cult surrounding his life grew and Myra became a centre for pilgrimage. He became a saint through popular acclaim; in those days, there was no official canonisation process. The first life of St Nicholas was written by St Methodius, the patriarch of Constantinople, a prolific author who died in 847.

The church in Myra was destroyed by Arab invaders, but under the patronage of Constantine X was rebuilt in 1043.

During that time, with the Byzantine Empire in its very protracted death throes, the cities of Venice and Bari, ports in what we now know as northern and southern Italy respectively, vied for maritime influence and ascendancy. Venice had stolen a march on its rival in 828 when Venetian merchants plundered the body of St Mark from his tomb in Alexandria. They carried it off in triumph back to Venice, where a magnificent basilica was built for it along-side the Doge's palace. Through the centuries thereafter, the relics accrued enormous religious, political and commercial advantage. Rarely has crime been so munificently rewarded.

After 1071, when much of Asia Minor was lost to the Seljuk Turks, opportunist citizens of Bari saw the chance for some plundering of their own. Merchants anchored at Myra and made straight for Nicholas's church, which was guarded by four monks. The merchants firstly tried to persuade them to hand over the body; then tried to deceive them, saying that Nicholas had appeared in a dream to the Pope, asking to be re-interred in the Holy Roman Empire. The monks weren't fooled. So, both strategies having failed, the merchants resorted to brute force. They overpowered the monks and broke open the sarcophagus.

As they seized the body, an oily substance was said to flow from the tomb. (Some have thought this was myrrh, since Myra is associated with the Greek name for myrrh, although it is doubtful whether it was produced in the region at that time.) The Bari adventurers collected it in vials before making off with the holy relics. The looting and the desecration of the tomb naturally caused the local people enormous grief.

On 9 May 1087, the merchants arrived back in Bari with their spoils. San Sabino was instantly demoted from his position as the city's saint to be replaced by San Nicola, who was entombed in the church of St John the Baptist while more suitable accommodation was prepared. One hundred and ten years later, in 1197, the Basilica di San Nicola was consecrated.

The oil flowing from the tomb, now termed Manna di San Nicola, was apparently unaffected by the long journey through the eastern Mediterranean. Known for its medicinal properties, it reputedly continues to flow to this day (which explains the saint's enduring association with perfumers). Again, pilgrims were attracted from across the world – a further example that, so far as the medieval church was concerned, crime didn't merely pay, it reaped boundless reward.

During the centuries, the myths surrounding St Nicholas and his life mushroomed. He came to be regarded as a thaumaturge, or wonder-worker, and was adopted as patron saint of countless professions and places. According to some versions of the tale of the three dowryless daughters, the bags of gold that were lobbed into the house landed in the girls' stockings. The detail launched the legend. So it is that, every year, St Nicholas's alter ego, Santa Claus, arrives to deliver presents directly into children's houses and, by custom, into their stockings.

St Nicholas is today one of the most industrious figures in the Christian church. He is charged with ministering to the needs of, amongst many others, children, sailors, travellers and pawnbrokers, as well as perfumers and those wrongly accused. He has been entrusted with safeguarding the entire populations of Russia and Greece, not to mention all those on the island of Manhattan.

But, despite the wonders associated with his name over the centuries, it must be pointed out that in the work by St Methodius – the original biographical source – the only miracle attributed to him is the overturning of the death sentences on the three soldiers. So, for all the great host of supplicants, it is the wrongly accused who have the prior claim on his saintly favours.

THIS BOOK relates the stories of English lives that have been destroyed by malfunctioning criminal justice processes. In theory, wrongful conviction should not necessarily ensue from wrongful arrest and charge, but in practice there is a dismal inevitability about it. The trial process is supposed to be the mechanism for separating the guilty from the not-guilty; but it has been battered, betrayed and broken, in the most part through imprudent political meddling.

However, the book is not just about the failure of the criminal justice process. It is also about the failure of journalism – a triple failure. It is not merely that the media fails to draw attention to wrongful convictions when they occur; it is not just that trials leading to these injustices are misleadingly reported; it is that in some instances the media itself has played a key role in bringing about the wrongful conviction.

But beyond the failures of the criminal justice process and of contemporary journalism, what these cases also represent is the failure of England: the failure to protect and preserve what was decent and best in the country; the failure to recognise that some traditions had an almost sacred significance and needed to be properly nurtured.

Apart from the fact that those wrongly imprisoned, or someone on their behalf, asked for my assistance with their case, there is nothing to connect them. I have tried to explain the personalities involved, and their interrupted lives; and the circumstances in which, on a particular date when their destiny was changed forever, they were tossed into the maelstrom of the criminal justice system; and what happened next.

These are real lives that are being destroyed by errors in criminal justice proceedings; and yet after the trial, when the wrongly-convicted person must engage with both prison and the appeal process, an implacable refusal to countenance error becomes the dominant theme. The inertia which is the central feature of England's criminal justice machinery is there for a reason: to sap the spiritual and material resources of all those who would wish to challenge it.

Just about all of us who were students at the end of the 1960s knew about the *Desiderata*, Max Ehrmann's inspiring prose poem ('With all its sham, drudgery and broken dreams, it is still a beautiful world'). There wasn't an internet in those days, but *Desiderata* went viral anyway. One of its most affecting ideas was that everyone had their story to tell. So here are the stories of some of those who have not had the opportunity to tell them themselves; up until now, their stories have been falsely told. Whether those lives are ordinary or extraordinary, here they are.

The lives chosen did not have to be these; there could have been an entirely different selection. As the twenty-first century unfolds in the UK, there are many, many to choose from. St Nicholas's workload gets heavier and heavier.

Chapter 1

The phone set to discreet

Glyn Razzell's story

1

On Tuesday 19 March 2002, just after 9.00 in the morning, Linda Razzell disappeared. She parked her car near where she worked at Swindon College, but never arrived at work.

Linda and her husband, Glyn Razzell, had four children, but their marriage had ended acrimoniously. Linda had twice made allegations of violence against her husband that led to criminal proceedings. Divorce proceedings were well under way and both were living with different partners.

About sixteen hours later, shortly after one o'clock in the morning, Wiltshire police knocked up Razzell and his partner and questioned them. This house was searched, as were their cars – although Razzell explained that during the day he had not been using his own Ford Galaxy but his friend's Renault Laguna. So that car, too, was searched. The home that Razzell had shared with Linda was searched. Police cut holes in the carpet, broke up the paving slabs on the garden path and patio, took the waste-traps from the bath and sinks and removed the filter from the washing machine.

From all these investigations, no evidence emerged.

The following year, however, Razzell was convicted of his wife's murder. Blood spots had been found in the Laguna, albeit only at the fourth inspection. Having been sentenced to life imprisonment, Razzell continued to protest not just that he hadn't murdered his wife, but that she wasn't even dead.

Nor were these empty assertions of innocence. The fact that he had been driving his friend's car that day became an absolutely key feature of the case. It meant that there was only one day on which he could have murdered her – and Linda was seen alive the day after.

THE ELDEST OF four children, Glyn Razzell was born in Chelmsford, Essex, on 18 July 1959 and brought up in the nearby village of Ingatestone. His father worked in insurance in the City of London, a career path that Razzell followed when he left school in 1977. He too went to work in the City, at the head office of the Midland Bank, though within a year he had joined a firm of stockbrokers.

He took a keen interest in orienteering and had been part of the British junior team at events in Austria and Switzerland in 1975. Returning from a Duke of Edinburgh Awards expedition to the Brecon Beacons on 17 April 1979, he met Linda Davies on a train. Linda, who was born on 12 April 1960, was returning from her home in Carmarthen to Reading University, where she was a first-year languages student. He helped her with her luggage. They exchanged addresses. They got on well with each other.

As part of her course Linda spent the 1980-81 academic year in Paris, where Razzell visited her about once a month. Soon after moving there she began to suffer panic attacks, which were initially attributed to tachycardia (an abnormally fast heartbeat). She lived in fear of having a heart attack, her mother having died from a heart problem when Linda was seven. She was then diagnosed with anxiety nervosa, for which she was prescribed beta-blockers and tranquillisers.

Her illness became worse after she returned to England. She became agoraphobic and had a great deal of time off sick. She took her finals in the university medical centre. Over the next few years, she was treated at both Goodmayes Hospital in Essex and the Seymour Clinic psychiatric unit in Swindon.

Razzell felt he couldn't desert her and believed her medical problems would abate. There were no emotional problems with the relationship; Razzell respected Linda's intelligence and found her good company. In March 1984, he got a job with Dunbar Bank, part of Hambro Life Assurance in Swindon. With this new financial security, and a generous relocation package, they were able to buy a house and get married.

However, Linda was unable to work. She stayed at home and was kept under medical supervision. In August 1985, she suffered a particularly tragic bereavement. At the wedding of her eldest brother in Llandaff, near Cardiff, she accompanied her father into the vestry to sign the register as a witness. Suddenly the guests heard her scream. Linda's father had collapsed. Having suffered a massive heart attack, he was certified dead on arrival at hospital.

Her health began to improve after Catherine, their eldest daughter, was born in December 1987. Over those next years, the stock market was booming and Razzell's career went well. He moved to the unit trust division of his company. The family began to take holidays in France and in 1992 moved to a larger home in Highworth, just to the north of Swindon. That year, Linda started helping to run a local playgroup as deputy to Jolanda Gingell. This was something she kept up for several years.

After the deregulation of the financial market in Sweden, Razzell saw an opportunity to sell investments there. He helped to set up a Stockholm office, and from 1993 until 1996 regularly travelled to the country.

With Razzell's absences, the marriage came under strain. It became especially difficult after the birth of their fourth child in 1996, perhaps because Linda had become very frustrated about her situation. While her husband's career was going well, she had never even had a career and was now unable to break away from childcare, though Razzell also recognised that she may have felt stifled and have come to regard her relationship with him as unexciting and unfulfilling. Nor did she share many of his interests, like walking.

With a growing family, they still needed more room and, in 1998, embarked on building an extension to the house. It was the following summer – in August 1999, at the time of the total eclipse of the sun, when they were on holiday in France – that Linda admitted to Razzell that she'd had an affair with one of the builders.

She had also told a close friend. It seemed to have been, for her at least, a torrid relationship. The friend stated:

[Linda] came round for coffee and blurted out that she was having an affair with one of the builders who was working on their extension ... She was besotted with [him] ... She had sex with him in the house, she would go upstairs with him while the children were downstairs ... on one occasion she locked herself in the garage with him ... She told me she had sex with him at a mobile home near Lechlade ... One day she persuaded me to go for a walk with her because he was working nearby ... She would park outside his house ... [she would] follow him home if she saw the van ... she was crazy about him.

However, Linda belatedly learned that her lover had a reputation locally for bedding married women while their husbands were out at work.

After that, the marriage swiftly disintegrated. In May 2000, Linda initiated divorce proceedings and in June she disappeared. It turned out that she'd taken the children with her to Wales. She'd told friends that she had to move out as Razzell was beating her up – an allegation that he emphatically denied. She returned after a few days but then disappeared again in the second half of July. This time, she was away for a fortnight; she had again gone to her family in Wales.

Shortly after her return, with Razzell about to take out a court order against her, she alleged that he had kicked her. He was charged with common assault. She then made an affidavit which listed a series of alleged violent attacks on her. The case was heard in February 2001. After the magistrates had heard that Linda's allegations had been made straight after court papers had been served on her, and that there were numerous inconsistencies between her affidavit and a statement she had given to police, they acquitted Razzell.

By then, he had found a new partner in Rachel Smith, a much younger work colleague. In August 2000 he had moved out to rented accommodation.

Linda had started work, for just a few hours a week, as a learning support assistant at Swindon College. She began a new relationship with Malcolm Fereday, the husband of one of her closest friends. Razzell found out when Angela Fereday, in some distress, phoned to tell him. Again, Linda confided in the friend to whom she'd spilled the beans previously, as the friend recalled:

She said it's Malcolm, we've fallen in love and he's moved in with me. I remember being stood there open-mouthed. I was really shocked, I remember saying, 'Angela's husband?'

I didn't agree with what Linda had done. Angela had done so much for her, and for Linda to have a relationship with her husband was wrong. That was the last time I spoke with Linda … I felt that I couldn't support her any more. I couldn't condone her and Malcolm being together.

Fereday moved in to the house that had formerly been the Razzells' family home. He was there in the early evening of Saturday 19 May 2001 when Razzell arrived to drop off one of the children. There was some friction and Linda angrily stood in front of the door to remonstrate with Razzell as he was leaving. He tried to get past her, and she fell backwards through a glass panel in the porch. As she did so, she grabbed his arm for support, with the result that the second finger of his right hand was badly cut on the jagged edge of the broken pane.

They were both taken to hospital. Razzell had fourteen stitches put in the finger and was then arrested. Linda had made a statement, corroborated by Fereday, asserting that Razzell had violently attacked her and pushed her onto the broken glass.

Razzell's friends were alert enough to notice that, while the police took photographs of Linda, they took none of him, which completely distorted the evidence-gathering process. So they took timed and dated photographs of his arms and hands. The case was then set down for trial at Swindon Crown Court, but would not be heard for several months.

Razzell's company, by now part of Zurich Assurance, had announced a number of job cuts across the UK and at the end of the year he was one of those made redundant. He would be due a redundancy package of £68,700 and could keep the company car until March 2002. As he was not receiving a salary, however, his maintenance payments to Linda stopped.

With a criminal trial hanging over him, he was in no position to seek work immediately, so he and Rachel went on a four-week walking holiday in New Zealand.

The assault trial began on 18 February. A doctor specialising in glass injuries had studied the photographs and had access to the hospital records. He described Linda's injuries as 'superficial cuts' and said that, had the accounts of Linda and Fereday been accurate, then he would have expected to see more serious, and different forms, of injury; whereas Razzell's account was consistent with the medical and photographic evidence. Razzell was again acquitted.

During the week beginning Monday 11 March, Razzell made travel arrangements for two trips abroad: the first, to the Le Mans 24-hour car race in France with two friends, one of whom was Mike Sutcliffe, a colleague who had also just been made redundant by Zurich (the three of them had also been to Le Mans together the two previous years); the second, a three-day trip to Prague for a stag weekend as part of his brother's forthcoming wedding celebrations. Razzell was to be best man. Meanwhile, a third trip was being planned. Sutcliffe booked ferry tickets for himself, Razzell and another friend for a day-trip the following Tuesday. On this occasion, they were going only as far as Calais in order to stock up with French wine and other provisions.

Thursday 14 March was the first day of the divorce hearing, with financial issues on the agenda. Linda's lawyers asked for an order freezing Razzell's redundancy money, but the judge refused to give it. The next day, Friday, Linda's lawyers applied again and this time it was granted – despite the fact that Razzell was not informed about the hearing and was given no chance to respond. In these circumstances, hardly surprisingly, there was a mix-up and the judge froze the wrong bank account (Razzell's current account, not the one containing the large redundancy package). Even so, Razzell, who found out about the order on the Saturday morning, obviously needed to get it unfrozen straightaway.

He spoke to his lawyer on Monday morning. She advised him to be ready to get back into court at a moment's notice; with luck, she'd be able to get a hearing for the next day. Accordingly, he had to pull out of the day trip to France. His friends would go without him. As his Ford Galaxy people-carrier was the largest of their vehicles, he agreed to swap cars with Mike Sutcliffe, who owned a silver Renault Laguna. These were company cars and there were no insurance problems. While Sutcliffe took the Galaxy across the Channel, Razzell had the Laguna for almost exactly thirty-one hours, from 2.30pm on the Monday.

On Tuesday evening, 19 March, at the Pheasant Inn near Hungerford, Razzell met the others on their return from France. The ferry had been delayed by about 40 minutes, and by then it was 9.30pm. They took back their own cars and, as it was a wet evening, drove back to Sutcliffe's house in South Cerney to share out the wine and food.

As they were doing so, the police were already starting inquiries into Linda's disappearance.

THAT MORNING, LINDA and Fereday left home a little late, at about 8.40. Linda dropped off three of the children (the other one walked to school with friends), as well as Fereday. It must have been just after 9.00 when she parked her car, a red Ford Escort.

During the morning Fereday attended a school function for the youngest child and afterwards phoned Linda to ask if she needed any shopping. He got no reply. Towards lunchtime, he said he rang the college to speak to her, but was told that she was unavailable as she was with a student. In the afternoon, he went to the Honda factory, where he worked, to begin his shift at 3.30.

Catherine, who was then fourteen, telephoned at 6.24 to tell him that the two youngest children had not been picked up from their after-school club. While she arranged for them to be collected, Fereday immediately rang his local police station to report Linda missing. That call was made at 6.28. He then made arrangements to leave work immediately. (His shift was due to finish at midnight.)

Once the children were all back at home, they began texting their mother. One of their texts read:

All we want is for you to come home, but if you feel you can't, that's fine.

At 9.33 Fereday again contacted police to say that he knew where Linda parked her car, and that he was going to look for it. At 10.15, he rang Catherine to say he'd found the car, in its customary position, and then at 10.17 he called the police to tell them he had found it.

Three hours later, at a quarter past one in the morning, Wiltshire Police called on Razzell and Rachel Smith. Despite the anti-social hour, Razzell tried not to be impolite. He got in stepladders from the garage so that they could look in his loft. They asked if Linda had disappeared before, so he told them about the two occasions in 2000 when she had suddenly gone to Wales.

During Wednesday afternoon, Razzell was questioned again, this time for four-and-a-half hours. Scene-of-crime officers arrived to search both the house and the cars (his own and Rachel's). They took away the shoes and clothes that Razzell had worn the previous day.

At the same time, the police spoke to Fereday at the house where he was now living with Linda. While officers were talking to him, scene-of-crime experts were searching his home address. They took away a number of exhibits, but it is what they did not find that is of the utmost importance: they did not find a blood-stained T-shirt under the bed.

That same afternoon, also, Mike Sutcliffe found two detectives waiting for him when he got home at 4.30. They interviewed him and briefly inspected his Renault Laguna. Then, at 6.50 that evening, the car was properly examined by a scene-of-crime team. Again, what is important is what wasn't found; as they reported, there were 'no signs of blood or recent cleaning'.

However, there was a key development in the case at that time. At about 5.00 that afternoon, Linda's mobile phone was found close to garages in the alleyway she would have cut through on her way to work.

There was, though, an oddity about this: the phone was set to discreet (or quiet). This didn't make sense. If Linda had been carrying it on her way to work, why would she have set it to discreet?

The police decided to examine the Laguna properly. They asked Sutcliffe to drive it to Swindon Police Station. He did so, and it was in police possession from 10.15 in the morning on Thursday 21 March. It was taken to the forensic examinations bay where specialist officers undertook a five-hour inspection of the car in ideal conditions. In the course of that, thirty-six separate exhibits were taken and the officers used four different techniques, including ones with special chemicals and ultra-violet equipment, to look for blood. At the end, there was no evidence of Linda's blood, or indeed any blood at all, in the car.

Meanwhile, the police held a press conference about Linda's disappearance, at which Fereday made an emotional plea for her safe return. By then, his house had also been searched by police.

On Friday 22 March, officers arrived at Razzell's home and questioned him for eleven hours. His computer and mobile phone were taken for analysis.

On the Sunday, having held the Laguna for three days, police returned it to Sutcliffe. Nothing had been found to connect the car with Linda's disappearance. By then it was in a grubby state, with fingerprint powder and various chemicals covering many surfaces. Sutcliffe used it to take his dog for a woodland walk and also took the household rubbish to the local site. Then, on 26 March, he cleaned it thoroughly.

Undeterred by the absence of incriminating evidence, the police arrested Razzell on suspicion of murder. He was taken to Swindon Police Station on Wednesday 27 March and held for forty-eight hours while he was further questioned and his house examined again. One of the items police now found was a makeshift noose in the loft; Razzell explained that, in a state of utter despair about the recent upheavals in his life, he had momentarily toyed with suicide.

At the end of the week – it happened to be Good Friday – he was released at 5.30pm. The previous day, however, police had taken in the Laguna for a fourth examination. It was a week after the previous inspection. Wiltshire Police have never revealed what led them to take what must at the time have seemed an entirely pointless action.

This time, they found blood spots. A DNA profile for Linda was obtained from a local hospital and a partial match was obtained with the blood in the car.

That scientific evidence led to Razzell's arrest seven weeks later. There was still no information about what had happened to Linda.

No trace of her had been found. Nevertheless, on 16 May, the day before he had been due to go to Prague for his brother's stag weekend, Razzell was charged with her murder.

He was remanded into custody and had to remain there for several weeks while his lawyers sorted out bail. An attempt to get him bailed in June was defeated after the Crown Prosecution Service told the judge that he had tried to contact key prosecution witnesses from prison and that, because he had been applying for work in Eastern Europe, there was a high risk of his absconding.

It is extraordinary that the CPS can put forward nonsense in an English courtroom with complete impunity. In fact, Razzell had never contacted anyone in Eastern Europe or applied for work outside the UK; and the only potential prosecution witness he had tried to contact was Mike Sutcliffe, merely in order to tell him where he could find the tickets for the Le Mans trip.

'I later heard that the CPS had written to the judge to apologise for misleading him', commented Razzell. 'No one has yet apologised to me.'

2

Bail was finally granted on 19 July on the condition that Razzell resided at his elderly mother's home in Crewkerne, Somerset. One evening, just after midnight, the doorbell rang. Razzell answered it. Two police officers were on the doorstep.

'Bail check and the time is 00.07', said one. The other made notes.

They had arrived to check that Razzell was adhering to his bail conditions. They did this for four consecutive weeks, much to the annoyance of Razzell's mother who complained, firstly, about being woken up at that hour and, secondly, about the folly and waste of the entire exercise.

Razzell and his mother assumed that her phone was being tapped. This was subsequently confirmed when, buried among paperwork, Razzell found a note from Wiltshire CPS confirming that this had been the case. However, it was not this surveillance that concerned Razzell, but rather the covert eavesdropping of private conversations with his solicitor.

At one stage while he was being held at the police station, Razzell was talking to a lawyer (not his trial solicitor but another member of the same practice). It was one of the very few times they were together. In an idle moment, as a way of easing the tension, they started light-heartedly discussing how one might actually dispose of a body so that it could not be found. Razzell said he'd thought of a good ruse; he'd go to a graveyard, find a newly-buried coffin, unearth it and bury his victim beneath.

Some months later, Razzell was going through all the unused material in the case when he noticed that, after he'd had this private conversation, the police had instigated a series of enquiries 'with funeral directors … re interments and lists of gravediggers'. One detective constable had been assigned to make enquiries at local graveyards. A statement was taken from a gravedigger. He spoke about how muddy people got when digging graves and added that it would be impossible for anyone to disturb a grave without it being noticed.

Tracking back through the paperwork, Razzell also noticed that these inquiries appeared to have been set in train by an anonymous tip-off to the Crimestoppers phone-line. An informant claimed to have overheard Razzell talking. Yet Razzell knew he had not said this, whether seriously or in jest, at any other time. There was really only one logical explanation.

'The only time I had such a conversation was at the police station with the solicitor', asserted Razzell. 'If a call was made to Crimestoppers it must have been by an officer, or someone acting on his behalf, as a way of covering up the fact that they were acting on information they'd obtained illegally.'

Conversations with solicitors are, of course, subject to absolute confidentiality. Sometimes in the past, if these strict legal conditions have been breached, then convictions have been declared unlawful.

IT TOOK SEVENTEEN months for the prosecution to prepare the case for trial. The time it takes to prepare a case for trial is often a reliable guide to its validity: the longer the time, the weaker the case. However, there had clearly been considerable acrimony in the marital relationship and, whatever had happened, Linda had certainly disappeared.

By the time the trial began at Bristol Crown Court in November 2003, the prosecution case was that after Linda had parked her car that morning, Razzell had abducted her in the alley where her mobile phone was found and subsequently murdered her and disposed of the body. The Crown lawyers argued that the noose in the loft showed that Razzell had been conscience-stricken about what he'd done and had therefore contemplated suicide. They described him as 'a good chess player' and 'a methodical man who planned everything in advance'.

The trial went badly for Razzell. On 13 November 2003 the jury brought in a unanimous verdict of guilty. He was given a life sentence with a term of sixteen years.

The prosecution case had rested entirely on the evidence of those blood spots in the car. Blood was found in a number of places. There were spots, for example, on the underside of the parcel shelf and on the sides of the boot; a stain on the top of the parcel shelf; and one on the right-hand side of the front passenger foot mat.

But hadn't there been three previous examinations of this car? The police explained that on this occasion they had used a different forensic method. They had used the chemical Luminol. This is viewed as a last-resort chemical because it is a once-for-all test that eradicates the original sample.

There are, however, serious problems with this explanation. Firstly, the bloodspots were clearly visible. Some officers even referred now to 'heavy bloodstaining'. So how could specialist examiners have missed them previously? Nor, secondly, was there the correlation one would have anticipated between areas in the car which reacted to the Luminol, and areas where the Forensic Science Services (FSS) in Chepstow subsequently found blood.

Some areas to which Luminol reacted did not turn out to be

blood (not surprisingly, as Luminol will react with a number of substances, including cleaning fluids and plant materials).

The position of the blood spots is also intriguing. There was the stain on the grey front passenger footwell mat. (Again, this stain, on a light surface, was clearly visible.) With the mat positioned on the floor of the car, the stain was close to the central console – yet there were no corresponding stains on adjacent carpeted areas. One explanation of how the stain came to be on the mat but not on the immediate surrounding area could be that the blood got onto the mat when it was outside the car.

In the boot, there were spots on the underside of the parcel shelf. There were corresponding spots on the sides of the boot, but only up to the level of the parcel shelf. If anyone had struck Linda while she was in the boot, and the back was open (and so would have been six feet up in the air), then other parts of the back area should have been bloodstained. So this suggested that any spattering must have occurred when the hatchback was closed, with the parcel shelf in place.

Similarly, there was no blood on the floor of the boot. The prosecution argued that this was because it had been covered. However, the spattering on the sides of the boot was only high up. There was no spattering on the sides lower down, as would have been expected if the Crown case was valid.

Nor was there blood on the door handles or the driving controls or the seat belt. Nor was there any other evidence – no hairs, skin, fibres or fingerprints – that matched Linda. Apart from the bloodstains, there was nothing to indicate that a body had been in the car. Nor was there corresponding evidence. Despite the lengths the police had gone to in taking the waste-traps from the basins at his home, there was no evidence of blood on Razzell or his clothing or in his house, nor signs that he might have washed any away.

Sutcliffe provided a list of who had travelled in the vehicle. After they had all been eliminated, there were still seven unknown types of DNA in the car. While some could be explained by mechanics who serviced the car, it was intriguing that unknown DNA was found on the back door handles inside the car.

The amount of blood found in the car could not be quantified,

but it would certainly have been in the range of about ten millilitres – that is, the amount that a syringe might hold.

Bearing this in mind, it is intriguing to consider a stain on the
upper side of the parcel shelf where it came into contact with the
back seat. Suppose someone holding an object like a syringe had
gone into the back of the car and needed to pull the seat forwards
in order to gain access to the boot. This would have required two
hands, one to release the catch and one to pull the seat forward; so
the syringe would have been put down. This stain on top of the
parcel shelf was exactly in the position in which someone would
have placed it while gaining access to the boot area.

So the evidential integrity of these blood spots is in serious
doubt. Yet the overwhelming objection remains: there had been
three previous examinations of the car. The CPS cannot be so
selective in its appraisal of the evidence as to ignore that fact
altogether.

The first was, admittedly, a cursory one by officers, who weren't
looking for anything specific. They did, however, examine it in
daylight. The second examination was conducted by specialist tech-
nicians who were specifically looking for blood and they found,
as they clearly reported, 'no signs of blood or recent cleaning'.
The latter point has also been disregarded but, again, is of obvious
importance. Had Linda been abducted or carried in the car, then
an assailant is likely to have tried to cover his tracks by cleaning out
the car. The third was the thorough examination under ideal conditions on police premises. Specialist officers had everything that
they needed, and all the time they needed, and they found nothing.
No signs of blood or of recent cleaning.

And why were the police so interested in this car anyway, so
soon after the alleged abduction? It was because Razzell had
straight away volunteered the information that he'd used the car
that day.

Yet if he had any kind of abduction and murder plan, he would
certainly have wanted to use his own car; after all, any of Linda's
DNA or hairs or fibres in their Ford Galaxy would have been evidentially valueless, as she had been in it so often.

The 'blood spots in the car' is the evidence on which Razzell was convicted; but it is precisely the evidence that makes no sense at all.

IF RAZZELL HAD INDEED been 'a methodical man who planned everything in advance', as the prosecution alleged, then he would never have done what they accused him of doing. There would have been no point in trying to harm Linda or remove her from the scene. Razzell would have known that he could never benefit financially from his wife's disappearance. With his professional background and training, he would have understood precisely the consequences that would follow – namely, that the existing financial difficulties would not be resolved but only become intractable. In missing person cases, insurance companies still adopt their traditional policy of not paying up for seven years. There could have been no financial incentive for him to have brought about Linda's demise.

If Linda were murdered then, in view of the friction and her previous allegations, the finger of suspicion would be bound to point at him – which is exactly what did happen. Even if he were out of the country, even if he had gone on the trip to Calais, he would still have been suspected of involvement.

Nor could any of this have been planned in advance. The events leading up to the disappearance were triggered by Linda herself, in taking out the court order to freeze his account. The process server delivered the order on Saturday morning. It was only on Monday lunchtime, while he was with Mike Sutcliffe, that Razzell – having had further phone conversations with his solicitor – decided to pull out of the trip to France. It was then at Sutcliffe's suggestion that the cars were swapped.

If Razzell was, as the prosecution stated, 'a methodical' man and 'a good chess player', then he would presumably have planned the crime carefully. Yet there was no evidence whatever of planning. Linda had only just started at Swindon College when Razzell left the family home and her hours of work had changed since then. There was no evidence he knew how or when she got to work.

17

There was no evidence that he had reconnoitred the scene of the alleged crime. No witness ever placed him there at any time.

Nor did he have the time or the opportunity to abduct her. At 8.24 that morning, he took the call on his landline at home from Rachel. As a rule, in order to be at work for just after 9.00, Linda should have been parking her car by about 8.45. It would have taken Razzell about fifteen to twenty minutes, depending on traffic, to reach Alvescot Road, where she parked her car, from his house. Had he been planning an abduction, he would have wanted to be prepared and ready in position for her. It is inconceivable that he would have cut it so fine.

Moreover, if he had been travelling there, and if he had cut it so fine, then he would have needed to reach the scene by the quickest route. Consequently a police action was initiated, 'to identify and seize any CCTV along vehicle route'. The police visited all commercial premises along all possible routes and took CCTV footage from twenty-four sites. Four officers then spent about a month going through it all. Five of the cameras had clear views of the road. The Laguna, the car that Razzell was driving, was on none of them.

If Razzell's car wasn't being driven towards the abduction site, is there any evidence about where it actually was? There is indeed. It was parked in his driveway. His next-door neighbour said that it was there at 9.30 when she left the house to go shopping and was still in the same position when she returned at 11.00. She owned a Renault Laguna herself, and so had specifically noticed the sudden arrival of another.

Further, a passer-by had seen the Laguna outside the house at 10.30. This must have been Razzell's car; it could not have been the neighbour's because she was on her shopping trip. This was very inconvenient testimony for the prosecution, so the police checked the neighbour's shopping receipt from the local ASDA supermarket in order to verify the information. The timing was correct; her account of her shopping trip was accurate.

That morning, Linda would have driven her Escort eastwards along Upham Road. She turned left through a narrow alleyway between garages into Alvescot Road. At the end, she turned right and straight away parked the car. She would then have walked back through the alley. Her normal routine would have been to walk through Queen's Park on her way to work.

Anyone planning an abduction is likely to have eliminated the location instantly: too many passers-by; too little getaway potential. It would have been unwise for a potential abductor to wait around and risk being seen. The alley itself was too narrow to have turned a car round and to have reversed out would have attracted attention. So a car could only go in the direction it was already heading. There was only one way out, and always the possibility that that might be temporarily blocked.

After the discovery of Linda's mobile phone, the police did a fingertip search of the alley and found nothing more to suggest an abduction had taken place there. Nor did the abandoned phone suggest, as it might have done to a casual observer, that a struggle had taken place. The evidence actually pointed to the opposite conclusion. Linda would have had a briefcase-style bag with her, as well as her handbag. Had there been a struggle, one would have expected other items to be dropped. Also, the mobile was found under a piece of wood. In other words, it was unlikely to have fallen where it was found. The impression of the head of the scene-of-crime team was that it had been 'placed' there. Another recorded in his notebook, 'Alley has been made to look like abduction site'.

The abduction of a middle-aged woman in broad daylight is the sort of thing that people are likely to notice. This was a residential area with, in the main, semi-detached houses lining the streets. It was busy at that time in the morning with people on their way to work. The roads were used by many Swindon commuters as they were among the closest to the town centre to allow unrestricted parking. There is also a playschool nearby, and at that time mothers pushing buggies were arriving to drop off their children. Of all those who were in the vicinity at the relevant time, no one saw Razzell or a silver Laguna or heard or saw anything suspicious.

In any event, how could he have accomplished anything on his own? Bearing in mind the level of animosity between them, Linda would only have got into his car against her will; he would have had to use force. Despite the fact that houses overlook the whole area, no resident or passer-by heard screams or anything to cause them concern.

On the other hand, four witnesses did see Linda and recognised her as the woman they'd previously seen walking there at that time of the morning. None of these saw her come to any harm.

Of these four, one man's evidence was especially significant. He observed her, and knew that she regularly parked outside his house. He saw her lock her car and walk towards the alley. He then got into his own car, reversed out of his drive and followed her down the cut-through in order to walk his dog. His evidence was important in three respects. First of all, he said that no pedestrians or vehicles entered or left the alley through the Alvescot Road entrance after Linda had walked into it. Secondly, he must have been only about sixty to seventy-five seconds behind her. Thirdly, he was adamant that nothing untoward occurred.

Recognising that he was a potent witness for the defence, the prosecution placed him under surveillance. All they found out was that his routine was more or less as he had described it, and that it took him on average about 65 seconds from opening his gates to turning into the alley. It would have taken about 37 seconds for Linda to have walked from her car to the point where the mobile phone was found, so this allowed only about 30 seconds in which she could have been abducted without this witness seeing anything – and even then, of course, the whole idea is impossible because there would have needed to be a car heading towards him; and there wasn't.

Nor was anything happening at the other end, the Upham Road end, of the alleyway.

That morning, a driving instructor had parked there, waiting to start a lesson. He was there for several minutes. He, too, noticed nothing out of the ordinary.

Another witness saw a woman whom she thought was Linda walking along Upham Road. She too recognised her from previous mornings, and described her clothing accurately. She said that Linda was:

walking fast and looking flustered … I got the impression she was nervous.

So, when this woman saw her, Linda had walked safely through the alleyway.

In any case, there is excellent evidence that she was not abducted there, or anywhere else, that morning. She was seen alive the following day, Wednesday 20 March.

Jolanda Gingell knew Linda well, as they had worked together in the children's playgroup. She explained in her statement:

I saw her most days, usually to just say hello but sometimes we had a longer chat.

That Wednesday morning, at 11.15 (she could be certain of the time because of her work schedule), she saw Linda driving a silver Ford Fiesta. As she related:

I thought, 'Oh, it's Linda, good for her she's got a new car'. I made eye contact, she didn't need to turn her head to see me and I put up my hand in acknowledgement. She didn't wave back and I thought that she looked cross and wasn't happy to see me.

By the time she made this statement, Jolanda was well aware that Linda had, as it were, officially disappeared the previous day. She ended it by commenting:

Even knowing what I know now, I am sure it was Linda.

THE CRIMINAL Procedure and Investigations Act 1996 gives police the responsibility for investigating all aspects of the case including those favourable to the defence. For this case, however, the police put enormous energy, resources and commitment into trying to find a body; they put virtually no effort into trying to trace a living Linda. Similarly, while they tried hard to find an evidential basis to undermine Jolanda Gingell's sighting, their investigations into Razzell's alibi were feeble.

In searching exhaustively for a body, the police examined about two hundred sites in and around Swindon, particularly in the areas where Razzell might have gone to on the Tuesday. They flew over the countryside using specialist equipment such as ground disturbance detection. They contracted divers and searched drains, rivers, canals, ponds and lakes. They used specialist contractors to search old tunnels. They examined railway cuttings.

By contrast, what steps were taken to try to verify Razzell's alibi?

He was questioned within twenty-four hours of Linda's disappearance and gave an account which he has consistently maintained. At 7.45am that Tuesday, 19 March, he went out to put some petrol into the Laguna. This part of his account was subsequently confirmed by CCTV. He was back home at about ten past eight. At 8.24, Rachel, who stayed at her mother's on Mondays, telephoned to say hello. The call lasted just one minute 43 seconds.

His solicitor had earlier advised him to draw up a formal letter of complaint about the way the police had handled Linda's allegations against him. He'd been intending to do it that morning but, being reluctant to get down to work, decided instead to go for a walk round Lydiard Park.

He left about 9.00, returned about 11.30, had a long soak in the bath and then some lunch. He picked up voicemail on his mobile at 2.11pm. At 2.28 he returned a call to his solicitors, who said that an affidavit regarding the unfreezing of his accounts was ready for him to sign.

He left home at about 3.00. His pay-and-display ticket at a town centre car park was timed at 3.13. He was at his solicitor's offices until about 3.45, when he phoned Rachel. They decided to go for a light meal at the Red Lion in Avebury after she finished work.

Razzell then drove to Barbury Castle, an iron age hill fort which is at the western end of the Ridgeway Path and a favourite area for walking. He walked round there and then picked Rachel up at ten past five. They drove to Avebury and were at the Red Lion until 7.30. He dropped her back at her workplace so that she could pick up her car. He then had a message from Sutcliffe to say that the ferry had been delayed, so he bided his time at Membury service station on the M4 motorway with a cup of tea and a copy of *Autosport* magazine. He met the others at about half past nine.

Cell-site analysis of the masts through which his mobile phone calls were routed allowed his whereabouts to be broadly established. There are accordingly about six hours in the day (from approximately 8.30am until just before 2.30pm) during which he was unalibied.

His walk through Lydiard Park that Tuesday morning became the focus of bitter and protracted dispute with the police. By Wednesday morning, having been questioned in the middle of the night, Razzell already realised that he might need to prove his whereabouts. Therefore, a mere twenty-four hours later, he retraced his steps, deliberately looking for CCTV cameras which would have recorded his movements. He noticed cameras at six particular sites.

Then, the police said they needed to check for potential alibi witnesses, so Razzell agreed to do the walk yet again and accompany them on the Thursday morning. However, the officers arrived three hours late so the precise point of the exercise was lost.

Nevertheless, they undertook the walk together. One of the points of dispute arising afterwards concerned the state of their shoes. At that time of year, the park was muddy. Razzell noticed that while he occasionally strayed off the path to avoid especially muddy areas, the officers chose instead to walk straight through. Afterwards, the officers declined the opportunity to clean off their shoes, as our mothers taught us when we were children, and as Razzell did, by rubbing them through blades of grass.

Razzell was astonished when this episode emerged at his trial as 'evidence'. In the Crown's opening speech to the jury, it was claimed that this undermined his alibi. He couldn't have done the walk as the police had as his shoes would have been muddied as theirs were:

> The officer noted that in the course of his walk his shoes had got very muddy and this contrasted with the clean state of the shoes which the defendant produced as being those he had worn during the walk.

The fact that this was included in the prosecution's opening speech provides a fair indication of the hollowness of its case.

Might dog-walkers have seen Razzell that morning? The police seemed to have some details but had not passed these to the defence. At a directions hearing in March 2003, a judge ordered the police to disclose full details of these potential witnesses. This, it appears, spurred the police into action. The defence then belatedly learned that one witness said he may have seen Razzell but, because of the time that had elapsed, he could not be sure. This was hardly surprising; the man's statement was taken only after the judge's intervention – in April 2003, *more than a year afterwards.*

Nevertheless, there was something that should have provided clinching evidence. Of those CCTV cameras that Razzell had noticed, one was of prime significance.

'During my walk', he told police, 'I went past Westlea Police Station. You have CCTV outside so you will be able to verify what I am saying'.

The camera was positioned high up under the eaves. It would have had a perfect view of Razzell as he walked past at about 9.15, and again on his return at about 11.15. However, the police subsequently told him that the cameras outside the station were not recording at that time. Of course, Razzell cannot possibly have known that.

'At trial, I produced photographs showing those cameras outside the police station', said Robbie Ross, Razzell's trial solicitor. 'They were pointing straight at where he would have walked past. I don't think anyone in their right mind would have claimed they'd walked past if they hadn't.'

Even without this, Razzell felt that the police had ample opportunity to substantiate his alibi. What about the other cameras? Factories and businesses along Razzell's route had their own security systems. Yet, as with the dog-walkers, essential investigative work was carried out either belatedly or not at all. No videotapes were seized. Statements were only taken months later, when memories had dulled and (more importantly) tapes had been wiped over.

Further argument concerned Razzell's mobile phone. He took it with him on the walk, but it was not switched on and was not receiving calls. The prosecution alleged that he had turned his phone off to prevent his location being established.

Razzell maintained that the phone tended to switch itself off, and this is what must have happened; others who owned that model had reported the same tendency. The prosecution expert confirmed this. 'The bottom line', he wrote, 'is that the phone does appear to switch itself off.'

WHEN POLICE EXAMINED papers and documents they had taken from Razzell's home, they had noted the name of Debbie Gasson. She was a girlfriend from about 20 years earlier. Razzell's and Debbie's mothers had been friendly and still exchanged Christmas cards. Obviously, one of the matters that was bound to go against Razzell at trial were Linda's previous allegations against him; so he wanted Debbie to be called as a character witness on his behalf.

The police made inquiries and then informed Razzell that they had been to see Debbie Gasson and her mother and father. All had denied knowing him. With the trial date looming, this was further depressing news.

It was in 2005 that Debbie Hameed (née Gasson) was astonished to read an article about Razzell's conviction. She contacted the family and then went to visit him in Gartree Prison. She said she would certainly have spoken up for him and couldn't understand why no one had got in touch with her before the trial. When Razzell responded that he thought they had, Debbie reiterated that no one had contacted her and no one could possibly have spoken to her father because he'd died in 1982.

Even though Gasson is one of the easier surnames to trace, the police had incompetently contacted the wrong family.

Linda's maiden name was Linda Jane Davies. The surname is the sixth most common in the UK. If Linda had been planning to start a new life, she is highly likely to have reverted to her maiden name, both because it gave her a far greater chance of achieving that and also because, bearing in mind her animosity towards her husband, she would not have wanted to retain his name.

Virtually the only checks the police carried out were for Linda Razzell. They asked the Passport Office to let them know if Linda Razzell were to apply for a new passport. Her existing one remained at home. Not surprisingly, she didn't. Then, when one woman reported seeing Linda on a KLM flight from Schiphol airport in Amsterdam to Bristol, her sighting was dismissed by police because 'no one by the name of Linda Razzell travelled on that flight'.

Checking records for 'Razzell' is straightforward; checking for 'Davies' is well-nigh futile. For example, when police did try to check in her maiden name with the utility companies, npower responded that they had 1,200 L.J. Davies's on their database. Other agencies didn't bother to reply.

Linda was a fluent French speaker. Had she requested a new passport in her maiden name in advance, done a vanishing trick and then slipped out of the country, no one would know to this day because no checks have ever been carried out. Amazingly, the police couldn't even check whether she had flown out of the country. Getting such information out of the major airlines was, according to an internal police report, 'not a viable proposition'.

And what if she had changed her name by deed poll? The police discovered:

> There is no central registry for those [who] change their name. Any solicitor in the land can facilitate a change of name by deed poll and there is no requirement to register this.

On the other hand, the police tried every which way to account for the small silver hatchback car that Jolanda Gingell had seen the day after Linda went missing, in order to try to undermine her evidence. They studied her work records, but found only that her schedule was as she described it. They tried to find a car like the one she had described with a driver who looked like Linda. They took to the trial women who may have been driving similar models in the area around that time.

Yet the prosecution would not call Jolanda Gingell. The defence could have called her, but opted instead to have her statement read into the court record. That may have been a tactical misjudge-ment, but it should be understood that it is always difficult for hard-pressed defence lawyers to anticipate what the right tactics are going to be.

Ultimately, her evidence could not be discredited. The idea that she could have been mistaken is fanciful. She had known Linda for about ten years. She was only about twelve feet away. She had no doubt that it was her.

3

The case remains a major unsolved crime mystery. Could Linda have plotted her own disappearance with the dual objective of escaping her problems and creating huge difficulties for her estranged hus-band? There were indications that this may have happened.

She did have problems. With Razzell's maintenance no longer coming through, she had already defaulted on the monthly mort-gage repayments. Her life at home appeared stressful. There are suggestions that the children thought their mother had had enough. She was allowing her own difficulties to interfere with her work. One internal email from the college makes it clear that her position as a member of the student support staff had become anomalous, since it was she who appeared to need emotional support from the students.

In missing person cases, there is an obvious first step in police inquiries: they check the money. If a woman has disappeared and her bank accounts and savings are untouched, then murder may be indicated. In this instance, the day before she went missing Linda had visited *three* banks or building societies in Swindon.

Amazingly, no evidence has ever been produced that the police even inquired what these banking transactions were.

There are indications that Linda may have been about to fake a disappearance. She had to wear a college identity badge to work but, that day, left it at home. She actually had two mobile phones, one of which was an emergency number, reserved solely for con-tact with the children. She left that at home, too. On the kitchen calendar, there was a question-mark against the very date, the 19th, on which she disappeared.

She had drawn up a to-do list for the previous day's trip to the town centre. One of the items on this list was:

Collect travel tickets

That morning, they were late leaving the house; one of the children could not find her homework. Fereday said that it was about 8.40, which would have meant that Linda was going to be late for work. The children said that, although she would normally have been stressed about that, on that morning she was more easy-going. In a video-recorded interview Catherine remarked that on the morning of her disappearance her mother had been 'in a good mood, more cheerful than usual'.

Catherine went on:

Normally, she'd say, 'See you at six', but that day she didn't, which I thought was a bit odd.

One of the other children added:

Mum used to have stresses, she sometimes said she couldn't cope with it … We were sure she might walk out.

If she had been planning to disappear, then she would have needed someone to help her carry it off. Since, at that stage, the whole thing could perhaps have seemed little more than a semi-malicious adventure, Fereday may have been happy to assist.

'I even wondered if Malcolm could have had anything to do with Linda disappearing', one of Linda's relatives commented, 'I thought he might have helped her plan to disappear to get at Glyn.'

Certainly, there are numerous indications that Fereday may have been involved. Here are some of them:

He was the last adult who knew her to see her alive (according to the Crown, since they discounted all subsequent sightings).

In the two weeks before Linda's disappearance, he had been effectively spying on Razzell. He had been to his house a number of times to check up on his movements. He admitted having been there on a Sunday earlier that month, either the 3rd or the 10th. He agreed that he was outside the house on Saturday 9 March. Mobile phone cell-site analysis also placed him in the vicinity a week later, on 16 March. A digital photo of Razzell's house was loaded on to Linda's computer on Sunday 17th, just two days before she disappeared. Fereday claimed that Linda's solicitors had asked him to assemble evidence about Razzell's relationship with Rachel. This explanation was palpably untrue, since no solicitor would ask someone personally involved in a legal dispute to gather covert information.

Fereday's explanation of what happened the previous day when he and Linda went into Swindon together is lacking in detail. That day was supposedly the last that he and Linda were together. One might have thought that, only a couple of days later, he would remember it clearly. But what could he say about what happened after they went to the banks? He said they 'browsed round various shops'. Oh, which ones? the police naturally asked. Fereday, they reported, was 'unable to recall which shops'.

He cannot satisfactorily explain why they needed to visit three different banks or building societies. In the Woolwich, for example he withdrew forty-two pence (£0.42p) and closed the account. Asked what had prompted Linda to write 'collect travel tickets', he responded that she was compiling a 'fictitious' list, hardly a convincing explanation.

Fereday was the one person who did know where she parked her car in the mornings before work.

One witness said she saw him sitting on a wall close to the supposed abduction site and very close to the entrance to Queen's Park at about 9.30 that morning. She described him accurately. Fereday maintained that she was mistaken because he was wearing a white T-shirt that day and she described different clothing; but her description matched those of witnesses who saw him at the school performance an hour later. The police nevertheless wondered whether it may have been Razzell whom she had seen, and so an officer was sent to check the sighting. He reported back, 'Witness is sure she saw Fereday'.

Then, there was the matter of the lunchtime telephone call to Linda's college.

Fereday said that at about 12.30, having failed to contact Linda through her mobile, he telephoned the college and asked to speak to her. Someone called Sarah then told him that Linda was in a room with a student. That was his evidence.

The police investigated this call:

> Extensive inquiries have been made at the college in order to identify the member of staff he spoke with, but this has proved unsuccessful, with no staff members recalling such a conversation.
>
> It should be noted that when Mr Fereday's landline and mobile telephone billing is examined, there is no trace of a telephone call being made at the time specified by Mr Fereday.

One inference to be drawn from this is that Fereday had invented the call and the conversation, together with the information that Linda was apparently safe at college. If so, the reason must have been to give her more time to effect her getaway.

Then, his reaction to Catherine's call was completely unnatural. She called him at 6.24; he called the police at 6.28. So within four minutes of the start of his conversation with Catherine – in which she has told him merely that Linda had not yet picked up the children – and *without making any other phone calls at all*, he phoned the police to report her missing. It is as if Fereday knew she was going to go missing and was waiting for the signal to start the search.

What might a natural reaction have been to Catherine's call? He might have worried about the situation for a few moments, and contemplated alternatives. He'd have rung Linda's mobile himself. He'd have rung round family and friends. He'd have worried some more. He'd have waited for some people to call him back. Only after establishing that no one had any news is he likely to have taken what would have seemed the alarmist step of telephoning the police.

Nor was that the only strange aspect. When he phoned the police, Fereday did not ring 999. He telephoned the police station direct. He had the number already keyed in to his telephone memory.

By four o'clock the following morning, less than 24 hours after her disappearance, when there might still have been an innocuous explanation for what had happened, he asked Wiltshire Police why they had not arrested Razzell. So it was Fereday who both initiated the missing person inquiry and quickly tried to turn it into a murder inquiry.

That afternoon, Wednesday 20 March at 1.30, Fereday was interviewed at the Razzell family home. While this was happening, scene-of-crime officers searched his home address.

Crucial evidence emerges from all this. Firstly, Fereday gave police the names of three friends of Razzell. The fact that they discussed his friends would suggest that at this stage the police believed – correctly, the defence would say – that it would have been impossible for him to abduct Linda on his own.

Fereday mentioned three names to police officers. But how would he have known the names of Razzell's friends? Two of the three were character witnesses for Razzell at his trial a few weeks earlier. Fereday had been in the public gallery and so would have learned their names then. But the third friend, noted simply as 'Mike', was Mike Sutcliffe, the owner of the Laguna. This is the point of singular interest.

Having searched Fereday's home, officers bagged up and took away some items. These included hairs for analysis that they'd picked up from the carpet by the bed. Although nothing of interest was found, police searched his house again on 3 April. This time, they found a yellow bloodstained T-shirt in a bag under his bed. The bloodstains were on the front, shoulder and side. Analysis confirmed that it was Linda's blood.

Asked to account for this, Fereday explained that he had been wearing it on the day when Linda fell into the glass door in May 2001 and so the spots must have been deposited when he took her in his arms and comforted her.

This is strikingly implausible. The distribution of the blood spots did not support that explanation. Moreover, even if the explanation had been plausible, it would be hard to understand why, in the intervening ten months, Fereday had not either thrown it away or washed it.

So the vital point here is the astonishing coincidence regarding Linda's blood: police did not find the bloodied T-shirt during the original search of Fereday's house – even though it was under the bed, exactly where police search teams naturally look and even though we know that the police had looked there (because they took the hairs away for analysis); and nor did they find Linda's blood in Sutcliffe's car during the original searches, even though they had specifically looked for it and even though they described the bloodstaining as 'heavy' when they did find it. In murder investigations, coincidences are always instructive; coincidences concerning the victim's blood should sound a thousand alarms.

One logical explanation of the failure to find either the blood spots or the T-shirt during the original searches is that they weren't there.

We know from the police interview notes of 20 March that Fereday knew of Sutcliffe. So how did he know him? This remarkable entry appears in the police case log:

> Message from Malcolm Fereday, 26 June 03. Phones office to advise that he thought he had dealings with Mike Sutcliffe in 1987 relating to purchase of life insurance. Check by DC. Negative.

What was going on here? There is no record of any officer having asked Fereday about this. So why would Fereday phone police fifteen months after the original inquiries to tell them this? Why phone police to give them the answer to a question they haven't asked?

One can only surmise. Perhaps Fereday realised that he had mentioned Sutcliffe's name to police at the outset of the inquiry and thought that they might need an explanation of how he knew him.

However, the information was untrue. Sutcliffe had never sold policies. He worked in a different part of the company; he was not involved in sales and had no contact with clients. The police checked Fereday's information and found out for themselves it was untrue.

What can be inferred from this is that Fereday was aware of Sutcliffe at the outset of the investigation; and that it must have been important to cover up exactly how he came to know of him, else he would not have misinformed the police.

The police obtained Fereday's mobile phone records up until 20 March. It is a great shame that they did not obtain records for the period from 24 to 27 March – the period during which the blood spots appeared in the car.

ONE MASSIVELY RELEVANT point about the evidence relating to Fereday is that he had only a very limited alibi. In the morning, from about 9.45 until 10.30, he was watching a school performance by one of Glyn and Linda's children. Even this is strange; there can't have been many fathers present, and Fereday wasn't even the child's father. It almost seems as if he was deliberately creating an alibi for himself for that period.

Then, he went to the Co-op and bought a few items. He texted Linda (unsuccessfully, obviously). In his statement, he said:

> I sent a text message to Linda to tell her that the assembly had gone OK and to see whether she wanted anything from the Co-op.

This was not correct because the timings of his phone record and the supermarket receipt show that he only sent the text message *after* he'd done the shopping.

Otherwise, he was not alibied until he clocked on at work at 3.28pm. The police interviewed those living in the neighbouring houses, and recorded that:

> None of the occupants or recent visitors to these premises can confirm either Mr Fereday's or his vehicle's movements on Tuesday 19 March.

It would be fair comment that, although Fereday does not have an alibi, neither, because his was never properly investigated, does Razzell. However one can examine the surrounding evidence to see how well their respective accounts are supported.

There was plain evidence that Razzell's car was in his driveway. The CCTV evidence showed that the car was never somewhere he said it wasn't; on the other hand, the Laguna is on CCTV that afternoon and evening on four occasions in locations where Razzell said he was. The petrol consumption of the car bore out his mileage; he had, he said, driven approximately sixty miles that day and about sixteen the day before. Although Razzell's phone was switched off in the morning, calls to and from the phone during the rest of the day were routed through masts that confirmed his account.

By comparison, Fereday's account is, at key moments, not borne out by other evidence. At 9.30, he said he was at home repairing his oven; but a witness placed him close to the supposed abduction site. There were no neighbours to verify his account. In the middle of the day he said he was at home. However, he sent two text messages just after 1.00pm. An analysis of the cell-sites through which these were routed indicated that he is likely to have been not at home, but in the area around Lechlade, north-east of Swindon.

Fereday said that he left home at Highworth at about 3.00 and drove straight to work at the Honda site, which is south-west of Highworth. Cell site analysis again indicated that this was not true. A call he made at 3.11 was from a location other than where he claimed to be. 'I find it difficult to believe', reported the defence analyst, 'that the user was anywhere in Highworth or south of Highworth during the time of this call.'

Fereday told police at 9.33 in the evening that he was going to look for Linda's car. One wonders why he hadn't carried out such checks *before* phoning the police. Yet he didn't go directly there. At 10.00pm, he made a call to his workplace which was routed through a cell site that was not compatible with his having driven direct to Linda's car from his house. In fact, his phone records over previous weeks showed several calls to his workplace all routed through the same mast; this particular call to the Honda factory was the sole one routed through a different mast. The analyst believed that the call was made from a moving car on the A420 or possibly the B4019, both of which are east of Highworth.

Tantalisingly, all this evidence – which places Fereday not where he said he was, but to the north and east of Highworth – connects with the area around Lechlade. We know that one location of

Linda's trysts with the builder was a mobile home near Lechlade. It is also known that, the previous month, one witness saw Linda driving towards Lechlade early one morning, at a time when she should have been on her way to work.

It is, though, what happened at 10.15 when Fereday reached Linda's car that the available evidence is at its most riveting.

When he found the car, Fereday opened it and looked in the driver's door pocket for Linda's mobile phone. At 10.15, he telephoned Catherine. At 10.17, he phoned the police to say that he'd found the car. That call lasted for one minute forty-six seconds. It was *exactly at that time* that Linda's mobile phone, which was supposedly lying by some garages, received a call routed through a cell-site that was different to those used in all other calls.

Between 11.05am on 19 March and 4.45pm the following day, there were forty-three calls to Linda's phone. Of these, forty were routed through the same mast. Two were routed through another mast – probably, a technology expert believed, because a passing car had momentarily interfered with the signal. Just that one call, at 10.17, was routed through a different mast entirely.

A defence phone expert visited the site to test signal strength. He found that there was no signal from this third mast at the exact location where the phone was found. At that moment, therefore, the phone must have been somewhere else.

Altogether, there are four significant pieces of evidence in this one small part of the story: the 10.17 phone call was routed through a different cell-site; that call lasted for four seconds only before it was disconnected; when the phone was found in the alleyway, the phone was set to discreet or quiet; and Fereday's DNA was on the keypad.

So this is what the defence believe happened: Fereday arrived at the scene at 10.15. He phoned Catherine and took Linda's mobile from her car. As he walked from the car to the alley with it in his hand, he used his own mobile to phone the police to tell them he'd found the car.

Now comes one of those dramatic moments which are usually the hallmark of crime fiction rather than crime fact. While Fereday was talking to police, Linda's phone suddenly rang. He momentarily panicked, but quickly reacted by closing off the call. He then set the phone to discreet in case it rang again. One can imagine his relief at having averted the danger. He then planted the phone in the alley where police found it the next day.

That is the scenario that would explain those four pieces of hard evidence.

LINDA MAY HAVE found it convenient to ask Fereday to help her disappear, but there is nothing to indicate that she contemplated any kind of elopement with him. In fact, their relationship may not have been going smoothly. According to a police family liaison officer, Catherine had commented, 'Mum would come home if Malcolm wasn't here'.

However, there is evidence that she may have been moving on to a fresh attachment. There are three sightings of a beige car, probably an old-style Rover or Nissan Bluebird. On 15 or 22 January 2002, in Stratton St Margaret on the outskirts of Swindon, a driving instructor who was waiting in a pub car-park with a pupil, said he noticed a woman he identified as Linda in a clinch with a man in a beige car. They separated, she got into a red Escort, and both cars were driven off in the direction of Highworth. The pupil commented, upon being shown a photograph of Linda, that the hair was exactly the same although he hadn't seen her face.

At 6.50 on the morning of the disappearance, there was a sighting of a beige car and a red Ford Escort together in a lay-by near the Swindon exit from the M4. A female witness described a woman she saw standing there. The description certainly fitted Linda and the witness additionally described a handbag that the woman was carrying. What made this particularly interesting was that the children confirmed that Linda did have such a handbag — but that it had disappeared.

Just over ninety minutes after this sighting, a beige car, probably a Nissan, was reported waiting in Alvescot Road at about 8.30. There was a man in the passenger's seat. Police recorded that the woman who reported this was a 'very good witness'.

When Linda's Escort was recovered and examined, DNA from an unknown male was found on the gear-stick. There was also an unidentified fingerprint found in Linda's car on the rear-view mirror. This is where police generally look for fingerprints, as the surface is particularly retentive, and any new driver getting into the car will automatically adjust the mirror. As ever, what matters is the steady accumulation of points of evidence. Individually, these points could mean little; altogether, they are compelling.

4

Linda was an avid reader of crime fiction and at the time of her disappearance had been reading *Trial and Retribution 3*, the novelisation of a television drama series created by Lynda La Plante.

The police were so struck by this that one officer was commissioned to write a report on the similarities between the book and Linda's real-life disappearance. He concluded:

> There were several similarities in the story line… The missing girl disappeared on a Tuesday morning during a paper round. The route she used was a recognised regular route. [She]… disappeared after leaving the house, seeming to disappear without anyone seeing her. She was later discovered to have been approached by a driver in a vehicle whom she knew and bundled into the boot.
>
> Linda was three-quarters of the way through the book and would have read all of the above scenarios.
>
> My impressions were that if Linda had staged her own disappearance, as a result of reading the book, she would have gained clues on police inquiries into missing persons. Especially the immediate enquiries at the scene, including door-to-door inquiries and the use of search teams; also ideas on a person being abducted from a known recognised route.

Yet if it is the case that Linda was inspired to turn crime fiction into crime fact then, remarkably, the central motif of the story may in turn have become crime fiction again. Nicci French (the successful writing partnership of Sean French and Nicci Gerrard) wrote

Secret Smile, the book that became a television drama starring Kate Ashfield and David Tennant. The story concerned a woman faking her own disappearance in order to revenge herself on her partner and, indeed, send him to prison for life for her 'murder'.

And then there was *Gone Girl*, Gillian Flynn's phenomenally successful thriller, published in 2012, that became an instant classic of crime fiction. This was developed into a major film, directed by David Fincher and starring Rosamund Pike, who received an Academy Award nomination for her performance as Amy Elliott Dunne, the central character, and Ben Affleck as her husband. As with *Secret Smile*, the storyline of *Gone Girl* concerned the disappearance of a wife in circumstances that suggested that her husband had murdered her – in circumstances that replicated, whether or not Flynn herself was aware of the coincidence, the real-life case of Glyn Razzell.

'It's rather extreme, framing your husband for your murder', writes Amy in her diary, 'I want you to know I know that.'

But how might such extreme developments – not in fiction but in real life – have come to pass? It is conceivable that what Linda was reading chimed with hitherto far-fetched ideas of her own and encouraged her to put them into practice. So, after two previous attempts to incriminate her husband had come to nought, she may have been planning something more dramatic. Her own initial thought may have been to disappear for a period and then return, perhaps accusing him of having attacked or kidnapped her; alternatively, she may have been seeking an entirely new direction in her life, which her fluency in French and the boyfriend in the beige car gave her the opportunity to grasp.

Of course, it seems unthinkable that a mother of four would simply leave her children. However, if the former scenario were correct, then she would not in any case have been contemplating a permanent separation from them; but her plan may have been taken far too seriously and events, from her point of view, had spiralled out of control. If she is still alive, she would not be able to reappear without incurring a lengthy prison sentence herself for having perverted the course of justice in the most spectacular way.

If the latter scenario is accurate, then she must indeed have envisaged a long-term separation. However, as a child, Linda had herself been deprived of her mother. After her mother's death when she was just seven, she was sent away to live with her aunt's family. She knew that her own children would be looked after by her family in Wales.

There were about a million people unaccounted for at the last census. Despite the Big Brother aspects of daily life, disappearing is much easier than it would seem. Each year more than 250,000 people are reported as missing in Britain. The majority are swiftly found, but every year more than 16,000 names are added to the list of the long-term disappeared. These include the young, the old, sons, daughters, fathers and, yes, mothers. It happens.

Ultimately, the idea of a mother abandoning her children may be no more surprising than that of the abandoned children texting to their absent mother the message:

> All we want is for you to come home but if you feel you can't, that's fine.

IN OCTOBER 2012 Christopher Halliwell, a 48-year-old taxi-driver, was found guilty of the murder of Sian O'Callaghan, a 22-year-old office worker who had disappeared from the centre of Swindon in the early hours of 19 March 2011. Records showed that her mobile phone was in Savernake Forest, about ten miles south of Swindon, when a text message was received from her boyfriend. This information enabled police to focus their attention on vehicles travelling along the road that skirts the forest. As a result, the movements of a green Toyota Avensis were thought to be suspicious, and this led to the identification and arrest of Halliwell.

He confessed not only to the murder, but also informed police that he had killed a second woman some years earlier. There was speculation that this could be Linda Razzell.

In fact the second victim was 28-year-old Becky Godden-Edwards. Halliwell could not be charged with her murder as Wiltshire Police acted illegally in denying him access to a solicitor and additionally there was 'inappropriate' police contact with the media. However, Halliwell did receive a life sentence, with the recommendation of a minimum twenty-five-year term, for the murder of Sian O'Callaghan.

Subsequently, in May 2014, police found O'Callaghan's boots, together with a bundle of women's clothing, in and around a pool in Ramsey, Wiltshire. It is not known what led police to search the area.

This discovery led police to believe that there could be five other victims. 'A buried cache of clothing is unlikely to be fly-tipping', commented one detective. There was renewed speculation that Linda could be one of these victims.

Clearly, her disappearance is an ongoing mystery. No one knows what happened to her. In view of this factor alone, Razzell should certainly not be in prison today; the doubts surrounding the case are enormous. My own feeling is that Linda is still alive. But Wiltshire police, having briefly considered the possibility that she could have faked her own disappearance, abandoned it.

It seems this was never a viable theory for them; they already had their theory. Tanner Bolt, the lawyer in *Gone Girl* whose speciality 'was swooping down in high-profile cases to represent men accused of murdering their wives', observed to the husband, 'Most cops, they decide on a suspect and they don't want to veer at all'.

While Razzell's life wastes away in prison, it is no solace to him to reflect that his story is one of the most tantalising of real-life crime mysteries, albeit one that the judicial authorities in the UK appear determined not to resolve.

Chapter 2

Fire in Snowdonia

Jong Yoon Rhee's story

1

On 15 April 1997, soon after 4.00am, Jong Yoon Rhee and his wife Natalie, the only guests in a cottage in Snowdonia, north Wales, were awoken by a loud bang. Rhee opened the bedroom door and was hit by a blast of heat and smoke. The cottage was on fire.

Jumping out of the window was the only possible means of escape. It was fastened tight. The room was quickly filling with smoke, they were both choking, so Rhee grabbed the duvet off the bed, wrapped it round his hand and smashed the window. He then placed the duvet over the jagged glass at the bottom of the window and told Natalie to jump. She was scared; it was pitch-black and they weren't sure how big a drop it was. They agreed that he'd go first so that he could catch her from below. He got up on to the sill and jumped. He landed safely and called back to her. He heard her call his name and thought he heard her gasping for breath. He called back to her again and again. Smoke was billowing out of the window.

He ran along and knocked frantically at the kitchen door. It was opened by the guest-house owner, Nerys Williams. Rhee rushed through but found he couldn't reach the bedroom from inside as the stairs were ablaze. She grabbed a bucket, which they filled with water and he threw it at the fire, an entirely token gesture. They ran outside. She mentioned ladders, so he grabbed the nearest one but so many rungs were broken it was impossible to reach the bedroom. By this time, flames were shooting out of the window.

They tried calling 999, but the landline was dead. Rhee's mobile was in his car. He grabbed a curtain pole and used it to smash the window of their Citroen and retrieve the phone. There was no signal. He and Williams ran up the mountain until there was a connection. Rhee punched in the numbers and then passed the phone to Williams so that she could give the precise address and location.

The fire brigade arrived with exemplary speed, eleven minutes later, and started to put out the fire. They found Natalie's body under the window in the bedroom. Rhee and Williams were both taken to hospital and treated for smoke inhalation.

Jong Ho, Rhee's brother, came to collect him and took him to his in-laws' house outside Oxford. The following day, Rhee's father-in-law, Air Commodore Lloyd Doble, drove them all back to Wales, and Rhee and Doble went to the police. The officer who saw them recommended that they should be legally represented at the inquest. It seemed there was a possibility of civil litigation.

On 28 April, Doble and Rhee together went to see a solicitor in Oxford to discuss civil litigation. However, police attention was soon focused instead on Rhee himself. Six weeks later, they arrived at his home early in the morning, smashed down his front door, and arrested him. He was questioned and charged with his wife's murder.

He was then thirty-four and had lived in England since he was seven. His time in the country had certainly been chequered. This was the second serious fire he'd experienced. It would also be the second time he'd stood trial for murder.

JONG YOON RHEE was born on 3 May 1963 into a moderately well-to-do family in Seoul, South Korea. His father, Yung Shik, was what the country refers to as a *yang ban*, someone who is equally gifted in academic and sporting fields. He attended one of the country's elite schools, played for the national baseball team and went on to study international law at Seoul National University. He was one of the golden generation of Koreans. His contemporaries founded Daewoo, Hyundai-Kai and Samsung.

Yung Shik himself was recruited into the Korean Tungsten Mining Company – tungsten being one of Korea's most important natural resources. He married his wife, Hwa Suk, in 1958 and they had four children: two girls, Yung Mi and Yung Joo (born in 1959 and 1962); Jong Yoon and his younger brother Jong Ho, who was born in 1966. (Korean first names are traditionally formed of two parts, each of one syllable.)

Jong Yoon remembers a 'generally joyful' childhood, collecting stamps and playing tennis and football for his school, with summer holidays in Pusan, a popular resort on the south coast. Some weekends they went trekking up mountains to reach Buddhist temples; his parents were the only Buddhists in their family.

At the time of Jong Yoon's birth it was still unknown for anyone to have left Korea; but the country was beginning to engage with the world beyond. In 1971, Yung Shik was appointed European director of his company on a six-year contract. He also became South Korea's commercial diplomat at the UN, working in Geneva and New York. His brief included getting the best possible price for tungsten on the world market.

The family moved to England and rented a large house in Bromley, south London. At that time it was impossible for them to buy property because Koreans were not allowed to take money out of the country. It was a great adventure for the children, even if, initially, schooldays were difficult. With the assistance of a language tutor at home, they all became fluent in English. By the time Yung Shik's term was up, the children all wanted to stay. Indeed, they were all thoroughly assimilated into English culture and the educational system and would have found it very difficult to return.

As Yung Shik needed to go back for a year, he and Hwa Suk took Jong Ho with them, while the three older children stayed in England. The girls were looked after by guardians, and Jong Yoon went for a year to Launceston College in Cornwall, and afterwards to school in Eltham.

Yung Shik had wanted to return permanently to Korea, but for the sake of his family agreed to return to England. He took a potentially perilous path and left the company for which he'd worked for twenty-five years, and set up an import-export business in London. He also advised Korean businesses that were then just beginning to be established in Britain.

With his network of contacts, the import-export venture went well. When Rhee left school in 1979, he went to work for his father. He also took a Saturday job, at a jeans boutique in Bromley, working for a Chinese businessman, Jovan Wong. The wage was tiny, but most of his money was on commission. Rhee was a good salesman, so was soon earning a good wage to supplement the income from his father.

The following year, he happened to be driving past the shop late at night when he saw the lights were still on. Puzzled, he stopped and went to look. But there was something strange. The front door was open and no one answered Rhee's calls. He went upstairs to the stock room and found Wong lying in a pool of blood.

'I knelt down and turned him over. I placed my arm under his shoulder and head', recalled Rhee. 'I saw the wounds in his neck and realised he was dead.

'I panicked. I just went out of the shop and drove home. My family were all asleep. I told no one. As the hours passed, the longer I kept it a secret, the harder it got to tell anyone.'

Towards midday, the police came to the house; they were contacting all those who worked in the shop. The seventeen-year-old, by this stage in a state of overwhelming panic, denied having been anywhere near the premises.

The officers asked for Rhee's clothing. They noticed blood spots on one arm of his jacket and on the soles of his shoes. He was arrested. He told them the truth but by then, of course, it was too late.

'It was prize-giving day at my school', said Yung Joo, 'I was leaving the sixth form. I got home and was told that Jong Yoon had been arrested. It was a huge shock. We were living a quiet middle-class suburban life. As children, we were studying hard at school and doing what was expected of us. Nothing on that scale, nothing as devastating as that, had ever happened to our family.'

Rhee was remanded in custody, but after a month his lawyers succeeded in getting him bail. The case then went to trial at the Old Bailey.

'All of us went and sat in the public gallery every day', said Yung Joo. 'The atmosphere was very difficult. After all, we were a Korean family, this was a nasty crime and there could have been great hostility towards us. I remember our barrister working hard to get across the respectability of our family. He pointed out that I had won a scholarship to a private school – that sort of thing.'

Wong had been stabbed over thirty times. The defence was able to show that there was no motive for Rhee to have committed the crime, and that the sparse bloodstaining on his clothing was hardly consistent with someone having carried out such a bloody attack. Moreover, by the time the case reached trial, the defence team had found out that Wong had not only been living a dangerously gay lifestyle, but that he had business connections with the Triads.

It took the jury only fifteen minutes to bring in a not-guilty verdict.

'I never spoke about it again', commented Rhee. 'There's a stigma attached merely to the fact that you have stood trial for murder, no matter that you were cleared. During the following years, I made many, many new friends, but the only one I ever entrusted with the secret was Natalie.

'But not telling her parents about my past proved to be a huge mistake. I can imagine their shock at finding this out straight after I had been charged with their daughter's murder. It would under-standably have made them believe that I was guilty.'

AFTER THAT, Yung Shik sold his business and put just about everything he had into a new venture, a restaurant. It was sited in a Grade II listed townhouse just off Bond Street in Mayfair. There were dining rooms on four floors, with a total seating capacity of sixty, though a terrace provided an additional twenty covers during summer months. It was called Korea House Restaurant. The actual running of the business quickly became the responsibility of Jong Yoon and Jong Ho.

'We were there pretty much twenty-four seven', said Jong Ho, 'and sometimes we did sleep there.'

The moment was auspicious. There were very few Korean restaurants in London and Yung Shik, with his extensive network of connections in the Korean community, was able to attract a significant number of high-profile Koreans. Embassy parties would be held there. Then the Seoul Olympics in 1988 helped to bring a new fashionableness to all things Korean.

During this time, Yung Mi was working for the Bank of Korea. After graduating, Yung Joo had gone back to Korea to teach. She then returned to London to do a postgraduate journalism course at City University, and worked part-time as a waitress at the restaurant.

The business didn't enrich the family, but it did run success-fully throughout the 1980s. Then, one night in 1990 there was a serious fire. It was known that developers had wanted to move into that exclusive part of Mayfair. Nevertheless, the family were not suspicious about the cause of the fire, which was attributed to an electrical fault in the basement. The fire, though, did end the business. 'We got the insurance settlement, which wasn't great', said Jong Ho. 'After that, it wasn't really viable to reopen it.'

It was in the aftermath of the fire that Rhee met Natalie. She was born on 11 March 1972 and was then just nineteen. She was born into a service family in Steventon, Oxfordshire. Her father, Air Commodore Lloyd Doble, was a serving officer in the RAF based at Bentley Priory in north-west London.

Rhee was actually introduced to her by her then-boyfriend in a Soho nightclub, Les Scandales. They talked for an hour, at the end of which she left with her boyfriend. By then Rhee was completely smitten. It was like Alain-Fournier's *Le Grand Meaulnes*. He had found her only to lose her. He returned time after time, hoping to see her again.

Six months later, he did meet her there – and the news could not have been more uplifting. Not only had she dumped the erst-while boyfriend, but she'd visited the club herself several times on a complementary mission: hoping to meet him there. They swiftly began a relationship, and she introduced him to her parents at the end of the year.

At the time, she was still a student living in north-west London. Rhee was living in Crystal Palace, south-west London, with his brother. One day, after they'd been together a few months, Natalie turned up outside the brothers' house with a suitcase. She said she'd decided to move in.

They soon moved together into the flat in Elgin Avenue that Natalie shared with her sister, and Yung Mi got her a job with the Bank of Korea. Rhee and Natalie were engaged in 1993. He bought her an engagement ring of Baguette diamonds and emeralds and she bought him a Rolex watch.

After the closure of the restaurant, Rhee drew unemployment benefit for a time. Then he could only find work in a succession of menial catering jobs, and had to claim benefits to supplement his low wages. He decided that he needed academic qualifications, so he went to Middlesex University as a mature student to do business studies.

The wedding, in July 1994, was morning dress. The reception was held on the banks of the Thames, near the family home in Oxfordshire. They honeymooned in the Maldives where Natalie was able to indulge her passion for diving.

She moved on to the merchant bank, S.G. Warburg's, earning a modest salary which helped to subsidise Rhee's degree course. They sold the flat in June 1995, which brought Natalie and her sister a profit of £43,000 each. She and Rhee then purchased a nearby run-down flat which they had found in an auction catalogue. Rhee renovated it, and when they sold it in November 1996, after paying off the mortgage, had a clear profit of £52,000. The money was put into a joint account.

Rhee graduated in 1996, and was offered a job at an international hotel in Beijing, which he turned down. He and Natalie wanted to start a family in England. She became pregnant that summer, only to suffer a miscarriage.

All this time, Rhee had a secret: he was a gambler. He had shared the secret of his Old Bailey murder trial only with Natalie, but he kept his gambling addiction even from her. His brother knew a little, but certainly had no idea of the extent of it. Rhee regularly played the tables at the Golden Nugget casino in Piccadilly and the Grosvenor Victoria in Edgware Road. Gambling can be a serious addiction, and Rhee became seriously addicted.

'I started going when I was nineteen or twenty', admitted Rhee. 'Occasionally I would win a large amount, which tempted me back. I still feel foolish and ashamed every time I have to think about it.'

There were enormous fluctuations in his fortunes. He'd win a lot and then, all too predictably, lose a lot. He made several trips to pawnbrokers in New Bond Street. He pawned the family silver – or at least a canteen of cutlery that must have been a generous wedding present – before experiencing an upturn in his fortunes and redeeming it. The pattern of pawning and redeeming was repeated time and time again.

Naturally, he had to tell lies to cover up. Once, for example, he said he'd been held up at knifepoint in the Edgware Road and was forced to withdraw funds from his account at an ATM. So Natalie remained unaware.

At the end of 1996, he hit a real winning streak. On 20 December, he won £29,300 and, eight days later, a further £42,500 to add to the proceeds from the sale of the flat. The balance in his and Natalie's joint account was now very healthy indeed. He bought a BMW car.

Of course, he carried on. He very quickly had to sell the BMW. In order to explain his strange decision to sell the car he'd just bought, he had to tell Natalie he'd made a profit on the deal, but in fact he'd lost £347. It was all downhill after that. By the time that he and Natalie returned from another holiday in the Maldives, just three months later, their account was down to £127. Rhee had lost their nest-egg.

On the other hand, a joyful story seemed to be developing. Natalie bought a home pregnancy kit. She tested positive. It was very early stages, so they decided to keep the news to themselves until it was confirmed. Natalie, now at the Royal Bank of Scotland, had just been promoted at work. She suggested that they go to Snowdonia for a weekend break and take another home pregnancy test there.

On Friday 11 April 1997, they drove to Natalie's parents' house in Oxfordshire. They stayed overnight there before driving up to north Wales the next morning. They had not booked anywhere in advance, but that afternoon booked in for two nights at Nerys Williams' guest-house. They walked and toured in the area. Natalie bought four Portmeirion vases as gifts. They had such a pleasant time that they asked to stay over for a third night. That third evening, after a day's walking, they went out for a meal in Betws-y-Coed. They returned and said goodnight to Nerys Williams at about 11.00.

2

Fire crews were on the scene promptly. They came from Llanrwst, on the edge of the Snowdonia National Park, and arrived just eleven minutes after the call to the emergency services, which was timed at 4.30. The officer in charge, Arwel Hughes, saw flames coming out of the bedroom window and noticed that the fir tree outside the window was on fire. Rhee, who was dressed in boxer shorts, and Nerys Williams were both outside the cottage. Rhee tugged at Hughes' tunic, and indicated that he should go to his wife. Hughes described him as 'in shock … [he had] tears in his eyes and panic in his voice'.

A two-man crew with breathing apparatus went round the back and up the guest stairs. The fire at the top of the stairs was raging. Almost as soon as they entered, the ceiling and roof ahead of them collapsed. The bedroom was engulfed in flames. They described the heat as 'intolerable'. One of the men said that he'd been a fire-fighter for ten years and this was the hottest fire he'd ever been in. They had to withdraw to replenish their oxygen cylinders, while two members of a second team from nearby Betws-y-Coed, who had arrived at 4.47, continued to damp down the flames.

The police and ambulance services had arrived at the scene. One of the police officers noticed the curtain pole by the smashed window on the driver's side of the car. At 5.09, Rhee was given the inevitable news: Natalie's body had been found, between the bed and the wall. He and Williams were taken to hospital.

Nerys Williams did not live there alone but it happened that on that evening her partner, Mike Rothwell, was away.

The police spoke to Rhee at some length at about 8.30am. He told them what had happened. The account matched what he had told Gwenllian Parry, one of the ambulance crew, three hours earlier and was essentially the account given at the start of this chapter. There were some additional details: he said that he pulled out the plugs of all appliances (except possibly the television) before going to bed; and that, having found that the cottage was on fire, he attempted to kick the bedroom door shut as smoke entered, but it had failed to latch, and was open when he jumped out.

While Rhee was being interviewed by police, Arwel Hughes went back to his office and attended to the paperwork. He filled in the fire report. He ticked to indicate that the fire was not multi-seated.

That day, Doble and Rhee's brother, Jong Ho, drove up to Wales. Later that day, they all drove back to the Dobles' house in Oxfordshire, arriving at about 10.30. Lloyd Doble described Rhee as 'distraught'.

The next day Doble drove Natalie's mother and Rhee to North Wales. Naturally, there were discussions between the family and the police about the cause of the fire. The initial view of the fire service inspectors was that the fire was caused by a problem with the electrics. A faulty junction box was mentioned.

By now, police had driven the Citroen to Llanrwst police station. A local firm provided fresh keys and also replaced the window. The car was handed back to the family, and they drove back to Oxfordshire in the two cars. The local firm in Wales hadn't cleaned out the car, so Natalie's mother and sister had to clear up the pieces of glass. The Portmeirion vases were still in the boot.

Doble made an appointment to see a local solicitor on 28 April.

The day before that meeting in Oxford, there was an extra-ordinary development in the case back in North Wales. Nerys Williams made her first statement. Her account of what had happened was totally at odds with the one Rhee had given.

Williams described being awoken by 'choking fumes' that 'caught her throat'. At that point, she said, she 'smelt petrol'. She said that she had walked into the guest lounge where the fire was raging. She added that when Rhee had first knocked on the door and she had let him back into the house, the hallway was clear of smoke and fire so that he could easily have walked through and rescued his wife if he'd wanted to. Moreover, far from assisting, Rhee had hindered her attempts to deal with the fire. She said that she was the one who had taken the initiative and had phoned the emergency services.

By now, the police knew that Rhee, as he had acknowledged, had a secret gambling addiction; and also, as they found out from criminal records, that he had previously stood trial for murder. So they asked for a report on the cause of the fire from Dr Stuart Crosby.

He was one of the most experienced fire investigators in the country and had worked for the Home Office at the forensic science laboratory in Chorley since 1982. He concluded that there was no evidence that the fire had been started deliberately.

This should have set matters on their way to a proper resolution, but unfortunately the Crown Prosecution Service had already got the bit between its teeth. So they did what bureaucrats often do when presented with an inconvenient report: they ignored it and got an alternative one. In fact, they commissioned two fresh reports about the cause of the fire; but neither of the men they now approached was as well-qualified or had the level of expertise of Dr Crosby.

The new experts were Patrick Sheen, an electrical engineer, and David Hughes. The former's qualifications for this particular task were somewhat obscure. The latter was a full-time fireman. Indeed, he was the station officer at Llanrwst Fire Station, whose vehicles had attended the fire. He had arrived on the scene at 6.00am. He was a local man who knew both Rothwell and Nerys Williams. Later, when giving evidence, he referred to the latter by her Christian name.

Hughes and Sheen both said that there were two seats of fire – in the lounge and in the bedroom – and, therefore, the fire was started deliberately. There was, of course, a significant difficulty with this opinion: the original report completed by Hughes' colleague and namesake, Arwel Hughes, stating that the fire was not multi-seated and had not been started deliberately. So David Hughes attended to the problem. He changed the report to read that the fire *was* multi-seated and had been started deliberately.

With this supposedly scientific analysis as a foundation, the prosecution then brought a murder charge against Rhee. In April 1998 he stood trial for Natalie's murder at Chester Crown Court. The judge was the Hon. Mrs Justice Ebsworth.

The prosecution case was that he had restrained his wife and then used an accelerant to set two fires – one in the downstairs lounge and one in their bedroom upstairs – before jumping to safety himself. He then did his best to prevent the fire being put out.

Rhee's conduct after the fire, the Crown said, was not that of a grieving husband, but of a man obsessed with financial considerations and insurance claims. He and Natalie had joint life insurance policies totalling £250,000, having increased the sum shortly before the tragedy. The prosecution counsel told the jury that the motive for the crime was financial: 'When he had spent all her money and she was of no further use to him, he insured her in order to ensure his own financial future'.

Part of the case was that Rhee had chosen an isolated cottage after turning down accommodation elsewhere in the area because those properties had smoke alarms. He set the fire on the last night because he knew Mike Rothwell would be away overnight. Rhee had clearly planned it; when the fire broke out, his phone, cash and credit cards were all safely stowed in his car.

Among the fire debris, scene-of-crime officers found a bolt with the tongue extended in the locked position. The Crown argued that this bolt came from the bedroom and, because its tongue was extended, provided evidence that Rhee had locked Natalie inside the room. One police officer also gave evidence of having seen a green petrol can in Natalie Rhee's Citroen.

Nevertheless, the prosecution opening speech was at key points studded with vagueness: it was 'almost a certainty' that Rhee started a fire, before 'somehow' subduing Natalie and leaving her 'possibly unconscious'. The prosecution even told the jury that, when police had searched Rhee's house, they found a video of *Backdraft*, the Robert de Niro film about arson and fire-fighting.

THE GUEST-HOUSE WAS a seventeenth-century stone cottage that had been extended in 1984 to allow Williams and Rothwell to start a small Bed-and-Breakfast business. There was a model of the farmhouse in court to assist the jury. As it happened, it could not have assisted them at all because it was wrong, although that would not be realised for several years.

Rothwell was a builder and so carried out much of the work himself. The electrical work at the house was done by three contractors. When it was finished, there were problems over the bill and the electrician who'd rewired the old part of the house had to sue Rothwell for the money he was owed. According to a HOLAB (Home Office laboratory) report for the police, 'the owner may have had electrical problems'. No specific examples were provided, although inspectors reported instances of bad practice.

One of the exterior lights on the valley side was not connected, so there would have been no light on that side of the house. This bore out what Rhee was saying, which was that there was no alternative but to jump out into the pitch blackness and hope – which explained why Natalie was apprehensive.

Because suspicions were aroused only slowly, it was not treated as a crime scene for some time and so was not sealed off. David Hughes made a number of visits. He met Nerys Williams and read her statement as well as Rothwell's. He didn't have any contact with Rhee. He argued that there were two seats of fire. He said he could tell that the fire in the lounge had started at the gable-end wall because a piece of skirting board had been totally burned away. There was also a fire in the bedroom, which started under the bed. He examined the holes in the floor at the end of the floorboards where the fire had burned through. This was, he said, consistent with the use of an accelerant.

The other Crown expert, Patrick Sheen, also considered whether these sharp-edged burn marks in the bedroom indicated the use of an accelerant. He suggested carrying out an experiment to test this theory. The results showed that the burning pattern would have occurred naturally during the fire. Having witnessed the experiment, Sheen withdrew his conclusion about the fierce burning at the butt ends.

He stuck to his guns, however, in saying that there were two seats of fire. His conclusions were based, as the judge emphasised, 'quite significantly' on Williams' evidence. She said that the hallway was free of fire and smoke when she and Rhee first tried to fight the fire and Sheen accepted her testimony at face value. 'I cannot reconcile the time it would take the fire to get up those stairs and consume the bedroom', he told the jury, 'if there was no fire on the stairs at that point ... The most probable conclusion is that a separate fire had been started in the bedroom at or about the time at which the fire in the lounge had started.'

As the trial went on, there were deepening concerns about the expertise of both Hughes and Sheen. Hughes was roundly criticised for having altered his colleague's fire report. Referring to the doctored report, the judge said:

> That, you may think, is a very unsatisfactory document, however you look at it ... and he [Hughes] couldn't really tell you when he filled it in or why he filled it in in that manner ... What is said to you about him is somebody who approaches his duties in that way, who is so cavalier about how he records causes of fire, is not to be treated as a reliable witness.
>
> That's the first criticism of him. The second criticism is that, in any event, if you look at the basis on which he has reached his conclusions, they cannot live with the evidence of the other fire experts.

One of the reasons for this was Hughes' original assumption that the fierce burning at the butt ends of the floorboards indicated the use of an accelerant. Michael Jones, the defence scientist, was asked about this theory. He explained that at the point where boards butt, there is going to be more air available, and so this will feed the fire. The judge said that this appeared to be 'a matter of common sense'.

There were criticisms of Sheen too. There was a television set in the lounge. The other scientists could tell from the fire damage where the television had been: on shelves by the side of the fire-place. In his report, Sheen had placed it on its own legs in a corner of the room. The judge commented bluntly, 'We all tended to assume that he must be wrong about that'.

However, Sheen and Hughes were further compromised by something for which they were in no way to blame. They had both pinpointed the seat of fire in the lounge by the absence of a section of skirting-board which, they concluded, had been totally burnt through.

In fact, that skirting-board section still existed. It was exhibited in the courtroom. It had simply been removed by police. The fact that the experts were kept in the dark about it was especially surprising as Sheen had faxed the police beforehand on precisely this point:

> The fire damage to the [skirting-boards] has some importance ... As part of the skirting-board is missing, it will be necessary to have statements from those who cleared the debris to prove that the missing skirting-board was a result of the action of the fire and not simply because those who cleared the debris dislodged it.

Even though he had attempted to pursue the matter, he and Hughes were both misled. This was another feature that made this case so extraordinary: the prosecution's withholding of essential evidence from its own experts. The judge commented:

> So Mr Hughes got a false impression of the scene, and nobody told him, any more than they told Mr Sheen ... How it happened that nobody told [them] about that, you may wonder about, but it is a fact, and [they] reached that false conclusion.

Nevertheless, Hughes maintained his original stance. Even though he accepted under cross-examination that if the skirting-board had not burned away then that would affect his conclusions, he did not amend his conclusions. He continued to argue that, through a process of elimination, the fire had been deliberately set.

Nor did Sheen amend his conclusions, although he did alter the basis for them. He said in cross-examination that firemen in the bedroom had referred to 'flare-up', the phenomenon whereby flames, having been dampened by water from the hoses, suddenly flare up again. Sheen averred that this was evidence of the use of an accelerant.

While this could be true, other factors can also account for flare-up. In fact, a major criticism of Sheen was that he had crossed the boundary from scientific objectivity to witness subjectivity. A number of his faxes were produced in court. These suggested that he was, as the judge put it, 'trying to prove a particular case rather than looking at the evidence and asking what the answers are'. She cautioned the jury: 'You have to ask yourselves whether he has approached this matter open-mindedly or whether he's approached it from a partisan point of view'.

Dr Crosby (whom the Crown called as part of its case, although his evidence did not benefit the Crown) said one possibility was that the fire was caused by the Calor gas heater in the lounge, though the severity of the damage precluded any possibility of saying where or how it had started. He couldn't find an electrical cause of the fire either. He found signs of less than ideal practice, but his general view was that the system was adequate.

He regarded spread from the lounge to the bedroom as 'the most likely scenario': in other words, there was just one seat of fire. Most importantly, there was no evidence to indicate the use of an accelerant. None was detected on the floor in the bedroom, nor were there any signs of burning by an accelerant.

Perhaps hinting at her own private thoughts about the calibre of Sheen and Hughes, the judge told the jury that Crosby's evidence was 'obviously important'. She added, 'You may have thought that he was a totally dispassionate witness'.

With Crosby's evidence so much in Rhee's favour, the defence felt it needed to call only one scientific witness, Michael Jones. He thought by the time the bedroom door was opened, the fire in the lounge would have been burning for about fifteen minutes. He said that, in the absence of evidence, arguing for a deliberate cause on the process of elimination (as Hughes had done) was dangerous because no one could tell whether what had been consumed in the fire might not have been the cause of it. He gave a straightforward answer to the only question that really mattered.

'Can you say from the scientific evidence if the fire was started deliberately?', he was asked.

'No, not at all', he responded.

FOR THE DURATION of the trial, Rhee's family – his parents, sisters and brother and brother-in-law – rented a cottage outside Chester in order to be able to attend court every day. As the trial unfolded, their hopes were raised. Much of the evidence had been knocked down; and one particular juror appeared very favourably disposed towards the defence.

'There was this one guy on the jury', explained Yung Joo. 'We thought he could see through it all, he had insight about how emotive the prosecution case was. So it was going really well.

'That's when, as I saw it, the prosecution played the race card.'

What happened was this. There was evidence that, when he was recovering in hospital in the immediate aftermath of the fire, Rhee passed a number of comments to two police officers which showed that he was not in any genuine distress in the hours following his wife's death. Far from it. These were the alleged remarks:

'I never liked white girls and now I am burying one'
'I used to joke with her that she was that pure, that if I was a pimp, I'd make her a good prostitute'
'She always wanted to be cremated'
'Did you find her jewellery? – she always had £7-8,000 of jewellery with her'
'Could it have been a Welsh extremist – do you think it was a petrol bomb?'

There was what is termed a voir dire, a preliminary hearing in the absence of the jury in order to determine the admissibility of the evidence. The judge disallowed the second of the five, the prostitute remark, but said the other four could be presented as evidence by the prosecution.

These alleged remarks played a critical part in undermining Rhee's credibility in the courtroom. There were gasps in court as one of the officers read them out. The family was horrified. As far as they were concerned, this was the turning-point of the trial.

'You will of course have to be sure that [the remarks] were made', Mrs Justice Ebsworth cautioned the jury. With reference to the key remark (about never liking white girls), she added, 'No evidence was actually called to support the suggestion that the police officers got that wrong'.

The problem was that Rhee did not go into the witness-box to give evidence in his own defence.

'I remember going into the room where we had our legal con-ferences', said Yung Joo, 'and the barristers advised us that Jong Yoon shouldn't go into the witness-box. It was such a shock. They just said they didn't think it was such a good idea.

'Obviously, one of the concerns was that it may well have emerged that Jong Yoon had previously stood trial for murder, but we didn't think there would have been any problem about that. Those questions could have been answered. Jong Yoon didn't have a problem with giving evidence. There was such a lot he wanted to say.'

Nevertheless, Rhee did not give evidence.

By this stage, there were only eleven jurors. The twelfth man was stood down after other jurors complained about his personal hygiene. Before sending them out to consider their verdict, the judge said to them:

> The Crown's case is, and always has been, that there were two fires started quite deliberately – one in the lounge and one in the bedroom … That is why I say to you that you have to be sure the defendant started a fire in the bedroom as well as in the lounge …
>
> You may well reach the conclusion that, taken at its highest, no individual fire expert is saying to you, 'I am sure there was a deliberately-started fire'. No individual expert is saying to you, 'I am sure that the fire was started in two separate places' and no expert is saying to you, 'I can say how it was started'.

The jurors engaged in some preliminary discussion and then returned into court with three requests. They wanted Nerys Williams' witness statement and a transcript of her evidence in court. They asked for the written reports of the fire experts and transcripts of their evidence. Finally, they asked for a copy of the evidence of the police officer who claimed to have seen a petrol can in the Citroen.

Anyone familiar with the trial process would have been able to anticipate the answers, which were no, no and no. The jurors were refused everything.

The court is held to be an arena in which what matters is the direct unimpeded visual contact between the main protagonists in the courtroom, and especially between the witnesses and the jurors. The latter see the former. They must observe and listen carefully, both to what they are saying and their demeanour and expressions as they are saying it. The judicial process has developed as an oral tradition, and that is how it remains. Access to written forms of evidence, it is believed, will invalidate the purity of the process. The jurors may want various statements and transcripts, but they are not going to get them.

If the jurors needed to be reminded of particular areas of evidence, the judge told them, they would have to let her know. 'Then what I would have to do is to read to you everything a witness says', she explained to them. 'But I'm afraid we can't give it to you in written form.'

So the jurors were disappointed. There are twenty-eight pages of additional transcript when the judge dealt with their requests and went over points of the evidence for them again. On the Friday afternoon, one juror pointed out that he had a job interview on the Monday afternoon, but the judge refused his request for the court to adjourn for an additional day after the weekend. So they returned into court on the Monday morning. After further deliberations, they were given the majority direction. They then returned forty-five minutes later with their verdict: guilty, by a 10-1 majority, the dissenting juror presumably being the one in whom the family had set great store.

Dame Ann Ebsworth, the judge, was, sadly, to die of mesothelioma (the form of cancer that is usually caused by exposure to asbestos) in April 2002 at the age of sixty-four. According to her obituary in the *Guardian*, 'She cared deeply about the law, but even more deeply about justice'.

Notwithstanding some complicated areas of evidence, her summing-up is one of the clearest I have ever read. It seems to me that she was doing her best to nudge the jury in the direction of an acquittal. Perhaps, as she sentenced Rhee to life imprisonment, she may have reflected that she was upholding the law, but thwarting justice.

3

Two main areas of evidence underpinned the Crown's case: the testimony of Nerys Williams, the guest-house owner; and the testimony of their fire experts, Hughes and Sheen. Intriguingly, these were not self-contained areas of evidence, as they should have been. The Crown experts had based their findings on the supposition that William's evidence could be relied on.

This was a major shortcoming. In May 1998, just a few weeks after his conviction, Rhee wrote to Dr Zakaria Erzinçlioğlu, the former director of the Forensic Science Research Centre at Durham University. Erzinçlioğlu was astonished that Sheen had been allowed to give evidence in the way he did:

> One does not need a forensic scientist to repeat what a witness has said ... Mr Sheen starts his report by referring to [Williams'] statement that she smelt petrol. He then begins to argue from this that petrol must have been used to start the fire ...

But was it safe to rely on Williams' evidence?

She had not been injured in the fire. She was, however, kept in hospital for five days, presumably for observation. Afterwards, doctors diagnosed post-traumatic stress disorder. Her first statement regarding what happened was taken on 27 April, the thirteenth day after the fire. It contained a number of very intriguing features. She began by saying that she was awoken by 'a strong smell, a toxic smell, burning materials and substances'. She described the fumes as 'choking' and added, 'I thought I was dying'.

She mentioned that she could smell petrol. She continued, 'As I started to wake up, I heard a series of bangs and shouting, Jong's voice. My first thoughts were that Jong and Natalie were having an argument. I could hear Jong calling my name from outside the house.'

She grabbed her dressing gown and ran down the stairs. Rhee was shouting, 'Open the door, there is a fire'.

When she opened the door, she said, Rhee was outside. He was naked, with 'his hands crossed over his private parts'.

She described going upstairs to the guest lounge:'I was horrified to find that the lounge door was on fire. It was slightly ajar, however, enough for me to be able to enter the guest lounge. As I did so, I could see that the curtains and furniture were on fire and the flames were licking across the top of the carpet. Everything in the room seemed to be on fire. I stepped back into the hallway.

'I was shouting at Jong. The stairs to the bedroom were clear, there were no flames on them.'

She said that the guest bedroom door was 'closed' or 'closed to'.

'I could see the door', she emphasised. 'There were no flames. There was nothing to stop anyone going up the stairs. There was no smoke on the stairs. There was fire in the lounge, not anywhere else. I said, "Get Natalie out". I shouted it repeatedly. He made no attempt to do so.'

She said that they filled a bucket of water and threw it at the fire. She then told Rhee to get the ladder to reach the bedroom, but he appeared with a broken wooden ladder rather than the aluminium one she had indicated. They tried the phone, but the line was dead. Rhee said that his mobile phone was in the car, so he tore down a curtain pole, ran to the car and smashed one of the windows to reach in and grab the phone. There was no signal, so they ran up the mountainside and eventually got a signal, and were able to phone the emergency services.

That was her first recorded account. By the time she came to give the account at trial, it had changed in a number of key respects. She did not say she had heard voices and as a result thought that perhaps Rhee and Natalie were arguing. She no longer maintained that she went *into* the burning room, but had instead stood in the doorway. She now said that, when she was given the mobile, she ran up the road to get a signal because she knew you couldn't get a signal by the cottage. Rhee didn't go with her. 'She was quite confident', explained the judge, 'that Rhee had not been with her when she went up the road with the mobile'.

Another of the significant departures in Williams' trial evidence from what she had said in the witness statement was the omission of any reference to having smelt petrol. The defence argued that this was because she had come to understand that if she had actually smelt petrol from her bedroom, in a separate part of the building, then the fire would have been a conflagration from which none of them could have escaped.

Her account of how she awoke was strange. Her bedroom was in the main part of the house. There was fire in the lounge in the guests' accommodation, which was an extension to the original property. Consequently, the smoke that she said woke her needed to pass out of the guest lounge, through the hallway, down the stairs to the kitchen, through a corridor and into the main lounge, up the stairs at the other end of the building, onto the landing and into Williams' bedroom. It is hard to understand how the 'choking fumes' which were so uncomfortable that 'I thought I was going to die' could have reached her.

It is far more likely that she was awoken by Rhee's desperate shouts. Why did she omit all reference to that at the trial? A possible reason, one might suggest, is that it hardly squared with the account she was going to give of Rhee being unconcerned about rescuing Natalie.

Mrs Williams said that she and Rhee left the cottage through the hallway door. Due to the heat, however, they would not have been able to do that. In any case, a fire officer found that the door was locked when he attempted to enter. On this point also, Rhee's account, that they entered and exited from the kitchen, must have been accurate.

Mrs Williams made the baffling suggestion that she went into the guest lounge, where the fire was raging. Obviously, this could not have happened. So she changed her account at trial. 'I didn't mean to say I went in', she said, 'I stood on the edge of the doorway, between the frame. I didn't go in. There were flames everywhere, the room was ablaze.'

However, this would have been equally impossible, because of the heat from the fire. 'If there is a fully developed fire in the lounge', Jones pointed out, 'then you couldn't stand in the doorway. [Williams] cannot have been standing where she said she was.'

The judge agreed. That was something, she told the jury, which 'your common sense, as well as the evidence of every fire expert, tells you she would not have been able to do'.

Mrs Williams said that at that key moment, the hallway was clear of flames, but that Rhee failed to save Natalie when he had the opportunity. She said, 'There was nothing to stop anyone going up the stairs'. If this evidence is taken at face value, and there really was nothing to stop anyone going up the stairs, it begs an obvious question. If Rhee wouldn't do anything, why did she not attempt to rescue Natalie herself? Again, her story makes no sense.

The judge pointed out to the jury the 'discrepancies' between what she said in her statement and the evidence she gave at trial. 'If [Williams] has changed what she said originally', she said to them, 'then you have to make a judgment about whether that affects her reliability'.

In fact, the variations in her account is just one of the features that brings into question her reliability.

According to Rhee's account of what happened in the initial stages, she was like a headless chicken. Some of the incidents (for example, throwing a bucketful of water at the raging fire, a hopelessly futile act) do tend to suggest a state of blind panic. Williams suggested that Rhee had ignored perfectly serviceable ladders and instead used an old, broken ladder. Yet she and Rhee were in pitch blackness on a Welsh mountainside. The wooden ladder was near at hand; the aluminium ladders were the other side of a stone wall.

She stated that she had run up the hill with the mobile phone to get a signal to call the emergency services and that Rhee had not assisted her. At trial, the defence QC handed Williams the phone and invited her to call 999. She took the phone and put it down while she got out her glasses.

'On that night', he asked, 'did you put the phone down while you put your glasses on?'

No, she conceded, she hadn't.

So she tried in court without glasses. The first problem was how to switch it on. She couldn't manage to do that. She couldn't even slide the cover down to reveal the numbers. So she handed it back. It was switched on and then given back to her. She struggled for a while with the buttons and eventually managed to dial 000.

'It is not unfair to her to say', the judge subsequently commented, 'she obviously hadn't the faintest idea how to use … that phone.'

This obviously supported Rhee's account – that he had dialled 999 and handed her the phone, already connected to the emergency switchboard, merely so that she could pronounce the Welsh place-names correctly. She had not called the emergency services herself. Nor, as we will see, was the phone switched off at the end of the call.

Nerys Williams said that when she saw Rhee he was 'naked' and was 'holding his hands crossed over his private parts'. Rhee said this was untrue; he was wearing his boxer shorts. So here, again, there is a complete difference of opinion between them. Under cross-examination, it was put to Williams that she must have got it wrong. 'No', she insisted, 'that is how he was when I remember first seeing him'.

Again, the evidence supports Rhee's account and not hers. Rhee was certainly wearing his boxer shorts when the fire services and the police arrived; there was unanimity among the witnesses on that point. So, if he had been naked but had put on his boxers in the meantime, where had he got them from? Obviously not from the bedroom, where his underwear is likely to have been.

Eyewitness testimony is one of the most bedevilled areas in criminal justice. However, this is no ordinary point of evidence. In any hierarchy of points of evidence that are most likely to be remembered accurately by eyewitnesses, whether someone is naked comes more or less at the top of the list. The fact that Williams has a mistaken memory about this therefore suggests that she comes into the category of the least reliable witnesses of all.

It is also known that personal stress is a factor tending to make eyewitnesses less reliable; and these circumstances would have been very personally stressful for her.

At one point, Nerys Williams was asked about the threat of civil proceedings against her. Was she perhaps, the judge asked rhetorically in her summing-up, deliberately giving a false account to protect herself?

The guest-house extension to the cottage was put up without planning permission. It was in one of the country's national parks, where planning restrictions are generally tighter than elsewhere. When a previous owner of the cottage had been seeking to develop it in 1973, he did obtain planning permission (with a number of conditions) – so he had been fully aware of the position. Mike Rothwell told the court that, because they were not changing the roof line, 'there was no need for planning consent'. In fact, the consent of the Snowdonia National Park Authority would have been needed.

As a rule, those developing their properties will get planning permission and then ascertain that the proposed development conforms to building control regulations. In this instance, there was no planning permission and nor did anyone from the building control department of Conwy County Borough Council inspect the works. The extension may not have been built to standards of the time.

The jury specifically asked Williams whether health and safety regulations were adhered to in the construction of the extension. She replied that she was not required to comply with regulations as the house accommodated fewer than six guests.

There was significant flooding in the area in 1990. Housing was damaged, claims were submitted, and as a result insurance premiums escalated. The higher rates were prohibitive for Williams and Rothwell, who allowed their policy to lapse. At the time this happened, therefore, they were not insured.

Inspectors reported 'several faults and aspects of bad practice in the wiring of the old cottage'. Perhaps the fire may have been caused by electrical problems. Nerys Williams may have been vulnerable to legal proceedings. The failure to obtain planning permission would have seriously compromised her defence of any civil action, which would undoubtedly have been ruinous for her as she was uninsured.

However, as Rhee was prosecuted, she did not suffer any difficulties as a result of the fire and was even able to obtain a grant of £39,481 from Conwy Council towards rebuilding the house.

The timing of Williams' original statement, made on the *thirteenth day* after the fire, is remarkable. The police told the Court that there had been previous discussions with her about what happened, but that no record of those conversations was taken. It then emerged, quite by chance, that the information wasn't true. In the third week of the trial, it came to light that day-by-day notes of the conversations *had* been taken. The police revised their stance, and now said they weren't available because they had been 'lost'.

So we do not know what occurred during that vital thirteen-day period between the fire and her first statement. What we do know is that the situation, as it was relayed to the jury, is not credible. If Williams was aware that Rhee, in order to murder his wife, had burned down her property – her uninsured property – it is unimaginable that she would not have wished to draw this to the attention of the police straightaway.

After the call to the emergency services, the mobile phone was not switched off. The line remained open. Most users would automatically have pushed the button to end the call. So this was of some minor interest in providing further evidence of Williams' inability to handle mobile phones. It was, though, of major importance in providing evidence of the ensuing exchanges between Rhee and Williams. Obviously, neither had any idea that their words were being overheard and, indeed, recorded.

There was nothing in what passed between them to support Williams' contention that Rhee was responsible for the fire. Indeed, the situation was the reverse of what she claimed. He was upset and angry and clearly blamed her. She is heard to ask, 'What happened?' He snapped back at her, 'You should know – it's your house'.

There is, moreover, the additional evidence provided by that first statement made by Williams. Referring to these same moments, after they had phoned and while waiting for the fire service to arrive, she stated:

On returning to the house, flames were now coming out of the roof. Jong was now sitting on the grass with his head in his hands. I approached him and the first thing he said was, 'Natalie's dead, Natalie's dead, she was pregnant as well, you know'. I put my arm around his shoulder to comfort him, but he shrugged it off and now seemed angry.

It scarcely needs restating but by this point, according to the testimony which Williams would give on oath at trial, this is what had happened: Rhee had set a fire in her house in order to murder his wife. This had led to most of her uninsured property being burnt down. He had not helped her to fight the fire and indeed had been obstructive. He had not helped to phone for the emergency services. Knowing all that, what did she do? *I put my arm around his shoulder to comfort him.*

Altogether, it would be foolhardy to place weight on her evidence. Yet that is what the two prosecution fire experts, Hughes and Sheen, had done.

Setting aside her evidence, it becomes possible to piece together a logical picture of what must have happened. It is probable that the time between Jong Yoon and Natalie Rhee and Nerys Williams being awoken, and the arrival of the fire services, was about twenty minutes: the fire crew arrived eleven minutes after they were called, and Rhee reckoned that up to about eight minutes elapsed before the call was made.

Six of the firemen attending the scene independently noticed that the guest lounge was 'smoke-logged' – that is, totally burnt through – when they arrived. By contrast, the bedroom fire was raging. It was, said one, 'engulfed in flames from floor to ceiling'. Another said that it was 'the hottest fire' he had experienced in ten years. In fact, it took so long to put out that the frontline crew fighting it had to withdraw to replenish their oxygen supplies. The air in their cylinders usually lasts for about ten minutes.

It would normally take about forty minutes for a room of the size of the lounge to reach a smoke-logged state. So the bedroom fire seemed to be running significantly behind the lounge fire. Not only does this entirely contradict the theory that they were separate fires started at more or less the same time, but it is evidence that fully supports the view of Crosby and Jones – that the fire started in the lounge and spread naturally to the bedroom.

These crucial timings, however, were never explained to the jury.

Nor was the significance of the pathology ever explained to the jury. The carbon monoxide level in Natalie's blood was 79%. This is massively important information. A person lying on the floor during a fire will not have a carbon monoxide level greater than 50%; in a fire, hot air will rise over cold, so the more toxic gases of the fire will not be concentrated at floor level. Had Natalie been on the floor before the smoke and fire penetrated the bedroom, it would have been impossible for the level to have reached 79%. (Inhalation cannot, of course, occur after death.) So this is clear evidence that Natalie was standing up when she was overcome – evidence that is fully consistent with the defence case.

This also brought into perspective the weakness of the Crown's argument that Rhee had 'somehow' subdued Natalie before leaving her 'possibly unconscious'. Natalie's body was found on the carpet by the window, with her head just under the edge of the bed. She was on her back, which was not burnt, nor was the carpet beneath her. Her legs and arms were free. There were no signs of pressure having been applied to the neck. All toxicology tests proved negative. She had not been drugged. Alcohol tests showed that she had consumed no more than two units. There was nothing to indicate that she had been either attacked or forcibly restrained.

The Crown had to admit that the pathologist 'could not find any evidence of any act other than fire as the cause of death'.

OTHER AREAS OF evidence were massively contentious. The Crown told the jury that Rhee had looked at other guest-houses, but had turned them down because he could see they had smoke alarms. He had chosen this one both because of its remote location and because it was not fitted with smoke alarms.

This was reported as fact in many national newspapers but, like much that is reported as fact, it is untrue and even absurd. Rhee and Natalie had previously looked at one hotel. It was next to a main road and there were a couple of uncouth-looking characters at the bar. They turned it down. They then went to the tourist information centre where they selected a guest-house, this one, from photographs. Staff there booked it for them straightaway. Obviously, Rhee could have known nothing of the adequacy or otherwise of its fire precautions.

In order to try to create the impression that he had turned down other accommodation, the Crown brought forward evidence that a couple had rejected a guest-house room elsewhere in the area at about 4.00 that Saturday afternoon. Rhee and Natalie were not identified as the couple in question. This was not surprising. After all, it couldn't have been them because by that time they had already arrived at Williams' guest-house. They got there at about 3.15 or 3.30, as Nerys Williams herself testified. With some under-statement, the judge observed that it was 'a little difficult' to see how these pieces of prosecution evidence could be reconciled, and how Rhee and Natalie could be in two places at once.

The suggestion that this property had been chosen because of its remoteness is also disingenuous. Probably a high percentage of cottages in Snowdonia could be described as 'remote' – but this one wasn't; after all, the fire brigade attended within eleven minutes.

Then, the prosecution argued that it was significant that Rhee's mobile phone, cash and credit cards were in the car; he had previously been the victim of burglaries, they said, and so was especially security-conscious and would not normally leave them there overnight.

Here, again, the Crown was putting forward inconsistent pieces of evidence. They had spent some time arguing that Rhee deliberately selected an isolated cottage in order to carry out the crime. So while he would certainly have been very concerned about security in London, he may well have been less circumspect on a Welsh hillside. The defence explanation – that as the couple would be departing the next morning, Rhee had already packed a few items away in a rucksack in the car – was perfectly adequate.

The Crown suggested that Rhee had deliberately chosen that evening to set the fire as he knew Rothwell would be away. But if Rhee had been an arsonist and murderer, why would that have mattered? Rothwell and Williams slept in a different part of the building; they were unlikely to be able to lend effective assistance.

Then there was the bedroom door bolt, in the locked position. This may on the surface have appeared incriminating; the locked door has been a feature of many Hollywood crime thrillers. In this instance, the situation was completely different. The lock was a sliding bolt. So, if Rhee had locked Natalie in the bedroom, she could have unlocked it simply by sliding the bolt back.

But that hardly got to the bottom of why this evidence was so misleading. Supposing a fire had been deliberately set outside the room, then, if the bedroom door had been securely fastened, that could only have been *very helpful*. As one expert put it, 'a closed bedroom door offers a considerable degree of protection from the toxic smoke for an extended period'. Alternatively, if there were fires both inside and outside the room, as the Crown asserted, then it would have made no difference whether the door was bolted or not.

The bolt was not recovered from the door. It was recovered weeks later from the general debris outside the house. The area was not treated as a crime-scene for some time after the fire, so items of detritus could have been interfered with. There is no evidence whatever that this bolt came from the bedroom; the prosecution merely asserted that it did. The judge's advice to the jury was unequivocal: 'to actually place serious weight on exactly what was found when, and how it was labelled, would be unwise'.

So the locked door idea was of no value evidentially. This description also applied to another area of testimony, the green petrol can. The evidence was merely that one police officer said he had seen such a can, containing a small amount of liquid, in the boot of the Citroen car. When questioned, Rhee told officers that there wasn't a petrol can in the car. He was slightly uncertain, however, saying, 'If there was one, I don't recall one'. This was presented as evidence of his evasiveness on the issue, though one could alternatively argue that it was indicative of some puzzlement and a desire to give an honest answer.

There is no contemporaneous evidence about the petrol can. No statement was made at the time. The officer who said he saw it didn't make a statement until 27 April (coincidentally, the day that Nerys Williams made her first statement).

He had not actually opened the boot. The keys to open it had been consumed in the fire. He attempted to see what was in the boot by pulling down the rear seat and looking behind through the crack. He said there was a small amount of liquid in the bottom of the can. But it is hard to understand how he could have known this. Presumably, he can only have done so by reaching behind the seat, taking out the can and shaking it; but he said he didn't do that.

Although he said he saw a petrol can, what is rather more significant is what he didn't see. He did not notice bulky items that were in the boot: Natalie's full-length woollen winter coat, and the four large ceramic Portmeirion vases. According to him, these items, which one would have thought impossible to miss, were not in the boot.

No other police officer ever saw a petrol can in the car. The other officer who was searching the car with him made a statement. He could not corroborate the evidence; he said he was searching a different part of the car and had not seen the petrol can in the boot.

As Williams had retracted her original evidence about smell-ing petrol, this was now the only evidence of petrol in the case. Yet there are several reasons why we know that this was not a petrol fire. None of the firemen smelt petrol. There was no petrol detected in the debris. If petrol had been used, then the whole house would probably have gone up in an inferno which neither Rhee nor Williams could have survived.

The postmortem on Natalie provided further information about this. If someone dies in a rapid flash fire, such as one started with petrol, then there will be pulmonary oedema, or damage to the lower respiratory tract, as a result of breathing in hot gases. Natalie's body showed no damage of that kind. Secondly, there will be a relatively low carbon monoxide level in the body, as such fires produce little carbon monoxide, but the level in Natalie's body was especially high.

Apart from the evidence of the solitary police officer, there is no evidence at all of the existence of this can. The situation is odd. Police officers are professionally trained to notice things that aren't quite right. This officer was attending a fatal fire; and there was, he said, an almost-empty petrol can in the car. So wouldn't it have been professionally diligent for him to take in this information, note it down, and draw it to the attention of colleagues? Yet he admitted not only that he didn't remove it or pick it up, but even that he 'didn't register it as being of significance'.

What was supposed to have happened? Had Rhee, having started the fires, leapt from the window, petrol can in hand, and then placed it back in the boot? But he couldn't have done that; he didn't have the keys.

So, viewed in its totality, this is a grossly misleading area of evidence. Whether there was an empty petrol can in the car or not, it was clear that a can of petrol was not used to start this fire.

What about the race remarks evidence? On that first day, in the hours after the fire, the officers wrote reports of what happened when they were with Rhee. Those reports contained no mention of the remarks. Nor were they referred to in their notebooks. There was no contemporaneous reference to them at all. At trial, the officers conceded this. In explanation, they said they had omitted them because, at the time, they did not consider them to be of any significance and, in the circumstances, it seemed unnecessary to refer to such distasteful comments.

However, there was no credible context for the remarks. Indeed, there was no context of any kind. The officers were unable to say what conversation had led up to such remarks or what had flowed from them; or when, in relation to other occurrences (like the arrival of the nurse or doctor), the remarks had been made. They simply said that Rhee had made them.

After his early years in South Korea, Rhee had enjoyed a solidly middle-class upbringing in England. He had been immersed in English culture. He had never had a Korean girlfriend; all his girlfriends had been white. His family adamantly believe that such thoughts would never have entered his consciousness, let alone been uttered as gratuitously offensive remarks to complete strangers. All the supposed remarks, they believed, were illogical and unthinkable. They had no doubt whatever that they were untrue.

Six weeks after the fire, Rhee was interviewed under caution for over nine-and-a-half hours about his supposed crime. Not once in all that time did the officers – one of whom was one of those to whom the comments had supposedly been passed – mention the remarks or allude to them in any way. That is so extraordinary it inevitably raises additional queries about the integrity of the evidence.

So Rhee, who maintains that he was unaware of the alleged remarks until committal papers were served, was given no opportunity to rebut or make any comment about them. His family believed that it would have been of inestimable importance to his defence for him to have gone into the witness-box himself. The jury would have had the opportunity to see how inaccurate the prosecution's characterisation of him was.

However, lawyers are trained to think differently. Indeed, I often feel there is a huge gulf between the legal process as lawyers view it and as the public – and therefore jurors – perceive it. Defence lawyers are trained to ensure that points of evidence are countered and all roads to a guilty verdict are barred. There must be no route through to a conviction. That is the approach that lawyers adopt. The imperative is not to lose. It is the equivalent, in football terms, of playing for a goalless draw.

From that perspective, it made no sense for Rhee to give evidence himself. There was the risk that, once the jury got to hear about it, the previous murder charge would assume a wholly unwarranted saliency. So no risks were taken; the goalless draw mindset prevailed.

However, that approach entirely ignores the countervailing risk: that jurors who haven't heard from the defendant will imagine the reason for his non-appearance is much more detrimental than it actually is. Moreover, this risk has been significantly magnified since the Criminal Justice and Public Order Act 1994 allowed adverse inferences to be drawn from a defendant's choosing to remain silent and not give evidence at trial. The judge had said, 'You may think that if he had an answer to it, he would have gone into the witness-box to tell you what it is'.

The arguments which the defence gave for his client's non-appearance in the witness-box were that the evidence was so thin and unreliable it did not call for an answer; and that Rhee had said it all before and the jury had already heard his account at considerable length.

In recent years, some unfortunate developments have impaired the trial process. One of these is that the defence case is initially heard as part of the prosecution case from the mouths of prosecution witnesses. The record of the interview which the defendant gave after his arrest will be laboriously read out as part of the interviewing officers' evidence. That is what the defence counsel was referring to. Nevertheless, if the defence offer no resistance, it gives the Crown the double advantage of being able to present the crux of the defence case itself without the jurors hearing it at all from the defendant.

The family vehemently maintain to this day that this was one of the main reasons for Rhee's conviction; he should have gone into the witness-box, both specifically to rebut the race remarks and more generally to allow the jury to hear his own first-hand account.

The police probed into Rhee's background, perhaps expecting to find unedifying details, but there were none. Friends spoke positively about Rhee and Natalie's relationship. Air Commodore Doble said that his daughter was deeply in love with Rhee and seemed very happy. Rhee and Natalie had consulted a financial adviser and taken out life insurance. Witnesses pointed out that there was nothing remotely sinister about that; had Rhee predeceased Natalie, then the level of cover would have provided no more than a modest income for her and any children.

The fact that Rhee had lost a great deal of money in gambling did not in this instance provide a motive for murder. There are cases where the pressure of unmanageable debts has had tragic outcomes, and led to murder or suicide. But people respond in different ways. Mario Puzo paid off his gambling debts by selling the film rights to a book he hadn't even started writing, the book which became *The Godfather*. In Rhee's case, there were no debts. He had certainly lost a lot, but he had not lost more than he had.

The phone evidence is instructive not simply because of Nerys Williams' comical attempts in court to dial a number. When Rhee was first suspected of murder, investigators believed he would have cut the phone line. This proved not to be the case. British Telecom engineers confirmed that Rhee had not tampered with it; the landline was dead because of a short circuit caused by the fire. It was therefore fortuitous indeed that Rhee's mobile was in the Citroen and was available. Had he been an arsonist, it would have been easy enough for him to have left it where it was not available – in the bedroom.

The basic crime scenario never did make any sense. It was hard to believe that someone in that situation would light two fires – wouldn't one have been enough? – especially as lighting the second may have jeopardised his own safety.

The account of what happened at the start of this chapter is the one given by Rhee. In describing other cases, I have tried to ensure that the account given initially is as neutral as possible. On this occasion it cannot be done. It is impossible to synthesise the witnesses' statements. One must accept either Rhee's account or Nerys Williams'. As the judge put it, their accounts 'cannot live together'.

Two aspects of his account remain particularly instructive. He emphasised in his very first statement that he had turned off all the electrical appliances before going to bed. Yet he knew from his own first-hand experience that major fires could be caused by electrical faults. If he had been an arsonist, wouldn't he have wanted to leave open the possibility that the fire was caused through some electrical malfunction?

This similarly applies to his continuing insistence that Natalie was pregnant when she died. The pathologists refuted this suggestion and said that they had discovered no evidence of pregnancy when they examined her. So the matter was presented at trial as evidence of his dishonesty. Then, in summing up, the judge said:

> Natalie was not pregnant, whatever may have been said by the defendant ... [When he] was saying, 'Natalie was pregnant', that wasn't true ... There couldn't be a mistake about that because there was a hysterological examination and she was not pregnant.

This was wrong. Indeed, it was probably the only mistake that Mrs Justice Ebsworth made. There hadn't been what she termed a hysterological examination; just a postmortem. Gynaecological signs of early pregnancy may not be revealed at postmortem. Would the very tiny foetus have been seen by anyone not specifically looking for it?

Rhee is adamant that she had tested positive, and there can be no reason to doubt him. If he were guilty, why would he wish to emphasise this point, which would only have exacerbated his crime?

The fact is that, in view of Natalie's earlier miscarriage, they decided not to jump the gun in relaying the news to their families. They had told both Jong Ho and also a friend who lived in Greenwich, south London with his wife and three daughters who, on hearing this news, gave Rhee and Natalie a congratulations card. This card, bearing the message, 'You must come and see us soon with your new baby', was found in the Citroen after the fire.

4

Dr Zakaria Erzinçlioğlu began to correspond with Rhee and carefully read through the bundles of case papers that Rhee sent him. On 18 December 1998, he visited Rhee in Gartree Prison and afterwards wrote:

> I spent two hours with him and we discussed the whole case. I asked him all the questions I had prepared. When I arrived home that night, I wrote in my diary, 'Jong Rhee is innocent'.

Zakaria was an Armenian Jew born in Hungary to Turkish parents. He became the UK's foremost forensic entomologist, spending much of his career at Cambridge University. He seemed, to those of us who knew him, one of the genuinely good people in the world, combining a gentle disposition with a fierce desire to tackle injustice. He concluded his examination of Rhee's case by noting in his diary, 'For my part, I will not give up the struggle to redress this monstrous iniquity'.

His own part, however, was to be sadly cut short; he died of a heart attack in September 2002.

By then, however, he had asked Michael Green, the now-retired professor of forensic pathology at Sheffield University, for his views on the case. Green reported:

There is nothing to show that Mrs Rhee had been incapacitated or 'subdued' before the fire started. I am satisfied that the levels of carb-oxyhaemoglobin would have been sufficient to cause rapid incapacity. If cyanide [from furniture materials] was present in the products of combustion, as it almost certainly would have been, incapacity would have been even more rapid.

One has to consider the effects of fear and the production of dense smoke which would both impede vision and cause respiratory distress … However my personal opinion is that the heat, smoke and toxic fumes alone would have produced rapid incapacity.

The case was next examined by Christopher Milroy. He was one of Green's successors as professor of forensic pathology at Sheffield University and is now a forensic pathologist in Ottawa, Canada. Milroy concluded that 'the pathological findings … provide sup-port for [the] contention that Natalie Rhee died in an accidental fire'.

A further opinion was sought from Dr Roger Berrett, of Forensic Access. He had been a forensic scientist for thirty-five years, was a former principal scientist at the Metropolitan Police forensic science laboratory in Lambeth, and had specialised in fire investigation since 1988.

Dr Berrett said that the fire started in the lounge, and had spread to the roof space and from there to the bedroom. He said it should have been treated as a single-seat fire. He was highly critical of the professional standards of the prosecution's experts, Patrick Sheen and Station Officer Hughes. He said that Sheen had 'leaned over backwards' to support the prosecution case; that his conclusions were 'simply wrong'; and that he was 'dangerous in the criminal courts'.

He was emphatic that the views of these Crown witnesses were 'scientifically flawed' and that there was no scientific evidence to support the prosecution's assertions either that there were two seats of fire or that an accelerant had been used. He added that the investigation itself contained many breaches of Home Office guidelines for the investigation of fires.

Then Professor David Purser came into the case. He has advised the British government on fire safety issues for over twenty years and has given evidence in trials in both the UK and US. He holds visiting professorships in the UK, US and New Zealand. His particular expertise, as a fire expert with additional qualifications in pathology and neurophysiology, is the interaction of fires with people. He uses pathological and toxicological evidence, together with the information about the fire, to establish the causes of incapacitation and death.

His first observation was that no expert evidence had addressed the important question of smoke (though Professor Green had alluded to it). Large domestic fires will produce dense smoke. Purser described it as 'inconceivable' that the lounge fire would not have been producing 'a large volume of dense, hot and highly toxic smoke in the lounge and hallways area'.

He also noticed a vital point which the original witnesses had either failed to register or failed to draw to attention: the bedroom window was open. We know the window was open because the fire had reached outside to set a fir tree alight, as members of the fire crew noticed; there were shards of clean broken glass on the ground beneath it; and because the notion of Rhee jumping through the window, and somehow stopping in mid-air to shut it behind him, is ridiculous.

This means that, if there had been a separate fire in the bedroom, it would have been supplied with air from the open window and would quickly have become very hot. This would only increase the inevitability of the victim suffering extensive burns, but having relatively low concentrations of carboxyhaemoglobin in the body. As this was not the case, it was another powerful pointer to the fact that there was not a separate seat of fire in the bedroom.

The level of carboxyhaemoglobin in Natalie's bloodstream in itself proved there was not a separate seat of fire in the bedroom. Together with the absence of respiratory tract damage noted at postmortem, the 79% level showed that Natalie had died from the smoke. Purser said her death was:

> ... typical of cases in which the victim is exposed to smoke from a fire in a different room in the same house and where the door to the victim's room is open ...

The further you are away from the source, the more likely it is that you will die from the smoke rather than the flames. You lose consciousness, but have to have lived for a while to continue to breathe in the toxic fumes …

He addressed the absolutely central issue in the case: how had Rhee managed to escape from the fire, while Natalie perished? He reported:

The conditions in the bedroom would have been sufficient to cause collapse within approximately one-and-a-half to three minutes. The time available for escape is very limited. The time between Mr Rhee escaping and Mrs Rhee becoming incapacitated could have been a matter of seconds and almost certainly less than one minute.

Once Mrs Rhee had been overcome by the asphyxiant gases she would continue to breathe in an unconscious state. After a minute or so the concentrations of carboxyhaemoglobin and hydrogen cyanide in her blood would be sufficient for respiration and circulation to cease and she would have died.

Natalie's momentary indecision about jumping had proved fatal.

Purser was one of the international experts who in December 1986 had investigated the major Dupont Plaza Hotel fire in San Juan, Puerto Rico, which led to the deaths of ninety-seven people. In that case, there was a parallel tragedy. A couple went to the window to jump. The man jumped and survived, but his female companion failed to jump. She was among the fatalities. Indeed, Purser knew of several cases in which 'two people were together in a fire from which one escaped and the other did not'.

In Purser's report, he included a caveat to the effect that no scientist could be absolutely sure because of variables such as the precise structure of the building, the materials used in its construction and the ventilation conditions at the time. He suggested that the only way to assess and eliminate all possible variables about the spread of the fire was to construct a computer model.

It took years, but finally the Rhee family managed to raise the thousands of pounds to carry out this work, which was conducted at the Building Research Establishment in Watford.

The computer modelling bore out the defence case. There was only one seat of fire. It started in the lounge and, having consumed the lounge, the most likely scenario is that it spread rapidly to the bedroom through the unlatched door. Had the bedroom door been closed, then the fire could not have broken through in the time available.

The only person who had ever suggested the bedroom door was closed was Nerys Williams. But she had not consistently said that. At one point she said it was 'closed'; and at another that it had been 'closed to'. In the context of a raging fire there is, of course, all the difference in the world between the two; if the door was 'closed to', then it was ajar. It is indicative of the poor levels of case analysis in UK courtrooms that this vital distinction was never addressed or, perhaps, even noticed.

Because of the heat and the smoke, it would not have been possible for Williams to stand where she said she stood – whether in the lounge (her original version) or just outside it (her changed version). The plume of thick black smoke pouring out of the lounge and filling the hallway area also means that the bedroom door would have been obscured and Mrs Williams would not even have been able to see along the passage to it.

However, the computer modelling further illuminated this aspect of the case. After the cottage was in effect reconstructed from the original plans for the computer, the scientists realised that the three-dimensional model used at trial for the jury was incorrectly constructed. It gave a false impression of the critical hallway area. Because of the curvature of the passage wall, Mrs Williams would not have been able to see the bedroom door from where she said she was standing. The jury was misled. Irrespective of the density of smoke, she could not have seen it.

The computer modelling demonstrated that, with all possible fire scenarios, there was one consistent factor: in every instance, there was thick smoke in the hallway at the time that Rhee and Mrs Williams returned into the house.

If accelerants had been used, then there would have been a rapidly developing fire and, again, Natalie would have suffered very severe burns prior to death. Even if low levels of an accelerant had been used, so that the fire had remained non-hazardous for a little while, there would still have come a point when it would have developed into a hot fire. In that case, again, Natalie would have received serious burns to the body and to her upper respiratory tract. Again, this was not the case; again, this was an indication that no accelerants were used.

If Natalie had been incapacitated or restrained in any way, and a fire ignited in the bedroom, then she would have died from burns and her body would have contained only a low level of carboxyhaemoglobin

So the computer modelling bore out all the work conducted by the genuine experts: Crosby and Jones at trial; and Green, Milroy, Berrett and Purser post-trial. The Crown's scientific case now rests on the views of one man, the electrical engineer Patrick Sheen – a man who has been described as 'dangerous in the criminal courts'.

DURING THE PERIOD that Purser was conducting his research, there was heightened interest in a similar case in the United States. On 23 December 1991, Cameron Willingham, a 23-year-old car mechanic, was the only survivor of a house fire in Corsicana, just south of Dallas, Texas, that killed his three young children. This was an unmitigated tragedy for him and his wife, Stacy, who at the time was out of the house buying Christmas presents for the children.

The tragedy was to be quickly compounded. State prosecutors argued, on the basis of no evidence whatever, that Willingham had been abusing his children (in fact, Stacy told investigators that he would never have harmed them) and had started the fire deliberately in order to cover this up. Willingham was put on trial for murder.

It is intriguing to note that in both these cases the prosecutions used parallel strands of emotive evidence: in the Willingham case, as with the Rhee case, prosecutors said that the fire was multi-seated, with an accelerant having been used; and also called witnesses to testify that Willingham would not go back into the house to rescue the children, even though there was the opportunity to do so. As with the witness in the Rhee case, this evidence was intrinsically irrational simply because it raised the question of why, if this was so, witnesses hadn't rescued the children themselves – although this point wasn't emphasised sufficiently at either trial.

Willingham was convicted and sentenced to death.

There was also other 'evidence' against him. Just prior to the execution, by which time the scientific case for arson was fast unravelling, a State prosecutor argued that the testimony of a prison informer, who claimed that Willingham had confessed to him in prison, was on its own sufficient to prove Willingham's guilt. However, on 28 February 2014, the *New York Times* reported that newly-found documents in the case files showed that the jailhouse snitch had actually struck a deal with the authorities. He had been promised a lighter sentence in return for assisting the State case. *(see Note re jailhouse snitch, page 468)*

Willingham, protesting his complete innocence to the very end, was executed on 16 February 2004. In the years since, internationally respected fire investigators have argued that the prosecution case was completely wrong and that the cause of the fire was not arson. The Texas Forensic Science Commission asked Dr Craig Beyler, of Baltimore, Maryland, to provide an independent assessment. He delivered a scathing report in which he stated that the original State fire 'experts' had botched their investigations.

ON 28 MAY 2015 Jong Yoon Rhee was taken from his cell at Gartree prison, near Market Harborough, to Heathrow airport where, accompanied by three guards, he was put on a Korean Air flight to Incheon airport, Seoul.

The UK Borders Act 2007 stipulates that all non-EEA citizens sentenced to a prison term of twelve months or longer would face mandatory deportation. However, the government is routinely criticised by the media for failing to expel those labelled as malefactors of various kinds. Here, the authorities reckoned, was someone who could become a statistic to help placate the popular press.

It would be the first time ever that someone was deported from the UK to South Korea. In enforcing this deportation, the UK government was sending Rhee to a country where he knew no one, a country that he had left as a seven-year-old and had had no contact with in the forty years since.

It was only through a diplomatic oddity (or, some might argue, administrative disingenuousness) that Rhee never became a UK citizen. When the family first arrived in the country at the start of the 1970s, they were welcomed. 'Indefinite leave to stay' was stamped on their passports. It was explained to them that this was an absolute guarantee of their freedom to live and work in the UK and that further accreditation was unnecessary. If it had been, family members would have applied – and would certainly have been granted citizenship.

Now Rhee has been driven to the very edge of mental despair, not just by his long incarceration for a crime he didn't commit – a crime, indeed, that never happened – but also by the knowledge that he has been able to demonstrate his innocence over and over, and yet all his entreaties have been brushed aside.

'I produced so much fresh evidence to prove my innocence', he wrote from Seoul, 'and could never understand why the judicial system rejected it each time.'

Despite the overwhelming evidence that his conviction was wrongful, the UK authorities turned a blind eye to his case before – the final betrayal – irresponsibly abandoning him to an uncertain fate.

All that is certain is that he will never see his mother again. Like the rest of the family, she lives in the UK; but he will now not be allowed back into the country and she is too frail to be able to leave.

'The only wish that I now have', Rhee wrote to me, 'is to establish my innocence.'

Chapter 3

His own petard

Emma Bates' story

1

On 12 April 2009, at two in the morning, Emma Bates arrived home to an empty house. It was the early hours of Easter Sunday. There was no sign of her partner, Wayne Hill. He had gone, and seemed to have taken some of his clothes. She saw that the bed-room was in disarray, with the wardrobe doors and dresser drawers flung open. She also noticed that, mystifyingly, the knife sharpener was on the kitchen table.

She rang his mobile. The call didn't connect. She rang again and this time he spoke to her.

'Ha ha', he laughed, 'I've got your car'.

She looked out of the window and was dismayed; he had indeed taken her car. She hadn't used it herself because she had gone out drinking. But at least she could drive. Wayne couldn't; he'd never passed a driving test. So he had no licence or insurance – and he had been out drinking most of the day. Emma was understand-ably alarmed (though she'd have been much more alarmed if she'd known that he was nearly three times over the drink-drive limit and had also taken cocaine).

'If you're not back here in ten minutes, I'll call the police', she said.

'Go fuck yourself', he replied. 'You can have the car back in the morning.'

'No, bring it back now or I'm phoning the police.'

He responded by slamming the phone down. In her anxiety, she rang round his friends to ask them to impress upon him that, for his own safety as well as others', he had to bring the car back. She called Danny Westlake, his closest friend, who said Wayne wasn't with him and he hadn't seen him. She also called her own friend, Nicola Giles.

'She said, "You won't believe what he's done"', recalled Nicola. '"He's taken the car". I said to her, "Emma, he's been out all day, he's drunk, he hasn't got a licence, phone the police". She said, "I've given him ten minutes to bring it back". Obviously, she was giving him a chance. I said, "If he starts anything, just phone the police".'

In fact, Hill did then return. Emma looked out of the window and saw him 'come screeching up the road' and then getting out of the car. Even from inside the house, she could hear the car door being slammed. He was in an ugly mood.

As he let himself in, Emma went towards the living-room door.

'Have your fucking keys', he said, throwing them at her. They flew past her and landed on the sofa in the living-room.

He seemed about to leave again but, as Emma chided him for being so senseless, he suddenly turned back.

'I'll show you fucking trouble', he said.

He grabbed her, ripping her T-shirt. He was often aggressive towards her, especially when he had been drinking. In the narrow hallway of Emma's house, he cupped her chin in the palm of his right hand and swung her round, lifting her up against the stairs.

Initially she was aware of, rather than saw, something glinting in his left hand. He pinned her against the spindles of the bannister, so they were now at eye-level. He momentarily lowered her while he changed his hold. He gripped her left arm with his right hand, and again lifted her up.

'He said I should not go out', Emma remembered, 'or come to the pub and embarrass him in front of his friends'.

As he pulled her closer to him, the knife became visible.

'I thought, my God, he's going to use it', she recalled. 'I have never been so frightened.'

She kicked out against his shins and put her hand over his, trying to push him away and prevent him thrusting the knife into her. They pushed and pulled in the confined space. As they struggled, his left elbow was momentarily caught in the spindles. Then, his arm broke free. And so it happened in a micro-second as unforeseeable circumstances coalesced, with Emma pushing his hand away just as he'd jerked his arm free and was striking downwards.

He collapsed to his knees, and stayed doubled up.

'You fucking bitch', he muttered.

Emma didn't realise what was the matter. Then, he fell backwards. Suddenly there was blood everywhere.

There was just a single wound, but it was fatal. The ambulance took Hill to the City Hospital in Birmingham. He was pronounced dead at 3.20am.

Seven months later, Emma was put on trial for murder. She was convicted, sentenced to life imprisonment and told she must serve at least fifteen years.

To calm public fears about yobbish youths carrying knives in violent gangs, the government had lately announced a crackdown. One of those quickly ensnared in its tough new policy was this five-foot-one-inch mother who had never carried a knife in her life.

EMMA BATES WAS born on 24 January 1979. She is the older daughter of Linda and Keith, who are both Birmingham born and bred. Keith worked shifts as a porter and driver at a local hospital; Linda, by the time these events unfolded, was a nursery assistant at Busy Bees nursery, where Emma also worked.

Linda and Keith married in 1970. They found a house in Great Barr, a densely populated area of north Birmingham alongside the M6 motorway. There is relatively little social mobility. People tend to stay close to where they were brought up. Emma's closest friend is Nicola Giles, whom she has known virtually all her life since they started nursery school together. They both went to the same secondary school, Great Barr Comprehensive, which is today the largest single-site school in the country. Its alumni include Martin Shaw, the much-respected actor; and Steve Winwood, the much-respected musician.

When Emma left, she took an NVQ in nursery nursing and, in July 2000, was taken on at the local Busy Bees nursery. Looking after children was her metier; she'd loved children all her life and this was exactly the job she'd always wanted.

Her own two children – a son and daughter – were born in 1999 and 2001 respectively. Her relationship with their father broke down soon after their daughter's birth. This disappointed Emma's parents, although they could understand the situation.

'He was a stable person, very hard-working', Keith reflected, 'but that was the problem. He had to go out and earn. As well as his day job, he was also in the Territorial Army, so he was not just working all week but was away for a lot of weekends. So, as a family, they had little time together.'

Emma, with her children, briefly moved back in with her parents until she found rented accommodation, a semi-detached three-bedroom house, at Tideswell Road. Soon afterwards she found a new partner in Arran McLachlan, a chef who was working at Sloan's, a night-club in nearby Sutton Coldfield.

'I met Emma, who was there with her friend Nicola, at the end of one night', Arran recalled. 'At the time, I thought she was a lovely, beautiful girl, and that's how I still feel about her.'

They went out on a few dates, and then Arran moved in and helped Emma to raise the children. They became friendly with Andrea McGivern and Steven Hands, a couple living a few doors away. After the night-club was taken over and Arran found himself out of work, Steven, who constructed aluminium towers for scaffolding, suggested that he should help him out for a day.

Arran was scared of heights but, needing work, took him up on the offer. So the solitary day's work turned into a four-year job, although he never did overcome his fear of heights. The work, on building sites, entailed early starts, which was convenient because he could finish early. If Emma was working late at the nursery, as she often was, he could pick up the children and look after them and have dinner on the table for when she got home. However, in the summer of 2007, after she and Arran had been together for six years, Emma was hospitalised with a painful kidney illness. When she recovered, they decided to part.

Shortly afterwards, Emma was having a drink with friends at The Cup in Sutton Coldfield when she met Danny Westlake, who told her that his close friend, Wayne Hill, had long had a 'thing' about her.

Wayne had also attended Great Barr school – 'though the school was that big', explained Nicola, 'that, if you didn't actually have classes together, you never really met'. In fact, Emma had had a one-night stand with him about a decade earlier. It now seemed that Wayne had been carrying a torch for her ever since.

Westlake telephoned Wayne there and then, and Emma spoke to him, suggesting that he should come along to the pub, but Wayne lacked the nerve to take up the invitation. Some days later, he did ask her out and they went to JDs, another pub in Sutton. So the ill-fated relationship developed, although from the start it seemed a mismatch. Emma was petite, docile, and socially outgoing; Wayne was boorish, socially ill-at-ease and a heavy drinker. In the late autumn of 2007, he moved into her house in Tideswell Road.

'Right from the start, he was possessive', said Nicola. 'The very first time he was there with Emma and me and some of her friends from nursery, he went on a big strop because she was speaking to her other friends. Obviously, if you've got a new partner, and you go out with their friends for the first time, it can be a bit awkward, but you learn to get on with everyone. Wayne could never do that.

'There was one time when we were all at Drake's Drum. Wayne was inside with his friends, but I left early. Emma walked to the corner of the road with me, we were just chatting. The next thing you know, he's there with us, saying, "What're you doing?"

'Emma said, "I'm just saying goodbye to Nicola". He stood over us, so we couldn't talk. I just had to say, "OK, then, 'bye".'

'He was always in a bad mood', agreed Donna Plester, who was also a nursery nurse and a close friend. 'He'd be having a moan, and being stroppy if she was going out with friends.

'But Emma would never say anything back. She never wanted conflict, she hasn't got that temperament.'

'He wouldn't ever talk to me', commented Andrea McGivern. 'If he saw me coming, he'd cross the road to avoid me. He wouldn't look you in the eye; he wouldn't interact with you in any way.

'When we came out of our houses, Emma and I would obviously speak to each other. But if she came out with him, she wouldn't look at you. It's as though she wasn't allowed to have contact with anyone.

'There was the time when the wing mirror was broken on her car. Steve went out and said, "It's OK, Emma, I'll fix it for you".

While he was doing it, we could see Wayne looking out of the window. Steve felt as though he shouldn't be doing it – but he did it anyway, for Emma. We later heard he'd given her a load of grief for letting Steve fix the mirror.'

Anne-Marie Mason, who worked with Emma for five years, re-called a social function when Emma was talking to Nicola's brother.

'I could see Wayne getting more and more agitated', said Anne-Marie 'He said to me, "I'm gonna punch his head in". I said, "Wayne, she's just talking".'

On one occasion, Emma went with Wayne to the house of one of his friends, Terry 'Geezer' Gosling. She was shocked to see that one of the rooms was decorated with knives, swords and other such memorabilia. The knife fetish, she soon understood, was shared by Wayne and Geezer. They were especially fond of *300,* a violent film taken from a graphic novel which was based – well, very loosely based – on one of the most famous battles in ancient history: the last stand of 300 Spartan warriors facing the Persian Army at the Battle of Thermopylae in 480 BC.

Within just a few weeks, it was clear that this affair wasn't working. He would constantly be quizzing her: who was she with? what was she doing? 'His jealousy was impossible to deal with', Emma said, 'so I ended the relationship.'

Towards Christmas, she resumed her liaison with Arran. After all, he always got on well with the children, and her then-six-year-old daughter virtually regarded him as her father; and he was by now best mates with Steve. Wayne, however, refused to go away. When he found out about Emma's renewed relationship with Arran, he 'went nuts', as Emma put it. She was concerned both for her own safety and also for Arran's. Once Wayne went round to the house and hammered on the door but, Emma admitted, 'I was too afraid to answer it.'

On Christmas Day 2007, Arran was away; he had family obli-gations in Swindon. Emma's children were at their father's and she was alone in the house. Arran kept in regular telephone contact with her during the day, and was alarmed to learn that Wayne had arrived with Danny Westlake and the latter's girlfriend. Arran was so concerned he decided to drive back in the middle of the night.

It was 6.00 on Boxing Day morning when he let himself in. He was confronted by a scene of devastation. The bedroom was in disarray and much of the house had been trashed. Emma was lying asleep on top of the bed. She was naked and had bruises on her arms. Her phone was in pieces on the floor; Arran assumed it had been smashed to prevent her contacting friends and calling for assistance.

During the day, Emma dissuaded Arran from taking the matter further; but that evening Wayne turned up at the house again and started threatening Arran from outside, so he did contact the police. Officers came to the house, and the incident was logged, but Emma refused to make a statement and no further action was taken.

Soon afterwards, Arran and Emma re-affirmed their original decision — a more-or-less amicable split — and he moved out to his mother's house in Walmley, Sutton Coldfield. A few days later, Emma told him she'd packed the belongings he'd left behind into a bag and left it in the upstairs wardrobe. When Arran picked up the bag, he noticed to his horror two samurai swords lying at the bottom of the wardrobe.

'Where have these come from?' he said to Emma. 'What are they doing here?'

He imagined that Emma had been too frightened to challenge Wayne about them. Arran said he didn't dare think what might have happened if the children had found them. So he put them into the boot of his car and drove off. Not wishing to face possibly awkward questions at a police station (as Arran puts it, the police seem to bring him 'bad luck'), he passed them to a friend of unquestioned respectability to hand in.

About a week later, he was at his mother's house when he heard banging and shouting. Wayne and Danny Westlake were trying to kick in his mother's front door.

'What's going on?' he shouted from the relative safety of an upstairs window.

'I want my swords back', Wayne yelled at him.

Arran said they'd already been handed in. Wayne's anger intensified. Arran called the police and then his mother, warning her not to return to the house. Neighbours gathered in the street to see what the commotion was about. The police arrived at almost the same time as his mother, who had naturally ignored her son's warning. The officers sent Wayne and Westlake on their way and, again, no action was taken.

Despite these episodes, Wayne moved back in with Emma. She did love him and she tried to make the relationship work for both of them. She encouraged him to get his life together – for example, by persuading him to resume contact with his young son from a previous relationship. She told him that he needed to face up to the problems with his jealousy and uncontrollable anger and the fact that he couldn't deal with social situations.

But he wouldn't take her advice. If ever she went out, when she returned he'd want to know who she'd 'got off with'. Whenever she did go out, she had to be discreet. 'Don't tell anyone I've been to yours', Emma said to Anne-Marie as she left her house.

As Arran still worked with Steven, he would drive his car over to his house every day, and they then went to work in the firm's van. After they returned, Emma and Andrea would sometimes arrange for him to see the children at Steve and Andrea's. 'If Wayne had known that Arran was here with the kids', explained Andrea, 'God help Emma'.

Emma kept Wayne's outbursts and violence largely to herself. They had an arrangement that whenever he'd drunk too much, he would stay overnight with Brian Levitt, a work colleague, and sometimes that happened. Meanwhile, she was always loyal to him publicly. 'She wouldn't ever slag him off to other people', said Donna, 'she wasn't like that'.

Nevertheless, as the weeks passed, the situation became increasingly obvious to all who knew Emma.

'There was the time when you suddenly couldn't get hold of her', remembered Rachel Bishop, who worked with Emma for five years at Busy Bees. 'That was when he'd taken her phone because his own was broken.

'At my son's Christening, Emma was godmother. She worked her backside off helping us prepare, but when Wayne didn't turn up, she went back home to see where he was. When she came back, it was clear she'd been crying. He was supposed to have been getting ready, but he was asleep on the settee.'

When Emma had a black eye, she made out to friends that she'd had an accident at her parents' caravan. 'But I'd been in a domestic violence relationship myself', explained Rachel, 'so I could tell what was going on.'

Another friend made a statement about Wayne's treatment of Emma.

'She would ring me at two in the morning', she recalled, 'sobbing down the phone, saying, "Wayne's gone mad again"… [she] told me that Wayne was becoming more abusive to her after he had a drink … I noticed her black eye – it was very bruised. I asked her about this, but she said that she had hurt herself. Emma would not say anything else, except told me not to tell her Mum anything. Deep down, I knew that Wayne had hit her.'

'She was able to confide in me', said Steven, 'and when she had the black eye, she told me that Wayne had grabbed her and pushed his fist into her face. I wanted to go round and have it out with him, but she begged me not to.'

Rachel recalled her first meeting with Wayne, when he saw her baby son and realised he was mixed-race. 'I saw his face drop', said Rachel, 'he muttered "hello", but wouldn't say another word.'

Anne-Marie's first meeting with Wayne, when he did go out one night and met some of Emma's friends, was unforgettable. As they were talking, Anne-Marie expressed a liking for the music of Snoop Dogg. Wayne instantly objected.

'That's black music', he said.

A startled Anne-Marie asked how he felt about black people.

'He said, "I don't like them, I think they should all be shot"', she remembered.

'I could see Emma kicking him under the table.

'So I said to him, "Oh. What about the police? What do you think of them?"

'"I don't like them either", Wayne said.

'"Well would it surprise you to learn that I'm married to a black policeman?" I asked him.'

That did surprise Wayne.

'She wanted to go on to the internet and do a profile on Facebook', remembered another friend, 'but she told me that when she went to do it, Wayne went off on one and stopped her.'

In addition to her job at Busy Bees, Emma had a part-time second job as a playworker for the local church. For a time she also made evening collections for a credit company – a dangerous job, especially as she could end up carrying thousands of pounds in cash, for someone as petite as she was. 'She did it just for the income', her father explained. 'On dark nights, I'd go with her. We were really worried about her. In the end, we talked her out of doing it.'

Wayne worked as a tiler, doing sub-contracting work mainly in small businesses like restaurants but in September 2008, after the worldwide financial crash, he lost his job. As he not only didn't have a car but couldn't drive, finding work was not easy. He got a provisional licence and Emma started teaching him to drive. Her family also tried to help. Linda, her mother, spent time at her computer, making him business cards to attract clients. This was to no avail.

'The cards never left the house', she said.

On 25 October 2008, Wayne again rowed with Emma about her wanting to see her friends. He became so angry that he punched the kitchen door. As a result, he injured his hand and had to phone Levitt, who took him to Accident and Emergency at Good Hope Hospital. A fracture of a bone in his right knuckle was treated.

Soon, Emma couldn't stand the inevitable confrontation and simply stopped going out. Not that this was any solution. As she later commented, 'This didn't stop Wayne from being paranoid about me having friends'.

Wayne did pick up the children from school, which allowed Emma to work overtime. Arran, on his return after a day's work with Steve, would sometimes notice Wayne in the road, a can of Stella inevitably in his hand.

As Wayne had been self-employed, he could not claim benefits and so had no income at all. He paid rent when he first moved in, but now Emma was the breadwinner in every sense. Her parents were buying the car for her, but she paid for everything else herself.

She also funded Wayne's mobile phone, which she'd bought for him. She even bought his cigarettes on the basis that if he didn't have them, he would just be more aggressive towards her. She would not pay for his drinks, though. Yet, after he became unemployed, Wayne spent most of the time drinking. Friends bought him drinks, but that couldn't explain everything. Emma's parents became increasingly concerned.

'At one stage, the three of us were all working overtime just to keep our homes together', Keith explained, 'while he spent all day drinking. We didn't know where he got the money.'

It was only later, after Emma was remanded into custody, that her parents realised what had been going on. They went through her papers and saw that, while Emma was at work, Wayne had been using her bank card to take out small amounts on almost a daily basis.

'Whatever money Emma was making and putting in the bank', said Linda, 'he was taking out.'

As Easter approached in 2009, Emma was really stressed. However hard she worked, she never seemed to be out of debt; her weight dropped to six stone. She was also beset by domestic problems. The hob on her cooker wasn't working; the gas was getting through to the oven, but not the hob.

'I said to her, "you'll have to get someone who knows what he's doing"', Linda recalled, 'but she was worried in case it was an expensive job'.

On Maundy Thursday, 9 April, she went to an end-of-term get-together with other nursery staff. In the pub, she was introduced to just the man she needed to meet: a Corgi-registered gas-fitter. She chatted to him – he was called Carl – about her cooker. This utterly innocuous conversation was to prove the catalyst for the tragedy that unfolded over the following two days. Unbeknown to Emma, as she spoke to the gas-fitter, Geezer and his girlfriend were watching with interest from the other end of the pub.

On Good Friday morning, all was calm. As usual, Wayne went out for a drink. During the day, Emma's brief conversation with Carl was relayed to him; his friends were stirring it. Winding Wayne up was good sport, and as easy as shooting fish in a barrel.

When he got home that evening, he was livid.

'Who was he?', he wanted to know.

Emma tried to explain, but the incident seemed to drive him wild.

'He said I had no right to go out and that I wasn't allowed out again', she said. 'He said, "What were you doing speaking to Carl? If I ever cop you talking to him again, I'll slit your throat and I'll slit his".'

Later, Nicola phoned Emma: 'She told me he'd been kicking off, going berserk because she'd been talking to Carl in the pub', she explained. 'Wayne told Emma that she was not allowed to go into that pub again or talk to anyone else.

'Knowing how possessive he is, I didn't think this was unusual.'

Previously, Emma had arranged for all of them – Wayne and herself and the children – to spend the Easter weekend at the family caravan near Tenbury Wells in Worcestershire. Now the situation was so bad that a relaxing weekend break was inconceivable.

On Easter Saturday, Hill simply told Emma that he planned to go out with Geezer. He said nothing more. Emma took her car to the garage to get a new tyre fitted. When she returned, Wayne was gone. She presumed Geezer had arrived to collect him. Andrea arrived then; she and Emma had Easter eggs for each other's children.

Afterwards, Emma and her mother went shopping to Asda. Linda told Emma that she thought she looked ill.

'You've been working hard all term', Linda said to her, 'why don't you at least go out with Nicola tonight, and me and your Dad will have the children?'

This was a stressful time for Nicola as well. She was a metalworker, making fittings for shops and bars, but the company had just gone bankrupt.

'Seventy per cent of the workforce were let go the day the administrators came in', she said. 'I was one of those who were kept on, but we were thinking we had only another week, maybe two at most.'

In the end, a new company came in and took on all those who were still there, so Nicola would be fortunate; but at Easter, she was facing an uncertain future. The two of them decided to go out for the evening. Donna Plester was also invited.

Emma phoned Wayne to let him know. At that stage, he was in Star City. This was a large-scale leisure complex built on former industrial land close to the M6 motorway. It sometimes attracted an unsavoury clientele. There had been a number of incidents, and some locals now referred to it as Stab City.

Wayne told Emma he would not be going home but, as she got ready, he phoned to ask why she had to go out.

'What's your fucking problem?' he said to her.

'He went off on one', recalled Emma. 'He cut me off, so I called him back to talk to him as I did not want to end things on a bad note. One minute, he seemed in a good mood; I think he thought that if he was nice to me, I wouldn't go out with Nicola and Donna. But I was firm: I said I was going out with my friends.'

Emma took the children to her mother's.

'She brought them round about eight o'clock', Linda recalled. 'That was the last time we saw her, as it were, properly saw her.'

Emma, Nicola and Donna had one drink at home, and then went out to the Drake's Drum pub. They soon realised that Wayne was now there, in the other bar; so they left quickly. They went to The Old Horns. Donna drove them there, but then left as she had an early start at work the next day.

Emma and Nicola decided to go to a club in Sutton Coldfield and called a taxi. As Emma was short of cash, they asked the driver to take her home first of all. She picked up her bank card and also a jacket to lend to Nicola. She then noticed that Wayne had left his keys. Was he coming back or not? If he was, he wouldn't be able to get in. She'd better phone and tell him. Wayne told her to bring the keys to him.

So they went back to Drake's Drum. Emma went in on her own while Nicola stayed in the taxi. Far from being grateful, Wayne was very angry.

'Where do you think you're going?' he shouted. 'You should be at home with the children.

'I suppose you're going to flaunt it with Nicola', he berated her. The barmaid had to ask him to cool it. Once more trying to avoid confrontation, Emma left quickly, but he aimed a volley of verbal abuse at her and followed her outside. From the taxi, Nicola saw him climbing onto one of the outside benches, gesturing angrily. Emma got in. 'Just drive', she said to the driver.

Nicola looked back and saw Wayne, in the middle of the car park, glowering as the taxi pulled away.

Emma and Nicola went to JDs in Sutton and then to Fever, the club across the road. They spent almost the whole time on the dance floor and finally relaxed. They had a thoroughly enjoyable time.

2

Emma's call to the emergency services was timed at 2.29am. Like all calls to the emergency services, it was recorded, so there is a complete transcript of what followed. Throughout, Emma was sobbing uncontrollably.

Hill had collapsed with his legs in the hallway and his head and shoulders in the living room. He was slightly on his side, but in a prone position. The operator told Emma that she needed to apply pressure to the wound in order to control the bleeding. However, he was 204 pounds, fourteen-and-a-half stone, and too heavy for Emma to turn over. She kept crying and the operator kept trying to calm her down.

'I can't calm down', she said.

When it became clear that Wayne was simply too heavy for Emma, the operator told her to 'knock on a neighbour's door' to get assistance. Emma ran to Andrea's.

'I heard banging on the door', said Andrea. She and Steve responded, although not instantly. 'It took a little while', she admitted. 'You know when you're asleep, and you think you're dreaming, you don't react straightaway. Then, Steve and I had to get our clothes on.'

Emma's presence would later be confirmed by the bloodstains on the front door, although she quickly returned to tell the operator she could not get assistance.

'OK, really big push', said the operator, 'just get him on his back for me'.

But Emma couldn't move him.

'I'm trying, I'm trying', said Emma, 'I can't push him over. I'm gonna get done for attempted murder, oh my God, there's loads of blood.'

Andrea was now looking out of her window to see what was happening. She saw Danny Westlake casually coming up the road, a cigarette in one hand and a can of beer in the other.

He texted a message to Wayne: *Im at the door.*

As Emma had left the front door open after returning from her failed attempt to get help, he walked in. Emma was kneeling on the floor with Wayne's head in her lap, the operator having told her to lift his head in order to make it easier for him to breathe.

'Get the fuck up', Westlake roughly told her.

Then he saw what had happened.

'You fucking dickhead', he said.

He then snatched the phone from her.

'Hello', he said, 'we need an ambulance really quick'. Westlake was then able to turn Wayne over. The operator asked where Wayne had been stabbed. Westlake in turn asked Emma, who didn't know. After checking, Westlake said, 'I think it's where his heart is'.

At that point, when it was 2.41, the first police officers arrived. They had to tread through the large pool of blood in the hallway. Wayne was by this point covered in blood; his eyes were fixed open and he was starting to turn blue.

The ambulance crew arrived and the scene was cleared. Andrea and other neighbours were watching as Westlake went back outside. He, too, had blood all over him. He was very angry.

'You could hear him shouting, "You slag!" and "Rot in hell!"', said Andrea. 'He was sitting on the bonnet of a neighbour's car, and was then pacing up and down outside the house.

'The police were trying to calm him down. They took him down the road when they brought Emma out.'

Because Westlake was, as the police noted, 'abusive' towards Emma and 'clearly angry', a police inspector instructed his officers to protect Emma by taking her to the station immediately.

The conversation in the police car taking her to Thornhill Road Police Station in Handsworth was also recorded.

'Keep your hands down', said one officer, 'because you're covered in blood at the moment'.

'I'm gonna go down for murder and I didn't mean to do it.'

'Alright Emma, you're safe here now'.

'No, I'm not; no, I'm not', responded Emma – instinctively distrusting police platitudes, even in her anguished state. She was clearly going into shock and her words and sentences became scrambled.

'He came with me at my knife and I didn't know what else to do … I didn't know what, he took my car, every name under the sun and he came with me at knife … I'm gonna go to prison, I'm gonna go to pri …'

At 7.15 in the morning of Easter Sunday, Emma was told that Wayne had died.

'Oh, no, I've killed him', she said.

One of the other things she said, according to a police officer who was placed outside her cell, was, 'I was just defending myself, but I don't think people will see it that way, I think I'm going to end up in prison'.

The police took her clothes, but would not allow her to shower, so while she was being questioned, she still had Wayne's blood all over her: in her hair, and on her hands and feet. She was interviewed three times on Sunday evening. A medical examination on Monday morning revealed an area of blueness on the inside of her left armpit, which would correspond with where Wayne had gripped her when he lifted her up.

She was then interviewed four more times, though her solicitor (she was allocated the duty solicitor) advised her to give 'no comment' answers, and for most of the time Emma acceded to that advice.

After being charged with murder, she was bailed and spent the pre-trial period with relatives in Kidderminster.

Meanwhile, her family had to clean her house.

'We asked the police', Keith Bates recalled. 'They said, "It's down to you, nothing to do with us". They recommended industrial cleaners, which we couldn't possibly afford. In the end we had to do it ourselves.

'The police had left such a mess – they'd trampled through everything. The blood was everywhere. We had to scrape it all off the walls and the floor. It took us a week of solid work.'

3

The trial began at Birmingham Crown Court before Mr Justice Mackay on 18 November 2009. The scenario presented at trial was a vastly different one to that which Emma's family and friends had anticipated. Events, to their way of thinking, were turned upside down and inside out.

The prosecution case was that Emma had deliberately murdered Wayne, by luring him back to the house. She armed herself with a knife and lay in wait for his return. Why otherwise, argued the prosecution, would she have been so desperate for Wayne to return to the house? Why did she want him to drive any further when she knew that he was already very drunk? Conversely, there was no evidence of Wayne springing a trap for her. As the judge said, 'Wayne never once phoned her that night'.

The three main witnesses supporting the Crown case were those who had been Wayne's close friends. They gave sworn testimony that on a number of occasions, Emma had 'produced a knife'. Geezer said that Wayne told him of a time when Emma held a bread knife to his throat. During cross-examination, he said that Wayne might have said this happened a couple of times. 'Wayne was not fazed by it', Geezer added.

His evidence suggested that Emma was prone to outbursts of uncontrolled anger. 'She was all right when [we] all went out together', he testified, 'but sometimes her mood would change and she would snap'.

Levitt told the court that Emma would let herself be chatted up by other men. He was not specific about her conduct, simply saying, 'She did have a reputation'.

He said that Wayne had told him of three separate occasions when Emma had used a knife against him – the first was when Wayne was in the pub and they'd had a row, and she put a knife to his neck; the second was just before Christmas 2008, Wayne said he was in bed, he rolled over and she had a replica sword from the film *300* pointing at his chest. Levitt added (though he only remembered this part after being allowed to refresh his memory from his statement) that Wayne had told him that she had said to him (Wayne) that if he cheated on her, 'I will stab you'.

According to Levitt, Wayne said, after he recounted this, 'Do you think she's a bit nuts?'

The third, Levitt said, was when Wayne said they were having a row about money, and she put a kitchen knife to his chest. However, the only actual violence Levitt had first-hand experience of was the occasion when he had to take Wayne to hospital after Wayne had broken his own hand. According to Levitt, however, on that occasion Emma had apologised to Wayne for winding him up.

'I know 100% he would not hit Emma', Levitt told the court.

Westlake said that Emma 'became argumentative when she'd had a drink'. He spoke of one occasion when Wayne said to him that, at home, Emma had threatened him with a knife. It seems this was the only incident Wayne ever mentioned to him.

Most of the prosecution case came from these three witnesses.

'You will be careful, I know', the judge said to the jury, 'to allow for the fact that these were old friends of his from way back in his childhood days'.

There was something else that the jury needed to be careful about. Almost all of this evidence was hearsay. For hundreds of years, throughout the history of jury trials in Britain, hearsay was not admissible evidence in the courtroom. Evidence had to be first-hand; you could not pass on what someone else had said to you, for the very good reason that the veracity of the supposed remarks could never be tested. The jury are supposed to be able to evaluate the truthfulness of a witness who is giving evidence before them; but they cannot possibly ascertain from witness A the truthfulness of witness B. It was an illogical proposition.

First of all, was witness A actually telling the truth about what witness B had said to him? There was not necessarily any way of testing the evidence. More importantly, even if witness B actually had said what was being reported, was *he* being truthful? Perhaps he had just been concocting a story out of bravado, embarrassment, fear or some other reason. Again, the jury had no way of divining which it was.

A subsidiary problem was that the evidence could, and usually would, become very confusing. Working out who was supposed to have said what to whom was rarely straightforward.

For such reasons, hearsay was disallowed in the courtroom. The Criminal Justice Act 2003 then overturned centuries of practice to enable hearsay evidence to be given. There were warnings at the time that this would debase the judicial system, lead to the conviction of the innocent and, correspondingly, allow the guilty to escape justice; but the Labour government disregarded the warnings. As a result, Emma was now being prosecuted almost entirely on hearsay evidence.

SO WHAT happened to Wayne on that Easter Saturday?

Geezer acknowledged that he and Wayne were drinking together for about eight hours. (In fact, the drinking period seemed to last from about midday almost to midnight.) They started off in local pubs, and during the afternoon went to Star City before returning to their local – Drake's Drum – in the evening.

The barmaid there recalled having asked Wayne to keep it down, when he was haranguing Emma, but said that he wouldn't behave aggressively towards her, adding, 'He wasn't that type'.

During the day, Wayne had periodically called Westlake and Levitt, though neither bothered to return his calls. It was nearly midnight, at 11.43, when Levitt did get back to him, by which time Wayne was at home. He told Levitt that he'd had enough of Emma and was leaving. Could he stay with him for a while? Levitt said that would be OK.

Wayne also then succeeded in contacting Westlake. He told him he was definitely finished with Emma. He wanted Westlake to help him steal Emma's car. Westlake declined. He was concerned with the behaviour of his own girlfriend, who was dancing with another man; he was not happy about that – so he told Wayne he'd have to do his own car-stealing.

At about half past midnight, Wayne arrived at Levitt's house. At home, he'd taken some clothes and Emma's car and then driven the few miles to where Levitt lived. He arrived with some of his belongings and told Levitt that this time he had definitely finished with her. Levitt said Wayne told him that in the pub she'd thrown the keys at him, and told him that she was going off to get fucked by someone else.

They talked for approximately an hour. Levitt said that Wayne wasn't excessively drunk, saying he was 'upset, heartbroken but not angry'. Wayne went on complaining about his situation. Then, at about 1.30, Levitt announced that he had to get to bed because the next day was Sunday, an access day for him; he was due to see his children. (Levitt said he knew nothing more until he was awoken by phone calls at four in the morning, informing him that Wayne was dead.)

After Emma and Nicola had been happily cocooned together at Fever, the desperate reality of normal life quickly reasserted itself on the way home. 'I kept saying to Nicola, he's going to go mental when I get back', recalled Emma. 'He didn't look very happy in the Drum, in fact he looked furious.'

So, on returning home, she straightaway tried to contact him in order to avert problems. At 2.12 she succeeded in reaching him. He was then on his own at Levitt's, though she did not know that; when he told her that he'd taken her car, she imagined that he was in it. Terrified at the thought of him driving round in his state of inebriation, she then rang round, trying to ensure that both Wayne and the car got back without mishap. At 2.24 she rang Westlake's girlfriend, who passed the phone over to Danny. Emma told him that Wayne was missing, and that he'd taken her car.

Westlake said in his testimony that he then called Wayne, and the call stayed live for three minutes. In other words, he heard the entire event over his mobile phone. He said he could hear that the television was on in the background; that Emma walked away and came back again; and that there was noise like a knife being taken out of a block, with metal scraping on metal.

When he reached the house, he said that Emma let him in. He said he did not hear or see Emma on the phone to the ambulance service when he was there. The phone was there, he said, but Emma wasn't using it.

Afterwards, he spoke to an officer outside the house, explaining that he was on the phone to Wayne at the time of the tragedy. He said he'd heard Wayne say, 'You better put that down' and also, 'You better call an ambulance'.

The testimony of Wayne's three friends was effectively the only evidence, apart from that relating to the knife wound itself. There was, the judge commented, 'relatively little or no dispute about the evidence of the pathologist in this case'.

The pathologist was Dr James Lucas. He testified that the wound was consistent with 'a downward stab by a right-handed person'. He added that he 'could not conceive of a scenario where the knife would go in accidentally'.

He also said he would expect to see signs of injury if Wayne had lifted Emma off the ground by her neck in the way she described, and there were no signs of injury. Accordingly, this suggested that her account was false.

The defence case was distinguished only by its brevity. Ten statements of mothers whose children attended the Busy Bees nursery were read on Emma's behalf. Giving evidence herself, she testified that the account she gave in her interviews on the Sunday evening, while covered in Wayne's blood, was accurate. She has consistently maintained that the death was an accident, brought about by Wayne's use of the knife. Her story has never changed.

However the clarity of her defence was obscured, not least by the fact that it was disputed by her own legal team. The judge explained this in his summing-up:

> Her case was it was an accidental injury ... She said [under cross-examination] 'I didn't push it down into his chest. He accidentally stabbed himself. There was no way I could overpower him ... It was an accident'.

> [The defence barrister] does not let go of self-defence. He says it is
> still something he maintains on her behalf … [He says] it is clear she is
> hopelessly confused and not aware of what she is saying.

With such a lack of focus among her own legal team about how to
conduct the defence, Emma's chances of winning her case would
be seriously hindered. But things got even more muddled than
that.

There are, clearly, a range of possible explanations of a death
in these circumstances. These include accident, self-defence, manslaughter, and murder under provocation. No one at all suggested
that the latter – provocation – applied in this case; yet the judge
told the jury that he was 'under a legal duty' to set it out for them.
He said that there was a route map to a finding of murder by
provocation: did she kill Wayne unlawfully? When she unlawfully
killed him, did she intend either to kill him or cause him very serious injury? Could the jury be sure that she was provoked? And was
the provocation such as would have caused an ordinary person to
act as she did? The judge then emphasised to the jury, in an awkward phrase, that the 'touchstone issue' was: who had the knife?

This was the key point. Yet all that is actually known is that,
although the sharpener was taken from its drawer, the knife was
not sharpened. Beyond that, the evidence is non-existent. No one
knows who had the knife that night. The prosecution asserted that,
in these circumstances, it couldn't have been Wayne who had the
knife; you do not stick a knife like that in your pocket or down
your trousers, they told the jury.

The jurors retired to consider their verdict.

During and in the aftermath of contentious trials, there are
regularly concerns voiced by family members and others about
whether all jurors were paying full attention. Usually, these concerns are brushed aside by both lawyers and journalists. In this case,
exceptionally, the trial had been halted while counsel discussed
with the judge a tricky problem, which was that at one point two
jurors appeared to have been asleep. The outcome was that the trial
continued. Remarkably, one of those two jurors was now elected
as foreman.

The jury returned to ask for the written statements of Gosling, Westlake and the barmaid. In accordance with the rules of the adversarial system, this request was not granted. The jury also asked for further help on the definition of provocation, so the judge went through all that again for them.

They retired and then, on 27 November 2009, returned into court to give a unanimous verdict of guilty.

4

When first arrested, Emma was allocated the duty solicitor from a practice in central Birmingham, and she stayed with that firm throughout. Not having had any previous contact with the criminal justice system, she had no conception of how it worked. It is an enduring problem that the innocent will have no prior knowledge of how they should be faring within the system; whereas those who do have past experience of it – that is, the guilty, likely as not – are far better able to function inside it.

So there were several cock-ups. The solicitors allowed the police to interview Emma about Wayne's death in traumatic circumstances, when she – the newly-bereaved partner – was still covered in his blood.

Nevertheless, in three interviews, she answered fully everything that was put to her. Then, the solicitors advised her not to answer further questions. This is fairly routine. The police will attempt to make progress by asking their suspect the same question at different times in the hope of catching out him or her by getting different answers; solicitors will then recommend to their clients that they do not respond at all. So, the next day, there were four no-comment interviews. However, it was during these that the police put to Emma the highly damaging suggestions of Wayne's friends that she herself carried knives and used them in a threatening way. These allegations could have been easily, plausibly and firmly refuted. Her refusal to answer – on legal advice – created wholly avoidable difficulties for her.

It is customary for those facing murder charges to benefit from the services of a QC. This is one aspect of the principle of the equality of arms that underpins the adversarial system. Emma's solicitors, however, did not succeed in engaging a QC to represent her. The upshot was that she was defended by a junior barrister but prosecuted by the very senior QC who was Leader of the Midland Circuit.

Some key changes in criminal trial procedures were introduced in the Criminal Procedure and Investigations Act 1996. This established a kind of *pas de deux* for pre-trial manoeuvres. Step one: the prosecution provides the outline of its case to the defence; step two: the defence provides the key defence case statement, explaining exactly what its case is; step three: the prosecution then provides disclosure of the remainder of the relevant case material.

In general, this procedure allows the prosecution to disclose vital material at such a late stage that the defence is handicapped from the start. In this case, although the postmortem was carried out on 13 April, the report of the pathologist, Dr Lucas, was not handed over to the defence until, the barrister stated, 'just a couple of weeks before the trial'.

That was bad enough. However, his report did not refer to the explanation of the death or address the defence position in any way – as Emma's lawyers quickly pointed out. So the first time Dr Lucas even addressed the matter was in a vital fresh statement, dated 17 November, which was first served on the defence on 18 November – the day the trial started. This evidence was the crux of the case; yet the defence had had no opportunity at all to consider and assimilate it. Even a first-rate defence team would have been up against it in such circumstances.

However, that was step three and by then Emma's prospects had already been seriously jeopardised by step two: the defence case statement (DCS). This statement, produced on her behalf by her solicitors, was inept, inaccurate and incoherent.

It began by stating that Emma gave six full-comment interviews to police. This was untrue. As the solicitors were supposedly advising her during these interviews, it is shocking that they did not know how many there were, or whether or not they were full-comment, and still more shocking that they lacked the initiative even to check the case papers.

Describing the hallway incident, Emma's lawyers wrote:

> Suddenly, arm which was slightly bent at the elbow when holding the knife seemed to bend further, then up in the air.

That's it. That's what they wrote and handed in to court. This is the absolutely key part of the DCS. This is precisely where, if the solicitors were to have a chance of successfully defending Emma, their attention to detail needed to be at its most careful; but it was where the DCS was at its most careless.

The DCS also states:

> Before the ambulance arrived, Danny Westlake arrived and tried to calm the defendant.

Now the defence lawyers were just making it up. The police recorded that Westlake was 'abusive towards Emma Bates' and 'clearly angry'. Neighbours also saw what happened. As Andrea, for example, looked out of her window, she saw and heard some of Westlake's threatening behaviour and his invective against Emma. In any case, his attitude towards Emma (together with his untruthfulness) was evident from the taped log of the 999 call. As a result of his hostility to her after Wayne's death, the police arranged for Emma to be quickly driven away. So this part of the defence case statement is wholly false.

Another part read:

> [Wayne] held her by the throat and produced a kitchen knife, which was in his left hand. During the altercation, to protect herself, she twisted his left arm and the knife pierced his chest. She acted in self-defence at all times.

Leaving aside the fact that this was absurdly terse, there are, in this single passage, four key errors or misconceptions.

Firstly, Wayne did not grip Emma by the throat. She made this clear, at an important stage of the police interviews when she interjected in order to correct the interviewer and clarify the position:

Police: So he's lifted you by your …
Emma: I was off the floor.
Police: Chin, under your chin, round your neck …
Emma: Sorry, he didn't grab my neck. He grabbed my chin.

Secondly, Emma did not 'twist his left arm'; at no stage had she said that.

Thirdly, what happened in the hallway was not an 'altercation'. An altercation is a heated verbal argument that, by its nature, is sustained and can certainly be a prelude to physical confrontation. But this was not an altercation. It was not sustained – the drama was all over in less than two minutes – and, in any event, it takes two to create an altercation. Emma momentarily remonstrated with Wayne for treating her so appallingly, but she had said only a few words before he turned on her saying 'I'll show you fucking trouble' and attacked her.

The defence team's use of the word 'altercation' was a serious mistake: it gave the momentary incident a depth it did not have; and it made Emma seem complicit in the hallway drama when she had been, characteristically, largely submissive.

Fourthly, the suggestion that Emma had 'acted in self-defence at all times' completely muddled what should have been the crystal-clear defence position. The problem with the phrase 'self-defence', when applied in a criminal justice context, is that it implies that the person defending him or herself is consciously making a choice. A component of self-defence is some foreknowledge, however split-second, that one's action will cause harm to the other party, albeit that it is necessary in order to protect oneself. In this situation, there is no such foreknowledge. Nor did Emma do anything that, in routine circumstances, was likely to cause Wayne harm. Nor did she exercise any choice, other than to try to extricate herself from the situation. She was petite and passive; Hill was heavily-built and aggressive. She would not have been able to defend herself against him; self-defence was not an option.

In many other respects, the defence case statement was skimpy and failed to put forward Emma's case adequately; in other words, it comprehensively failed to achieve its purpose. It becomes easy to understand how demoralised she must have felt in the courtroom.

Yet there were still more defence errors. At the postmortem, Dr Lucas considered it anatomically possible for the knife to have caused the wound had it been in Wayne's left hand. He took a photograph which bore that out. Emma's lawyers then instructed Dr Peter Acland to carry out the defence postmortem. Acland agreed that it could well have been an accident. He pointed out that the angle of entry was consistent with the knife having been held in the victim's left hand, that the knife had not gone in up to its hilt, and that only 'mild to moderate' force would be needed.

Although this was very helpful, Dr Acland's own position at this stage was unhappily compromised. Seven weeks before carrying out the postmortem, he had faced a disciplinary tribunal. The outcome of that hearing was due. In the event, he carried out the post-mortem on Hill on Wednesday 15 April and on the Friday, within forty-eight hours, was suspended from his post. As a result, the defence were unable to use him at trial.

So they now needed a second pathologist. Unfortunately, this second choice, Dr David Rouse, was equally unhappy. He would be criticised for his work in the case of a Royal Navy officer, Daniel Purcifer, who was testing helicopter equipment in Germany when he died in his sleep. Dr Rouse attributed death to postural asphyxiation, with alcohol as a contributory factor.

Purcifer's widow, Samantha, campaigned for a fresh postmortem. This showed that death was due to heart disease. The coroner told Dr Rouse that he 'could not rely on the findings of your post-mortem examination' and that he would be contacting both the General Medical Council and the Royal College of Pathologists. Because of this case and a previous one in 2006, Dr Rouse was given an official warning that was to remain on his file until 2016. He resigned.

In Emma's case, however, he was not instructed until several months after the incident. He never saw the body, or the scene, or even the key photograph. He was also incorrectly briefed, as he was told that Wayne 'grabbed Emma's neck', which didn't happen. On the basis of this misinformation, he thought that Wayne could not have killed himself.

In response to Dr Rouse, Lucas then made a second statement, the one provided to the defence on the trial's opening day. He said that 'if Emma had been forcibly grasped round the neck and lifted clear of the ground, it is more likely than not that marks would have been apparent on … her neck'. Yet there were none. Lucas continued: 'nor have I been provided with any information that she complained of hoarseness or a painful throat, symptoms one might expect if her throat had been forcibly grasped'.

Lucas acknowledged that, 'It was clear from my [original] post-mortem examination that the fatal wound could have been inflicted by a knife held in Wayne's left hand. However, I find it difficult to conceive of a plausible scenario whereby the knife would have accidentally penetrated the chest'.

When Dr Lucas's second statement was submitted on the first day of the trial, the defence really needed an adjournment in order to consider the matter and obtain fresh defence reports. However, the judge gave the defence barrister merely a couple of hours to 'sort your case out'. Lucas then said in evidence that he could not conceive of a scenario where the knife could go in accidentally in 'the sort of altercation' that Emma had described. The judge told the jury that 'there was relatively little or no dispute about the evidence of the pathologist'.

But what had gone wrong? Why had the medical experts ultimately resolved that the accident theory was untenable? The problem is that pathologists, like all others involved in a case, cannot themselves illuminate a darkened scene. They are guided by what they are told. Lucas was incorrectly briefed at the outset, on the morning of 13 April. An officer told him that Wayne had grabbed Emma's neck and she had twisted his arm. Neither point was correct. In fact, at that stage, Emma was still being interviewed. Nor had Emma described any 'sort of altercation'.

The next morning, a different police officer wrote an entirely accurate report of the incident, but no one seems to have noticed that. Instead the misinformation that infected the case from the beginning was passed on and used as the foundation for further evidence. There were indeed no marks on Emma's neck, and no complaints of hoarseness or a sore throat, but there was a very good reason for this: she was never lifted by the neck. She made that clear in her original interviews (when she could have had no idea what subsequent medical examinations would or wouldn't find).

So Dr Lucas was in no sense to blame. On the contrary, he specifically asked for 'a more detailed description' to enable him 'to consider this further', but additional information was never provided to him.

What the Court needed was a robust defence team, pointing out where mistakes were being made and the case was being pushed in the wrong direction; but that was never likely to happen in this case, when the defence was just as culpable as everyone else of adducing misinformation.

Once the misinformation is removed, it becomes clear that the pathologists who originally saw and examined the body believed that death could well have been caused accidentally. When the correct pieces of information are drawn together, everything falls into place. Emma's arm was bruised, from where Wayne had held her off the ground; the postmortem showed that there were bruises on his mid-shin consistent with Emma kicking out at him as she was suspended; and, most importantly, there was a bruise on his upper left arm, perhaps showing where it got stuck between the bannister spindles. Further, Wayne had no defence injuries (which occur when someone being attacked attempts to defend him or herself by blocking the weapon). These would have been anticipated if it had been Emma wielding the knife.

In June 2011, Dr Acland carried out a fresh analysis of the evidence. 'It does seem that there has been a significant misunderstanding of the mechanisms of the stabbing', he stated, 'where the court, including the judge and both counsel, assume that [Emma] "overpowered" [Wayne] during the struggle, whereas she has merely deflected a thrust initiated by his force.

'In my opinion', he concluded, 'the injury could have been caused in the way she has described.'

Dr Hugh White, a pathologist who was fresh to the case, examined the evidence in February 2013 and also concluded that the death 'could have occurred' in the way that Emma described.

The Department of Forensic Medicine at the University of Dundee has produced some authoritative material over the years.

In one of their reports, they examined stab wounds leading to fatalities, and concluded that homicidal stab wounds will usually be 'multiple' and 'widely spread' on the body, and that the evidence for murder will also be supported by defence injuries. Accidental stab wounds will be 'mostly single'. So the academic research also bears out the likelihood that this fatality was an accidental death.

The prosecution acknowledged that the diminutive Emma would not have been able to overpower Wayne and so suggested either that he could have 'passed out' or that she had taken him by surprise. Yet, plainly, neither could have happened. The physical evidence from the scene buttressed Emma's account. There are clear signs of what happened: Emma's T-shirt was ripped, where Wayne had forcibly gripped her and lifted her up; and a framed photograph on the hallway wall – of Emma as a baby, with her grandmother – had fallen behind the radiator, its picture hook broken. This had happened as Wayne had swung Emma round in the narrow hallway. In any event, according to the prosecution's own evidence, Wayne could not have passed out because Danny Westlake had phoned and heard what he was saying.

The defence muddle carried through to the trial itself, with Emma's defence barrister – who was understandably guided by Dr Rouse's unhelpful report – attempting to put the case in a very different way to how she had put it herself. However, his bald suggestion that she was 'hopelessly confused' was extraordinary, because she was consistent from start to finish.

As if all this was not damaging enough, there was the judge's insistence that he had to put the defence of provocation to the jury:

> I am under a legal duty as the judge in this case to direct that [provocation] is at least theoretically available as part of the defence.

So it wasn't his fault. One can also accept that the law was refined in this way in order to benefit defendants. Nevertheless, in this instance, the raising of this completely irrelevant matter obviously served only to make the legal fog still more dense. The fact that the jury actually returned to ask for further guidance on the matter of provocation simply proved that their deliberations were now all at sea.

IF THE LEGAL FOG over the case had lifted, then one aspect would have stood out like a beacon, and that is the timing. Whatever had happened, had happened very, very quickly. The boundaries can be fixed by Emma's call to Westlake's girlfriend's mobile phone, a call which was made at 2.24am. The girlfriend simply passed the phone over to Westlake. She then heard Emma saying something like, 'Get him to bring the car back now'. The call ended after one and a half minutes. It was only after Emma had completed the phone call that she heard Wayne drawing up in the car and looked out of the window to see him parking it. At 2.29 Emma called for the ambulance. So there is a gap of, at most, three-and-a-half-minutes in which all this happened.

One aspect of the Crown case was that Emma must have lured him back because she was the one calling him. As the judge put it, 'Wayne never once phoned her that night'.

This extraordinary comment created entirely the wrong impression. Wayne didn't phone Emma because he didn't make any calls at all; he couldn't. He had no credit on his phone. Emma paid for his mobile, just as she paid for everything else, but now he had run up an outstanding debt of £200 which he was obviously unable to pay and so Orange had placed 'call barring' on his number.

These were the particular circumstances at this time; but they were also the routine circumstances. Wayne never made calls from his phone. He wouldn't spend his money; he'd rely on his friends spending theirs. He'd borrow phones, leave messages, and hope someone would call him back. The documents in this case included 290 pages of his itemised telephone activity over the previous two years. He would send texts (frequently of a crude or racist nature), but in all those 290 pages, he didn't make a call to anyone. For the judge to tell the jury that he 'never once phoned her', as if it were a specific and relevant point, was highly misleading.

Given that there was a struggle in the hallway, who would have been the more aggressive? Wayne had been drinking almost all day and, as everyone knows, alcoholic consumption is associated with aggression. His blood alcohol level was 182 milligrams per 100 millilitres of blood. His urine sample gave a reading of 224 milligrams. (In order to be fit to drive, the level must be below 80 milligrams per 100 millilitres.) Wayne also had cocaine in his blood-stream; the drug's come-down effects, as is also well known, include feelings of anxiety. Wayne, of course, did not need his anxiety and paranoia to be fuelled any further; it was already near-impossible for him to keep a lid on his feelings of jealousy.

On the other hand, Emma's blood/alcohol test was, as the judge put it, 'clear ... it was negative'; there was no trace of alcohol in her bloodstream. Her urine sample gave a reading of 39 milligrams, so she would certainly have been fit to drive.

However, because Emma's samples were not taken until 10.25 the following morning, the prosecution tried to back-calculate what her level might have been at the time of the incident. They based these calculations on a series of assumptions, as the judge put it: 'assuming that she had last passed urine six hours before the sample was taken, at four or five in the morning ... or if, on the other hand, she had urinated more recently than that ...' On the basis of such assumptions, the judge told the jury, her alcohol level 'could have fallen within a range of levels from mild intoxication to drunkenness'.

The first point to note about this is that it wasn't evidence at all. The information not having been collected at the time, the Crown Prosecution Service should not have been allowed to speculate what it might have been if they had had the forethought to collect it.

More importantly, however, the jury was again being seriously misled. If Emma had shown signs of inebriation, then the cus-tody sergeant who booked her in at Thornhill Road Police Station would have been bound to mention that in his report. It would have been negligent not to have done so. Likewise, the doctor whom police called in to examine Emma at the police station specifically reported that she 'showed no signs of intoxication'.

The reason why Emma's blood alcohol level was clear would have been appreciated had the real evidence been heard. Emma, in fact, did say in her testimony that she may have had ten measures of vodka during the course of the evening. That is merely a typ-ical example of her compliant nature. It is Nicola who can explain what actually happened.

'We didn't have a lot to drink', she recalled. 'We did have a drink at Emma's before we left, and that may have been a large measure, because we poured it ourselves. After that, we bought drinks at the Drum, but left them because we realised Wayne was there and left hurriedly. We had another at The Old Horns, but didn't finish that either because the taxi arrived.

'We had a drink at JDs, but didn't finish that because we joined the queue at Fever. There, we had two vodkas and a bottle of Smirnoff Ice, which I don't think we finished.

'But the fact that we didn't finish several of the drinks – that wasn't mentioned in court.'

The speculation of the prosecution and the judge that Emma might have been intoxicated was based on the idea that she passed water during her time in custody. However, she hadn't. From the moment she arrived at the police station, as the custody record confirms, there were precise instructions 're female not having access to washing facilities including toilet, with evidence preservation in mind'.

Throughout the night, everything that Emma said and did was carefully logged; she did not go to the toilet. So West Midlands Police knew exactly what the position was; but the jury was misinformed.

IT WAS ALWAYS FELT by legal observers that as soon as hearsay evidence was allowed then injustice would swiftly ensue. In this prosecution, the case was based on hearsay evidence. Just one of the problems with hearsay in situations like this is that it allows evidence to be given with impunity. It would be impossible to bring a perjury prosecution afterwards because, logically, the hearsay evidence about someone who is deceased can never be disproved. Witnesses know they can say whatever they like.

The defence view was that, irrespective of whether Wayne had ever said such things, none of the supposed events had ever happened. However, there are criteria that can be used to ascertain whether the evidence is likely to be true. Examining the hearsay evidence as a whole, a few points stand out. Firstly, it appears that, in the testimony, the roles have been reversed, with actions and behaviour ascribed to Emma that one would instead have expected of Wayne. Secondly, there is no corroboration for any of it even though there are moments where, had the events happened, one would have expected corroboration. Did Emma draw a knife in a pub? The sheer unlikelihood of that happening is only reinforced by the complete absence of witnesses. A *woman* brandishing a knife aggressively is the sort of thing that, if seen, is likely to be remembered; yet, apart from this witness, no one at all did see it.

Similarly, Emma, according to Levitt, is supposed to have yelled to Wayne that she was going off to get fucked by someone else. Yet no one heard that. The first-hand witnesses heard only the opposite (Wayne berating Emma). According to what Levitt reported, Emma taunted Wayne outside the pub; but there is CCTV evidence showing that Emma was behaving passively, walking away and trying to avoid confrontation; it is Wayne who is ranting at her. Again, the hearsay evidence given in court is contradicted by the genuine evidence. Also, Emma's subsequent behaviour that evening certainly did not suggest that her objective was to 'get fucked by someone else'. There were countless witnesses to the fact that her behaviour was natural and unexceptional.

Thirdly, the hearsay witnesses struggled to remember what they'd said earlier. This can often be a sign of fabricated testimony: if something has happened, then witnesses should have no problem in recalling it; if, however, they have invented the incident, they may be unsure what they said on the earlier occasion. Here, there are several contradictions with earlier statements. This explains why the jury specifically asked to see the statements of Westlake and Gosling (though Levitt also had difficulty in remembering what he'd previously said).

Altogether, the hearsay evidence is so riddled with implausibility that one is surprised the judge allowed it to be given. Having said that, his problem was that there was no other significant prosecution evidence, so disallowing the hearsay would have been tantamount to throwing out the case entirely. Certainly, that is what he should have done, but it is something that judges strive to avoid.

The testimony of both Gosling and Levitt appears unreliable. The latter said, 'I know 100% he would not hit Emma', a remark which most of those who knew the couple found astonishing. It is Danny Westlake's evidence, however, which is the most contentious. There is, most startlingly, his extraordinary claim that he was on the phone to Wayne for three minutes from 2.27; in fact, as the entire episode unfolded.

WITHIN A FEW MINUTES OF WAYNE'S DEATH, Westlake approached PC Cooper outside Emma's house. Cooper, one of the first officers to arrive at the scene, recorded what Westlake said to him:

> Westlake started saying that he had been on the phone to [Wayne] at the time of the stabbing. He heard him and his partner, Emma Bates, having an argument. He told me he heard him say. 'You better put that down', before he heard some noise followed by him saying, 'You better call an ambulance'. At this point Hill told me *he carried on walking* to his house. (italics added)

At trial, Westlake gave different evidence:

> Q: Where were you when you started to make that call?
> A: I was in my house.
> Q: In your house, yes. Did you get through to Wayne?
> A: Yes.
> Q: Were you able to speak to Wayne?
> A: Yeah.
> Q: What did you say to him?
> A: I asked him where he was … He said he had just got back home now …
> Q: We see that that phone remained as a live call for three minutes, 180 seconds. Were you listening to it the whole of that time?
> A: Yes.
> Q: Where were you when you were listening to that?
> A: I was standing in the living room.
> JUSTICE MACKAY: You were what?
> A: Standing in my living room.

In these circumstances, with Westlake having *immediately* spoken to an officer outside Emma's house, he cannot have been confused or forgetful about this. So he told police one thing; and then said something different under oath at trial.

This is, however, by no means the only reason for the deepest scepticism. Westlake's report of this event changed each time he was asked to provide it. At one time or another a number of details were incorporated into his account: the television was on in the background; he claims to have heard Emma leaving and then returning (when, he is implying, she went to the kitchen to fetch a knife) and to have heard the metallic sound of a knife being drawn from a block; he claims to have heard Wayne saying, 'You better put that down' and, then, 'You better call an ambulance'.

It is evidentially significant that Westlake's call was meant to have been made at 2.27, and stayed active for three minutes, and Emma called the ambulance at 2.29. So Westlake's account can be tested against the log of the overlapping minute. From this, it can be seen that almost nothing that Westlake claimed to have happened did, in fact, happen. There is no background television heard on the 999 tape. There was no possibility that he could have heard the sound of a knife being drawn from a block. Emma's block was not metallic; it was wooden. Knives came out noiselessly.

When interviewed by police, Westlake contrived to say that Wayne was 'more chilled out than normal … he was so *chilled out*'; and also that his intention would have been 'to bring him to my house and *calm him down*' (italics added), comments that obviously contradict each other.

Surprisingly, he asserted that Emma was not speaking on the phone to the emergency services when he arrived:

Q: Whilst you were there did Emma pick up that phone?
A: No.
Q: Do you recall her using the phone at all?
A: Not while I was there no … She wasn't on the phone when I got into the house.

Obviously, this was untrue. He also said that when he arrived at the house, Emma let him in. In fact, the door was already open as she had left it open after returning from knocking at Andrea's door.

Although Westlake said he overheard what happened, his behaviour afterwards did not suggest that. Having supposedly heard Wayne say 'You better call an ambulance', he didn't rush to the aid of his friend. None of the witnesses who followed his progress up the road suggested that he was hurrying to the scene. They watched him sauntering up the road, with a can of beer in one hand and a cigarette in the other.

At 2.32 he phoned Virgin. He had topped up his credit on Saturday morning. 'Done!' Virgin responded, 'we've topped you up. Your Virgin Mobile airtime balance is £5.06p at 11.57am.' Now, it seems he was probably checking how much was still available. Then at 2.34, he sent Wayne a text:

Im at the door

But if he'd heard the 'ambulance' remark, and therefore knew that serious injury, at least, had befallen him, why send this text?

Westlake, one deduces, had earlier declined to assist Wayne, but had now gone to offer him a bed for the night. He didn't want to see Emma, and so simply texted for Wayne to come out to him. So the hard evidence of the text itself refutes the idea that Westlake had overheard what happened. He sent the text because *he didn't know* what had happened.

In any case, the remarks of Wayne that Westlake supposedly overheard – 'you better put that down' and 'you better call an ambulance' – reek of implausibility. Those who knew Wayne point out how uncharacteristic such comments would have been. In everyday circumstances, let alone life-or-death ones, his language is likely to have been more profane and more in line with Westlake's (whose own comments to Emma at this time, as recorded on the 999 tape, were 'Get the fuck up' and 'You fucking dickhead').

However, there is no need to wrestle with evidential points such as these, because technology has provided an important means of checking the veracity of such evidence. One can simply refer to the automated log of someone's telephone calls.

In the list of the calls 'made, received, missed or attempted' from

Westlake's phone, the text to Wayne's phone at 2.34 is listed; but there is no record of any call from him to Wayne at 2.27.

Further, in the *Chronology of Events* drawn up by the police, the key telephone calls during this episode are listed; according to this, there was no call from Westlake to Wayne at 2.27. It is clear that Westlake's telephone activity has been taken into account because the 'Im at the door' text is included.

If one searches diligently, one also comes across in the documentation a statement from a police liaison manager at Virgin Mobile's corporate office. He points out, with commendable restraint, that at the request of West Midlands Police he has been asked for the itemised outgoing call data for Westlake's phone on three separate occasions: on 30 April, 21 May and 30 June. It's as if the police were hoping that if they asked the same question enough times, they might get a different answer.

Perhaps the explanation of whether Westlake made the call while walking down the street, or while he was still at home, is that he instantly invented this account after Wayne's death, but subsequently reasoned that his story would be more credible if he said he'd made it from his home – forgetting he'd already told police that he'd made it whilst walking along the street.

Had the call not happened, then this would explain all other discrepancies. If one does take this view, then the impression is that from the very first moment, Wayne's friends were attempting to steer the police investigation in the way that suited them. *(see Notes, page 463)*

5

'When all this happened', said Rachel Bishop, 'I became pregnant with my second child. Straightaway, I asked Emma to be godmother again. By then, she was in prison, but that's how much I trusted her. I trusted her with my child's life.'

Emma was a non-violent woman. As the judge had put it, the 'touchstone issue' was: who had the knife? There is no reason to suppose that Emma had it. Despite the picture that Wayne's friends attempted to create through the hearsay evidence, it would have been completely out of character; whereas it was entirely *in character* for Wayne to have taken it with him.

The defence argument was that, when Wayne returned to the house to take some clothes and steal Emma's car, he took the knife and got out the sharpener, but didn't use it (perhaps feeling the knife was sharp enough already, but probably because he was distracted by the phone call from Levitt).

According to the prosecution, he didn't take the knife with him when he left.

'The prosecution suggests', said the judge, 'that, frankly, you do not stick a knife like that down your trousers or in your pocket'.

This was another remarkable comment in the summing-up. The police know only too well that youths and young men *do* stick knives like that down their trousers or in their pockets. Unfortunately, it happens every day. One favoured method is to place the knife behind the trouser belt so that it can be conveniently concealed and carried in the small of the back. (In theory, it can be easily accessed with either hand; in practice, most people will always use their dominant hand.)

How do we know this? We know this because the police have made a public service video about it. In the interests of public safety, they have made the video available to all on the internet. So when the prosecution suggested in court that 'you do not stick a knife like that down your trousers or in your pocket', police officers the length and breadth of the UK would have known that it was untrue.

The experience of Nicola Giles further illustrates the ways in which the criminal justice process can distort reality. Nicola was a vitally important witness. She and Emma had met on their first day at nursery school, and so had known each other for thirty years, seeing each other on an almost daily basis.

Arriving at court to give evidence for Emma, she was naturally apprehensive, and her anxiety was exacerbated by the fact that she was not greeted or approached by anyone from Emma's legal team and indeed was left by herself in the waiting room. When finally called to give evidence, she was understandably ill-at-ease, nervous and less forthcoming than she would otherwise have been.

What should have been key points of her evidence – that she knew Emma was in an abusive relationship; that she knew Wayne was intimidating when he was angry and especially intimidating when he was drunk; that Emma had told her Wayne had threatened to slit her throat; that Emma had been telling her throughout that Saturday that Wayne was particularly argumentative and aggressive; that Wayne was particularly angry as they left the Drake's Drum pub, followed them outside, jumped up on the picnic bench and gesticulated angrily after them; that as they returned home, Nicola was especially worried for Emma's safety and begged her to call the police if there was any trouble – all these points were either skated over or not brought out at all. Nicola did say that Emma told her that Wayne had threatened to slit her throat, but the point was not pressed home and wasn't even mentioned in the judge's summing-up.

Afterwards, she was critical of the defence team for not putting her at her ease beforehand. There was, however, one problem. Unbeknown to her, that was not the fault of the defence, because she was called *as a prosecution witness*. The prosecution can list her as a witness, even though nothing in her evidence will assist its case, and it is a very effective way of neutralising a strong defence witness.

The jurors had been fed a diet of misinformation: Emma was an aggressive woman who carried knives; there was 'relatively little or no dispute' about the pathology; Wayne had never once phoned Emma that night, as though that were unusual and significant; because the prosecution couldn't tell how often she'd urinated during the night (even though they knew that she had not), she may well have been intoxicated; Westlake overheard the hallway drama on his mobile phone (even though the key phone records contradicted this); young men do not conceal knives down their trousers (even though they do); and Emma's best friend was a witness for the prosecution (even though that was the last thing she thought she was).

The one element that was kept out of the court case altogether, and which the hearsay evidence was calculated to subvert, was any appreciation of Emma's character. She was submissive throughout her relationship with Wayne; she was always ready to take responsibility, even if she herself was the victim. It was three years before she was able to explain what had happened in the caravan.

'I was making the beds and Wayne came in and asked me to go and get him some cans of beer', she wrote, 'I refused and the next thing I knew his fist was in my face.

'I carried on making the beds through my tears. When the children saw my black eye, Wayne told them I had accidentally hit myself with the mobile phone plug, and that I was a clumsy Mummy. Turning to me, he said, "Isn't that right, Mummy?" If anyone asked, that had to be the story.'

In the courtroom, she was acquiescent. She naturally deferred to others. She would fall in line with whatever authority figures suggested. Her evidence was not as forthright as it should have been. She could see Wayne's family sitting in the public gallery and regarded them with a mixture of feelings: she didn't want to increase their all-too-obvious distress, and specifically didn't want to upset his mother.

In any case, she was scared of the family, as were others. One witness who came forward in 2013 in the hope of bringing new evidence to bear on the case insisted that, 'I do not want Wayne's family to know of my involvement ... I am very scared of them and do not want them to be present at court if I have to give evidence'.

Police documents referred to the 'threats by the deceased's family' against Emma, and the fact that she could 'come to harm'. So, when giving evidence, she didn't exacerbate the friction – she was well-practised in defusing potentially tense situations – and denied that Wayne was ever violent towards her.

'Her response was one most women would adopt', wrote Helena Kennedy QC, 'when confronted by an attack on their integrity and values: to retreat to a non-combative position.'

In fact, Kennedy wrote that about a different woman in a different case, though it could equally have applied to Emma.

Emma, having experienced all this, has now learned to stand up for herself. The Criminal Cases Review Commission was unmoved by her case, as with all those in this book. When, in December 2013, members of the Commission gave a talk at her prison, she was emboldened to approach them afterwards. As a result, the Commission agreed to meet her to allow her to put forward her own case to them. They visited her in prison on Wednesday 26 March 2014. Even then, she could not bring herself to relate what happened in the Christmas Day incident, explaining that it was still 'too painful'.

AN INSTRUMENT USED in warfare in the sixteenth century was a heavy iron contraption that would be filled with gunpowder and then fastened to gateways, entrances or defensive fortifications in order to blow them up. This was called a petard. Naturally, setting off the explosion could be a dangerous undertaking, and many an engineer who fired the petard would himself be blown up by it. This gave rise to the expression: hoist with his own petard. It refers to someone who intends harm to others but instead suffers the consequences of his own trap. The idea was popularised by Shakespeare in 1601 in *Hamlet* – ''tis the sport to have the engineer hoist with his own petard' – and remains in vogue today.

It applies precisely to this case. Wayne took the knife, intending to harm others, though specifically Emma and the man (Carl, perhaps) who, in his jealous rage, he imagined she'd be with. Instead his scheme backfired and his weapon inflicted harm only on himself. When all the evidence is properly examined, accident is the only logical explanation of what happened.

Two changes of recent years facilitated the catastrophic courtroom outcome: the decision to allow hearsay evidence into the courtroom; and the significant reductions in legal aid payments to defence solicitors. The cuts were so stringent that some of the country's leading practices felt unable to continue doing legally-aided work for the defence. They reluctantly accepted that, as the funding available would not allow them to perform their job to adequate professional standards, then they had better not do it at all.

Although some practices heroically continued in the field, some of those who took on the mantle were ill-equipped to do so. The inevitable result, as this case illustrates, is that greater numbers of people will now be wrongly convicted of serious crimes. Funding saved on legal aid expenditure is instead devoted to keeping innocent people locked up.

The criminal justice process having inverted reality, Wayne Hill is now not perceived as the graceless bully he was. He is officially viewed as the victim, and his family as the bereaved. They will have received significant financial compensation for his death. In years to come, they will be informed and consulted about Emma's release from prison. They may put up objections to her release; they may be able to get it postponed, so that she serves a longer term. They may also be able to stipulate, for example, that when released she is not allowed to return to her home area but must live elsewhere in the country.

Such are the ways in which victims and the bereaved have been empowered in recent years. There is nothing wrong with that, of course; it is just that it makes it more imperative that the system correctly identifies the victim and the aggressor rather than, as happened here, getting them the wrong way round.

Chapter 4

One good turn deserves ...

Geoff Hyde's story

1

On 27 February 2006, at 6.30pm, Geoff Hyde received a call on his mobile phone. The caller explained that he had a lorry that had developed brake problems. He said he'd found a mechanic. Would it be all right if the repair could be carried out at the yard?

Hyde, who ran a haulage company based at the Tamchester Yard in Chertsey, said it should be fine but he'd first need to check whether there was sufficient space available. At that point, he didn't know. He had spent the day at home in bed, suffering a bout of 'flu. However, he'd been intending to go in, just to check that all was well at the end of the day, so he got ready and drove in to the yard. He ensured that there was enough room; he gave the caller the go-ahead.

Shortly afterwards, he noticed a white van – the mechanic's, he presumed – and then a lorry being driven in. On his way home, he stopped to buy medicine and looked forward to an early night.

Meanwhile, back at the yard, the lorry driver and the 'mechanic' were unloading seventy-seven kilos of cocaine from the lorry into the back of the van. However, the yard was under surveillance. No sooner had the van been driven out than it was stopped by a convoy of police vehicles. Another police team in the yard stopped the lorry and grabbed the driver.

Not surprisingly, the lorry-driver and the 'mechanic' were charged with conspiring to supply cocaine. Rather more surprisingly, Hyde was also charged with the same offence. Indeed, when the case went to trial the prosecution told the jury that he had played the most important role of the three.

Having been found guilty, he was given a twenty-two-year sentence. He was sent to Brixton Prison. He was now not merely a convicted criminal but, he soon found out, the most serious criminal held at that prison. Nor was that all he faced; his family was also put at risk. The prosecution also applied for a confiscation order and soon the judge ordered the seizure of almost £1million-worth of his assets.

As if all this wasn't bad enough, his lawyers told him that, as he had been convicted on so little evidence, they could see no grounds on which he could appeal.

HYDE WAS BORN in Chelsea, London, on 13 September 1947. Today, Kensington and Chelsea is London's wealthiest borough; in the immediate post-war years it had a more motley character and was home to working-class families, like Hyde's, who were struggling in difficult times. He grew up, the second of four children, in a small council flat.

After leaving school, his first job was as a baker's assistant earning four pounds ten shillings (£4.50p) per week. He then worked for a time as a shop assistant at a greengrocer's in Ashford, Middlesex.

While there, he bought a Lambretta – a motorised scooter – which, in those days, branded him a mod. The mods were natty dressers. They thrilled to the music of the Rolling Stones, the Who, the Small Faces and the Yardbirds; and they drove Vespas or Lambrettas. Those mid-'60s years were marked by periodic gatherings of thousands of mods, usually on bank holiday weekends, at Britain's coastal resorts.

'We would spend a lot of time riding to seaside towns', recalled Hyde, 'especially Brighton, which is where I got my tattoos – something I've always regretted. I've often thought of having them removed, but never got round to it.'

Hyde went to work for British Railways and was briefly a fireman, but the death-knell of the steam engine had already sounded. When his depot went over to diesel ('which was pretty boring'), Hyde handed in his notice. He then got a job as a gold leaf gilder in Fulham. About three further jobs followed, before a friend talked him into working as a minicab driver for a firm called Dial-a-Car in New Southgate, north London. After about a year, the owner asked Hyde and his friend if they'd like to buy the company. So they did. Then they found larger premises where they had the space to set up a second company, a car repair business.

It was while running these companies that Hyde met his first wife. They married in 1970 and their first child, Karen, was born in February 1971. A second daughter, Nicky, was born in August the following year.

By this time, Hyde's younger brother had emigrated to Australia. He ultimately settled in New Zealand and became a prison officer. In 1973 the rest of his family – his parents, sister and David, his elder brother – decided to join him there. Hyde stayed behind in England, but decided to leave the businesses to his friend and start afresh.

He got a lorry-driver job with an agency in St John's Street, Clerkenwell, central London. It was a night run, picking up newspapers and delivering them to Heathrow airport. After about a year he bought his first lorry, a thirteen-ton box-shaped Mercedes, and took over the business himself. So, in September 1974, Hyde Transport began.

Having failed to settle, Hyde's parents and brother arrived back from Australia. Hyde and his father then started a second transport company which they called Merlin Freight. After about a year, however, his father decided not to continue with it and instead became a driver with Hyde Transport. Hyde himself continued with the night run to Heathrow for five years, while picking up jobs with other companies during the day.

He also developed another sideline after a friend asked him to put in some money to help set up a hairdressing business in Richmond, west London. Hyde agreed, and they called it Fellini's.

In 1980 Hyde's wife developed serious mental health problems. For years, her illness was, if not untreatable, then certainly untreated. (More recently, it has been diagnosed as circumstantial schizophrenia.) As her condition deteriorated, so relations with most of her family broke down. One family member commented, 'She made it extremely difficult for you to be around her'.

The family broke up. While his wife went into hospital, Hyde moved out and the children were looked after by his brother's family. The family got back together when his wife was discharged, but she stopped taking her medication and had to go back into hospital. Hyde then looked after the children. She came out again, but there were further problems. Under the pressure of her instability, the marriage collapsed. They divorced, although Hyde agreed that she could remain in the home that he continued to pay for.

Hyde Transport had begun to expand in 1979 when the transport manager of one of the companies Hyde was working with offered to go and work for him. With this stimulus, he started buying more lorries and recruiting new drivers. He acquired fresh contracts, some of which – one was with a large plastics company – proved of lasting benefit. Hyde's father retired as a driver in 1989, but continued to be involved with the company. He still went to the office several times a week to help with admin work.

From 1987 the company was based at the Tamchester Yard where Hyde, along with several other companies, rented space.

HYDE WAS INTRODUCED to Gillian Allen in 1982 at a rock'n'roll music venue just off Leicester Square in the west end of London. At that point, they were both just coming out of relationships that had proved intensely emotionally draining – albeit for very different reasons. Hyde's had been with his ill wife; Gillian's was with the folk-jazz guitarist John Martyn, a musician as talented and charismatic as he was wayward and self-destructive.

Gillian found herself in the rock'n'roll world through the contacts of her brother Jeff, who started off as drummer for the rock group East of Eden. One night, with a group of friends after a Lou Reed gig, she met Martyn.

'I loved his music', she said, 'and fell passionately in love with him'.

Martyn was then breaking up with his first wife, Beverley, with whom he had three children. He and Gillian began a relationship. It was to last for three turbulent years, during a time when Martyn, even by his standards, was particularly troubled. He was then recording the album *Grace and Danger*.

Gillian found a cottage in Roberton, in the Scottish borders, where they lived for a couple of years. Then Gillian found out that she was expecting a baby. 'I was deliriously happy about that', she said, 'and because I was pregnant, I stopped doing the rock'n'roll stuff – the vodka-and-oranges at breakfast, and all the rest'.

Martyn, however, had wholly embraced all the excesses of the lifestyle and had no intention of letting go. By the time their son Ruari was born, the relationship was crumbling fast.

'Things were going badly', recalled Gillian, 'and I bailed out.

'Geoff was a completely different personality, someone who wasn't in the music business. He is very shy when you first meet him. Friends of mine said it would never last; but my mother knew it would, she said "You've got a good one there"'.

Gillian bought a flat in Richmond, but they lived together in Woking and then Kew. These were, recalled Hyde, 'some of the best times of my life'.

He and his Richmond partner then decided to add on a children's clothes shop to the hairdressing business. They called this Fellini Kids, and it was run by Gillian and the partner's wife.

The partner then bought Hyde out. With the windfall, he could contemplate buying a property for himself and Gillian. They got a flat in Sheen Court, Richmond and then bought a house with a large garden in Effingham, Surrey. In the short term, this created serious difficulties. The housing market collapsed at the start of the '90s and for some time they were not able to sell the Sheen Court flat so Hyde found himself struggling to pay the bills on three properties. However, they weathered the storm.

They had married in 1987, after they had been together for five years, so that Geoff could formally adopt Ruari. 'He never called Geoff "Dad" before he got adopted', said Gillian, 'but has done so ever since. They just have the best relationship.'

IT WAS HYDE'S SUPPORT for the Chelsea football team that led to an unexpected expansion in his social horizons. Having been born locally, he had supported Chelsea all his life. He first saw them in 1969 at Stamford Bridge, their home ground, when they lost 2-1 to West Bromwich Albion in a sixth-round FA Cup tie. His early heroes were the forwards Peter Osgood and Ian Hutchinson and the goalkeeper Peter Bonetti. As soon as finances permitted, he became a season ticket holder.

In the early '90s, at Pyrford Golf Club, near Byfleet in Surrey, he was introduced to Osgood. A firm friendship between their families quickly developed. Hyde and Gillian went on to share many social occasions with Osgood and his wife, Lynn. Affectionately remembered as 'the King of Stamford Bridge', Osgood had had an illustrious Chelsea career, albeit one frequently interrupted by injury, from 1964 until 1974, and again from 1978 until his retirement in December 1979. He now organised annual charity events at the Meon Valley Hotel and Country Club, near Southampton, which Hyde and Gillian always attended.

It was through his friendship with Osgood that Hyde met many other former Chelsea players, including Hutchinson, Tommy Baldwin and Ron 'Chopper' Harris. The latter had started a commercial holiday venture Hunter's Moon in Warminster, Wiltshire, and for a couple of years, Hyde and Ruari (who by now preferred to spell his name Rory) went there as Harris's guests.

Chelsea's fortunes revived and they competed again in Europe. By this stage, Osgood had already helped Hyde get executive suite tickets for himself and Rory. They watched home games together and also attended matches across the continent with Harris and others. They were all together in Stockholm on 13 May 1998 when Chelsea won their second European Cup-Winners' Cup.

Hyde went on golfing holidays to Spain with Osgood and Harris. He was also introduced to one of the most publicly prominent of Chelsea supporters, the colourful MP Tony Banks, who invited him to the Houses of Parliament.

In September 2002, Hutchinson died after a long illness. Osgood started organising memorial horse-racing days for him – more charity events – at Windsor racecourse and Hyde made the winning bid at an auction for a bronze statuette of Hutchinson delivering one of his trademark long throw-ins. Osgood had been sacked as a match-day hospitality host after a dispute with the previous owner, but was rehabilitated at Stamford Bridge after Roman Abramovich bought the club. He resumed his job and Hyde and their friends watched home games with him.

Towards the end of the 1990s, Gillian, who was by then a manager for the technology company EDS, contracted bronchial problems that she found impossible to shake off. However, the doctor did notice that her condition improved whenever she was in a drier climate. As a result, she decided to buy a small apartment in Spain – near Denia on the Costa Blanca, where one of her friends owned a house. Hyde and Gillian had spent their wedding night there with Rory in 1987 and been back every year since. (Hyde never took more than one week's holiday at a time, with one solitary exception: a trip in 2001 to visit his family in New Zealand.)

Gillian moved there permanently in February 2004 to see if her health would improve. Fortunately it did, and she was able to start a small business, the Frock Exchange. The overall plan was that Hyde would visit for long weekends every month and, ultimately, would retire there.

In this, as in all other matters, he had encountered difficulties and got through them. By 2006, he was an English paterfamilias; family matters revolved around him. There were always spring and summer barbecues at Effingham, usually arranged to coincide with important football matches. They were always much anticipated by family and friends.

'I remember we once had seventeen sleeping over at our house', said Gillian.

She and Rory were looked after and financially supported by Hyde, as were his daughters, his father, and his first wife. He was able to do all that because of the steady way in which he'd built up his business. His hard work had paid long-term dividends and, since 2000, he had paid himself a six-figure annual salary. By 2006, he had twelve vehicles and employed thirteen men – a small, though very loyal, workforce.

He was the kind of businessman whom politicians affect to admire: someone who had started with nothing, who had never looked to the State for assistance, and who had built his own prosperity which he had used to create jobs for others and support an extended family. He had never been in trouble and, indeed, had always been on the right side of the law. A thank-you letter from Customs & Excise testifies to the assistance he had given the authorities in a cigarette smuggling operation in 1999.

2

Hyde received the fateful call on his mobile at 6.30pm. It was almost unheard-of for him not to be in work, but this 'flu had laid him up for two days. The caller – let us call him Greaves – seemed to be English. He claimed to know someone else who rented space at the yard, Mick Barnes.

'I had a storage and distribution company', Barnes told me, 'distributing marble and granite from Portugal, Spain and Italy; Geoff was one of my hauliers.'

At this time, however, Barnes had closed down his company and so was no longer working at the yard. But Hyde instantly knew to whom Greaves was referring. Having gained his confidence, Greaves went on to say that he had a 'foreign' lorry whose brakes needed fixing – could a mechanic do it in the yard?

He would always help out colleagues in the business, essentially because it was in his nature to be helpful. Of course, it also made good sense; after all, you never knew when you might need a return favour.

Tamchester Yard was just off the M25, and conveniently situated for haulage companies. Lorry drivers not just in Britain but across the Continent seemed to know about it. Overseas drivers used it all the time, usually without bothering to ask. They would regularly stop there, whether for rest and relaxation or just to use the toilets.

Ultimately, it was used so much that overnight parking became a problem; space was often so restricted that the companies based there found it difficult to get their lorries away in the morning.

The obvious solution – locking the yard overnight – was not available. The land was owned by British Gas who needed 24-hour access to the site. So those using the yard improvised. They wound a chain round the gates and put a nut and bolt through it. That way, it appeared to be locked. Those familiar with the site would be able to get in at any time; those who weren't would probably be deterred. Secondly, a notice was put up requesting drivers not to park overnight. Because the problem was mainly caused by overseas lorries, the sign was printed in four languages.

So, that February night, Hyde told Greaves it would be OK providing there was space available. Despite feeling unwell, he then went in to the yard. Normally he would go in every day; he liked to satisfy himself that everything was ticking over. He also needed to book online a flight back from Spain for Gillian. He started out at 6.59 and phoned Greaves to tell him he was leaving.

On his way there, Greaves phoned again. Hyde merely said he hadn't got there yet; Greaves would have to be patient.

Hyde got to the yard at 7.40. He and one of his drivers, Liam Carey, re-parked two lorries. They needed to create space for another driver, Barry Barwell, who was on his way back from Manchester, and also to make room for the 'foreign' lorry. Hyde had to ensure that, if the brake problem could not be remedied and the lorry was immobilised, it was not going to hinder the movements of other vehicles in the yard. Then Greaves rang again (at 7.52) and Hyde confirmed that there was indeed space.

Hyde then went into his office. He'd recently had a satellite tracking programme installed on his computer. This would allow him, once he understood how to work it, to check the locations of all his lorries that were on the road. Other staff were still teaching him how to use it. He was briefly preoccupied in trying to figure it out on his own. Still feeling unwell, he didn't bother booking the flight.

He stayed for only about twenty minutes and left at two minutes past eight. As he drove out, he noticed a white Vauxhall Astra van arriving. The lorry was just a couple of minutes behind.

Hyde then phoned back Greaves. 'Just to let you know', he said helpfully, 'your lorry's just turned up, and there's a fitter with him.'

Hyde stopped to get his medicine and then, back home, got yet another call from Greaves. The time was now 8.51. Barwell had got back from Manchester. Greaves wanted Hyde to phone him to reassure him that there was no problem with the 'foreign' lorry being there. By this stage Hyde was beginning to consider Greaves a bit of a pain, but it was no problem to ring Barwell.

At 9.39, Greaves telephoned again. He said he couldn't now make contact with his driver. Could Hyde throw any light on the situation? Hyde said he couldn't. However, he quickly found out what the situation was. His next call was from Barwell, who had some troubling news: there had just been a police raid on the yard.

The lorry had been carrying a cargo of bagged salad leaves for English supermarkets. Underneath, in a secret compartment, was its illegitimate load: seventy-seven kilos of cocaine.

It took about forty-five minutes for two men to unload the cocaine into the back of the van. They were able to work without interruption. Almost all the staff had gone home for the night; Barwell had stayed in his cab to catch up with the day's paperwork.

The van drove off at two minutes past nine. Then, as the lorry was manoeuvring, Barwell noticed that it was about to reverse into a barrier. He jumped out of his cab and yelled at the driver to stop. He was helping him with the reversing, a couple of minutes later, when the police appeared. There were about a dozen of them. Some had hidden in the adjacent car park; others arrived in cars. In a matter of seconds, Barwell found himself pinned to the ground by officers.

Meanwhile the van was stopped just a short distance away by several police cars.

Barwell was asked to account for his movements. After he'd done so and had provided personal details, including his mobile phone number, the police released him. He immediately phoned Hyde to tell him what had happened. Shaken and perplexed, he then drove home.

At about 10.15, Barwell's phone rang. It was the police. They said they needed to get into the office. So, astonishingly, they wanted Barwell to contact Hyde for them, to ask him to go to the yard with the office keys. Barwell rang Hyde again. Hyde reluctantly accepted that, in view of everything that was going on, he had better go to the yard. Picking up his mobile phone as he left, he drove back. It was 11.10 when he arrived.

He let the police into the office and sat down while they went through some paperwork.

Then, at about 11.30, they arrested him. They drove him in his own car to his house, with Hyde giving directions. While he put the car in the garage, they began a cursory search of his home. (It took about fifteen minutes.) They opened his briefcase and took his Filofax. They were interested to find a boarding pass from a flight to Spain. They were also interested to learn that he'd intended booking another flight that evening, but had not actually done so.

They then took him to Charing Cross Police Station and held him overnight. Hyde took some medicine and spent an uncomfortable night in a cell. In the morning, he requested medicine again but declined several opportunities to ask for a solicitor: what on earth did he need one of those for?

Then he was interviewed. He couldn't think clearly. He panicked as he began to realise that it was all much more serious than he'd imagined. The police dropped the bombshell that they were talking about the illegal importation of nine million pounds' worth of drugs.

Hyde was completely taken aback.

'Nine million pounds' worth of drugs?'

Confusing him further, the police misinformed him.

'You were able to tell your driver that it was a Spanish lorry', one officer put to him. 'So how did you know that?'

The officer reiterated: 'The important question is, how did you know that it was a Spanish lorry?'

This was untrue. All that Hyde had known about the lorry was that it was 'foreign'. But in his groggy state, with his accelerating anxiety compounded by illness, he believed that he needed to distance himself entirely from the drugs consignment. He denied having received the critical phone call; and said that he had spoken to the van-driver as he drove in.

Of course, the police knew from having spoken to Barwell that Hyde had received the phone call. In any case, they could access his mobile phone records. They also had the video surveillance of the yard and so knew he hadn't exchanged any words with the van driver. Any real drug-runner would have understood all that. But Hyde was undone by his naïvety. As far as the police were concerned, he had told two lies and incriminated himself. That was enough. The interview lasted a mere twenty-seven minutes. Hyde was then charged and remanded in custody.

At that juncture, the most immediate problem for his legal team was simply to get him out of prison. Many of those who knew Hyde were prepared to put up whatever they had – in some instances, their life savings – so that he could get bail. In the event, however, bail was refused. The prosecution argued that, in view of the seriousness of the offence, he might abscond. Hyde accordingly spent almost nine months in prison prior to his case coming to trial.

THE CASE WAS HEARD at Inner London Crown Court, at the Elephant and Castle, not one of London's most picturesque neighbourhoods. Hyde was charged with conspiracy to supply cocaine that, by the time of trial, was valued at £9.7 million. Two men had been charged with Hyde: the lorry driver, Francisco Ibanez Cantero; and the 'mechanic', John Town.

Ibanez Cantero pleaded not guilty. Town, however, had already pleaded guilty. From the moment of his arrest, he had made a limited confession. He told police that the van contained fifty kilos of cocaine, which he would have been paid £2,000 for transporting. Although it seems incredible that he should have risked so much for so little, it may well be true. He told them nothing more.

The fact that Hyde was charged together with Ibanez Cantero and Town created immense difficulties for him. Firstly, the prosecution asked to delay the trial (which had been due to begin on 30 August). They said they needed more time to translate documents relating to Ibanez Cantero. The judge granted them the adjournment. A knock-on effect of this was that Hyde lost his barrister, who was not available for the new trial date. A fresh barrister had to be recruited. He would have far less time to prepare his case than his Crown opponents.

Secondly, when the trial did start two months later, on 24 October, all proceedings needed translating into Spanish. As a rule, every criminal trial process is protracted and frustrating. With the need for simultaneous translation, this trial would be even more so. Perhaps the more important repercussion, however, was simply on the fluency of proceedings. Clear-cut argument would become even more difficult under such conditions.

Thirdly, whereas it makes sense for there to be co-defendants in cases (such as a robbery carried out by a group) where the defendants' cases are on all fours with each other, it made no sense for Hyde to be a co-defendant in circumstances such as these. He had never met, or had any contact with, Ibanez Cantero or Town, nor did the prosecution suggest that he had. His defence could only be seriously compromised by being charged alongside them. Ibanez Cantero was directly involved, whether wittingly or unwittingly, in the importation of drugs; and Town had already pleaded guilty. Unhappily for Hyde, this was made known to the jurors.

'You have been given this information', the judge told them, '[because] it's evidence which goes to prove that there was a conspiracy to supply cocaine.'

The prosecution counsel told the jury that the affair was a 'very sophisticated criminal enterprise'. He described the secret compartment where the drugs were hidden as:

> One of the most sophisticated lorry concealments that the customs officer had seen in his nineteen years working at Customs & Excise … So what does that tell you about the conspirators? That they are serious people, [who] are involved in this in a serious way.

Hyde's son-in-law, Paul Dietrich (Nicky's husband), was himself a journalist. So he attended each day, sitting in the press box and taking copious notes – indeed, paying far more assiduous attention to the evidence than other reporters would have done.

As he listened to the unfolding prosecution, two points of evidence particularly surprised him. The first occurred when one police officer was asked about the sign at the yard, written in four languages, requesting drivers not to park overnight. The officer told the court that there was no sign.

This is one of those moments for which a criminal defence team is inevitably unprepared. They knew that the sign was there; but had not anticipated that the prosecution would deny it. When that happens, it obviously creates logistical problems for a small and under-resourced defence team. It was important for them to be able to show that continental lorries regularly used the yard, and therefore that there was nothing necessarily out of the ordinary about the phone call that Hyde received; but was it important enough for them to drop everything, research this small corner of the case, and then protest vehemently to the judge?

In practice, in the context of a complex trial, the defence is going to be unable to challenge erroneous information of this kind. After the trial ended, the defence team readily obtained photographs of the sign *in situ*, and also the invoice from the graphics company that created it – but this evidence had not been made available in time for the trial. So the jurors were misinformed, and they stayed misinformed.

Then, the defence asked a female police officer about Mick Barnes, whose name Greaves had used to win Hyde's confidence. What attempts had she made to contact him? The officer told the court that she had put his name into Google. That was the extent, it seems, of the attempts to locate him.

'This is where the case became a bit of an eye-opener', said Dietrich. 'I think we'd all assumed that when police investigated cases, they followed leads exhaustively. But they hadn't got in touch with Barnes.'

The defence had other concerns with the way the case was being handled at trial. There were a great many surveillance videos. Looking through these properly is inevitably time-consuming. However, despite the fact that they had been available from the outset, they were handed over to the defence at such a late stage that it precluded any adequate analysis of them.

This problem was insignificant, however, in comparison to an issue with the mobile phone records. The first batch of case paperwork that the prosecution sent to the defence included the log from Hyde's own phone. According to this, *there was no incoming call at 6.30*.

According to these CPS documents, the first contact between Hyde and Greaves was at 6.57 when Hyde had telephoned. This was very important. It appeared as though it was Hyde himself who had initiated the dialogue with Greaves.

This led to anxious discussions between Hyde and his lawyers. Had there really been such a call at 6.30, he was asked? Hyde was emphatic that there had been but, faced with the black-and-white evidence of the phone records, he began to doubt himself. As he had been unwell at the time, he wondered if perhaps the call had come through earlier than he remembered. He was understandably wary of putting possibly incorrect information into his key defence statement.

As a consequence, defence lawyers suggested that it might be prudent not to be specific in any way, but for Hyde merely to say that he was contacted that day. The defence material was then sent to the prosecution.

Just before the trial started, the defence team received the prosecution's secondary disclosure bundle. This contained a fresh read-out of Hyde's mobile phone records – *which did now include the 6.30 call to his phone.* He had been right all along.

At trial, however, the Crown prosecutor used Hyde's failure specifically to refer to this in his original statement as a prime example of what he said was evasiveness.

'Also of significance is the damning contact [with Greaves]', he told the jury. '[Hyde] says, "I would have told the jury about that" – but, of course, he wouldn't. *It's left out of the defence statement that was handed to the Crown.'* (Italics added.)

During cross-examination, the prosecution counsel (who may not himself have understood the full background to this) pressed home his advantage:

> *Prosecution:* In your defence statement, you could have assisted by telling the truth. You were not telling the truth, you were still lying in July?
>
> *Hyde:* I'm not lying about it …
>
> *Prosecution:* You deliberately left out the fact that it was a call to your mobile phone, it's deliberately vague …
>
> *Hyde:* We didn't get the full phone calls until about two weeks before we came to court.
>
> *Prosecution:* Is this why you decided to make up this story about the [Greaves] phone?
>
> *Hyde:* I didn't make up the story.

At that point, the jury was sent out. There was then legal argument in the jury's absence, with the defence QC protesting about the line of questioning.

Defence: He [prosecution counsel] is inferring to the jury that this defendant has made up the account about the call he received.

Judge: He is entitled to …

Defence: He is making comments that he knows are wrong …

The judge allowed the prosecution to continue and the jury returned into court. Hyde was ground down by the questioning:

Prosecution: In the version [of the defence statement] you signed: on the 27 February Mr Hyde was contacted by a person who asked if a lorry with brake problems could use the yard. Did you ask for the reference to you being phoned to be taken out?

Hyde: I have admitted it …

Prosecution: If the Crown had not discovered these phone contacts, then the jury wouldn't have known about it, because you wouldn't have told them … Why not put it in the defence statement?

Hyde: I didn't think it was necessary. I said I was contacted.

Prosecution: Were you telling the truth?

Hyde: Yes, I was contacted by a person.

Prosecution: But not saying it was by phone … You would still be lying about it now if the link had not been discovered.

The paperwork had been tampered with in order to put Hyde into a compromised position. It appeared to be an example of dirty tricks.

The jury's deliberations on the case did not detain them for long. On 17 November 2006, both men were found guilty. Ibanez Cantero was given an eighteen-year sentence. Town, who was sentenced with them, received twelve years. Hyde, having been portrayed throughout by the prosecution as the ringleader, received a heart-stopping twenty-two years. Family and friends in court were weeping.

At this point in a case, the gulf between the court professionals and the distraught relatives is absolute. The barristers move on; they suffer the defeat but not the consequences.

'They looked a bit gutted', said Gillian, 'but they weren't as gutted as we were'.

The leading defence barrister then explained that he could see no grounds on which an appeal could be made. He told the family that they would just have to accept the situation and let Hyde serve his sentence.

'He's got to keep his head down', he told Gillian, 'and you've got to keep yours up.'

As an attempt to comfort a grief-stricken wife, it left a lot to be desired.

3

On that Monday evening, Hyde's disposition was hardly that of someone organising a multi-million pound drugs run. He received those two vital phone calls, from Greaves at 9.39 and from Barwell at 9.48 – with Greaves asking what was going on and Barwell telling him, giving him the dramatic details of the police raid.

Having received these calls, what did Hyde do? Did the first call create any anxiety? Apparently not. What did he do in response to the second? Urgently start ringing round criminal contacts to tell them the game was up? Again, he did nothing at all.

When he received a third call half-an-hour later, asking him to help the police in their investigation he did so, despite the late hour, the obvious inconvenience and his ill-health. He remembered to take with him his mobile phone, which would later become the key strand of evidence against him.

In key respects, the telephone evidence, although it was used to incriminate him, instead appeared to exculpate him. Firstly, there is a clear inference to be drawn from the fact that the police did not have his contact number, and so had to ask Barwell to phone him for them. Clearly, at that stage they could not have believed that he was tipping off one of the key personnel.

As the case progressed towards trial, much information was withheld from the defence under public interest immunity (PII). The defence believed that this material would have enormously strengthened Hyde's position. They wanted to show that he had never been placed under surveillance or been suspected in any way.

Further, any surveillance of the yard would have shown him working late each evening, catching up on paperwork, and frequently moving lorries around to ease congestion and create space in the yard – thereby confirming that what he did on the evening of the 27th was entirely routine.

Part of the prosecution case was that, in moving lorries around to make room for the 'foreign' lorry, Hyde was plainly assisting the traffickers. When an appeal in the case was heard (the appeal being against sentence only), the judges said:

> We have been told by counsel for the Crown that part of the facilitation lay in the applicant ensuring that the premises were cleared of other vehicles before the transfer took place – *a process which took some time.* [italics added]

If that was what the judges were told by Crown counsel, it was untrue. The police surveillance logs confirm that Hyde spent *in total* twenty-two minutes at the yard.

The brake warning light on the lorry's dashboard was lit – but its brakes were in perfect working condition. The obvious inference was that Greaves and the others had taken the precaution of giving some substance to their cover story, just in case Hyde had checked the lorry's mechanical problems himself. Again, this is crucial (albeit overlooked) evidence tending to show how the drugs traffickers planned to dupe Hyde, should it have been necessary.

The police had full computer and mobile phone records. Hyde had had his mobile phone for about five years and there was no evidence to suggest he had another. He used it for both business and personal calls. It was registered to himself. The ones actually engaged in this operation, the criminals, had used untraceable pay-as-you-go phones.

After Hyde was arrested, his house, office and car were all searched. From all that, not one shred of evidence emerged. There was no documentary or scientific evidence. There were no witnesses. Having been arrested and advised of his legal rights, Hyde immediately waived his right to a solicitor.

Did the investigators actually believe that all this was the behaviour of a major drugs baron?

BECAUSE THE POLICE were monitoring the telephone exchanges, we have a good idea of what actually happened. There were two key traffickers. The first was Greaves. A second man was also involved. We'll call him Wilson. Like Greaves, he was using an unregistered phone.

At about 2.15 that day, Wilson rang Town. This appears to have been the first contact of the day between the traffickers. The purpose of the call was presumably so that Wilson could tell Town that the lorry was on its way from Spain, and so the drugs run was going ahead later that day.

During the delivery of the drugs consignment, Wilson was in regular contact with Town; and Wilson and Greaves were in regular contact with each other.

From 6.22, things began to move quickly. Wilson telephoned Greaves, no doubt to tell him that the lorry was getting close. As a result, Greaves made the opening call to Hyde to win his confidence and, in effect, obtain his permission to use the yard.

However, the plans immediately went awry. Naturally, when Greaves rang Hyde, he would have assumed that Hyde would be at the yard and would straightaway be able to give the go-ahead for the lorry to 'have its brakes fixed'.

Yet when Greaves called, Hyde was not there; he was at home. That very day he was off sick – something that almost never happened. Hyde's illness, and consequent absence from the yard, appeared to have surprised them and created unanticipated difficulties. Although less than a disaster, it was more than an inconvenience. At 7.07, the gang had to park their lorry in a lay-by on the A317. They then had to wait, for what may have been forty-eight nerve-racking minutes, while Hyde drove to the yard, at his unrushed pace, and checked that there was indeed space available.

As a result, Greaves was becoming impatient; that was why he called before Hyde had reached it. He called again soon afterwards and Hyde was then able to reassure him.

After the forty-eight-minute hiccup, the plans were on again. Greaves telephoned Wilson, who then rang Town to tell him that all was OK. The van then reached the yard at the same time as Hyde was leaving it. The lorry was just two minutes behind.

At about 8.45, Town rang Wilson, presumably in some apprehension, to tell him that another of Hyde's drivers had arrived back in the yard. This was Barry Barwell. So, Wilson rang Greaves to get him to ring Hyde to ask him to ring Barwell.

Obviously, the gang had Hyde's number from the outset. However, this is not significant. As it was Hyde's solitary mobile, which he'd had for some years, hauliers throughout the British and continental industries would have had the contact number.

However, Greaves must have known that Barnes's name was an ideal one to put forward. Although Hyde would be reassured by the name, there would be no danger of him checking the information straightaway because Barnes himself was no longer involved at the yard. So, this did reveal a level of inside information. It could have been a useful lead, had any of the investigators bothered to follow it up.

'The police never contacted me', said Barnes. 'I found this strange.

'I could have said that what they found suspicious, the foreign lorries in the yard, happened on a daily basis. Whenever we worked late, which was quite often, Geoff and I would always help each other out. I've known him for a long time; he's a really honest person.'

AFTER THE TRIAL finished, the Metropolitan Police press office put out a statement:

> The operation demonstrates our determination to combat the supply of class A drugs in London by targeting the criminal networks responsible for bringing large amounts of cocaine into the capital.

Clearly, that was untrue. The situation was the exact opposite of what the press office claimed.

This had been – as the prosecution emphasised – a 'very sophisticated criminal enterprise'. One customs officer working on the investigation described the secret compartment in the lorry as one of the most sophisticated he had seen in his nineteen years' experience. Yet there was never any suggestion that Hyde – or indeed

Town or Ibanez Cantero – might have been responsible for that. The ringleaders, those who had planned and organised all this, got away scot-free. If this investigation is any guide, these authorities had no interest whatever in bringing to account those really responsible for importing cocaine.

They had clearly received inside information about this drugs consignment. That was why an expensive surveillance operation was mounted. A police helicopter had tracked the lorry from Dover.

A fortnight before this, on 14 February, the same Spanish lorry went into the yard, parked out of sight of the surveillance cameras, and left at 6.00 the following morning. The vehicle was entirely unhindered by police and Customs. During the trial, the prosecution claimed not to know what had happened on this occasion. It may have been an actual drugs operation, they said, or it may have been a test run. All we know for sure about this is that it was nothing to do with Hyde. He wasn't in the country at the time; he was with Gillian in Denia.

The police may have known of this earlier event either through surveillance or because Ibanez Cantero told them. Another of the unexplained features of the case is that the police interviewed him twice, each time with an interpreter present. The ostensible reason for the second interview was that the tape didn't record properly the first time. Yet such equipment is unlikely to fail and, in any event, it is easy to tell at the time whether it is functioning correctly. No notes or documentary records of the first interview were disclosed to the defence.

What we do know, from interviews conducted in Murcia, south-east Spain, where Ibanez Cantero's journey began, is that the company he was working for had just three lorries, two of which had lately been found to contain drugs. A month earlier, in January, another was stopped at Algeciras, the Andalucian port where transport arrives from Africa, and was found to be carrying a cargo of 170 kilos of hashish.

The reason usually given by the authorities for allowing illegal activities to continue is that it will give them the opportunity to apprehend more significant members of the gang; they need to net the bigger fish, they say. That did not apply in this instance.

Lots of police and vehicles were involved in the operation. There was also the helicopter with an infrared camera focusing on events below. The locations from which the mobile calls are made can be calculated. Yet those running this operation were able to evade capture without any difficulty. Greaves and Wilson vanished into thin air. From the surveillance videos, it can be seen that as the lorry moved out of the lay-by to go to the yard, a saloon car was being driven away at the same time. This may have been Greaves, or Wilson, or another trafficker. We just don't know. What is the explanation of this bizarre investigation? Was it simply completely inept? Or was something very murky going on?

In 1933, George Orwell wrote:

> It is easy enough, of course, to buy cocaine in Paris, and the smuggling would be quite simple in itself, only there is always some spy who betrays the plan to the customs or the police. It is said that this is often done by the very people who sell the cocaine, because the smuggling trade is in the hands of a large combine, who do not want competition.

That was written three-quarters of a century ago and yet the situation today is much the same. Drugs traffickers will allow some consignments to be seized in order either to eliminate competition, as Orwell wrote, or to allow even larger ones to get through.

There is also a widely-held view that those involved with drugs are often working in collusion with corrupt investigation officers. In the context of an investigation as disturbing as this one, it is not surprising that such theories should be generated.

There was the mystery of the twenty-seven-minute interview with Hyde. He was not interviewed again. Yet one imagines that if the investigators had actually been interested in nailing the drugs gang, they would have been keen to talk to him at much greater length. If they genuinely thought (as the prosecution had told the court) that these were 'serious people, [who] are involved in this in a serious way', then wouldn't they have wanted to know all about his contacts and how the shipments were arranged? Wouldn't there have been a multitude of questions they wanted to ask?

'Our feeling about this', explained Paul Dietrich, 'is they knew that if they investigated properly, it would just become more and more obvious that Geoff had nothing to do with it. So they didn't investigate.'

Here are other curious aspects of this case. There was no film of the actual unloading of the drugs. On 14 February, there was, or there may have been, a drugs run, but unfortunately the lorry parked out of sight of the surveillance camera so that whatever happened was not visible. On 27 February, the lorry and van parked in the same part of the yard – out of sight of the surveillance camera. As the ostensible point of the exercise was to obtain evidence against the traffickers that would lead to their arrest and conviction, why was the camera so poorly sited?

The surveillance camera, however, did catch one fascinating incident. Hyde's defence team only became aware of it years later, when they were at last able to study all the videos properly. On 27 February, at 4.02pm, a car drew up in the yard. Two men briskly got out, walked out of sight of the camera to the area where, later that day, the drugs would be unloaded, and then walked back to the car, got in and drove off. They had been there less than two minutes.

It seemed, in retrospect, as though they had been carrying out a quick on-the-ground check to ensure that there would be no problem in unloading the shipment a few hours later. Indeed, it is difficult to think of any other explanation for this hasty, yet clearly purposeful, visit. So who were these men? And why hadn't the prosecution mentioned them?

It is also strange that, although the authorities had been tipped off and so seemed to know everything that was happening in the drugs operation, there were no recordings of the telephone calls that they were monitoring.

Hyde seems to have been contacted because Greaves and the traffickers assumed, wrongly, that he was the owner of the yard. Coincidentally, the investigation teams seemed to be under exactly the same misapprehension.

Indeed this misinformation appears to be still present in the system. When the case went to appeal in June 2007, Lord Justice

Dyson said, 'The facts are these. The police conducted a covert surveillance operation in and around Hyde Transport, a haulage yard owned by the appellant in Chertsey.' But those weren't facts at all. The yard was not called that; nor did Hyde own it.

The key mystery is why Hyde was phoned at all on the 27th – bearing in mind that foreign lorries routinely used the yard, regardless of whether they had permission to do so, and that on the previous occasion the traffickers hadn't involved anyone else.

Who knows? Perhaps something happened on the 14th to unnerve the gang, as a result of which they decided that they would be better off having authorisation.

What we do know is that it would be unlikely for someone who was financially secure and had no criminal background suddenly to become involved in drugs smuggling at the age of fifty-nine. The investigators, too, would have known that. From the outset, the case against Hyde was intrinsically irrational. In fact, the only rational explanation is that there was collusion between some-one involved with the investigation and the drugs gang, and they needed a fall-guy.

HYDE'S ARREST CAME as the first half of a double tragedy in his life that happened within forty-eight hours. The second was the sudden death of his close friend Peter Osgood, who died of a heart attack. When Ian Hutchinson had died, Hyde had attended his funeral in Derbyshire. On this occasion, Hyde was in prison and unable to go to the funeral.

Had Osgood survived, his friendship and support would un-doubtedly have been hugely beneficial. Sadly, another member of the Chelsea brotherhood, Tony Banks, had died on holiday on Florida only the previous month. Again, had he lived, his support for Hyde could have been invaluable. 'Chopper' Harris remained loyal and visited Hyde in prison.

Not content with one major injustice, the British authorities set about perpetrating another. They applied for a confiscation order against the convicted men under the Proceeds of Crime Act 2002. Neither Ibanez Cantero nor Town had any assets, so the burden of this fell on Hyde. As the owner of three properties and a flourishing transport business, he initially faced a confiscation order of £2 million, although this was reduced to £900,000.

By this stage, Hyde was being represented by a different lawyer, who fought the confiscation order tenaciously. The wrangling went on for three years. The outcome was that the Crown lost. The Assets Recovery Agency was unable to show that a single penny of Hyde's finances had been earned dishonestly. In the end, the ASA defaulted on its timetable for delivering documents and the judge threw out the case.

That's the good news. The bad news is that this was not only a lengthy process but a particularly oppressive one. With uncertainty shrouding Hyde's homes and all his assets, the well-being of all his family was at risk. Not surprisingly, the protracted action, even though it ultimately proved abortive, created considerable stress for family members.

'Geoff is the man I always thought he was', reflected Gillian, 'the way he's coming through this. But it's very, very hard. The effects on the family have been appalling. Everyone has been under so much pressure.'

'A lot of people depended on him', said Nicky, his daughter. 'Now their safety net has gone.'

There were, inevitably, other huge costs of the wrongful conviction. The first thing to go was Gillian's business in Spain. She needed to be in England, not only to fight the confiscation order but to run Hyde's business.

At first, this went well. She had to close the original company (because of the conviction, Hyde lost his operator's licence) but set up a fresh one as a partnership between herself and Rory, although that necessarily involved considerable cost.

'The staff remained loyal, as did the banks and business partners', explained Gillian. 'I was completely open about what happened. I've had a fantastic bank manager, I told him everything after Geoff got convicted. In fact, everybody was brilliant and stuck by us.'

However, the recession that started in 2008 brought about the company's collapse. In such harsh business conditions, Gillian had neither the experience nor the contacts to pull it through.

'We lost our biggest contract in February 2009. The company had been with us for thirty years, but in the recession they just couldn't do it anymore. That's really what brought us down. We lost a lot of money and had to draw a line under it.

'Now I've had to sell the house to pay off the debts.'

There will be no more barbecues at Effingham.

'It's really heartbreaking that Dad's work is being taken away from him' said Nicky Hyde. 'That's all he's done, he's built his business up, that's his lifetime's work.'

The other aspect that continues to rankle with family members is the intrinsic irresponsibility in the system.

'We now know that, finally, the Crown have investigated his books for the purposes of the confiscation order for three years', said Paul Dietrich, 'and there's no money that can't be accounted for. Not a penny has been earned dishonestly.

'Wouldn't it have been useful for the jury to know that at the time?'

Or, indeed, for the jurors to be informed of that, even now. But there is no moral integrity in the process. There is no one to point out that this bit of the system doesn't match up with that one. The system is incapable of identifying, much less correcting, its own mistakes.

'Geoff is in the mess he's in for two reasons', said Dietrich. 'He did someone a favour; and then he believed in the criminal justice system.'

Chapter 5

'Forensically aware'

Andrew Malkinson's story

1

On 19 July 2003, Andrea Prestwood had a row with her boyfriend at his parents' house and told him she was going to walk home. She left melodramatically, slamming the door behind her and setting off the house alarm. It was about 2.30 in the morning. Her own house was six miles away.

About two hours later, she heard a man's voice coming from behind bushes. He said he had a gun pointed at her. She reacted by sending a text message to her boyfriend.

A little further on, a man jumped on her – 'possibly' the same man who'd shouted at her from the bushes. They rolled down a grassy bank. He then got on top of her, and tried to throttle her. She passed out.

At about 5.30, she scrambled up the bank and stopped a passer--by, telling him that she'd been raped. He took her into his house and called the police.

When two police officers heard Prestwood's description of her attacker, they said it immediately brought to mind a man they had spoken to about five weeks earlier: Andrew Malkinson. Two weeks later, he was arrested, charged with double rape and attempted murder and sent for trial. Malkinson had been in the country for less than six weeks. He'd left Britain more than ten years earlier to live abroad. Today he is in prison, serving a life sentence; so it could be said that the biggest mistake he ever made was to come back.

HE WAS BORN Andrew Strugnell on 23 January 1966 in Grimsby, on the Humber estuary, one of Britain's major seaports. He grew up with his mother, Trisha, and Phil, whom he believed was his father. One of his main childhood interests was the night sky. He would avidly read astronomy books. Phil bought him a pair of binoculars and together they would stand outside on bitterly cold winter evenings and gaze up at the stars.

He left school at sixteen and went to work in the docks. Usually it was cold, and the work was poorly paid, but it did allow him some independence.

In 1983 he had to leave home. Phil threw him out after an argument about the amount of rent that he was paying. He was able to go and live with Gary Foreman, a school friend, and his father. The circle of friends to which he and Gary belonged also included Dave Tindall, whose house they would often go to at weekends to listen to Pink Floyd, Rory Gallagher and Led Zeppelin records.

Andrew got a conviction for causing criminal damage by breaking a pane of glass – for which he was fined £35 and ordered to pay £15 costs – but otherwise his later teenage years were untroubled. He was working at a duck-processing factory, Cherry Valley Farms, when he met Jacqui Tyler. She liked Bob Dylan and Genesis and was seven years older than him, and they struck up a relationship. She had a mortgage on a small terraced house in central Grimsby where he moved in with her. In 1986, they went to Amsterdam together and, shortly afterwards, Jacqui announced that she was pregnant. The following year she gave birth to Andrew junior: little Andy.

'He was born at 9.00 on Saturday morning, 27 June', Andrew recalled. 'I'll never forget it. I went home and played the Rolling Stones' *Get Off Of My Cloud* over and over.'

The Amsterdam trip had given Andrew and Jacqui the travel bug. They talked of starting a new life together in Australia. Their plan was to go there for several months to find out if they liked it and finance their stay by taking short-term jobs. In order to do that, they needed work permits. Andrew applied and was asked to produce his birth certificate. He didn't have one so he went to the local register office. That was how he discovered he wasn't on the official register of births.

The assistant did some searching and soon realised the reason for the omission: he was on a subsidiary list – because he was adopted. This came as a complete shock to him. Naturally, he asked for his real parents' names, but the assistant said she could not divulge them. So he confronted his mother.

'I was pretty confused about all the secrecy', he said, 'and a little angry. But I also felt sorry for my Mum, for all the anguish she was clearly experiencing.'

Once she had got over her shock of Andrew's accidental discovery of the circumstances of his birth, she did provide him with the name of his father, Paul Malkinson, and also the story of what had happened.

He learned that there had been considerable heart-searching within the family over his arrival into the world. The '60s was the decade of the sexual revolution, but in 1966 it had yet to reach Grimsby. So, at the time, this was a small family scandal. Trisha was pregnant but unmarried; Andrew's father refused to succumb to the emotional pressure and do the decent thing. He went off to the United States.

'Both my parents were very young', Andrew explained, 'and I do not blame either of them for events unfolding as they did.'

Happily, his mother found a new partner in Phil; but in order to satisfy the bureaucratic niceties of the time, he could only adopt Andrew if his partner did too. So, bizarrely, Trisha became Andrew's adoptive mother as well as his natural mother.

Malkinson was an uncommon surname. A family by that name actually lived further down the street where Andrew and Jacqui were living. He composed a letter to them.

'This was no easy task', he said, 'writing to complete strangers on the off-chance that they could be related to you, and doing it in such a way so as not to cause offence, alarm or distress.'

A few days later, there was a knock at the door. It was, as it turned out, his grandmother, Iris.

'It was very emotional for all concerned', he recalled. 'In the weeks that followed, I went to visit and found out about that side of my family tree. Obviously, I had no prior knowledge about any of it. Iris was a strong-willed woman who was then in her seventies. She was very interested to learn about me. She told me that a Malkinson trait was stubbornness. Her husband, Pim, my grandfather, was an RAF World War II veteran. He was quite seriously ill with emphysema and in fact died shortly afterwards.'

After Iris had, as it were, introduced father to son, they were soon corresponding with each other. At this point, Andrew and

Jacqui were making plans to sell their home and go to Australia. Coincidentally, they found out that not only was Andrew's father now in Australia, but he was in the Northern Territory – one of the areas they had been hoping to visit.

Eventually, the house was sold and all the preparations were made. Andrew changed his and his son's names by deed poll. In June 1990, the new Malkinson family set off from Heathrow and flew to Darwin.

THEY ARRIVED in the middle of the dry season. It was cooler then, but even so the difference between the temperature there and in England was considerable. The sky was cloudless and an intense blue. Everything felt full of vitality and promise. Malkinson and Jacqui took little Andy in his buggy to see sights like the ruined town hall (destroyed by Cyclone Tracy in December 1974) and also to Doctors Gully by the harbour, where the clear blue water fizzed with mullet as they threw in pieces of bread. They got chatting to two locals who offered to take them to a beauty spot called Berry Springs, a small creek. The water, surrounded by pandanus palms, looked refreshing and inviting. Having been assured that there were no 'salties' (saltwater crocodiles) there, they all jumped in.

They caught an internal flight to Nhulunbuy. This involved flying across the landscape of Arnhem Land, which was marked by spectacular gorges and waterfalls and countless miles of ghost gum trees, spinifex and harsh red earth. They arrived at an airport which consisted of little more than a dirt airstrip chiselled out of the rock-hard red earth.

At the small reception area, Paul was waiting for them with his wife, Sue.

'I know Paul must have found it difficult, me showing up', reflected Malkinson, 'but he dealt with it wonderfully. He was the father I'd always wanted, my real father, but this was tinged with the knowledge that he wasn't there when I was growing up, so I was both incredibly happy and a bit sad at the same time.'

After leaving Britain, Paul had joined the US Army and fought in Vietnam. He had been decorated but, after a black friend had died in his arms, had thrown his medals away. Afterwards he travelled extensively; he'd lived in Malaysia, Palau, Guam and South Africa. He had two daughters: seventeen-year-old Bianca, who was born in Spain; and two-and-a-half-year-old Amber. They were, of course, Andrew's half-sisters.

Nhulunbuy was known as Gove to the very few English-speaking visitors who arrived there. (In fact, the peninsula is named after Pilot Officer William Gove, a young Australian airman who was killed in action in 1943 during the Second World War.) The area is home to some of the most pure-bred Aboriginal communities in Australia today. It has only been inhabited by any Europeans since 1962 when Swiss prospectors first realised the rich potential of the bauxite and manganese deposits. Today, the mining company controls many aspects of day-to-day life; for example, it owns all the housing.

The Arnhem Land plateau is a restricted area, so permits for travel in and across it need to be obtained from the Northern Land Council. However, permission for travel is not easily granted. The NLC takes the view that there must be some reason other than mere sightseeing or travelling round the perimeter of the continent. As his father lived and worked there, Malkinson had no difficulty obtaining permits if, for example, they wanted to go picnicking in the bush.

The government makes a monthly payment to the Aborigine people for the rent of their land. One of Paul's jobs was to take the cash in a briefcase to the community at Yirrkala, south-east of Nhulunbuy. The road was a corrugated track and, in case of bandits, he carried a sidearm.

Gove was wild in every sense. The town was simply hewn out of the bush and it merged back into it abruptly. There were no city limits signs; nothing to demarcate the edge of town – everything just walked straight through. Nature was rampant. Ants invaded everywhere. There were impossibly bright green mantises that turned their heads as anyone walked past and stared them out.

Paul got his son a job barramundi fishing on the Arafura Sea as a hand on a boat named the *Dugong*. It would, he said, make a man of him. There was just a three-man crew: Rudi, a Serb who had a reputation for being difficult, was the skipper; a New Zealander known, predictably, as Kiwi; and Malkinson.

With a coast lined with mangrove swamps in the background, they steamed over to the fishing grounds accompanied by a pod of dolphins. They dropped their nets in Buckingham Bay, but if the barramundi weren't biting they pushed on further west into the remoter parts.

There was no on-board toilet. Excretions had to be performed over the side. This required practice and skill. As soon as the turd hit the water, it boiled and thrashed as a thousand catfish fought for it. They couldn't see beneath the surface because it wasn't the clear turquoise sea of the open ocean but opaque mangrove water; and it seemed to be inhabited by every dangerous creature under the sun. The key piece of advice, inevitably, was: whatever you do, don't fall in.

They would lay the nets from a small aluminium outboard boat, by dropping one end with a small anchor and then slowly unwinding close to the mangrove banks and anchor the other end. They'd regularly go back to check the nets. If fish had been netted, they had to pull them in by hand, then relay the nets and head back to the *Dugong*, where they'd gut, skin, fillet and freeze the barra.

It was physically hard, gruelling and frequently scary work. They had a powerful searchlight to check the nets. As they used it to scan the banks of mangroves, the entire swamp would light up with the unmistakeable ruby-red eye-shine of saltwater crocodiles. Even if they were surrounded by crocs, they had to put their hands in the water to haul up the nets.

Malkinson, however, didn't stay the distance. Rudi, who kept saying he was going back to Yugoslavia to fight for his people (the Balkans conflagration was then yet to happen), teased him once too often. Relations became very strained and Malkinson asked to be taken off.

Arrangements were made. A local pilot would fly Malkinson to Elcho Island the next day, and from there he'd get another light aircraft back to Gove. He phoned Jacqui and Paul to tell them he'd jumped ship; the trip hadn't made a man of him. Paul wasn't sympathetic.

'Paul picked me up', recalled Malkinson, 'but hardly spoke to me on the drive back into town.'

In Gove, however, there were no recriminations; there was only warm-hearted crack. Malkinson spent many evenings simply talking to his long-lost father. Paul said he was proud of his son for going all that way to find him. They hugged each other a lot.

'In many ways', Malkinson said, 'it really was the best time of my life.'

The Malkinson family stayed in Gove for three months before they travelled on. They visited Jacqui's two brothers, both of whom had emigrated to Australia some years earlier. At the end, they returned to Darwin for their flight home. Malkinson phoned his father from the airport. It was a difficult call. He did not feel ready to leave and he could tell his father did not want him to leave.

ARRIVING BACK IN England was a big shock. Things between Malkinson and Jacqui were never the same again. They were both depressed. They started arguing.

'Everything that happened was my "fault"', said Malkinson. 'After Australia, I had changed. I now had an insatiable appetite for travel.'

He temporarily (as he thought) moved down south to look for work, but then got a phone call from Jacqui to say that she was now with his old friend Dave Tindall.

'Which was a bit of a turn-up' said Malkinson, 'but not a complete surprise.'

There was no animosity to the break-up because Malkinson now no longer felt at home in England in any way.

'I knew I did not belong and that I would go and find a better place to live. I went to Amsterdam again. I chatted in the Leidseplein with English lads who had just started to live and work there. It seemed an attractive option.'

He returned to Grimsby to visit Jacqui and Andy and his mum. Whilst there, he was attacked and beaten up in the street. As a crowd gathered, he was head-butted, shoved to the ground and kicked several times. The assailant was, Malkinson learned afterwards, out of his mind on steroids.

He thought he'd been targeted, ironically, because he looked like an outsider who was new to the area. The hospital asked if he wanted to report the incident. He certainly did. The police took photographs of his injuries, but he heard nothing more.

That was the last straw. Soon he was on board a ferry to Rotterdam with a one-way ticket.

He found out about a *uitzendburo*, or job agency, in the Hook of Holland, and from then on things got easier. He felt at ease in the country. He learnt the language, got his *sofinummer* (which enabled him to work legally), paid his taxes, had Dutch medical care and eventually got on to Amsterdam's housing list.

In 1995 Karin Schuitemaker showed up at the Hook. She was, like him, a committed traveller with adventure stories of her own, and they hit it off straightaway. 'It was me who learned so much from her', said Malkinson, 'we could "talk each other's ears off"', as she was fond of saying.' Karin found him, 'sweet, honest, a little naive, not very good at judging people, but good fun … he was curious about new cultures and liked being adventurous and exploring'.

With winter coming on, she suggested they go to the north, to Medemblik, where she'd been born, on the shore of the IJsselmeer, the largest lake in Western Europe. They could get seasonal work picking and packaging lilies. It was night-work, but they were saving for a trip to the Far East.

In March they flew to Bangkok and travelled overland from there. At the southern point of Malaysia, they took the causeway to Singapore. They knew from their *Lonely Planet* guides that Pelni ships went from there to all parts of Indonesia. They went due south to the Riau Archipelago and at Bintan Island caught a converted Japanese trawler bound for Surabaya. From there they headed on to Bali where they passed long and enjoyable hours in the Sari Club, which seemed a wonderful place to drink and meet people of all nationalities.

The relationship with Karin ended in 2000, but they stayed in touch. The next year Malkinson decided to go back to Thailand.

As he and Karin had previously done, he travelled through the beautiful coastline around Phang Nga, in the southern peninsula. While there he foolishly walked into the jungle wearing only sandals and shorts. He felt a couple of sharp needle-pricks in his right foot, causing him a sharp jolt of pain.

By the evening, he was running a high fever and a boat was needed to take him to hospital in Krabi. When he was sufficiently recovered, three days later, they cut open his foot. Thick whitish-yellow pus was drained out – though he never did find out what had stung him.

He had no travel insurance. By the time he'd paid for a week's hospital bills, he had no money left. He went to the international community of travellers around Phuket, hoping to find work but, as it was out of season, that proved difficult. Fortunately, a Japanese woman gave him $200 for his flight home to Holland.

When he returned to Thailand the following year, things did not end as auspiciously.

While trying to get casual work in order to stay on in the country, he was introduced to 'James', a Chinese-Singaporean man in his mid-twenties, who promised to get him what Malkinson understood to be hotel work. 'James' asked for his passport and two photographs, which he said were needed to employ him. Malkinson was suckered in; it turned out that his identity had been stolen and used for a credit-card fraud. A week later, he was arrested. He received a six-month sentence for the passport offence. It was clear that the authorities regarded 'James' as their main target; he received a much longer sentence.

Malkinson was brought before the chief of the local police station who asked if he had any money. Obviously, Malkinson didn't.

'Ha, ha, then you go to monkey house', he said.

James, of course, did have money. He was soon free.

Malkinson was taken to the so-called monkey-house. On the first day, the prisoners had to line up on their haunches in a semi-crouching position. A Laotian guard walked along, brandishing a large cosh.

'Are you scared?' he asked.

'No', responded Malkinson, who was absolutely terrified.

On several occasions, the guards used their coshes to mete out their own forms of punishment to those infringing the rules.

They bedded down in a huge cell holding about 150 people. The floor was concrete, though prisoners could wrap a towel round themselves if they were lucky enough to buy or scrounge one. They had to shower with filtered water from a large concrete vat using plastic bowls. It was generally believed this caused the painful ulcers that were even more painfully lanced with a scalpel. Malkinson also suffered a few bouts of jungle fever.

He served out his six months alongside three Germans who were sentenced to thirty years for trading small amounts of heroin; and other Europeans whose only crime was not to be able to afford the modest fine of about 100 baht (about £1) a day, for overstaying their visa.

He left feeling oddly reassured that, as terrible as the time had been, he at least knew he would never go to prison again.

2

The following year, on 16 May 2003, he flew from Schiphol airport, Amsterdam, for a spot of sunshine in the Canary Islands. He stayed on his own in an apartment on Gran Canaria and spent most days relaxing by the pool.

An English family, John and Angie Garnham and their son Neil were staying there at the same time. Every evening he would see them at the hotel; and every evening they asked him to join them. They were oppressively friendly. Malkinson was content with his own company, but didn't like to be uncivil. When they beckoned him over, he became resigned to the fact that he'd have to join them.

Several times they asked him to return to the UK with them. Malkinson responded that he was perfectly happy in Holland.

On 31 May, to his relief, the Garnhams flew back to England. They had exchanged contact details, but Malkinson thought them a strange family and assumed he'd never see them again.

The next day, he was robbed of all his cash and credit cards. Ironically, he'd taken the precaution of carrying everything with him, thinking it safer not to leave things in the apartment. He was destitute. He tried desperately to find work, but it was early in the season, and none was available. He had to sleep on the beach. He could have asked friends in Holland to help him out or he could have asked his mother; but immediately to hand were those contact details for the Garnhams. He took the fatal step of telephoning them.

They sent him through the air-fare and, on 11 June, picked him up at Leeds-Bradford airport. He was wearing a T-shirt, shorts and flip-flops. John Garnham said he could sleep on the sofa at their home in Manchester. Malkinson had never been to Manchester before. He envisaged getting a job for a few weeks to pay them back, visiting his mother and a few old friends in Grimsby, and then returning to Holland.

Straightaway, Malkinson noticed a change in the Garnhams' demeanour. Whereas on holiday, they'd been overly friendly, now, on their home ground, they were off-hand and even unpleasant. Malkinson soon realised he couldn't believe a word they told him. They clearly lived a semi-criminal, if not entirely criminal, lifestyle and were well known to local police.

On 14 June, he was out with Neil on his motorcycle, having been to the local shops, when they were stopped by community beat officers. 'There were four of them in an unmarked car', remembered Malkinson. 'One of them was gesticulating for us to stop. It was as though they had been waiting there. Of course, they knew Neil – they were on first-name terms.'

The police asked Malkinson for personal details – name and date-of-birth – which he provided and they checked.

He started work as a security guard at the Ellesmere Centre, the local shopping mall, in Bolton. The work was mainly dealing with shoplifters and trouble-makers and wasn't at all to his liking. Nevertheless, it was only short-term. When his boss found out where he was staying, however, he strongly urged him to move away, pointing out that the Garnhams were very bad news locally.

One of John's friends, Roy, turned up regularly at the house.

'They thought he was great because he was violent', said Malkinson. 'One day, they were talking, and John said to him, in front of me, that I'd been to prison in Thailand and didn't mind going to prison.

'I found all this really disturbing. I was in a rough place and didn't know anyone. I was wondering what I'd let myself in for, and kicking myself for trusting these people.'

On 4 July, Malkinson picked up his few possessions and left. He hadn't told his hosts, fearing they might turn nasty. He went to stay with a colleague, Simon Oakes. As far as he was concerned, he'd got out just in time; the Garnhams were throwing a party that weekend, and he didn't like the sound of it.

FRIDAY, 18 JULY 2003 was one of the hottest days of the year. After finishing work at about 2.00pm, Andrea Prestwood drove over to her boyfriend's parents' house in Atherton, on the north-west outskirts of Manchester, and spent most of the day there. At about 7.40, she went to Bargain Booze in Atherton to stock up with alcohol. When she returned, she and her boyfriend, Dave Houghton, together with a couple of friends, started to enjoy the evening. Houghton's parents later joined them and the drinking carried on into the small hours. At 1.30am, the weather was still so warm that they had a water-fight in the garden.

The friends left after that, and at 2.00 they went to bed. Prestwood, as she acknowledged, had had 'a lot to drink'. She and Houghton had been arguing all day, and now the ill-feeling flared up again.

According to Prestwood, this happened when he called her 'Joanne', the name of his previous partner and the mother of his children, and this infuriated her. Houghton contradicted this account. He said the animosity had arisen as a result of tensions over a different previous girlfriend, Cara. 'She [wanted] to have an argument about Cara', he said in evidence, 'and I didn't want to.'

Whatever the reason, they quarrelled.

'She was spoiling for a fight', said Houghton. 'I grabbed hold of her and pinned her on the bed.'

Towards 2.30, Prestwood left. She said she intended to walk back to her own house, six miles away in Kearsley, Bolton. It was a walk that no one in the family would have contemplated at all, let alone at night.

'I was astonished at her decision to walk home', Houghton said.

Walking alongside the A5082, Prestwood continually pestered Houghton, phoning him 'every five minutes' both on his mobile and on the landline. The calls to the house phone, needless to say, kept everyone in the house awake, including Houghton's parents; there was a handset for the landline in their bedroom.

At 3.02, she sent a text message which (with the spelling mistakes corrected) read:

I HAVE FINISHED WITH YOU AND YOU CAN TELL CARA IF I CATCH HER I WILL SMASH HER FACE IN YOU DICK, I FUCKING HATE YOU SO YOU CAN TELL HER WHAT A PSYCHO I AM YOU FUCKING FAIRY

This message appears to bear out Houghton's version of the quarrel between them, rather than her own.

During her walk, Prestwood did say that she thought of calling a taxi, but didn't want to wait for one. She could certainly have paid for one; she said she had over £200 in her handbag. She felt uneasy, she said, describing herself as 'spooked'.

Then, at about 3.40, she phoned Houghton again, this time on the landline.

'Don't worry, I'm fine', she told him. 'I've found somewhere warm and dry, no need to worry.'

'Why, where are you?' he said.

'I'm safe', she said, and hung up.

It was about 45 minutes later that, as she walked, she heard a rustling in the bushes and then a man shouted that he'd got a gun pointed at her. 'The voice sounded very close', she said, 'and was a local accent'.

She again texted Houghton. This message, timed at 4.26, read (again, with corrected spelling):

I'VE JUST HAD SOME MAN SHOUT OUT FROM THE
BUSHES THAT I HAD BETTER COME INTO THE BUSHES
'CAUSE HE HAD A GUN POINTING AT MY HEAD I'M SO
SCARED BUT WHAT DO YOU CARE COS YOU HAD LEFT
YOUR PHONE OFF.

She walked on but felt that a man was following her, some distance behind at first, but catching her up. She looked back and saw a man who was wearing a white shirt that was completely unbuttoned and flapping open. She said he seemed to be getting closer, although 'he kept his distance from me'.

Then she felt a sudden force behind her as a man grabbed her round the shoulders. Together, they tumbled down a bank on which grass and thistles were growing to a height of three or four feet.

She still had her mobile, took it out of her jacket pocket and tried to dial 999, but the attacker told her to get rid of it. She tossed it away, to her right.

The man pulled her knickers away. As she protested, 'What are you doing?', his thumbs came down on her throat.

'It was like he knew what to do', she commented.

She said that he didn't have his shirt on, but didn't know when he had taken it off. She then told him that she would be able to recognise him again, and at that point the pressure on her throat increased. She reached up with her left hand and scratched the right side of his face causing a 'deep scratch'.

She begged him not to hurt her and said she had two children. This caused him to increase the pressure still further. She then lost consciousness.

When she came round, she scrambled up the bank and stopped a dog-walker who took her into his house and called the police.

Prestwood was examined at 11.30, between six and seven hours after the alleged attack, by the deputy police surgeon, Dr Mary Anderson. The examination revealed severe bruising to the face and throat. Prestwood had a fracture of the left cheek, bruising around the left eye, and marks and bruising around her neck that could be consistent with strangulation. A purple mark on the side of her neck could have been a 'love bite'. Perhaps the most serious injury was to her left nipple, which was partially severed. Dr Anderson thought this could have resulted from a bite. The fingernail on the middle finger of the right hand was broken. Prestwood's hands were bloodstained but Dr Anderson 'could not be sure' how this had happened.

Dr Anderson noted marks 'consistent with recent penetrative sexual activity' and a split in the anus that was also consistent with recent penetration but, she added, 'other explanations are possible'.

That afternoon, Prestwood made a statement and described her attacker. She said he was white and tanned, with a flat stomach and a shiny, hairless chest. He had thick hair, which was dark brown verging on black. He was clean shaven, had high cheekbones and was in his early-to-mid 30s. He was 5'8" at the most ('two inches taller than me'). He was wearing a 'very smart' long-sleeved white shirt, which was unbuttoned and flapping outside his 'smart' black trousers. He also had 'smart' black shoes – 'like you have to wear to get into a club'.

In theory, there may have been three different men: the one who'd shouted from the bushes, the one who'd followed her and the one who'd attacked her. However, there was an assumption throughout that this was one and the same man. On what may have been the only occasion on which she was directly asked about this, she said that the man who'd shouted was 'possibly' the man who'd followed her, who was 'possibly' the man who'd attacked her.

Her description was clearly made on the basis that this was just one man. She said that the voice from the bushes was 'a local accent'. By the end of her account, she had modified this slightly, saying that the man's accent was 'local to Bolton, with a slight twinge of another accent'.

FIVE DAYS LATER, on Thursday 24 July, John and Angie Garnham turned up at the Ellesmere Centre demanding money from Malkinson. By then, he had given them back the air-fare, paid them rent and also paid for shopping trips to Tesco, but they wanted more. They blamed him for smoke damage in the kitchen caused when a toaster failed to switch itself off. Also, after an evening's drinking, he had urinated in his sleep. The Garnhams had demanded £200 for damage to the settee; Malkinson offered £50.

In view of their demeanour, Malkinson contacted the police. The next day, Friday, an officer called at the house to take a statement, but told him it was unlikely that the matter would be taken further.

That was the day that Malkinson received his wages and left the job. The next morning, Saturday 26 July, he caught a train to Grimsby, relieved to be putting all the unpleasantness he associated with Manchester behind him.

Later that same day, back in Manchester, there was a development in the case. In response to calls for public assistance following the alleged attack on Prestwood, a couple came forward on 26 July with what the police considered helpful information. Sandra Carson and Malcolm Fentham said they had been disturbed outside their house at about 4.00 in the morning of 19 July by a woman 'shouting and bawling' outside their house.

They got out of bed, left the house and drove round the streets, trying to find the woman to confront her. While doing this, they noticed a woman who could have been Prestwood and said they also saw a man striding behind her, his white shirt unbuttoned and flapping outside his trousers.

A video identification parade was arranged at Salford Crescent Police Station. It took place at one o'clock in the morning of Sunday 3 August. Prestwood and Carson were picked up and taken together, in the same car, to the station. Malkinson had been arrested in Grimsby about sixteen hours earlier, on Saturday morning, and then taken to Manchester.

In a video parade witnesses have to choose not between actual people, but between photographs. Prestwood selected No.4 (who was Malkinson) as her attacker; Carson picked out one of the others, No.1.

Five months later, on 14 January 2004, Fentham was picked up and taken to Little Hulton Police Station where a second video parade was held. This time, Malkinson's photograph was No.6. Fentham picked him out.

On 2 February, Malkinson went on trial at Manchester Crown Court before His Honour Judge Henshell. He faced four separate charges: of attempted murder; of attempting to choke, suffocate or strangle with the intention of committing rape; and of both vaginal and anal rape.

Prestwood herself gave evidence, and said that the attack had become 'a life or death struggle'. The circumstances of the case were such that a great deal of forensic science evidence could have been anticipated. Yet there was none at all.

There was no evidence of Malkinson on Prestwood's body or her clothing. In an attempt to plug this gaping hole in its case, the prosecution blithely told the jury that the explanation of the absence of scientific evidence was that Malkinson was 'forensically aware'. Therefore, he would have known how to avoid leaving scientific traces of himself when committing the crime. The fact that he had used a condom, the Crown pointed out, indicated 'forensic awareness'.

There was evidence from John and Angie Garnham. Both appeared to be tailoring their testimony to fit the prosecution case. They said Malkinson was restless and active at nights. Angie Garnham added that he 'didn't have a single hair on his chest'. Shown holiday photographs from the Canary Islands which proved that Malkinson's chest was hairy, Angie retorted that it didn't look hairy to her.

No doubt aware that the 'local accent' was a significant advantage for the defence, John Garnham said that Malkinson's accent 'sometimes sounded as if he came from Bolton'. He added that his accent 'could vary from Dutch to Australian to Bolton'.

The prosecution had to concede that their witnesses were not exactly upstanding members of the community; Garnham had convictions for threatening behaviour, and both of them had convictions for offences of dishonesty.

Around the time of the attack, there were many other sexual assaults in the area. Other names were put forward as suspects, generally by members of the public. Some had previous convictions for rape, or were registered sex offenders, or had previous convictions for sexual assaults – which, bearing in mind Prestwood's comment that 'it was like he knew what to do', was at least interesting.

When Malkinson managed to obtain details of the enquiries by Greater Manchester Police into other suspects (not in time for the trial; only a long time afterwards), he was struck by how cursory they were:

> Notes have been left for him to contact the police but he has not responded ...
> It has not been possible to trace [the suspect] ...
> ... said he couldn't remember his movements, but said he had not raped anyone ...
> [The suspect] has not made himself available for interview ...

Many suspects were never traced, let alone eliminated.

One theory about the case is that the Garnhams may have been police informers themselves; habitual criminals often are. They and Malkinson had parted on unfriendly terms, and the Garnhams' animus against him can only have intensified after he called in the police over their threatening behaviour towards him. After Malkinson had left the area, they perhaps took the opportunity to make his life a little more difficult by mentioning his name to police as someone who had latterly arrived in the country and who had suddenly and conveniently, or so they could have hinted, disappeared.

They may also have been deflecting attention from someone else. One of the more intriguing items of unused evidence was a report from a woman who said that one of her colleagues at work resembled the photofit and that, when he turned up for work on the Monday following the attack, he had scratches on the right side of his face. This suspect was only seen by police in October, two months after Malkinson had been arrested and ten weeks after the incident – by which time any possible scratches would have healed.

This suspect, remarkably, was a close relation of the Garnhams. So this would have given them a motive both for pointing the police in the wrong direction in the first place; and then for giving false testimony in court.

IN THE END, THERE WAS just the identification evidence. Prestwood had identified Malkinson; so had Fentham; and so, in a bizarre twist, had Sandra Carson. Or so she said.

Yes, she had picked out No.1 (someone else) at the video identity parade; but she had subsequently changed her mind and told the officer that she had really meant to say No.4 (Malkinson). However, her account of how this had come about did not match the officer's and, as we will see, this area of evidence raised a host of questions.

In fact, the judge said to the jury in his summing-up that 'Sandra Carson changed her mind at the identification procedure – is that a weakness?' But the judge was wrong. Although it may seem pedantic to be picking a quarrel over prepositions, this was a weakness not because Carson changed her mind *at* the identification procedure; she changed her mind *after* it.

Far more importantly, the judge told the jury this about Prestwood's evidence:

> She believed, undoubtedly believed, that she scratched his face on the right-hand side … Did she succeed in scratching his face in the way she clearly believed she did?

This was inaccurate. In reporting her evidence in this way, the judge was subtly changing and re-shaping her testimony. At no point had she said that she *believed* she'd scratched his face. There was no uncertainty in her testimony; she was adamant and she was consistent; she *had* scratched his face.

The defence case was simple: Malkinson slept through the night and turned up at work on time that Saturday morning. He was well rested and had no facial scratches. There was no forensic evidence of the offence on him, and no evidence of him on the complainant – but the prosecution had countered this with their 'forensically aware' argument.

At the close of the case, the jurors appeared to be in a state of real indecision. Having been sent out at lunchtime on 9 February 2004, they returned the following morning to ask the judge for a copy of his summing-up. That, however, is against the rules.

'Whilst in many ways that is quite an understandable request', Judge Henshell told them, 'juries are not given written directions in that form.'

He invited them instead to itemise the particular bits of the summing-up they wished to be clarified. So the jury then sent through a note from the jury room, saying they needed him to read again his instructions regarding the reliability of a witness's evidence; and those regarding the scratch which Prestwood had inflicted on her assailant; and also what he had said with regard to Carson and Fentham's evidence, which included the discrepancy between Carson and the police officer about how she had changed her identification.

They also required further direction about how they were supposed to be reaching their decision:

> ... and the definition of 'sure of his guilt'. Did the judge say we have to be absolutely sure of his guilt? If we are unsure of his guilt, does this mean he is not guilty?

The judge didn't want to open up a dialogue on this.

'We shouldn't encourage such discussions of the word "sure"', he said to trial counsel. 'Any dissection of the word will lead to problems for all concerned.'

The jury returned into court and the judge laboriously re-read all those parts of the summing-up which covered the areas that were troubling them. On the vexed question of what, in legal terms, 'sure' actually means, he told them:

> The question reads, 'Did the judge say we have to be absolutely sure of his guilt?'
> I did not.

The jury then retired again, before returning to say they were unable to reach a unanimous verdict. The judge therefore gave them the majority direction, saying that the verdict of ten jurors would be sufficient.

Then the jury sent in a note headed 'Sandra Carson's Statement'. This asked for yet further clarification regarding the change of identification by Sandra Carson, and asking again to be reminded of the conversation that had passed between her and the police officer.

This led to further legal argument in the jury's absence. If a statement had existed, the jurors would not have been entitled to see it. However she had never made a statement about this anyway. It was such a vital part of the case that the jurors were spot-on in anticipating that there should have been a statement; but there wasn't one.

So the judge reread yet again the parts of his summing-up that dealt with this aspect of the evidence. After the jurors had spoken to him directly in court, to ask for specific reminders about the words that were actually spoken, they retired again.

Finally, they returned with the verdicts. Malkinson was acquitted of attempted murder, though the sudden ray of hope was quickly eclipsed. He was convicted, on 10-2 majority verdicts, on the three other counts.

Judge Henshell then told Malkinson that the only 'appropriate sentence' would be life imprisonment.

3

The assumption at trial, obviously, was that Prestwood had been attacked as she testified. This belief was based on the evidence of a senior scientist with the Forensic Science Service. The judge explained:

> The evidence of [the forensic scientist] was that traces of condom lubricant were found in both the vagina and the anus. That evidence, when considered with the findings of the doctor, say the Crown, can only lead to one conclusion: that Andrea Prestwood was penetrated both vaginally and anally by an attacker wearing a condom.

The findings of the doctor were that the vaginal examination showed signs of 'recent penetrative sexual activity'; and the anal examination showed signs of 'recent penetrative activity, but other explanations are possible'. Prestwood acknowledged having recently had consensual sex. Consequently, the only evidence that this was a double-rape case was the presence of the condom lubricants. The complainant herself could not add supporting evidence. As she was unconscious throughout, she had no direct awareness of what occurred.

'I realised that something sexual had happened', she said. 'I felt I had been penetrated vaginally as my stomach was tight and sore.' As the judge put it, 'she has no recollection of being either vaginally or anally raped'.

So the entire basis for the case (because without it there was no evidence of a crime having been committed) was 'forensic awareness'. The circumstances in which the attack supposedly took place are these: the assailant rolled down a grassy bank with his victim; knocked her about and struck her face; straddled her; removed his shirt; was scratched by her; put on a condom; and then raped her twice over. Afterwards, Prestwood was given a thorough examination in hospital. Standard precautions were taken to preserve scientific evidence.

After all that, there was no evidence on Prestwood's body or her clothing of any assailant. No semen was found on the vaginal and anal swabs; there was no semen staining on her clothing; and no evidence was obtained from fingernail scrapings, even though Prestwood said she had scratched the attacker and drawn blood. There was an area of bloodstaining on the left cuff of her fleece jacket. A DNA profile was obtained from this. Similarly, there were saliva deposits on the left cup of her bra. Again, a DNA profile was obtained. In neither case, however, did the DNA profile match Malkinson.

An incomplete DNA profile was obtained from material, possibly saliva, from the outside of her T-shirt. Malkinson could have matched this profile, although so could half of the UK population.

The man had removed his shirt. The prosecution asked, Was this because he was 'forensically aware'? The question was rhetorical but, had an answer been required, then it would obviously have been, 'No'. An attacker who was forensically aware would certainly have known that wearing clothes (and disposing of them afterwards) would be a safer way of avoiding scientific discovery than removing them and allowing his body to come into direct contact with his victim's.

There aren't many hot and sultry nights in Bolton, but this was one of them. Sandra Carson gave evidence that, when she saw him, the attacker was 'sweating profusely' and his body was 'shiny' and 'glistening'. Prestwood said that she 'began to push his chest to get him off me'. An assailant who was 'sweating profusely' would not be able to carry out an attack in which there was such bodily contact, in such humid conditions, and not leave behind a microscopic trace of his presence.

The attacker was also supposed to have bitten Prestwood's left breast, leaving her with a partially severed nipple. This is another feature of the case that gives the lie to the suggestion of 'forensic awareness'. An attacker who was forensically aware would have appreciated the significant two-fold risk of acting in such a way and leaving behind excellent forensic evidence in the form of either teeth-marks or DNA from saliva.

Nor was there anything in Malkinson's background to suggest how he could have become 'forensically aware'. The idea is sometimes suggested in criminal cases. Despite the extraordinary technological advances in scientific evidence over the past twenty years (and specifically the development of DNA evidence) the Crown are sometimes confronted by the complete absence of evidence from semen, saliva, sweat or hairs or from fibre transfer; so they'll argue that the suspect was 'forensically aware'. It is the last refuge of a bankrupt prosecution.

THE GUILTY VERDICT was delivered by the jury on 10 February 2004. Less than a month later, on 8 March, the senior forensic scientist on whose work the case depended wrote to the authorities. According to his letter:

> A problem has recently emerged … As such the previously-reported results in relation to the possible presence of condom lubricants on the intimate swabs are *now regarded as unreliable.* (Italics added)

The Forensic Science Service had found traces of the material PDMS, the presence of which indicated (or so they had claimed) the use of a condom, in the swabs themselves. So the entire test procedure was invalid. The tests proved nothing.

The trial judge then used the rare procedure of issuing a certificate indicating that the case was fit for appeal; in other words, he effectively sent it to appeal himself. He wrote:

> In light of the letter of 8 March from [the forensic scientist] disclosing his previous findings of the presence of condom lubricants on the vaginal and anal swabs as unreliable (which evidence was unchallenged at trial and upon which penile penetration was inferred), the convictions on the counts of rape may consequently be rendered unsafe.

However, while the action of the scientist in reporting this may on the surface have appeared punctilious and highly commendable, in fact it was anything but. This was because the Forensic Science Service had discovered the problem, and so known that these tests were invalid, some months before the case went to trial. On 17 October 2003, the FSS circulated an internal memo, saying:

> We have withdrawn use of this test from casework

They added:

> We have informed all FSS staff, the CPS and other suppliers of forensic science services in the UK of the issue.

At trial, the Crown's only explanation of the complete lack of scientific evidence was that Malkinson was 'forensically aware'. By deploying this argument, the CPS was able to portray Malkinson as an experienced sexual predator who was used to stalking women – as was demonstrated by his cleverness in using a condom. But by the time the case was heard at court, both the CPS and the FSS already knew that the trial was predicated on unreliable evidence. The senior scientist was either negligent or dishonest in giving sworn evidence about the tests; and he was also conveying an erroneous impression by telling the judge after the trial that the tests '*are now* regarded as unreliable'.

There is a second point of great significance to emerge from his letter of 8 March. He refers to:

... the previously reported results in relation to the *possible presence* of condom lubricants ... (italics added)

This does not appear to have been the evidence that he gave at trial. The judge told the jury that this scientist's evidence:

... was that traces of condom lubricant were found in both the vagina and the anus ...

There is no suggestion there that the scientist had couched his evidence guardedly and referred only to the *possible presence*. It seems that he must have exaggerated his evidence at trial, and so misled the jury.

However, while belatedly alerting the authorities to the shortcomings of the scientific procedure, the scientist had neglected to alert them to his own professional shortcomings. So, remarkably, a few weeks later on 20 April, he was allowed to conduct fresh tests on case exhibits.

He said the results of his new tests from five areas of Prestwood's knickers were that:

Areas of fabric from the gusset of the knickers have given positive results indicative of the presence of silicone oil used in condom lubricants.

Once again, this appears to overstate his results, which actually indicated the presence of condom oils in only *one* area; a second area indicated the 'possible presence' of silicone oil; and the other three areas were negative. It also ignores the central controversy about these tests, which is that great care needs to be taken in the interpretation of the results because the silicone-based oils occur so widely in the environment. Numerous other products (for example, fabric softeners, hand creams, Vaseline, Nivea and moisturising lotion) could give similar results.

As we will see, it also ignores altogether the most extraordinary feature of the knickers.

So when the case was heard at appeal, the judges were given limited information about these tests, and were unaware of the full background. They heard fresh testimony from Prestwood herself, and described her evidence as 'convincing'. They then said they were satisfied that the conviction was sound and, in July 2006, dismissed the appeal. They said they were satisfied with the scientific evidence they had heard:

> Subsequent examination of her knickers revealed the presence of oil 'as used in condom lubricants'. These forensic examinations are not compromised by contamination.

Yet this part of their judgment not only ignores the ubiquity of these oils in the environment, but is wrong anyway. During the forensic science work done prior to trial, the swabs were in contact with the knickers. Professor Allan Jamieson, of the Forensic Institute in Glasgow, wrote:

> The results *are* compromised by contamination. There is no other conclusion. The fact that the swabs in the lab used to test the knickers had upon them the very substance being sought is evidence of that. The fact that another round of tests did not use swabs is irrelevant; the damage had been done.

So the Forensic Science Service had misled the court both at trial and appeal. However, the appeal court judges had the wool pulled over their eyes in a far more fundamental way. The argument deployed at appeal was that the woman had been sexually assaulted by an attacker wearing a condom, and she had afterwards resumed wearing her knickers, which was how they came to be contaminated with the condom oils.

However this could not have happened, as the scientists were aware, because the knickers were ripped down one side. Prestwood stated that when she came to:

It was daylight … My knickers were pulled right down and were attached to my right ankle

All the scientists who examined the knickers described them as 'unwearable'. At 6.05am, immediately after the supposed attack, they were handed to a police officer. According to the officer's statement:

Prestwood handed me a pair of briefs *which she produced from the right pocket of her fleece* (italics added)

So the knickers were not worn after the attack, and no relevant evidence could be gleaned about whatever substances were or were not on them.

In summary, the 'forensically aware' argument is untenable for four separate reasons: because there was no evidence whatever that Malkinson had any interest in or knowledge of forensic science matters, this was in any event a speculative assertion that had no place in the courtroom; because even had the assertion been plausible in some circumstances, it was not plausible in those circumstances on that unusually hot night; because the evidence given by the FSS at trial was invalidated some months before the trial started; and because the subsequent attempt to use the knickers to resurrect the argument was equally invalid as the knickers were not worn afterwards.

The complete absence of any forensic science evidence was the essential feature of this case. It should have led to an acquittal; but, by improperly deploying the 'forensically aware' argument, the Crown had deprived Malkinson of what would have been this virtually unassailable defence.

IN THE FINAL ANALYSIS, the judge told the jury:

The case against [Malkinson] *depends wholly* on the correctness of the identification of him by Andrea Prestwood, Barbara Carson and Malcolm Fentham … (italics added)

The video identification parade took place at approximately 1.00am on 3 August 2003. Prestwood and Carson were taken together to the station in the same police car. Fentham, the third witness, was not involved.

The outcome of the parade was that Prestwood picked out No.4 (Malkinson); and Carson picked out No.1 (a parade stooge). After each woman had made their identifications, they were taken to the same room.

There are, however, significant concerns about the parade. The first, of course, was the timing: one o'clock in the morning. Is it normal to hold identity parades then? Did the police expect witnesses' powers of recollection to be at their sharpest at that hour?

Moreover, the reason given for the non-attendance of Malcolm Fentham was that he had had a lot to drink and was in no fit state to attend. This merely underlined the problem. Given that one of the witnesses was unable to participate anyway, why was this key part of the case proceeded with at an irregular hour?

In theory, Prestwood's own identification of Malkinson should have been the crux of the case; in practice, much of what she said in her statement had already ruled him out. There were, most strikingly, the clothes. All three witnesses were in agreement about what the man was wearing. He was wearing, said Prestwood, 'smart' black trousers; 'smart' black shoes, 'like you wear to get into a club'; and a 'very smart' unbuttoned white shirt.

Those who knew him were unanimous about the kind of clothing that Malkinson wore; casual would have been the polite term. When he was arrested, all his clothing was taken for examination. This would not have taken long. He had arrived in the UK in T-shirt, shorts and flip-flops. His wardrobe was not extensive. The few items that he possessed did not include a white shirt or black trousers or black shoes. He was not looking to go clubbing.

Next there was the accent. Asked how he spoke, Prestwood responded that 'his accent was local to Bolton'. She did add that there was 'a tinge of something in it … but it was local'. Tinge or no tinge, it seemed unlikely that there could be anything 'local' about Malkinson's speech. He had never lived in the area or even been there before, and had lived outside England for the previous thirteen years.

Then there was the man's chest. Even before the attacker had removed his shirt altogether, he had it unbuttoned and flapping open so that everyone could see his chest which was, the witnesses said, 'shiny and hairless'. Malkinson's was not.

Then there was the height. Prestwood was very specific about this. She said the attacker was '5'8" at the most – two inches taller than me'. That was what she said: 5'8" *at the most*. Again, this ruled out Malkinson, who was 5'11".

Then there were the tattoos. Any acquaintance of Malkinson's who was asked to describe him would soon refer to the tattoos. He has large, very prominent tattoos running down both forearms – old-fashioned traveller's tattoos. In criminal cases, tattoos can often be very helpful; they can be damning evidence. Yet in this case, despite the attacker's removal of his shirt, and despite these tattoos being strikingly noticeable, Prestwood did not see any tattoos on her attacker.

She had scratched her attacker's face. 'I reached up', she said, 'and dug my nails into the right-hand side of his face and scratched in a downwards motion from his ear or cheek to his jawline'. At the end of her first police interview, she repeated this: 'I have caused a deep scratch in [his] face.'

The 'deep scratch' was an important piece of the evidence. There were no scratches on Malkinson's face. He turned up for work as usual the next morning – within a couple of hours of this incident. No colleague noticed a scratch; nor did the police when they saw him two days later.

Not only did Prestwood scratch her assailant's face, but they tumbled down a brambly bank together. This left her with significant cuts and bruises. So one would also have anticipated marks or scratches on the assailant's body. Again, there were none on Malkinson.

So there were serious concerns about her identification. However it emerged, when the case reached trial, that hers was not the only one. There was also a purported identification from Carson. She said in her testimony that, after the parade, she had changed her opinion; when she had said No.1, she had actually meant to say No.4.

It should be pointed out, firstly, that whenever Carson did change her mind, she was hardly the most reliable witness. Even before the identification process, she had given untruthful information. In her statement she said that she 'did not know' who the woman was who had woken them up by bawling outside their window. Of course, she knew. The woman appears to have been a former partner of Fentham's. She was named in his statement and they drove round to where she lived. According to him, it was actually Carson's idea to go looking for her as she wanted to tell her 'not to come to the house anymore'.

But when and why she did change her mind and identify someone different? That is the critical matter. With regard to the *why*, she said that she was confused and did not identify Malkinson straightaway because he had had his hair cut since the time of the offence; his hair was shorter in the photograph than when she had seen the attacker. But this was not true. He had not had his hair cut in the meantime. There was proof of this, as Malkinson had had a photograph taken at work for a security pass on 24 July.

Far more crucially, *when* did she change her mind?

This is what we know: the witness said that she told the officer she'd changed her mind when she returned to the witness room (where Prestwood was). However, the officer gave a different account. He said their conversation happened in the corridor 'more or less immediately' after they left the video suite.

What makes the disparity in their accounts particularly intriguing is the fact that there is no contemporaneous documentary evidence whatever to support the change of evidence. For example, there is no reference at all to this in the officer's notebook. That's astonishing. Something as exceptional as this should certainly have been noted down. Nor is there documentary evidence from the witness herself; as the jurors later discovered for themselves, she did not make a statement about her change of mind.

The duty solicitor accompanying Malkinson when the video parade took place was Shah Ali, from the Burton Copeland practice. Ali was certainly concerned about the propriety of the parade – so concerned that, just before the trial, he made a statement about it. He pointed out improper aspects of the parade: notably, that it took place in the early hours of the morning; and that the two witnesses were taken together in the same unmarked police car.

At that stage, he believed there was just the one identification. Had there been a second identification, it would have greatly strengthened the point he was making. It would have been grist to his mill, so he would have been bound to mention it. Yet, it is not mentioned.

When the police outlined the case for the magistrates, they too were unaware of a second identification:

> The result of the identity parade was that the victim positively identified Malkinson as the male who attacked her ... [He] was subsequently remanded in custody to appear before your worships today.

In the four-page case summary outlining the evidence against Malkinson, there was no suggestion that there was a second identification.

Months later, when the defence solicitor prepared the brief to counsel (which is the full exposition for counsel of the case that the defendant will need to meet at trial), only Prestwood's identification was mentioned. Even that late in the day – the brief was dated 22 December 2003 – the defence solicitor was unaware of a second identification. In the case documentation, the references that there should have been to the second identification are conspicuous by their absence.

In fact, there is only one reference to it. It is found in a statement from a police officer. This is dated 11 September 2003. However, it is a strange statement. For a start, the space at the bottom for a witness's signature is blank; this statement was witnessed by no one. Nor does anyone appear to have been appraised of either the change of evidence or this statement until just before the start of the trial. In all these circumstances, some might surmise that it was put together later on and then backdated.

Such thoughts are strengthened by the fact that this page referring to Carson's supposed identification is not paginated properly in the prosecution bundle. It is presented as page 45 — but there is already a different page 45. So there are two page 45s. In some circumstances, this might have been explained as a slipshod error; in these circumstances — where it concerns evidence which is not just critical, but around which irregularities have already accumulated — you don't need to be a lawyer to apprehend the dark clouds of doubt swirling around the case.

In fact, the jurors correctly understood the importance of this area of evidence, and were particularly concerned to have it fully explained to them; yet they were seriously misled about it.

The third identification was by Fentham who, by the time of the trial, was an important witness. Yet he had not seemed that at the outset. The original video parade took place without him; and he was not asked to attend one until January 2004. By that time, therefore, Fentham was purporting to identify someone whom he had seen for 'about five seconds' over five months earlier while he was driving a car at half-past-four in the morning. That is precisely the kind of identification evidence that brought the English criminal justice system into disrepute and created decades of problems. Yet a British court allowed that to be put before a jury as reliable evidence. Lord Devlin must be turning in his grave.

These problems were acute, but they were actually compounded by what the judge said in his summing-up. He told the jury that, 'the identification of any one of them can support the identification of the others'. Underlying that idea is the suggestion that different identifications, each of them unsatisfactory for various reasons, might be pooled in order to form a single strand of satisfactory identification evidence. That is, of course, a fallacious and highly dangerous way of assessing evidence.

Nevertheless, the judge did emphasise the key issue:

> You must be sure ... that the identification procedure has been carried out correctly.

If there was one UK police force that should certainly have been carrying out identification procedures correctly, then that force was Greater Manchester Police. In 2010 the GMP cooperated with the

BBC on a major three-part television series, *Eyewitness*, in which the reliability of eyewitness evidence was put to the strictest tests.

In the first experiment, ten unsuspecting people saw a murder take place in front of their eyes. They were not to know that it was a staged event which was being recorded. The unsuspecting witnesses were then asked to identify those involved. *None* of the witnesses identified the murderer. Indeed, only one of the ten even thought he was in the locality at the time. Two people identified a completely innocent man as the murderer.

Subsequently, there was a second staged crime – this time an armed robbery and kidnap. By now, witnesses were to some extent primed to expect the unexpected and to try to remember the details. Two picked out one robber correctly, and someone correctly picked out the getaway driver. However, witnesses again misidentified two innocent men. 'Despite having already witnessed one crime', said the narrator, 'our witnesses' memories are no more reliable the second time around'.

The programme also pointed out that while the careful sifting of the differing memories of a group of witnesses could allow investigators to form an accurate picture of what had happened, there were significant problems in cases where there were few witnesses, and where one witness was also the presumed victim.

Having examined the various difficulties in relation to eyewitness testimony, and how they could be overcome, the programme concluded by emphasising that GMP were on top of the problem. 'Greater Manchester Police are among the most modern practitioners of modern interviewing techniques anywhere in the world', the narrator said. 'Interviewing [is conducted] in state-of-the-art facilities by highly-trained officers.'

The programme drove home its message that techniques were now so sophisticated that judicial mistakes were reduced to an absolute minimum. 'The UK police are the envy of the world', said one GMP officer. 'The whole process of interviewing witnesses and victims is transformed beyond belief. It's something I think we can be rightly proud of.'

If Greater Manchester Police had adhered to their own guidelines, then this case would never have reached trial. As it did reach trial, then one can only conclude that the claims which GMP police and the authorities made on BBC television, that they can now elicit reliable witness evidence, are unmerited. Indeed, judging by this case, one is inclined to wonder whether there had been any progress at all in the hundred years since the Adolf Beck case.

The original purported identification of Malkinson by two community police officers was another aspect of the case that caused eyebrows to be raised.

The evidence was that at 2.00pm on the day of the attack two community beat officers, after hearing the description of the attacker, had 'immediately' and 'simultaneously' named Malkinson as the suspect. The apparent clarity of their joint recollections was astonishing. There are four specific reasons why their evidence is bewildering. Firstly, in almost all key respects, as we have seen, he did not fit the attacker's description. Why would anyone, having heard of the attacker's 'smart' clothes, instantly think of the generally dishevelled Malkinson?

Secondly, two days later, on Monday 21 July, the officers saw Malkinson at work. Police routinely liaised with security staff at the local shopping centre over matters of mutual concern – shoplifters, for example, or CCTV footage of suspects. That day, they talked amicably, and there was no suggestion that Malkinson was a suspect in a serious rape case.

Thirdly, it took two weeks after their supposed identification of him for them to arrest him, even though he could not have been difficult to trace.

Fourthly, neither of the two officers is mentioned in the contemporaneous crime records as having even part of the investigative team at the time they supposedly named Malkinson as the suspect.

WHILE THE QUALITY, or lack of it, of both the scientific and the identification evidence may lead one to conclude that this is a particularly unsafe conviction, some may go further and question whether the offence ever happened. Too many aspects of the alleged victim's account invite scepticism; and there is also the handbag mystery.

As has already been seen, her account of the argument with her boyfriend differed from his; and, judging by her text messages, his is the account to be trusted.

She was supposedly walking a very long walk home and yet, when she got there, she'd have been unable to get in. She didn't have her house keys with her. Houghton said in evidence that, as she was talking of leaving:

I said, 'Don't be silly', and tried to stop her … I made sure she couldn't get hold of her car keys.

He obviously knew she was in no state to drive, so he had sensibly hidden her car keys. However, Prestwood's house keys were on the same fob. (Cross-examined on this point, Prestwood said she would have had to knock up a neighbour for the keys. It seems reasonable to assume that the neighbour would not have been delighted to see her.)

There is also the matter of what happened to her at around 3.40am when she told her boyfriend that she had 'found somewhere warm and dry' and was 'safe'. Her calls were then discontinued for about 45 minutes. This is another unexplained part of the case.

There was the moment when she heard the voice from the bushes. Her account of this is astonishing. Someone was threatening her with a gun; she had her mobile phone in her hand. So what did she do?

She didn't phone the police. She didn't call for a taxi. She didn't run. She didn't try to attract anyone's attention. Instead, she composed and sent a lengthy text message to her boyfriend, who was obviously unable to lend immediate assistance. At trial, she could not even begin to explain that.

'I told [the man] … I was going to ring the police', she said, 'but I didn't do so.'

It should be added that there is no further reference in the case to a gun.

She said that she had scratched the right side of the attacker's face with her *left* hand and, as a result, had broken one of her nails.

'That's how the nail got broken', she testified.

However, it was the middle fingernail of the *right* hand that was broken.

Nor did she know how she suffered her facial injuries. Yet it is difficult to understand how facial injuries can have been inflicted on her while she was unconscious. Slapping someone about the face is the usual way of helping people to regain consciousness. Bringing her round was, presumably, not what the attacker wanted.

A major mystery surrounds her handbag. She said she was carrying it when she left her boyfriend's house. Among the items she said it contained were over £200 in cash, a camera that she thought may have been a Canon, a Pioneer car radio fascia, her bank card, driving licence, insurance certificates, lip gloss and her supply of insulin. Prestwood was a diabetic. There were also Citaloprim tablets (which it would have been unwise for her to be taking, since the drug can amplify the effects of alcohol). There were also two pens, one from Cancer Research and one from a local solicitor's.

Altogether, there was quite a lot in the handbag. She said that once she'd put her Diet Coke bottle on top, she was unable to close it.

As she tumbled down the bank, she said that her handbag was 'under my right arm with the strap over my right shoulder', but she added that it had 'fallen off'. When she came to, she said, she saw her bottle of Coke lying close by and she picked it up.

And the handbag? Where was it?

According to the first reports of what happened, she thought it had been stolen. In the original report of the incident, timed at 5.40am, she was saying that, 'a male attacked her … raped and assaulted her and stole her bag …' She told Dr Mary Anderson, who examined her at 11.30, that 'some possessions … had been taken'.

When she made her statement the next day, she listed the contents of her handbag. She was unable to recall what make of camera she had. Presumably, if the bag had been recovered, there need have been no uncertainty; she could just have looked.

So her statement was obviously drawn up on the basis that the handbag was stolen. Its contents were described in detail; and it is not normal police practice painstakingly to itemise the contents of a handbag that has not been stolen.

Yet the handbag was evidently not stolen. Malkinson was not charged with theft, nor were any items from the handbag associated with him. It was not scientifically examined, for fingerprints or traces of DNA. It played no part in the case. Although it is not mentioned in police statements, hearsay evidence suggests that it was found, possibly hanging from a fence-post at the top of the bank.

So it was not where the grass was flattened, or lying abandoned on the bank, where one would have expected it to be. Its contents were not strewn over the bank during the struggle. A team of officers spent over two hours combing the site and found nothing that belonged to her or had been in her handbag. They found a 'silver metal bar'. That was all. They found nothing else. The silver metal bar was given an exhibit number, but never became part of the case. Prestwood never listed it as among the contents of her bag and she was never asked about it. No one ever suggested that it belonged to her. It was presumably just an item of junk on the bank.

With regard to the handbag's contents, Prestwood's references to the £200 do not ring true. She said:

> I went to the bank and withdrew £200 in order to tax my car. I then went to the Post Office to tax the car, but could not do so as I had forgotten my log book.

She then bought alcohol, but was careful to say:

> I don't know how much I spent, but the money I used was not from the £200 I had drawn from the bank.

Despite 'not knowing' how much she had spent, she was able to say exactly how much money was in her bag when she was attacked: £220. According to her statement:

> Small black leather purse ... contained £210 in Bank of England notes and £10 in coin.

She said she had withdrawn the £200 to pay her car tax. Car tax falls due at the end of a month. The date was the nineteenth, so it seemed an odd time to be taxing the car. The excise duty at the time was £110 for a smaller car and £165 for cars with a large engine. There is an option to pay the tax at six-monthly intervals (and, thus, at half-rate). Whatever kind of car she had, she did not need £200 to tax it; and she hadn't taxed it anyway.

There is no subsequent reference in either Prestwood's testimony or the prosecution case papers to the bag or its contents.

It is difficult to reconcile the handbag evidence with the idea that an attack occurred.

Here is one possible explanation of what happened: after a night's heavy drinking, Prestwood had a serious argument with her boyfriend. That much, she had acknowledged. She also admitted that they had grappled just before she left the house. She said that he had 'pinned her on the bed'. The examining doctor recorded that, 'The bruising around her neck was consistent with strangulation. On the right side of her neck within the bruising was a deeper purple mark with some petechiae that could have been a love bite'. She had been 'spoiling for a fight' with him. She had also said that his mood that night reminded her of her former husband who was 'extremely violent' towards her.

So she angrily left the house at 2.30am, and then proceeded to harass him and his parents with a succession of telephone calls to their landline.

At about 4.30, she stopped to relieve herself and put her handbag by a fence-post, but then fell down the bank, knocking herself unconscious. Almost all of her injuries can be accounted for by having fallen down an overgrown brambly bank. When she was examined, the surgeon noted, amongst other things, 'fine superficial scrapes of the skin [which] resembled scratches from vegetation'; 'puncture marks of the right forearm [which] could have been caused by vegetation (e.g. hard twigs)'; and 'abrasions of the legs [which] are consistent with a scraping motion relative to a rough surface'.

The tear in her anus could have been caused simply by falling down the bank. As Prestwood said herself, 'I slid down on my bum'.

When she came to, she felt she would be ridiculed if she admitted to having injured herself falling down a brambly bank. It must have been tempting to try to cover her embarrassment. Also, fearing that, having kept her boyfriend's family awake half the night, she would not be welcome back at the house, she may have felt she had to create a sympathetic story. Perhaps her 'ordeal' would also serve the purpose of making him feel bad for not having been there for her (as her text messages had indicated).

To concoct an allegation, all she would have needed to do was to rip her knickers and throw away her mobile phone.

The defence needed access to her mobile phone records and the results of the tests for her alcohol level, which was checked when she was admitted to hospital. However, the prosecution withheld this evidence. If the defence had had full cell-site analysis of the complainant's phone calls, they could have established whether any of her calls indicated that she was somewhere other than where she said she was. Regarding her alcohol intake, the defence had no more information than that when she was examined at midday, she was still smelling of alcohol.

4

Remarkably, the Forensic Science Service was to have yet further involvement in the case. In November 2006, the police and Home Office officials told the government they believed that DNA techniques had not been pursued to their maximum in a number of serious cases. An ACPO (Association of Chief Police Officers) review was set up under Tony Lake, chief constable of Lincolnshire. The upshot was a recommendation that, in a number of cases, low copy number (LCN) analysis of retained samples would allow DNA profiles to be obtained from smaller amounts of material than had previously been possible. Accordingly, some cases which had failed to yield DNA results were reinvestigated under what was now termed Operation Cube.

The Prestwood case was one of those in which the FSS conducted further analysis. This in itself necessitated further deception by the Crown Prosecution Service. The general public was under the impression that cases being re-investigated under Operation Cube were 'cold cases' – that is, crime investigations which had been discontinued after a failure to resolve the case. The public was not told that the review embraced cases which had already been to trial and appeal. These were supposed to have been satisfied beyond all reasonable doubt; yet, clearly, considerable doubt surrounded this conviction – if not, why was public money being expended on renewed investigations?

So, there was that very weak DNA profile that fitted not only Malkinson but also half the UK's population. Could that now be enhanced? Fresh tests were conducted. This further analysis did indeed produce material from which a DNA profile was obtained. Just like the earlier samples, it was not Malkinson's. The scientists considered whether the profile did match someone on the national DNA database, but then decided that it probably didn't. The FSS conceded that it is impossible to know which bodily fluid it derives from, or whether it is associated with the case.

It was because of the partially-severed nipple on the left breast that the prosecution was able to emphasise to the jury just what a vicious attack this had been. Yet this evidence should be examined properly. There was saliva staining at the site, from which a DNA profile was obtained, but it didn't match Malkinson (though the profile could have matched the boyfriend); and the clothing on the upper body was not disarranged. Prestwood's fleece remained zipped up throughout and her bra remained in place. It would have been obviously impossible for Malkinson to have inflicted the wound without disturbing the clothing.

The most sophisticated techniques had been applied to the case – and there was still not a shred of scientific evidence that on that night Malkinson had been anywhere other than at home in bed. If he had been the assailant, he had accomplished the extraordinary feat of not only assaulting his victim and leaving nothing of himself on her, but also of simultaneously ensuring that the DNA of both her boyfriend and some unknown person remained. The prosecution case didn't rely on forensic awareness, after all; it relied on magic.

AFTER THE TRIAL, Malkinson's despair became complete when, bewildered by what he considered the abject performance of his legal team, he made a complaint to the Law Society, the body that regulates solicitors.

He then learned for the first time that, some years earlier, his lawyer had served a prison sentence for fraud and been struck off the solicitors register.

Unfortunately, this does not provide grounds for appeal.

The only course of action left to Malkinson was to complain to the solicitor himself. He was merely rebuked for his ingratitude. 'I would remind you', the solicitor responded, 'that the jury were out for over nine hours before they came to majority rather than unanimous decisions in relation to each of the convictions – I hardly call that incompetent or improper preparation of your case.' *(see Note, p 467)*

JUST BEFORE that ill-fated trip to the Canaries, Malkinson, a confirmed pacifist, was one of the thousands who, in February 2003, crammed into Dam Square in Amsterdam as part of the worldwide demonstrations against the imminent US-UK action in Iraq. Now, in prison in the UK, he recalled his years on the road.

'As time went on, I thought less and less about England', he reflected. 'I had a "rolling stone" life. The work you are doing is generally seasonal, so you're always looking to move on.

'You have your freedom but little else. Sometimes people are envious when you tell them of your travels, as though you've had more advantages in life than they have. But you aren't staying at the Ritz. More likely, you've paid a few dollars for a stinking hell-hole down the Khao San Road in Bangkok.

'The advantage is that there isn't time for things to go stale. You are always meeting new people and facing fresh challenges. Some might find it an insecure lifestyle, but it suited me.

'I left Amsterdam on 16 May 2003 with a return ticket to Gran Canaria. At that point, England to all intents and purposes did not exist for me anymore. In an ironic way what has happened has completely vindicated my reasons for leaving.'

Although Malkinson and Karin Schuitemaker separated in 2000, they remain close friends. It was Karin who contacted me from Holland to alert me to Malkinson's plight.

'I know him for twenty years now', she wrote in 2015, 'and I know for a 100% sure he is totally innocent. The details of the crime don't fit Andy. We worked and lived together and have been very close friends. He would never do the thing he has been accused of.

'Now Andy needs all the help he can get.'

Chapter 6

The missing missing person's inquiry

Gordon Park's story

1

On Wednesday 13 August 1997, two members of the Kendal and Lakes Sub-Aqua Club brought a bulky object to the surface of Coniston Water in the Lake District.

They had noticed it on the lake bed while diving the previous weekend and returned with lifting equipment to raise it. The bundle was well-wrapped and heavy and the cords holding it together were tight. There were problems attaching an inflatable bag; but, with considerable difficulty, they managed to drag the bundle behind them to the shore.

They cut open the outer canvas bag. Inside was another green bag. Inside that, covered in black plastic bin-liners, was a human body. The divers called the police.

Eight days later, the body was identified as that of Carol Park, a thirty-year-old schoolteacher who had been reported missing twenty-one years earlier. Her husband, Gordon Park, was also a schoolteacher. During the inquiry carried out at the time, in 1976, the police had bluntly told him that, should his missing wife ever be found murdered, he would be the prime suspect.

So it proved. Park was on holiday in France when the body was recovered. The dramatic events attracted enormous publicity. The papers carried pictures of his boat, and pictures of him arriving back in the country with his wife, just as though he were a fugitive returning to face justice. He was arrested and charged with murder.

To judge from the press coverage, it seemed a clear-cut case; but then, a few months later, a strange thing happened: the charge was dropped.

Nevertheless, Park did eventually stand trial for his wife's murder. The Crown Prosecution Service reinstated the charge in 2004, twenty-eight years after her death and more than six years after the recovery of the body.

Park was then sixty years old. The CPS argued that he had murdered Carol after becoming exasperated by her affairs. They said she had probably been killed with a small ice-axe, an implement which Park, a keen climber, possessed; as he had a boat, he would have been able to dispose of the body; clothes found at the bottom of the lake in the vicinity of the body belonged to Carol and a boulder used to weight them down had come from their house, as had a piece of Westmorland slate found by the body; there was evidence from a woman who in 2004 told police that in the summer of 1976 she had seen someone tip a bundle over the side of a boat; and there was evidence from two prisoners that Park had told them he had murdered the wife.

On Friday 28 January 2005, four days after his sixty-first birthday, he was found guilty and sentenced to life imprisonment.

BARROW-IN-FURNESS, where Gordon Park was born in January 1944, is a small industrial town in Cumbria. It lies at the top of the Furness peninsula, with the great expanse of Morecambe Bay to the south, and is sheltered from the Irish Sea by Walney Island. Directly to the north is the stunning beauty of the Lake District National Park.

After the arrival of the railways, Barrow became a centre for steel production as iron ore was transported there. Its natural harbour made it an ideal location for shipbuilding. From the 1890s onwards, warships for the Royal Navy were built there. Having the additional advantage of relative inaccessibility, it was in more recent times given the more politically sensitive role of building nuclear-powered submarines.

Park went to school there and, indeed, never left the town. From his childhood he loved walking the fells. He developed the climbing and sailing skills that are widespread in the area. Roger Mitton first met him in 1958 when they were both at Barrow Grammar School. 'We went hiking together in Chamonix, France in 1959', he recalled, 'and our friendship continued from then on.'

On 28 August 1967, Park married the twenty-one-year-old Carol Price.

'I'd known Carol since she was nine', said Alan Shaw, another fellow grammar school pupil who became a lifelong friend. 'She used to play the organ in church. In Barrow, being the place it is, we all knew each other, we were all friends and drifted in and out of relationships, as you do at that age, and have grown up together.'

Carol Park worked as a clerk at Barrow Town Hall after leaving school. By the time she married, she had taken a teacher training course at Matlock College in Derbyshire. She was an adopted child, and had been raised by the Price family who had two children of their own, Ivor and Christine. In April 1969, tragedy struck when Christine, who was then eighteen, was murdered by her boyfriend, John Rapson. He was convicted and sentenced to life imprisonment.

Christine had a daughter, Vanessa, who was just over a year old when her mother was killed. Gordon and Carol Park decided to take in and adopt the child. They then had two children of their own: Jeremy, born in 1970, and Rachael, born in 1971.

Park's parents ran a home decorating retail business in Barrow, and had four shops that they consolidated into one large store. DIY seems to have been in Park's blood. He bought a plot of land in Leece, just outside Barrow, and built a family home there. It was a three-bedroomed bungalow they called Bluestones. A stubborn piece of blue rock prevented the levelling of the ground to start the work. Finally, they had to dynamite it, showering the area with blue stones.

Despite his DIY expertise, Park felt he needed to do something more socially useful and in the early '70s went to teacher training college. From 1974, he was working as a primary school teacher at South Newbarns Junior School.

Carol gave up work for a couple of years when the children were born, before resuming her teaching career. She was attractive and vivacious and, from shortly after Rachael's birth, had a string of affairs. Park first became suspicious in 1972. He confronted the man about it and that relationship was ended. Then, in March 1974, he discovered that she had been having a relationship with a married man who lived locally and had children of his own. He told Carol he knew, and she packed her bags and spent the night with the man at the Swan Hotel, but returned the next day. The next month, she again left with a holdall one morning, only to return later the same day.

Then, she had two liaisons during a week-long Open University course at Keele in 1974. A boyfriend drove down from Barrow to be with her, so that would presumably have been pre-arranged; while there, however, she began a relationship with a fellow student, David Brearley, a teacher who had once been in the Durham police force. Two weeks later she left home and took a room in a guesthouse in order to be able to see him.

On 26 September 1974, she asked Park for a divorce, although she did not go through with this. That autumn, without telling Park, she tendered her resignation from her school, worked out her notice and then moved across the country to the north-east to live with Brearley. They bought a house and a car together. She took his surname and got a job teaching children with learning difficulties.

She tried to win custody of Vanessa, Jeremy and Rachael, but failed. In March 1975, magistrates in Middlesbrough determined that it was Carol who had left the marital home, and Park who was looking after the children responsibly; so this was one of those rare occasions when the father was granted custody.

'Basically, my Dad put up a good case', explained Jeremy. 'He said, "I've got family support, I've got school support, and it's better that the children should stay where they are". I'm glad they decided in Dad's favour, because I think Mum was unstable at the time and it was the outcome that we, the children, would have wanted.'

Carol was by now experiencing some mental problems. She was further depressed by the outcome of the custody hearing and was put on strong tranquillisers. During the Easter school holidays, she returned to Park. She spent a week back with him, before leaving again. She asked the babysitter, Judith Walmsley, to be kind to the children and help Park to look after them. Then she 'became hysterical', according to one witness, and 'wound up into a frenzy'. She grabbed objects and hurled them across the room. The upshot was that Brearley drove to the Lake District to collect her. He arrived that evening and saw 'broken glass and compost from the

210

houseplants' strewn across the floor. He took Carol back to the north-east with him.

Carol became more depressed by the separation from her children and began to see a psychiatrist, whose diagnosis was that she had 'a disordered personality' and was 'unstable in her relationships'. She seemed to treat Brearley as badly as she had done Park, and disappeared three times.

At the end of the summer term, she failed to arrive for work. Brearley wrote to the school to say that he didn't know where she was. After he reported her missing, a uniformed police officer made enquiries at Park's house. He hadn't heard from her either, but she was found at her mother's home.

She went back to Brearley and the children spent two weeks of the long school holiday there with her and her partner.

'I can distinctly remember it', said Jeremy. 'Dad dropped us off there. I can remember playing with David's son, Michael. I also remember David had a brown leather jacket and his car was a Vauxhall Victor or a Ford Cortina, one of those with wings on the back.'

At this time, Rachael was only four. 'I have this vivid recollection of seeing my Mum again after I hadn't seen her for a while, though I don't know how long that while was', she said.

'I was sitting in the living room and she gave us weebles.' (These were one of the briefly popular toys of the time; as the memorable jingle went: *weebles wobble but they don't fall down*).

'My brother got a plane, my sister had a boat, and I had a car. I remember sitting on the floor on this very thick white carpet playing weebles with my mother, and this guy, her boyfriend, whom I now know was David Brearley, hovering around in the background.'

'On the last day in Brearley's house, I wanted to stay', recalled Jeremy. 'We were baking cakes, and I thought, I want to stay here and bake cakes with my Mum. She got really upset, and that upset me. From an early age, I've had those feelings of rejection, as a lot of the time my mother seemed to be either going away from us or coming back to us.'

At the end of the summer she left Brearley. After that, he said, he never saw her again or even received a phone call from her. She left her job at the school, without explaining her departure to the headmaster, and returned to her family. In due course, Brearley sent her documents to sign. She made over the house to him and they sold the car.

Park was elated that his wife had returned and the children were naturally happy to have their mother back.

'It was a Saturday, it was sunny and bright, and my mum was laughing', said Jeremy. 'I remember feeling at the time, I'm really glad that she's back. I was only five but I do remember that strongly.'

Carol did not work that term, but found a new school job after Christmas and worked for the next two terms.

On 17 July 1976, the day after the end of the summer term, at almost exactly the same point that she had disappeared the year before, she disappeared again. She should have gone with Park and the children on a day's outing to Blackpool, but she made some excuse (probably complaining of a headache) in order to stay behind.

'I do remember that day', said Jeremy. 'She was still in bed; she said, "No, you go to Blackpool with Dad, you'll be OK", that kind of thing. My early childhood was punctuated with highs when she was in the house and was happy, and moments when she turned away from us.'

They had the day out at Blackpool, went to the funfair, and when they returned in the evening, Carol was gone.

'Where is Mummy?' asked Jeremy.

Her wedding and engagement rings were on the small dressing table in the bedroom.

Jeremy remembered his father seeming upset. He asked him if he ever cried.

'I am crying now', Park replied.

The next day, family friends, Malcolm and Angela Short, turned up at the house. As they recollected, Park told them that Carol had disappeared and not taken anything with her. They were 'asked into the house, but declined because [Park] seemed to have enough on his plate'.

Because Carol made a habit of disappearing, friends confidently expected her to turn up. When her absence became one of weeks, they merely thought that she had left to start a new life elsewhere.

Park simply assumed that she was 'in bed with another man'. It was only on 4 September, when she didn't return to school at the end of the long summer holidays, that he reported her missing. A missing person's inquiry was then initiated. As part of the investigation, police thoroughly searched Park's house and outbuildings and questioned him at some length.

At the end of the year, the local press arrived at the house to take a photograph of the three children standing next to the Christmas tree and pleading, 'Mum, please come home for Christmas'.

'As I recall it, the police and the press and the photographer were all in the house together', said Jeremy. 'The police had said to us, "You're going to have to make an appeal". That was the first time it was put to us that she probably wasn't coming back, which I found really traumatic, deeply disturbing.'

There were no developments and no news. In November 1978, Park filed for divorce on the grounds of Carol's desertion.

The children attended South Newbarns where their father taught, although he made sure they were never in his class. Outdoor adventures were readily available. As they were growing up, there was sailing and mountain-climbing. Park taught Jeremy to sail, just as his own father had taught him, and they would go sailing in small dinghies and luggers on Lake Windermere.

Jeremy and Rachael both recall helping their father with various ongoing projects from the age of about five. Having built his own house, Park's next major task was to build his own boat. This was the 'Big O', named partly because of his fondness for the music of Roy Orbison. It was a large dinghy, which was powerful and fast despite its weight. At 7'6", it was unusually wide, in order to accommodate lots of schoolchildren safely. He launched the boat in 1978 and sold it in 1982. Then he had a racing dinghy, before getting a larger yacht, the 'Lady J', which he bought in 1986 and kept on Coniston Water.

In 1981, Park had re-married disastrously. His new wife had five older children, so ten of them were squeezed into a three-bedroomed house. It led to what Park described as 'maximum domestic disharmony'. They soon realised it wasn't working and separated. The family breathed a sigh of relief.

'Collectively, we got our life back', recalled Rachael. 'From then on, we had a wonderful time. That period coincided with my brother's first girlfriend and my first boyfriend and it was terrific.'

There was, though, that nagging void in their lives.

'I was growing into a teenager', said Jeremy, 'but I still grew up feeling inadequate because you've only got only parent. I spent years wondering what had happened to her. I think we probably accepted as children that we were never going to know what had happened and, as I got older, the feelings of confusion and rejection arising from her leaving stayed with me as an adult.'

'I loved my mother', said Rachael. 'I missed her in the sense that everybody else had a mother and I didn't. That was quite painful at times. People would say to me, "Where's your mother?" and the answer to that was, "I don't know". It was only ever I don't know.

'My Dad didn't talk much about her. It wasn't a taboo subject in any way. But he always had the opinion that if you can't say something nice about someone, don't say anything at all. And he never wanted us to have low self-esteem because of our mother's reputation.

'My Dad was dad. But for important things like first boyfriend, first menstruation, for all of those sort of things I went to Dad, and he was wonderful. There was never a problem not having a mum because he was Mum and Dad rolled into one. He fulfilled the entire role of both parents.'

In 1989, Rachael went to Switzerland for what was intended to be a three-month stint in a small town, Delémont, working at a *ludothèque* and learning the French language. In due course, she got a flat and a job in Basle in the head office of a packaging machine manufacturer. Her three months in Switzerland became ten years.

On the day of their grandmother's funeral in 1992, the three of them – Vanessa, Jeremy and Rachael – decided to search for their mother.

'People have asked me, "Did you try to find her?"', said Jeremy. 'Well, yes, we did. But we didn't know how to go about it. I got a copy of her birth certificate. We asked around. We should have tried to look at the case files. That would have been useful. But we didn't approach the police, partly because they seemed not to know anything – they'd already investigated and got nowhere – and partly because when we asked around, we'd heard that the police might be involved. It was all gossip, and Barrow's a small town. Small town talk spreads quickly, and there were rumours that she'd been having an affair with a police officer.'

In 1993, Park married Jenny Marshall whom he had known for forty-five years since they were at junior school together. Jenny herself had two teenage children, Jane and Stuart, and was newly divorced from their father. It was Park's third marriage, but first suitable relationship; this would be the one that endured.

Having sold Bluestones in December 1991, Park moved in with Jenny to the house she bought after her divorce. Jeremy was by now at university and needed a base back in Barrow, but there wasn't room for him in Jenny's house.

'Why not build yourself a room of your own?' Park suggested to him. 'You can do a loft conversion.'

'So basically Dad told me how to do it', explained Jeremy, 'and bought all the materials for me. The first job was to jack up the roof, and I got a hydraulic car jack and turned round this roof beam. If it had gone wrong and the beam ended up out of position, the roof would collapse and possibly part of the walls, so it was a big responsibility. I did it while he was at school, so he was extremely relieved when he came home and it was all in place.

'But he'd trusted me and could trust me because he'd taught me all my life. I could fix things and build things. I knew how everything worked. One year, when I was fifteen, we were planning a trip round Europe in our Renault 14 and in preparation for this trip we rebuilt the engine. We completely stripped it and laid it all out, there were hundreds and hundreds of parts, and then put it all back together. It took us about two-and-a-half weeks.

'So Dad and I understood each other technically very well.

'I spent eight weeks that summer doing the loft conversion. Then I went back to university and Dad finished it off. When I came back at Christmas, I had somewhere to live.'

Park gave up work in 1994 and was soon busier than ever.

'He'd do loads of odd jobs for people', said Jeremy. 'He'd fix everyone's bathroom or kitchen or walls. Doing up people's houses was something he really enjoyed. If you knew my Dad, he'd come and do it. He did it for nothing. They gave him beer or wine, or sometimes bought him a book.

'He loved B&Q. It was his favourite shop. He was always in there buying bits and pieces for odd jobs he was doing.'

Park did some tiling work for St Paul's Church in Barrow, where he and Jenny were occasional worshippers, and for which, again, he refused to accept payment.

Music, too, played an important part in the life of the new family group.

'Dad would hum tunes and whistle all the time', Jeremy reflected. 'He loved a wide range of music. In the garage, he would always be singing, especially tunes that were inspired by what we were doing, like *If I Had a Hammer*, or *If I Were a Carpenter*.

'We had a lot of instruments between us. He played guitar, Jenny and Jane played piano, and Stuart played piano and guitar, so there was always a lot of music in the house. Dad bought a PA system, and also a five-piece drum set so he could play in school performances while Jenny played the piano. Around Christmas and Easter in Barrow, he and Jenny would go round old people's homes with guitars and recorders. They'd train a children's choir, and do carol singing and small musical productions. They could do two or three venues in an evening.'

2

The dramatic recovery of a body at the bottom of Coniston Water created enormous publicity. It was the middle of August, a time which used to be regarded as the 'silly season' for the UK press. Traditionally, when politicians, businessmen and lawyers went on holiday there was nothing for the press to fill its pages with, so matters that were otherwise too frivolous to attract notice were given headline status.

Yet some topics, and particularly crime mysteries, will still dominate the news agenda during August. The disappearance of three-year-old Madeleine McCann received incessant coverage throughout August 2007, irrespective of the fact that the child had disappeared three months earlier and there was no news about her.

Ten years before that, during the second half of August 1997, this unfolding drama had made all the headlines. The papers were particularly excited by the fact that the body was clothed in a blue baby-doll nightie. Needing a tagline to customise their story, and reaching by force of habit for the obvious cliché, they dubbed it The Lady in the Lake mystery.

In all the speculation, Carol Park was one of the names mentioned. At the time, Jeremy was working on IT contract work for a company in Scotland. Jane, his stepsister, telephoned to ask if he thought if it could be his Mum. Jeremy said he hadn't thought about it, though after the phone call he began to wonder.

By about the third or fourth day, the police had narrowed down the possibilities to two or three women. Vanessa phoned Jeremy to tell him the police wanted to speak to him.

Before ringing the station, Jeremy phoned his father, who was in France.

'I remember him telling me', he recalled, 'just tell them whatever you know, tell them the truth, we've got nothing to hide, help in whatever way you can.'

So Jeremy called the police and they went up to see him in Scotland. He couldn't abandon his work, so they stayed and interviewed him over two days, at lunchtimes and evenings.

'They were trying to find out what I could remember, what our lifestyle was like, they asked questions about boats. I told them what a good childhood we had, and that Dad was a lot of fun and was affectionate.

'I remember they asked how my Mum got to school. I said she drove. And they said, "What? Your father let her drive the car?" That's what they actually said. They'd built up this image in their mind that he was a domineering bully and she wasn't allowed to drive.

'I said, "Of course she was allowed to drive. She was allowed to do whatever she wanted. If she didn't have the car, she wouldn't have been able to get to work, to meet people and to have affairs". After a while the officers' body language changed. They realised I wasn't going to tell them anything that was going to convict my Dad and they just became uninterested.'

The police had decided that in order to confirm whether the body was Carol's, they needed to take DNA samples from both the children. Jeremy had to return to Barrow. He arrived at the station on Saturday morning and gave his sample. The needle and the blood proved too much for him. He passed out.

The police also wanted a written statement, which was taken over three days the next week. Jeremy suggested that he could draw up his own if they'd tell him which questions they needed answering. They told him they didn't work like that.

'So I'd had to have time off work', he said, 'They handwrote the statement. Eventually I got sight of this, and I didn't like any of it. I didn't like the language – it was written in their special phrases, the language they use in police stations where everything's dumbed down a bit. It didn't reflect what I'd said, it missed quite a lot out. It had taken all that time, and it was such a mess.'

ALTHOUGH PARK WAS BY THEN semi-retired, Jenny was still working full-time at the school. This meant they still needed to take their annual holidays at high season.

When the body was found, they were in Gascony on a cycling holiday, and naturally saw no reason to cut it short. The accommodation for their homeward journey was booked, and a ferry reservation had been made.

When it became clear that it probably *was* Carol's body, they were coming to the end of their holiday anyway. They cleaned the *gite* and packed and then embarked on the two-day journey home, with bicycles on the roof-rack and towing their trailer of luggage. On their overnight stop, they watched the television news with disbelief. The police were searching their home and carrying away black bin-bags of their belongings.

They returned to England late on the evening of Saturday 23 August. The police arrived at their house at 8.00 the following morning. Park was taken away for questioning, while the police continued to remove property from the house. 'They took away boxes and boxes', said Jeremy, 'the computer, floppy discs, CDs, photographs, documentation and all the rope and string they could find.'

Rachael and her boyfriend, Maximiliano Garcia, were each moving from their respective apartments in Basle when she received the news about the probable recovery of her mother's body. 'Max and I were surrounded by boxes', she recalled. 'We were just packing the last items because the next day we were setting up home together.'

She was unable to leave Switzerland straight away. Her boss was on holiday and out of the country. 'He flew back on Sunday the 24th', she said. 'He was totally supportive and told me to stay as long as I needed to. The next day, I got a flight to Manchester.'

Rachael then experienced at first-hand the climate of paranoia that a fired-up British media will instil in its targets. 'Alan and Sue Shaw [Park's schoolfriend and his wife] met me at the airport and drove me to Barrow', she explained. 'On the way, we liaised with Jez in a lay-by somewhere and I climbed into his car with my suitcase.

'Then we had the problem: how could I get home? It was a circus outside Dad and Jenny's house. There were thirty or forty journalists and photographers with their stepladders. There was even a fish-and-chip van parked round the corner to feed them all.

'Getting in to the house was a nightmare. We went through a neighbour's house and climbed in over the back fence.'

The next morning the police began the process of taking a statement from her. Her experience mirrored her brother's.

'They were asking me about my earliest memories, and how much did we talk about my mother at home. I didn't remember much. It's all very hazy because I was so small. The reason why the whole process took four days is that they would ask me a question which I would answer, in detail, to the best of my recollection. If it was anything vaguely positive, they would just sit there and not write a word. They were only interested in anything that could possibly be interpreted as being detrimental to my father.

'Every day, after eight hours of this, they would write out a statement. I would read it and I'd have to ask them to re-write it.

I'd be saying, "I didn't use that word, I never said that". They were constantly trying to put words into my mouth. So I kept refusing to sign it. The whole experience was very emotionally draining.'

The police took a blood sample from Rachael and it was on the basis of that analysis that they were able to announce that the body was definitely that of Carol Park.

After questioning, Park was charged with the murder of his first wife and, astonishingly, remanded into custody. He was then a fifty-three-year-old junior schoolteacher who was well-known in his local community and who had never been involved with any kind of criminality. Even if the prosecution had legitimate grounds for believing he'd murdered Carol twenty-one years earlier, he had obviously posed no danger to the public either at the time or in the years since.

'We all took our lead from Dad and thought that if we complied with the police investigation and volunteered information, everything would be fine', said Jeremy. 'Naively, we all thought that, having spoken to them, he'd be released and then there would be further investigations.

'So when the police came to the house to tell Jenny and the family that he was being charged, that was a real shock. I broke down at that point. It affected me quite badly for a couple of years afterwards. It's quite a scary thought that you might be under suspicion in whatever you do and could be arbitrarily charged with something.

'We thought, we're looking at a murder trial. This was the first time it actually occurred to me that he could be considered a suspect. All through my childhood we'd thought about my Mum, thinking she might be dead, and at no point did I ever consider that my Dad could be responsible. It just never occurred to me. That someone else might have done it – yes; that she'd gone off and come to harm – yes; but that Dad had done it – no.

'Only when he was arrested, did it twig. And we had to think: well, did he do it? I wonder if he has. Then every moment after that, I was thinking, well he can't have done it – because of this, because of that, because of his behaviour, because of the way he is.'

During that August, from the time of the discovery of the body, media interest was incessant – partly because it was an evolving news story with day-by-day developments, and partly because of the height-of-the-holiday-season factor. The family found the attentions of the media unbearably intrusive.

'I was being grilled by the police for four days', said Rachael, 'and meanwhile all these crazy articles were being written in the media. It really felt as if you were being raped in public. Nothing in my life was sacred. It was all there for the world to see. It feels afterwards as if you've lost all that part of your life; everything is sullied, everything is dirty. It really is the most awful feeling.'

Then, dramatically, media interest in their predicament was extinguished. In the early hours of Sunday 31 August, Princess Diana was killed in a car accident in the Place de l'Alma underpass in Paris. Amid the national grief and mourning, the Park family took crumbs of comfort from the tragedy and, ironically, were grateful for the lifting of an immense burden.

OBVIOUSLY, PARK HAD NO experience whatever of prison life. He was, though, specifically warned by his solicitor of the dangers of discussing the case with inmates or prison officers, all of whom had to be regarded as potentially untrustworthy. Park, who was hardly likely to be attracted by the social possibilities of his new environment, well understood.

He spent four days in the hospital of Preston prison, and was then put on F Ward, for vulnerable prisoners who might be attacked by other inmates. One day, sitting at a table by himself, he received a letter from Stuart, Jenny's son, with whom he had developed a close bond. Reading it, he welled up and then burst into tears. A prisoner named Steve consoled him.

'Steve came round from the other side of the table and just sat there quietly', Park wrote. 'He asked if I was all right and reassured me that everything would be OK. I did not expect to find human kindness in a place like that.'

After two weeks, Park's lawyers were successful in getting him bail, on condition that he lived outside the area. There was, of course, no reason whatever why he could not have been granted bail on these terms from the start.

'There was also a curfew, which he couldn't ignore', said Jeremy, 'if only because police regularly checked up on him. He had to be indoors from 9.00pm until 8.00am, which meant that he was prevented from going for his regular early-morning run.'

Though staying with his sister, Park was separated from his immediate family. Jenny could not leave her work or her children, and had to drive long distances at uncomfortable times to see him. Meanwhile, the Crown proposed calling both Jeremy and Rachael as witnesses at trial in spite of the fact that neither had anything to say that would assist them. By these means, the prosecution could increase the pressure on Park. Because of the proposed involvement of his children, he was not allowed to be in direct contact with them.

The bail conditions, though, were finally lifted in time for them to spend Christmas together as a family in a cottage in the Lake District.

The burden was lifted properly in January 1998 when the charge against Park was dropped.

'It was a brief moment of exhilaration', remembered Rachael, 'but funnily enough after that I totally went to pieces. Up until that point, I had been finding the courage to soldier on, thinking to myself, "You have to get through this". I was mentally preparing myself for the trial and everything that that entailed.

'When that was suddenly dropped, all of that pressure and the stress and emotion were released. Max scraped me off the floor and calmed me down. He took me to Bali for three weeks. The Balinese are such a gentle people, it's probably the least stressful place on the planet. It was an amazing therapy.'

Back in England, both Park himself and the whole family had been through a tremendously trying time. 'We were all screwed up by then', reflected Jeremy. 'We hadn't been allowed to talk to the press, but of course material leaked from the prosecution side had been appearing in the press throughout. That coloured everything that happened.

'As a family, we thought that everything we did came under suspicion. Dad was incredibly angry, and very suspicious. We didn't believe anything we were told, we all assumed the phone was tapped and he was being monitored.'

Even arranging a funeral for their mother proved difficult. Because they wanted to avoid something that they believed would be turned into an unseemly occasion attended by photographers and cameramen, they organised a secret service.

'We didn't know what she liked', said Jeremy, 'we didn't know anything about her private life outside of the family, we didn't know what she got up to as a child and where she liked to go, we didn't know what songs she liked. We just had a really quiet service. But by the time we left, the press had got wind of it.'

Later, Jeremy, Rachael and Vanessa scattered their mother's ashes on Birkrigg, the highest point on the Furness peninsula.

The fact that the charges had been dropped rekindled the media's interest in the case. Park and Jenny avoided the cameras and went into hiding.

'We're a very private family', reflected Rachael, 'we don't want to have these matters aired in public. My Dad's watchword was always dignity in the face of adversity. That's what we thought – that it was best to maintain a dignified silence. However, that just allowed the media to portray us as uncaring and unemotional.

'They never seem to realise that there's a family behind all this. It's terribly upsetting when your mother disappears, and is found murdered, and then there's this saga. As a family you're just struggling to get through the day anyway, and there's this constant added pressure of the media, of living in a goldfish bowl.

'Gordon Park was presented in a one-dimensional way; there was nothing of the loving, caring father that we knew him as. The people who knew my Dad were obviously aware of the vast difference between the real Gordon Park and the portrayal of him in the media; people who didn't know him and had never met him might have believed the media portrayal.

'The "lady in the lake" label was very upsetting. It seems to dehumanise the whole thing. I just wanted to get it into their heads: it's not the lady in the lake – *it's my mother.*

'What the media delivers is the barbarity of sensationalism – I know it happens to other people, too, but I find it sickening. The one consolation I had was that I didn't live in the country.'

Lawyers advised the family that, however perverse it seemed, the best way to tackle the problem of the media was to do an interview. They argued that if Park and Jenny finally spoke to one paper, then the others would leave them alone. Having no experience of PR or the media, they reluctantly assented to this strategy, and an account of their side of the story duly appeared in the national press.

However, this had no effect in curbing the hostile atmosphere, which was in due course exacerbated in a quite unexpected way. The BBC broadcast a drama series, *The Lakes*, which was set in the Lake District. The programme, which enjoyed great popularity, featured a husband murdering his wife, trussing up her body and going out in his boat to dump it in one of the eponymous lakes.

It is possible that the storyline was suggested by the case of Peter Hogg, an airline pilot who'd murdered his wife in October 1976. He disposed of her body in Wast Water; it was found unexpectedly in March 1984 after divers had been searching for a missing French student. Hogg was convicted of manslaughter and served fifteen months in jail.

It is far more likely, however, that the storyline was suggested by this case. The Hogg case was different: he hadn't lived in the Lake District; he lived in Surrey. Nor did he own a boat; he had merely bought a cheap inflatable dinghy on his way to the Lake District. (There are no boats on Wast Water.)

The dramatised case fitted the Park case – or, rather, what the media imagined the Park case to be – much more closely.

As if this wasn't bad enough, Channel 4 then broadcast a highly irresponsible documentary, inevitably titled *The Ladies of the Lake*, in which the Hogg case was associated with that of Carol Park. Inevitably, ITV then contributed its own documentary which, just as inevitably, was titled *The Lady in the Lake*.

'So you have the situation that, although the charges have been dropped, everyone is still being made to think he's guilty', said

Jeremy. 'When Dad was in B&Q, people would stare at him. The pressure got to him.

'He'd already semi-retired by the time he was charged, but after the charges he gave that up entirely and just did odd jobs for people, while Jenny still worked three days a week. He remained very suspicious and it took him years to come round. Only then, finally, could he actually begin to think, "It's all right, this has fizzled out", and they could spend time together, try to enjoy life and get over all this.'

One thing that never returned to normal, though, was Park's enthusiasm for sailing. He had sailed all his life but gave up after the discovery of Carol's body, when he realised how many times he must have sailed over it.

Rachael married Max in a ceremony in Spain that all the family were able to attend. Then Max was headhunted by a company that made packaging for pharmaceuticals, cosmetics and some foodstuffs. They wanted him to become managing director of their operation in China. It was a huge challenge which neither of them wanted to turn down.

Rachael, who already spoke English, French, Italian and some Spanish, had to go to school full-time for fifteen months to learn Mandarin.

'It's not an easy language to learn', she pointed out, 'but I didn't have any option. My husband is always with people who can translate for him, but that wasn't the case with me. We were living in the old quarter of Beijing where at the time there were no foreigners at all. So I absolutely had to learn the language to survive.'

One afternoon in January 2004, when she was four or five months pregnant with Hannah, their daughter, Rachael was sitting at her computer at home in Beijing, writing emails, when she received the phone call that would shatter their lives for ever.

'At all of these moments I remember exactly where I was, what I was doing, it's like a photographic image. Jez called to tell me Dad had been re-arrested.

'I remember being absolutely terrified. I was sobbing and sobbing and sobbing, I was worried about having a miscarriage because I'd already had a miscarriage just before getting pregnant. I was trying to calm down but I was alone. Max was a plane journey away, but he got back as fast as he could.

'By that point, we'd been through so much pain. I was terrified that it was going to be a guilty verdict. As far as the media was concerned he was obviously guilty, so there seemed to be only one outcome. I just thought: if the media perceives him to be guilty, then the general public believes him to be guilty, then the jury is going to find him guilty.'

Jeremy remembered the call that he'd received.

'It was a winter morning, the thirteenth of January. It was seven thirty, I was just getting out of the bath and there was a phone call from Jenny. I just felt darkness coming over me.

'Then it was the same process over again. They came to the house and took everything again – documents, computers, bits of string, photographs, CDs, anything with memory. They still hadn't returned the computer from last time. Now they took his new one. They've never returned that either.

'Then they started interviewing us all and going round and round, asking the same questions, trying to pick up inconsistencies, however inconsequential.'

A couple of times, Park did give answers in 2004 that were at variance with those he'd given in 1997. The interviewers deemed these highly suspicious; Park explained that, as preparation for the aborted trial, he'd carefully gone through all the case material. By reading other statements he had been able to refresh his own memory which was why, in a couple of small matters, he'd corrected himself.

Some months later, when their daughter was three months old, Rachael and Max came over to England in the lead-up to the trial. Rachael saw her father again.

'He looked old. I hadn't seen him for some time and was shocked by how much he'd aged. It was hard, seeing him like that. He was extremely preoccupied. Even when he was with us, he wasn't really there a lot of the time. He spent a lot of time upstairs, going through the case papers. He was very subdued and very worried.'

3

The trial began before Mr Justice McCombe at Manchester Crown Court on 22 November. The date had been inauspicious ever since the assassination of President Kennedy forty-one years earlier, in 1963.

The prosecution asserted that Park had murdered his wife on or about 17 July 1976 – in other words, at the time she disappeared, twenty-eight years earlier. Accordingly, the core evidence was naturally going to come from the extensive contemporaneous inquiries carried out by Barrow police in the wake of Carol's disappearance in 1976. That was the vital material; it was gathered at the time, when witnesses' memories were fresh.

However, the jury could not assess any of this evidence. It had mysteriously disappeared. All of it.

In its absence, the first area of evidence at trial was that obtained from the body parcel. It was discovered at a depth of some twenty-four metres, about 250 metres from the shore, near the edge of a ridge beyond which the water got considerably deeper.

This information is not precise because no one marked where the body was found. The amateur diver who discovered it afterwards returned with police divers, who then placed a buoy at that spot which they thought marked the location of the body. The amateur diver candidly said that 'it was difficult to say precisely where the body had been'. The critical aspect of his evidence was that he found 'nothing else in the immediate area' apart from the body.

On the day after the body was brought up, Dr Edmund Tapp carried out a postmortem.

He described the condition of the body as adipocere: having a white, soapy appearance, due to its having been in the water for so long. Carol was wearing a nightdress, and her body was tied up in a foetal position. There was a piece of medical dressing, with eyebrow and eyelash hairs attached to it, indicating the strong probability that her eyes had been taped over. What could also be ascertained was that the body must have been trussed up within two to three hours of death, before rigor mortis had set in. Inevitably, however, no one could give any idea regarding date of death.

It was not possible, either, to say how she had died. At the time of the original inquest the pathologists agreed that cause of death was unknown, and the evidence given at trial was essentially speculative. The facial bones had fractured into fragments, though parts of the face were missing. The upper part of her jaw was shattered and there were fragments in the cheekbones. Dr Tapp reckoned that those injuries were caused before death and that it would have required considerable force to inflict them. A broken finger on Carol's left hand could have been an injury that occurred when she tried to defend herself.

Dr Tapp said he thought Carol had been beaten about the face with a 'heavy blunt object, probably with a sharp edge'. The prosecution suggested that the implement could have been an ice axe, though the reason they suggested this was that they had found one when searching Park's home in 1997. An ice-axe is extremely light, designed to chip away at ice when mountain-climbing. It was an unlikely implement to have caused some of the wounds that Dr Tapp discerned. Realistically, even if he was correct about the injuries, it was impossible to tell what had caused them.

The body was wrapped in two bin-liners, a canvas bag and a large holdall. It was weighted down with lead piping, and all was bound together with rope which had been wound around the body at least three times. When Park was re-arrested, in January 2004, it was partly on the strength of evidence from a knot specialist, Mike Lucas, who concluded that Park had tied the knots on the body parcel.

In preparation for the trial, the defence commissioned a report. Its expert, Robert Chisnall, examined all the knots on the body and reached the opposite conclusion: Park hadn't tied the knots. Lucas read his report, accepted his conclusions and dropped out of the case – a man of integrity, clearly.

So the prosecution appointed a different expert, Roger Ide. The original thrust of the Crown evidence was now abandoned. Originally, they had tried to claim that there were *specific* reasons why the knots indicated that Park had tied up the body; now the

Crown said that there were *general* reasons why the knots suggested this. According to Ide's evidence, the knots on the body parcel 'demonstrated a skill in knot-tying ... [by] someone with a degree of knotting expertise'; and the knots on the ropes observed at Park's house and property similarly demonstrated 'knot-tying skill'.

The defence was unhappy with this evidence for two reasons. Firstly, it was so vague it was worthless. In an area like the Lake District, where sailing and mountain-climbing were popular, a significant percentage of the population possessed those same skills. On the basis of the Crown evidence, in fact, there was nothing to suggest that the two sets of knots had been tied by the same person.

More importantly, the evidence was intellectually dishonest. The original knot evidence was abandoned by the Crown because it didn't suit their case. Now they were trying to argue that the evidence was broadly consistent with their case. But the specific evidence now available wasn't simply neutral; it overwhelmingly assisted the defence.

From Park's house, garage and boat, the police had taken materials which in total contained 194 knots. Of these, there were more half-hitches (69, or 35%) than any other kind of knot; yet there wasn't a single half-hitch on the body parcel. Conversely, the most-used knot on the body was a granny (34, or 26%) – yet there wasn't a single granny knot found on Park's property.

This evidence by itself was highly persuasive of Park's innocence; a murderer who's disposing of a body in one of the UK's deepest lakes is hardly going to take the precaution of disguising his knot-tying habits in case it's discovered twenty-one years later.

The body was weighted down with lead piping – an inevitably jokey element of murder mysteries, because everyone remembers it as a possible murder weapon in the Cluedo board game. The lead piping around the body was also compared to lead taken from Park's house. As before, the evidence was in Park's favour; there was no match. They were produced by different manufacturers. They were not even visibly alike, as there was paint on the lead piping from Park's home, but not on that around the body. Impressions on the piping could have been made by any widely-available hammer.

The divers who found the body parcel on 10 August and recovered it on 13 August reported that there was nothing else of interest in the immediate vicinity. Nevertheless, the police conducted a series of further dives, specifically to search for items that might have been associated with the body. In dives on 14, 18 and 29 August, and in further dives on 1, 2, 4 and 9 September, nothing at all was found.

In a dive on 10 September, two women's shoes, one blue and the other black, a woman's leather boot and a small red dress were recovered. There was then a further dive on 30 September in which more items of clothing, including two matching pairs of shoes and also some cosmetics, were discovered.

During this dive – which was the eleventh in all – a rock was recovered. Well, a rock was purportedly recovered.

The Crown argument was that this rock had been used to weigh down a bundle of Carol's clothes that had been left on the lake-bed with the body. The items of clothing found in the water were, the prosecution suggested, Carol's clothes. They had been tied together and weighted down with the rock, but this second package had disassembled over the years.

A museum curator gave evidence that certain items appeared to date from the mid-'70s, although some items could not be dated. She had used *Vogue* magazines from the 1970s for her reference material. She had not gone back to the manufacturers to check periods of manufacture with them. That was just as well. It would have been a complete waste of everyone's time, since there was nothing to suggest that any of these clothing items were Carol's or that they were linked in any way to the body. There was nothing to contradict the proposition that these were just a few items of detritus that had collected on the bed of the lake over thirty years (perhaps having been borne on the wind, or thrown overboard from boats). A trawl of any comparable stretch of water might have yielded a similar haul.

Leaving that aside, the clothes, according to the Crown's theory, were meant to have been bundled together and weighted down with the rock which had been recovered from the lake bed and which could be linked to Park's Bluestones house.

Conveniently for the prosecution, one expert maintained that the rock matched four samples from the wall at Bluestones. He reached this conclusion because of the monazite that was common to all.

However, the forensic geologist Professor Kenneth Pye examined the materials for the defence and concluded that monazite was not present. So the prosecution expert then retracted his conclusion, and said instead that he could identify a substance called synchysite. However he had to acknowledge that no studies at all had been carried out in the area to establish the incidence of rock containing this material.

The sophisticated geological comparisons of the rock with the stones from the wall at Bluestones were evidentially meaningless. All that could definitely be concluded from those was that they came from the same general source and had been deposited in this glacial valley sometime in the last two million years.

More important than any of this, however, was the fact that there was no record anywhere of a rock having been recovered during this dive. There was nothing on the diving logs or the exhibits labels that referred to a rock. Pye asked for the statements relating to its recovery; there were none. There was no record anywhere of the recovery of a rock from Coniston Water.

The police diver who had conducted this particular search and who was accordingly supposed to have found the rock took the stand. 'When he was shown the stone', the judge, Mr Justice McCombe, reminded the jury in his summing-up, 'he fainted.'

The court was adjourned to give him a chance to recover. When it resumed, the diver said that he had no recollection of the rock at all. 'No recollection of recovering it', added the judge. 'Indeed, he said that if he had noticed a rock at all, he probably would have discarded it.'

On 4 October, this rock was seen on the floor of a cycle store, which was being used as a temporary exhibits room. At that point, a different diver was recorded as having recovered it. That, said the scene-of-crime officer, was a mistake.

So there were no records that it had ever been recovered from the lake. Nor did anyone at all say or suggest that they had taken it

231

from the lake. One imagines that, had someone gone to the trouble of bringing a heavy rock out of the lake to the shore, he would have remembered it.

Pye conducted further examinations of the rock. He pointed out that diatoms were commonly found on rocks which had been immersed in water for some time. Apart from one broken fragment, there were none on this rock. He concluded that there was no evidence that the rock had ever been in water at all.

To paraphrase: part of the evidence against Park, according to the prosecution, was a bundle of Carol's clothing that was weighted down with a rock that had come from Park's property and had been recovered from near Carol's body in the water. Every single aspect of this was false. There was no evidence that there was anything else in the vicinity of the body, or that the clothes were Carol's, or that there was ever a bundle, or that this rock had ever been in the water, or, even if it had, that it had ever had anything to do with Park.

Even apart from all that, there are two more considerations about this extraordinarily tendentious evidence. The suggestion that the rock could be associated with the items of clothing didn't fit the facts of the case. We know that the murderer had wrapped up the body so expertly that it stayed completely sealed for twenty-one years until it was accidentally discovered. So why, having made such a good job of dealing with this far more difficult package, would he have made such a poor one of tying the clothing together?

Secondly, if Park were the murderer, what would have been the point of disposing of just a few items of Carol's clothing? Indeed, if the clothing was evidentially significant at all, then it could only be on the basis that the murderer had needed to dispose of just a few items of her clothing. Logically, therefore, it must have been someone other than Park, who had wardrobes full of her clothing at home.

Then there was a piece of slate. This was Exhibit no.5. It had been recovered in Coniston on 27 February 2004, six-and-a-half-years after the discovery of the body. Again, the Crown wanted to associate this with materials found at Park's former home; again, they failed. It was not true slate, but a processed material that had been used for flooring or roofing. As there were no nail holes or signs of overlapping, it probably hadn't come from a roof. The defence expert said it resembled slates on walls he'd found around Coniston. He said that it could have come from there, or indeed from anywhere else. Once again, there was no evidence that it came from Bluestones. The Crown expert agreed that it could have come from anywhere and acknowledged that slate had been worked as a building material in the area for hundreds of years.

What was Exhibit No.5 doing in the case at all?

Then there was the evidence of Mrs Joan Young. After Park's re-arrest in January 2004, and the consequent fresh burst of publicity, she contacted the police to say that she remembered having been on holiday in the Lake District in 1976. She and her husband, John Young, arrived there on 25 July, and the incident as she recalled it had happened towards the end of their stay there. They parked their car on the lakeside, on the eastern shore, and she saw a man on a boat tip a large bundle over the side. She had remarked jokingly to her husband, 'Perhaps that's his wife'.

There seems to have been some diffidence among the lawyers about this evidence at trial – hardly surprisingly – and the judge only briefly referred to it in his summing-up. Mrs Young's evidence was supported by both her husband and her sister to the extent that they said they remembered her having mentioned this semi-comic, semi-dramatic episode at the time. She recalled the man as wearing a wet suit, having a moustache, and she thought he was wearing glasses. She said that the boat was white, with a cabin and a motor and possibly a mast.

She said that she particularly remembered that holiday because it was then that her husband had proposed to her. Immediately after she had given evidence, John Young came into the court to give evidence. Naturally, it was put to him that he'd obviously remember the holiday, even though it was almost thirty years ago, because it was then that he'd proposed to his wife. He looked startled. He had no recollection of that at all.

The topography did not fit. Although the Youngs had identified where their car was parked, the body site was more than a mile south, and in any event was out of line of sight because there was an island in the way. At that distance, Mrs Young, even if using binoculars (something which she wasn't sure about) would not have been able to see the details of what she claimed to have seen. John Young, who was sitting beside her, said he had only a vague recollection of 'seeing a man drop something over the side of a boat'.

Her description of the boat – a yacht, with a cabin, a motor and possibly a mast – did not fit. When the body was found, the press reported that Gordon Park owned a large yacht, the 'Lady J'. So, indeed, he did – in 1997. But in 1976, he had a 505, a fast and powerful racing dinghy designed for two sailors. Mrs Young's description of the boat was consistent with the boat that Park owned when the media were frenetically reporting the case, but not the one he had at the time of the murder.

Then there is the date. At this time, John Young had injured his leg and was on crutches. There were hospital records showing that he had received treatment (at home, in Scotland) the very week-end that Carol disappeared. Mrs Young said the man-on-the-yacht incident occurred towards the end of their holiday, which would have been the end of the month.

So this happened about two weeks after Carol's disappearance. It was always the Crown case that Park murdered her at more or less the time she disappeared: 'on or about' 17 July 1976. That was the charge on the indictment. So Mrs Young's scenario did not make sense. Park would have needed to murder Carol, to truss up the body straight away, very carefully, keep it around the house for about two weeks, and then dump it in Coniston Water in broad daylight – all without three lively children having been aware that anything was amiss.

Eyewitness evidence in the courtroom is naturally regarded with scepticism. A thousand and one studies have shown that witnesses will imagine they have seen things when they haven't; or will not notice what they have seen. If the evidence coheres with the rest of the case, then it may be valuable; where eyewitness evidence does not make great sense on its own account, and does not fit the prosecution's presumed facts of the case, and has been vouchsafed after a period of time (twelve months would be stretching it, let alone twenty-eight years) – then, in these circumstances, it was an egregious failing in the criminal justice process to allow this evidence to be put before the jury at all.

Then there was the evidence of two jailhouse snitches – that is, prisoners who suggest that the defendant confessed to them while in custody. *(see Note, page 468)*

After his first arrest, Park was held for two weeks in Preston prison in 1997. More than three years later, in October 2000, Michael Wainwright contacted police to say that Park had confessed both to him and another inmate, Glen Banks. This was not, however, unconnected to media reports of the case. Wainwright contacted police the day after the transmission of the Channel 4 documentary.

He made three statements – one when he first reported his evidence; a second in July 2004, and the third in November 2004, in the morning before he gave his testimony in court. He gave as his reason for not having come forward earlier the fear that Park might recruit someone to threaten him. This was despite the fact that Wainwright had to concede that he could turn violent himself.

He said that he was in the exercise yard in Preston prison when he became aware of other prisoners shouting names at Park. He then turned a corner and came across Park, who was mumbling to himself, 'She deserved it'. Later, Park approached Wainwright and asked if he could confide in him, because he had something he needed to get off his chest.

Park told him he had gone upstairs at home to find his wife in bed with another man. He put his hands round her neck until she passed out. In a subsequent account, however, Wainwright changed this and said that Park said he hit his wife with an axe that he used in mountain climbing. Of course, this change in his account meant that it now conveniently chimed with the Crown case.

He said that Park told him he buried the axe on the shore of Coniston Water, although that part of the story only came to Wainwright in 2004. Then he said that Park said he started to dismember his wife's body with an axe. This graphic, and one would have thought memorable, part of the story had slipped his mind when making his three statements. It wasn't even included in the one he made on the morning of the day he gave his evidence. It only came to him, it seemed, in the witness-box.

However Park, according to Wainwright, stopped dismembering the body and wrapped it up instead. He put the body in his car, drove to Coniston Water and went out in his boat to dump the body in the lake.

Even leaving aside the fact that Wainwright changed his account every time he was asked to give it, there are other notable problems with his evidence. Anyone inventing a story may well have assumed that, in order to reach his bedroom, Park needed to climb the stairs. Of course, that did not apply in this instance. Bluestones was a bungalow; there were no stairs.

Secondly, what happened to the man Carol was in bed with? This seemed rather an obvious lacuna in the story. Questioned further about this, all Wainwright could say was that he ran off.

Wainwright's mental state was a matter of concern. He complained about 'hearing voices' at the time he had first approached police. In all his many meetings with doctors and psychiatrists, he had never once mentioned his supposed conversation with Gordon Park. He had been a regular cannabis user for fourteen years and would, he said, smoke about fifteen joints a day. He agreed that he had difficulty remembering things.

One of the things he had difficulty remembering was why he was in prison in the first place. He said that he had tried to kill his stepson. Since he had only been placed on probation, however, it seemed unlikely that that was the offence. (Wainwright was actually in prison for breaching his probation order.) The judge commented that it appeared to be an example of his 'overdramatising'.

He said he had asked to be referred to hospital, telling doctors that he was going to kill himself; but they refused to believe him.

All of this, however, does not even touch on the main reason for scepticism about Wainwright's account, which is that there is no evidence that Wainwright and Park ever met.

The evidence is difficult to pin down because the relevant prison records had been lost. As far as could be ascertained, Wainwright was admitted to Preston Prison on 28 August, and appeared to have spent the first two weeks of his imprisonment there in solitary confinement. Since Park was released on 9 September, 12 days after Wainwright's admission, there would appear to have been scarcely any opportunity for them to have met at all.

Park said he had never seen Wainwright in his life until he walked into the Manchester courtroom to give evidence. The defence QC described him as 'a self-confessed attention-seeking liar'. It is, of course, impossible to say whether Wainwright had been influenced in any way by the £5,000 reward mentioned on the Channel 4 documentary.

When Wainwright gave police the name of Banks, the latter was living in supervised accommodation in Blackburn. Banks and Park certainly had met. They had shared a cell together after Park was remanded into custody and he had helped Banks with day-to-day problems in reading and writing.

On 12 June 2001, the police went see Banks and spoke to him in the presence of two social workers. These two had since married each other. Astonishingly, the wife gave evidence about this in court, but the husband did not. He said he could not remember anything about the interview.

At this stage, Banks appeared to be saying that when Park confessed to him, 'he said he put her down with bricks and a pipe'. No statement was taken, however, in view of Banks' obviously fragile mental health. It was not until 4 April 2002 that he was properly spoken to. The interview was videotaped. These are a few outstanding moments from the transcript:

Banks: They put Gordon Parker in my cell

Q: So this man that you call Gordon ...

Banks: Parker ...

Q: How long was he there?

Banks: I don't know how long it were, but he was in there for a few months.

Q: How long was he actually in with you?

Banks: Ages ... 'cause no one else would have him ... Then he started telling me all sorts ... He's just turned round to say, 'I got arrested for killing my wife' ... He went to Blackpool with his missus, right? ... whilst the kids were asleep at night ... and then when he came back, the kid's woke up ... and said where's his mum? ... and he says, 'Oh,

237

she hasn't come back' ... They had a drink on board on the pub ... on the yacht or something ... and they all went to Blackpool.

Q: Where was this motor boat or yacht?

Banks: I don't know if it was somewhere, er, in the bay.

Q: In the bay at Blackpool?

Banks: No, the boat wasn't at Blackpool.

Q: Where was the boat?

Banks: The boat was actually where the woman got killed ... In the bay, in the docks whatever you call them ... He told me, right, he said some white powder ... he put like a powder, he said he put it in her glass ... which no one could detect ... nobody can trace whatever it was.

Banks seemed to think that Park had poisoned his wife whilst they were on a boat somewhere, and knew that Blackpool was something to do with the story, although he wasn't sure what. He also said that the reason Park and his wife were together was that they were celebrating their fiftieth wedding anniversary.

A psychiatrist said that Banks was highly suggestible; in other words, he would adopt the words and ideas of others. In these circumstances, it was clearly a good idea to videotape the interview in order to allow for some objective assessment of the spontaneity or otherwise of his remarks. However, this aim was undermined by the fact that there were a number of unexplained breaks in the tape.

The psychiatrist added that 'problems with memory function' are a key feature of learning disabilities. There were suggestions that Banks should undergo a fresh psychiatric assessment in order to ascertain his competence to give evidence, but he refused. What is known is that he suffered learning disabilities, and in terms of intelligence was in the lowest two per cent of the population.

Coincidentally, he too appeared not to understand what he was in prison for. When it was put to him that he was in prison because he had been convicted of being equipped for theft, taking a car and burglary, he denied it. The judge commented that Banks 'probably was mistaken or confused about what he was in Preston Prison for'.

The one thing he was certain of was that he'd been on A wing. Except he hadn't; he was on F wing with Park. It was there they'd shared a cell. But Banks was clearly apprehensive about admitting publicly that he'd been on the vulnerable prisoners' wing (which is mostly restricted to sex offenders).

In giving evidence under oath Banks behaved unconscionably. But prisoners like these – like Banks and Wainwright – have been inured by a lifetime of drug dependency and the dehumanising effects of a prison culture to the consequences of their actions. All that matters to them is the shortest of short-term personal benefit. They are beyond the reach of conscience.

Because of Banks' fragile mental state, he gave his evidence by video link from elsewhere in the court building. The judge said that this was to enable him 'to feel more at ease' when giving his evidence. Accordingly, a witness whose evidence was patently fabricated was not only testifying but was mollycoddled and put 'at ease' when doing so; that highlights an almost incredible perversity in the UK's criminal justice process.

THERE WAS ONE particular weakness in Park's defence. When giving evidence to the custody hearing in March 1975, he denied having had an extra-marital liaison himself. It emerged that this was untrue. He had had a brief sexual relationship with Judith Walmsley, the babysitter. As he'd lied on that occasion, the prosecution suggested, his testimony could not be trusted.

Park was very upset by the way the evidence was used against him. There was also, to give a further example, the sailing log. The key question was whether he had had a boat at the time of Carol's disappearance in July 1976. In interview, he said he had sold his boat by then. According to the prosecution, however, his log confirmed that he had sold the boat that very month, so he would have had it at the time.

The defence countered that Park had filled in his log incorrectly. He had a 505, a fast racing dinghy. However, he attended a sailing course on Lake Windermere in May and June. At that time, one of the course instructors made him an offer for the boat which he accepted – so he *had* sold it by the time Carol went missing. The next year, September 1977, belatedly needing to complete the log details in order to qualify for his certificate, he had hazarded a guess and put in the wrong month.

The defence added that both the dates of the course and the fact that Park had sold the boat to a course instructor were confirmed; so the timetable fitted together.

Further, Park himself had volunteered the log. When police searched his home, even though they took boxes and boxes of documents, they had missed the log, not appreciating its significance. So Park had given it to them, because he thought it might be helpful and he wanted to show his willingness to assist the investigation. Would he have done so, the defence asked, if he thought that it was going to undermine his case?

Conversely, they pointed out, if he had murdered his wife, he would have been especially likely, as part of covering his tracks, to suggest he'd got rid of the boat earlier rather than later. He was hardly going to make it look as though he'd had a boat when he hadn't.

And while he was supposedly dumping the body, where were the children? During this time they were being looked after continuously by Park and were not taken elsewhere. How do we know this? *Because there was a missing person's inquiry at the time.* Park was a natural suspect. One of the first questions that police would have asked was: had there been any periods when Park offloaded the three children to family or friends? If there had been, then strong suspicions would have been raised and the inquiry was bound to have taken a very different course.

There is, though, a still more critical point: Park's boat was kept not at Coniston but at Lake Windermere. So, if he had been disposing of a body, then he would logically have done so either where the boat already was (Windermere); or, if he was going to the trouble of moving it, he'd have gone to a remote lake like Wast Water (where Peter Hogg had dumped his wife's body) and certainly not a tourist hotspot like Coniston.

Even if he had still owned the boat, it would have been locked in private premises. Park would have needed to get it out, unrig it, take it on a trailer to Coniston, to one of the only two places from which, at the time, it could have been launched – a boating club and a public jetty – rig the sails, launch it, sail it across the lake for about five miles, dispose of the body, and then do everything in reverse and take the boat back to Windermere. He would have had to do all that single-handedly in full public view at the height of summer without anyone at all noticing.

4

At the time of Carol's disappearance, there were three very important sightings. Firstly, she was seen by a next-door neighbour at the bottom of the drive leading up to the house. They had a brief conversation. Carol said that she was relieved the term was over and was looking forward to the summer holidays. The neighbour thought that this happened on the Saturday morning. (Obviously, the gist of the conversation, slight as it was, means it could not have taken place any earlier as term had only finished the day before.) It means that Carol was still alive after Park and the children had left for Blackpool and was, perhaps, looking out for someone.

Another neighbour saw a car drive up to the house. She did not recognise the man who was driving, although she could see that it was not Gordon Park. The car was a pale blue or grey Volkswagen Beetle (which was the one car model she could confidently identify). She said it was there for around fifteen minutes, and that she was surprised to see it because she knew the family had arranged to go to Blackpool for the day. Asked to time her sighting, she said it would have been sometime during the Saturday morning, lunchtime at the latest.

She was interviewed by police for the 1976 missing person's inquiry and again in the 1997 inquiry, when she made an intriguing comment. She said she was surprised that the police 'seemed to know about it [the car] already'. This could suggest that at this stage the police did have access to the 1976 inquiry.

Thirdly, and most persuasively, a woman who knew Carol saw her at the Charnock Richard southbound service station on the M6 at about six o'clock that Saturday evening. She said that as she went to the ladies' toilets, she saw Carol walking towards her.

Carol, she said, averted her eyes and did not acknowledge her. The witness said she was sure that Carol had seen her. 'Fancy her being stuck-up this far from Barrow', the witness thought to herself.

After seeing Carol's disappearance reported in the local papers, the woman went to the police at the time, in the summer of 1976, to make a statement. At Park's trial, the prosecution recognised that her sighting was fatal for its case, and so attempted to introduce uncertainty into the testimony. The witness knew that the sighting occurred as her own family was heading off on holiday but, on being pressed, stated that her husband could have left work early and so they had perhaps started their holiday on the Friday, the day before. In this way, this solid-gold piece of evidence for the defence was weakened.

However, there was no uncertainty. The original statement was buttressed by documentary evidence, because the husband had marked the Saturday in his diary as the first day of their holiday. In any event, the overwhelming likelihood is that he worked Monday to Friday and started his holiday on the Saturday. Moreover, the Crown should have known that this sighting could not have occurred on the Friday evening, because Carol's whereabouts on the Friday had already been established; she was in Barrow. This critical sighting must have happened on the Saturday.

The three sightings together form a coherent cache of evidence and suggest that Carol was alive after Park and the children had gone to Blackpool, and had made arrangements of her own that weekend.

The plain conclusion is that she was killed by someone else. One immediate suspect was John Rapson, the man who had murdered Christine, Carol's sister. He had, of course, been jailed for life for her murder, but in those days – the criminal justice system had not yet adjusted to the abolition of capital punishment – 'life' was interpreted very leniently. Rapson served a little over six years and was released into hostel accommodation in December 1975.

He is known to have been in Barrow at the time of Carol's disappearance. After his release, he was convicted of sexual assaults on children and imprisoned again. His ex-wife referred in a statement to his hatred for the Prices (Christine and Carol's family).

The fact that he was in the vicinity at the time highlights the illogicality of the CPS case. The Crown sought to draw attention to Park's knot-tying and boating skills, and deemed him a suspect on that basis; and yet excluded this man. Rapson was a local man who had been employed as an apprentice fitter for Vickers, the shipbuilders, in the Barrow shipyards. He would have had those same skills. As a convicted murderer who knew Carol, he should have been the likely suspect; Park, in contrast, was the most unlikely of suspects.

So, in prosecuting Park, the Crown believed that two sisters were both murdered by different men in different incidents. This in itself may seem unlikely, but when it is factored in that this happened in an area hardly known for criminality, at a time when the murder rate was very low, and there was a common factor in the murders – the eyes of both sisters having apparently been taped over – then the odds against this happening do seem to be unusually high. In these circumstances, even discounting all other considerations, it was unethical to put Park on trial unless Rapson could have been entirely excluded as a suspect – and there was no available evidence that he could have been.

Even so, there were other possible suspects. What the Peter Hogg case had shown was that anyone wishing to dispose of a body in the Lake District needed neither a boat nor particular local knowledge; just common sense and a small inflatable dinghy.

Roger Mitton, Park's friend from schooldays, was by this time a senior reporter, working in the United States as Washington bureau chief for a Far East newspaper.

'As anyone familiar with the case should know, there are many plausible suspects because Carol had a number of affairs', he said. 'I know from first-hand the way that Carol would indicate that she was sexually available. She was a woman who inspired high passions and unpredictable emotions, and who betrayed trusts.'

The defence did have a statement from one man who said that he had slept with her and knew several others who had done so. Three of those he named were local police officers.

A TRIAL IS ALWAYS an unequal battle. The prosecution has ample resources and vast powers; the defence has scant resources and no power. In this case, moreover, several matters additionally benefited the Crown cause. Foremost among these was the fact that it is difficult for anyone to defend themselves against something they are meant to have done twenty-eight years earlier.

There had been a contemporaneous inquiry into Carol's disappearance in 1976. Park had complained at the time that for weeks on end the police 'crawled all over my life'. So where was the documentation from that inquiry? Barrow police had lost it all – or should that be, 'lost' it all?

Obviously, missing person inquiries are considered to be still current while the person has not been traced. Consequently, the material ought not to have been destroyed. Jeremy Park attempted to trace what had happened and discovered about twenty police statements relating to its disappearance, all made in the period from 1997 to 2004. What is interesting is that one of the officers who had possession of the file was one of the officers with whom Carol had had an affair more than twenty years earlier.

'The file did exist until relatively recently', asserted Jeremy Park, 'and somebody has got rid of it, possibly someone who was involved with my Mum.'

There appears to have been nothing in that 1976 inquiry to implicate Park in his wife's murder. In 2004, his defence was seriously compromised by its unavailability. Its disappearance was so seriously irregular that the CPS should never have considered prosecuting him without it.

Nor was this all that was missing. The prison records for Wainwright and Banks had also disappeared. There were those gaps in the videotaped interview of Banks. The defence argument was that, during those gaps, Banks was being given what he termed as a 'bollocking' for not getting his story straight. We cannot speculate but what we do know is that, just as with the infamous gaps in US President Richard Nixon's Watergate tapes, missing parts undermine the integrity of the whole.

There was also another serious irregularity. In his summing-up, the judge made two references to the fact that as part of their analysis of the case the jurors would wish to take into account 'the evidence of your own eyes when you went to Coniston'.

Unfortunately, the wool was pulled over jurors' eyes. On 11 January 2005, as part of the trial, they were taken in a minibus to see the locations, including Bluestones and the parts of the lake where the body was found and where Mrs Young said she saw someone tipping a bundle overboard. This trip from Manchester to the Lake District greatly perturbed the defence team. Normally, anyone making that journey would come off the motorway on to the A6, turn on to the A590 and then the A5092 and, where that road forks, take the A5084 to reach the lake. That is the natural route; main roads all the way.

However, the minibus and the small convoy, carrying court officials, did not travel the natural route. The convoy firstly made an unnecessary detour east of the A5092 to go through small villages. Then, it returned to the A5092, but went straight past the fork with the A5084 (clearly signposted to Coniston) and so was then travelling away from Coniston. It left the main road to turn down a single-track country lane which passed between farm buildings. At one point, the track was so narrow that the hedgerows on either side were scratching the mini-coach's wing mirrors. The little convoy went down other little-used country lanes before reaching the A5084 and, finally, taking the road to Coniston.

It was a completely irrational route. So why had the valuable time of the judge, lawyers and court officials, not to mention the jurors, been wasted in taking them by the scenic route?

The defence believe that the journey was devised with the intention of giving the judge and jurors the impression that these locations were somehow remote and therefore would only have been known to a local man. But they weren't remote at all. The judge and the jurors were literally misled.

The matter immediately became a source of controversy but, giving evidence on oath, police officers denied that the route was an artificial one.

Another huge bone of contention at trial concerned a sum of £50,000, which was paid by the *Mail on Sunday* for the interview with Gordon and Jenny Park which appeared in the paper on 18

January 1998 after the murder charge was dropped. The judge had directed counsel that this should not be mentioned – clearly, it was not relevant to the case but was potentially highly prejudicial. It may have suggested that Park not only killed his wife but compounded the crime by benefiting financially from it.

Despite the judge's direction, however, this was mentioned. In cross-examining Jenny Park, the Crown barrister asked, 'So what about this £50,000 then?'

As with other aspects of this case, the jurors were then left with a false impression. The actual situation was this: firstly, the family had not received £50,000. They were naive, as anyone in that position is bound to be. The person who advised on and negotiated the deal had cut themselves in with a whopping 25% agent's fee. So the amount the family received was not £50,000, but £37,500.

Secondly, Gordon and Jenny had only done the interview with the utmost reluctance. They loathed the UK press and regarded any money accruing from it as tainted. So they bought a new car (their old one having all but expired after Jenny's long drives to see her husband when the bail conditions forced him to live away from home) and gave away the rest to family members.

After the £50,000 sum was brought up in court contrary to instructions, the judge told Park that he would consent to the abandonment of the trial and the empanelling of a fresh jury if Park wished. Of course, he had no desire to begin such a difficult and stressful exercise over again. So the trial continued.

AFTER BEING SENT OUT to consider their verdict, the jurors returned to ask a question about the analysis of hairs from a hairbrush recovered from the bed of Coniston. This had been alluded to in the closing speeches, but was not mentioned in evidence. So, the jury naturally wanted to know, what was the evidence?

The position, it emerged, was this: the evidence should have been read out in court as part of an agreed statement, but had not been. There then followed one of those episodes characteristic of English courtrooms, when the judge and counsel dug out all the authorities they could find to try to resolve whether or not they were permitted to allow the jurors to hear previously unheard evidence after their retirement.

What, first of all, was this evidence? It was a statement by a forensic scientist. In the jury's absence, judge and counsel read out for themselves:

> Several hairs were recovered from the hairbrush and the brush. These hairs do not match any of the hairs in the control sample relating to Carol Park and hence they are likely to have originated from her.

The judge was bewildered and said, 'It sounds as though it ought to be the opposite'.

Indeed it did. Clearly, the statement was written wrongly. It should have been 'unlikely', not 'likely'. A sloppy error. Nor was there just the one. The judge commented, 'It looks as though there is a further infelicity, because there is a reference to two brushes whereas I am sure that the witness probably only meant to refer to one'.

Eventually, the Court decided, on the basis of some authority or other, that what it deemed was the correct version of the statement could be read out to the jury.

This episode illustrated a number of salient features about courtroom practice. Most importantly, it showed admirable concentration on behalf of the jurors. Secondly, it said much about the lack of care with which cases are put together; important statements like the forensic scientist's may contain what are effectively schoolboy howlers. Thirdly, in the courtroom fastidious care was devoted to determining the admissibility of this entirely irrelevant evidence; conversely, little, it seems, was given to the truly devastating evidence, just about all of which – the jailhouse snitches, the eyewitness, the rock, the slate, the knots – would, if standards as rigorous as those prevailing at the end had been applied earlier, have been excluded. There would then have been nothing left.

Care had been taken with the evidence; that much is certainly true. However, the care had been expended on presentation rather than content. There was, in this trial, a great deal of geological evidence about the rock, and much psychiatric evidence about Banks, and such an impressive computer presentation about the parcel on the lake bed and the state of decomposition of the body, that anyone might have been fooled. Though paying close attention, the jurors could easily have been thrown off the scent. They may have thought to themselves: would the CPS have gone to all this trouble if they didn't know, albeit in some way that they can't tell us about, that Park was guilty? One can see how it is possible to hoodwink the court. As the prosecution laid out its evidence, with the stylish computerisations, the jurors should have realised that they were being asked to admire the emperor's new clothes.

On the other hand, pieces of evidence that really did matter didn't feature in the trial at all. There was a human hair in the body package that did not belong to Carol, or to Park, or to any family members. Whose was it? It was not identified. It could have been the murderer's. The jurors weren't told about that.

At 3.45 on the afternoon of Friday 28 January 2005, they found Park guilty of murder and he was sentenced to life imprisonment.

'Did I want to find out who killed my mother?', said Rachael, rhetorically. 'Yes, absolutely. Was there any possibility of ever finding out? Realistically, probably not. It seemed to all of us that the authorities had no interest in finding out who killed my mother; it was just a matter of framing my Dad.'

5

THOSE WHO KNEW HIM said that Park was kind and compassionate. 'He could have his off-days', said one neighbour, 'though there was nothing very serious even about those'. The surviving medical reports showed that Carol had specifically told doctors (even in circumstances where it would have been advantageous for her to exaggerate marital discord) that Park was never violent towards her, and had not even threatened violence. The judge referred to his 'non-violent nature'.

During the trial, Park had stayed in Manchester with Pastor George Harrison, of the Pendlebury Evangelical Church. They hadn't previously met, but Harrison's son taught at the same school as Jenny Park. 'He was a delight to have around the house', said Harrison. 'He didn't have an aggressive bone in his body.'

Park considered himself a practising Christian, though he believed that what was truly important was to live life according to Christian precepts. For more than a quarter of a century, he had donated to two charities World Vision and Save the Children through standing orders at his bank, and since 1979 had supported two boys in India in their training to become Buddhist monks. He was interested in Buddhist philosophies. At one point there was concern about a cardboard box taken from his house. It contained papers and tape-recordings of Buddhist teachings. His concern was merely that the police should not lose it, bearing in mind that a number of his possessions had been seized but never returned.

The prosecution understood neither his Christian outlook nor his forbearance. Carol was strikingly attractive, high-spirited and socially adept but she must also have been maddening. Wouldn't her infidelities and intermittent disappearing acts have made life utterly miserable for him at times? Why, prosecution lawyers wanted to know, would he have put up with so much from her?

'If you knew this girl', he told them, 'you could forgive her'.

In her absence, he just carried on raising his family. 'The care and stability of my children', he wrote, 'has always been my first concern'.

Such was Park's character, but nothing of that was ever reported. What was evident about the case was that the prosecution appeared to be guided not by the evidence but by the media myth. From the moment that Park was in France when the body was discovered, a story developed around him, with a myriad of enticing narrative details: *he had murdered his wife and put her in a baby-doll nightie (obviously a sex fiend), and then trussed up the body and gone out in his boat to dump the body. Now he had fled the country (obviously a fugitive from justice), with his third wife (definitely a sex fiend).* The story could be neatly fitted into one of the media's standard formats. They had a neat title, too, one they'd had for at least fifty years: the lady in the lake. So the story took outline shape in the papers and was then fleshed out in the BBC drama series and the Channel 4 and ITV documentaries. It was entirely untrue.

In 2004 the CPS, having originally reached the correct decision six years earlier, fatally reconsidered. And what was the basis on which it reversed its decision? What new evidence had emerged in the meantime? There was just the execrable evidence of the jail-house snitches and the rock.

When I produced television documentaries and we needed to illustrate the failings of nameless bureaucrats, we'd put in shots of the office blocks where they worked. We'd privately term these 'guilty buildings' shots. In this instance, the guilty building was Furness House in The Mall in Barrow, then the local base of the Crown Prosecution Service, from where the go-ahead for this iniquitous prosecution was given.

The fact that it led to a conviction does not vindicate the decision to press charges, but instead underlines the folly of prosecution. In this case, Park faced a media-made mountain of prejudice and hostility. There was a public presumption of guilt. He was never going to get a fair trial and should never have been exposed to danger. It was precisely to safeguard against such eventualities – to prevent innocent citizens being railroaded to trial – that the CPS was set up. In this instance, its failure to fulfil its *raison d'etre* was absolute.

AFTER THE CONVICTION, Park was sent to Manchester Prison. The family visited regularly, but visiting arrangements are inevitably stressful for everyone.

'We didn't talk about the case much in the visits', said Jeremy. 'He was just in shock and couldn't really discuss it.

'He put a lot of effort into making the visits pleasant for the people who came. He would spend the time joking and laughing, just trying to have a warm, normal relationship with us. That must have been hard for him. Sometimes you could see he was just numb with boredom, frustration and anger. It was just heartbreaking, and sometimes you came out of there sobbing.'

With the conviction, the whole family felt great unease.

'If they've convicted my Dad', explained Jeremy, 'then I'm the son of a murderer, Rachael's the daughter of a murderer and Jenny's married to a murderer. That changes all of us. It blights the family for generations.

'In spite of all the evidence that he's a good man, and all the lovely things he's done, and there's no genuine evidence that he's ever done anything bad, nobody believes us. So because you're not being believed, your behaviour changes. I've now got a security camera outside the house. If someone says, "You did such-and-such on this day", I can say, "No, I didn't, there's the proof". I've got some means of proving what I was doing at the time.

'That's the paranoia that stems from the trial and the investigation. It's a symptom of being wrongly accused and knowing that in some Kafkaesque way, the whole family is accountable to a court.'

Park lodged an official complaint with Cumbria police about their handling of the case. They ignored it, so Park then appealed to the Independent Police Complaints Commission (IPCC). They upheld the appeal and concluded there were four specific areas of complaint that Cumbria police should have registered and dealt with: that the original missing person file, the absence of which compromised Park's defence, was lost; that police officers, including one senior officer, lied under oath about the route by which the jurors were taken to the scene; that police officers improperly 'coached' witnesses (the IPCC put the word in quotes); and that exhibits from the lake bed (in particular, the rock) were not logged and recorded properly.

The upshot was that Cumbria police managed to get Park's complaint struck out on the grounds that it was out of time.

'It was difficult to organise a campaign', Jeremy reflected. 'There was loads of support, but people had different ideas about how to take the case forward. Some friends were so angry they just wanted to batter those they held responsible locally. Meanwhile, our solicitor had no funding for the case for the first year, so he was doing all his work on it in the evenings.'

Nevertheless, the campaign that they organised for Park did attract attention and was supported by, among others, the veteran Labour party politician Tony Benn.

'Five years on, we were all still writing', said Rachael, 'everyone was still very supportive. After all, writing is the only link. He loved

251

the letters, and would deliberately save them up to read at the weekends, when there are longer lock-ins.'

On 22 September 2008, Michael Wainwright, the first jailhouse snitch, made a fresh statement. He said that two police officers, whom he named:

> ... did put words into my mouth regarding Gordon Park ... They bought me drinks ... On the day of the trial they picked me up and took me to Manchester and paid for a night in the Britannia hotel ... I can say that the police told me what to say in court.

In a separate case Gill Beckingham, design services manager for Barrow Borough Council, was prosecuted for manslaughter after seven people died from legionnaires' disease. At the end of proceedings, one juror (who happened to be a former police officer) made an official complaint about the behaviour of two men who sat in the public gallery, in full view of the jury, and by means of gestures and mannerisms openly disparaged evidence that assisted the defence. The judge had them thrown out of court, saying, 'I've never seen such disgraceful behaviour in a courtroom'.

As a result of the juror's complaint, the men were named. They were police officers – the same two officers whom Wainwright had named.

Park's case took three years to get to appeal. When it did reach the courts, in November 2008, the three judges accepted fresh geological evidence about the rock, which thereby rendered the whole area of evidence about the rock and the bundle of clothes null and void. This was interesting because it left the evidence of the jailhouse snitches as the solitary reason why the CPS had taken the case to trial at all.

The judges said they were 'unpersuaded that the evidence about the rock was a crucial part of the Crown's case at trial'. They felt that the jury would have found it 'very difficult to [draw] conclusions from this area of evidence'. (Of course, this raised the question of why the trial judge had allowed the evidence to remain in the case at all.)

Overall, however, the appeal court judges concluded that there was a 'strong circumstantial case' against Park. The first point they mentioned in this regard was 'motive arising from the established evidence of past marital disharmony'. The rationale for this comment appeared to be that, wherever there was marital discord, there was a possibility that the husband would murder the wife – the most unfeasible of propositions. In any case, the judges had overlooked the key evidence of Carol herself, that Park had never even threatened violence towards her.

On the basis of the 'strong circumstantial case', however, the judges refused Park's appeal. It was another huge setback for him; even after all that had happened, he had still been placing trust in the system.

'We were all there at the courts in the Strand', recalled Jeremy. 'Jenny telephoned the prison and told him. It was a really horrible moment, he was sobbing down the phone.

'It absolutely crushed him.'

In Manchester Prison, Park had received regular pastoral visits from George Harrison. However, in September 2007 he had been transferred to HMP Garth, near Leyland, Lancashire, and the prison stopped these visits. Harrison contacted his MP and, after a while, they resumed but they were discontinued again in December 2009. It was difficult for anyone to perceive the sense in this.

'He's entitled to visits from his nominated pastor', explained Harrison. 'It doesn't cost the prison anything.'

When he requested an explanation from the prison, the Head of Security responded that the visits were redundant 'as the prison is capable of meeting Mr Park's spiritual needs'.

Rachael and her family came over from China to visit. Sadly, that merely led to another blow. On that occasion, the family didn't pass the prison's sniffer dog test. Dogs sniff incoming visitors. If they sit down, then the assumption is that the visitor has been in contact with drugs. Consequently, the visit must be a closed one; there is a glass screen between prisoner and visitors, and no physical contact between them. The sniffer dog test is essentially pointless: visitors are searched for drugs anyway (and, although drugs are in all prisons, they arrive there by other means); generally the dogs will be reacting to natural, ambient smells; and sometimes they're just wrong. But the prison rules are implacably enforced, even for a family that has come all the way from China.

'Dad was devastated that the visit had to take place in these conditions', Rachael recalled. 'The visiting time was much shorter. Then, we were all just sitting at what are opposite sides of a long counter with a glass partition. The acoustics are terrible, there are prison doors slamming. Conversation is difficult and the chances of a normal conversation are nil.

'So it was really distressing. That was the last time I saw him.'

'By the end, he was like Job, railing against the injustices he'd suffered', said Jeremy. 'He knew that he was being punished for something he hadn't done. But by then, he had no faith in the system which had betrayed him so much already.

'He was an outdoor man. He used to roam all over the Lake District. He'd sail to Walney Island and across the Lune estuary. He'd go camping, walking, mountaineering. Prison was intolerable for him. It was torture. He used to lie in his cell and listen to music and imagine that he was outside somewhere, walking the fells, listening to the birds.'

On 24 January 2010, Jenny had an almost unbearable conversation with her husband, who was crying down the phone. The next morning, he was found hanged in his cell. It was his sixty-sixth birthday.

AS IS CUSTOMARY in these circumstances, various reports were then drawn up by various officials who exonerated each other of blame. One concluded that, 'the prison did not manage the [matter] of the pastoral visits well', but that was as stringent as the criticism got.

'After five years, he just couldn't survive in there anymore', Jeremy reflected. 'He just couldn't take the pain anymore. I think part of his motivation was that it was just two fingers to the judicial system – he thought he'd rather die than serve another ten years in there to satisfy their corrupt system.

'But mainly I think he just wanted to take the onus off all of us working on the case and supporting him. He knew that it wasn't just his own life, it was taking up years of our lives too. Every minute he was in there we were thinking about him. He knew that was a drain on us. He didn't want us to suffer any more. He didn't want Jenny to suffer any more, I'm sure he wanted to take the pressure off her specifically.'

'Everyone was still very supportive', explained Rachael. 'That year, he'd got more than a hundred Christmas cards. He would probably have got the same number of birthday cards, but I don't suppose he ever saw them.

'It's so hard to see someone go through so much pain and be powerless against this system.

'At the end, I wasn't able to take him in my arms and give him a big hug and say how much I loved him, but he knew, I'm sure he knew. That's the only thing that gives me a tiny bit of peace. I think when he did it he knew how much we all loved him, and how much everyone loved him.'

Chapter 7

A man of proper good character

George Robinson's story

1

On 16 November 2002, at six minutes past two on a Saturday lunchtime, taxi-driver George Robinson picked up a disabled woman. He was to take her the short distance from her own home in Blyth, Northumberland to her boyfriend's house.

The woman, Hayley Fearney, was in a wheelchair, so he went slowly. The journey took twenty-one minutes and the fare was £5.30p. As Robinson helped her out of his cab, the boyfriend came out to welcome her. He gave Robinson six pounds and told him to keep the change.

Robinson's takings were shared with the taxi company he worked for – Phoenix Taxis – so he took home three pounds from that fare. His profit, after paying for petrol and the costs of car maintenance, would be negligible. The cost to him, however, was to be incalculable.

That afternoon, someone called the taxi firm on Fearney's behalf. The caller said that during the journey Robinson had asked her 'to lift up her top so that he could see her tits'. The caller twice asked how much compensation Fearney was going to get. The taxi company correctly said that any complaints of that kind should be made direct to police. So, someone then phoned the police station for her. However, the complaint was now a different one. During the journey, the caller said, Robinson had stopped and raped Fearney in the back of the cab.

An hour or so later, there was another call to Phoenix on Fearney's behalf, this time to book a cab for her for the following day.

As a consequence of the rape allegation, Robinson, a fifty-six-year-old grandfather, was prosecuted, convicted, sent to prison for nine years and put on the sex offenders register for life. It was just one short journey from which he had made almost nothing, but it had ruined his life.

ROBINSON was born on 7 February 1947. His parents were Arthur and Rene. He grew up, matured, and indeed has spent his entire life in Blyth, just as countless generations of his family had before him. His first home was one of the prefabs that were put up as short-term accommodation to meet the post-war housing crisis.

As a child in the early 1950s – days when children played naturally in the streets and in the countryside, and which many who remember them today would think of as halcyon – Robinson got into all the usual childhood scrapes, which could have proved fatal on a couple of occasions.

'In those days, cars were few and far between up here', he recalled. 'Only doctors and solicitors had cars.

'One day, a car arrived in the street. It was an Austin Somerset, the doctor's. As soon as we saw it, we were all over it. It was great fun.

'I clambered on to the back. I was holding this T-handle, which opened the boot. Suddenly the doctor got in and started the engine. Everybody scattered, but I was too small. I couldn't get down. The car moved off with me holding on. I saw us going past our prefab. I was just thinking, he can't take us away from my Mammy, I've got to let go.

'I landed on one of the cast-iron drain covers. The doctor just drove on, he didn't know a kid had fallen off the back of his car.

'My Mam had seen it all happen. A few neighbours saw it too, and they all came rushing out. They bathed us, I was screaming my head off.

'I hadn't broken any bones, but I had Blyth Corporation marks printed on my knees. They took years to fade away.

'Another time, I think I was eight, I nearly drowned. I was fishing with a net in the River Coquet at Rothbury. I stood on this stone and slipped and the next thing I was under the water. It was sheer luck that my cousin Tom, who was much older than me, was there with me. According to him, I'd gone under twice before I was able to grab his fishing-rod and he could pull us out.'

With their roots so firmly embedded in the local community, all of the Robinsons were passionate supporters of the local football club, Blyth Spartans, one of the most enduringly reputable of non-league teams. Home games were played at Croft Park, in the centre of town. Robinson's maternal grandfather, Robert, arrived home on weekend leave at Saturday lunchtime in the early days of the First World War. Competitive matches were still being played and no sooner had he arrived than he was off again.

'Susan, I'm just going to pop down and watch Spartans', he called to his wife.

Susan was working at the poss tub in the backyard. Washdays in that era must have been hard work. The water had to be ladled into a big drum which was heated by a fire underneath. When it was boiling, the clothes were put in together with carbolic soap, and then they were swirled around with a heavy poss stick. She threw a bowl of water over the fire.

'Hang on', she called back, 'I'm comin' wi' ye.'

They went out to the game together. The family remember the occasion because it was to be one of the last, if not the very last, game that he attended. He was among the one-and-a-half million soldiers killed at the Battle of the Somme in 1916. Rene, Robinson's mother, was born shortly afterwards, and so never saw her father.

Forty years later, Robinson's family were still dutifully attending all of Blyth's home games. Come hail, rain or snow, his paternal grandfather, who was also George Robinson, never missed a match. He was well-known and much-respected in the locality – like some other men of that generation, he prided himself on never having sworn – and worked as a master blacksmith on the quayside at Blyth docks.

'By this time', recalled Robinson of his grandad, 'he was long retired and would have been in his early eighties. He liked to sit in the stands, near the halfway line. Me Dad and me Uncle Joe stood behind the Kingsway Terrace goal. One Saturday in 1956, they were watching a match when the referee blew his whistle and stopped the game. He beckoned towards the dressing-rooms. My Dad and my uncle then saw this stretcher being taken directly across the pitch and into the crowd.

'"Someone's taken bad", they were saying to each other.

'Then one of the staff came through the crowd to find them.

'"Arthur, Joe, you'd better get to the dressing-rooms, your Dad's collapsed."

'They reached the dressing-room and found them trying to resuscitate him. A few minutes later, he died. He'd suffered a massive coronary.

'Dad and Uncle Joe walked back, and me Gran said, "Where's your Dad?" They just looked at her. She was a very dignified lady. As I understand it, she walked into her bedroom and closed the door.

'I remember me Dad coming home that night. He couldn't speak, it just broke his heart. I only saw him cry twice – that was one time; the other was not long afterwards, when it came on the news about the Manchester United air crash at Munich in 1958. It was just the thought of all those young players dying.'

When he was 15, in 1962, Robinson left school and found a job with Co-operative Dairies. The CWS (Co-operative Wholesale Society), known as the Co-op, traced its roots back to 1844 in Rochdale when weavers and other skilled workers allied together in a socialist undertaking to share the profits of the stores on which the workers relied for their daily needs. It had been a pivotal moment in the history of the Labour movement in Britain. At the time when Robinson was taken on, the Co-op was one of the major employers in the north of England.

He joined the union, USDAW (the Union of Shop, Distributive and Allied Workers). He'd have joined anyway, though in fact he had no choice. USDAW had a closed shop agreement with the employers, the CWS; jobs were only available to those who were, or became, members of the union.

Robinson met his wife Sylvia on holiday at Butlin's in Filey. She came from Chester-le-Street in Durham, but was happy to move the twenty miles north to ensure that the family traditions were perpetuated. They were married in St Cuthbert's Church in Blyth and had three children: Malcolm, Susan and Andrea.

He became a driver and got his HGV licence. He also became a union official and was formally elected as shop steward. He was based at Northumbria House, the major department store in Blyth.

He was also in charge of all the satellite shops – at that time, there were a dozen or more small grocery shops in the area.

'It was handy, being a driver', Robinson recalled. 'If anyone phoned in wanting a union rep, there'd be a message sent straight down to me and if I got a phone call, so-and-so wants to see you, I could nip down and see them.'

Most of his tasks were political in the broadest sense: just sorting out flare-ups or minor disputes, sometimes between employees, sometimes between the workforce and management. Once, a young recruit was sacked for using foul language to a female employee. Robinson was called in. How about, he suggested to the manager, if the lad makes a public apology to the woman in front of the staff? Everyone acceded to that, though the errant youth was not happy.

'If you let your pride stand in the way', Robinson told him privately, 'you're out that door. Summary dismissal. I can't do anything about that. But if you go in now in front of the staff and apologise to her, you'll keep your job. The choice is yours.'

So he kept his job, and was grateful afterwards.

'Thanks for comin' up, like', he said.

'Ay, just keep your language to yourself', Robinson advised.

So Robinson became well-known throughout the area. Colleagues tended to call him 'Bingo' – because he had a second job, working at the local bingo hall in the evenings. But, even as his union responsibilities increased, he fitted it all in. Every year he attended the Trades Union Congress annual conference, and he also became president of Blyth and District Trades Council, a body on which the different unions of the area were represented. Through that, he got to know a representative of the National Union of Mineworkers, Ronnie Campbell, who would later become MP for Blyth Valley.

In 1975, Robinson became an overnight hero. There had been a number of robberies of security vans in London, so the Co-op recognised that they needed to reorganise their own security. Being thrifty (to put it politely) and with the intention of cutting as many corners as they could (not to put it politely), they decided to do things their way.

'They got one of the vans from the transport department, an

263

Austin A55', said Robinson. 'Then they got a craftsman in the garage – because there were some good lads up there – to devise a lock for the back door that was worked by a switch from the cab. He did it really well. It was foolproof. No way could you pull the doors open.'

Robinson was told he'd be driving the van, with an older man, Jack, as his mate.

'They just said, "We've got a job for you". It was a full-time, six-days-a-week job. There was no training for us, and certainly no salary increase.

'We used to pick up all the takings from the satellite shops – Wallsend, North Shields, Newbiggin, all round – and take them into the office, then we'd pick up the full amount and take it to the bank.

'One day I went through the shop in North Shields upstairs to the office. They gave me the bag with the takings. It was an old-fashioned doctor's bag and it was chained to my wrist.

'I went downstairs, but the moment I walked outside there was an almighty screech of tyres. Jack screamed at me, "Get back in, it's a raid". He ducked down behind a car.

'It happened so fast. This guy chased us back into the shop, with an iron bar in his hand. You had to go virtually to the back of the shop to get to the stairs. So he chased us through the shop, past the washers [washing-machines] and that. I was just screaming, "Get the police!"

'The gang were in a Ford Transit that they'd stolen. They were trying to open the back doors – because they were trying to open both together, they were locking. Of course, with Transits, you have to open one and then the other. They were reversing down Bedford Street, but the kerbs are very high, so they scraped the van on the kerb. That, and trying to get the doors open, gave me the few hundredths of a second I needed.

'I didn't realise at the time, but I went up the stairs three at a time. The one thing that was going through my mind was, I can't let them catch us, because the only way of getting that bag off my arm that I could think of, was to chop my hand off. That thought was what propelled me up the stairs that fast.

'Upstairs, they'd heard the commotion and opened the doors. Solid oak doors. I rushed straight through and they slammed the door shut. In fact, when I started going up the stairs, he gave up, but I didn't know that, I wasn't looking. I was focused on one thing: getting through that office door.

'The police were there within a couple of minutes – the place was crawling with police. They found the Transit on the quayside. They must have got away in another car.

'An inspector came in. I was shaking, really shaking. They gave us a cup of tea with some whisky in it. The gang members were never caught.'

A couple of days later, Robinson and Jack were summoned to the manager's office.

'"You did a good job there, lads", the head manager said to us. "There was £25,000 in the bag. In recognition of the good work you did, we'd like to give you something."

'He passed across two white envelopes. We both opened them. There was a ten pound note in.

'Jack was really angry. He said, "Look, son" – he was actually much older than the manager – "the Co-op needs that more than I do. You can find someone else to risk their neck for you, 'cos I'm not risking mine for ten pound". And he threw it back across the desk at him.'

Robinson was taken aback. 'Sylvia and I could really have done with that ten pounds, but I felt I had to follow him. "The same goes for me", I said, "I'll go back on the trucks".'

The internal security job disappeared. The Co-op went back to its old system of using an outside firm.

'It was a frightening experience', said Robinson. 'I got this rash, skin blemishes – I still get it today whenever I get stressed. That was when it started. The doctor said, it's the anxiety. But that was 1975 and it's still happening today.'

Five years later, after a fire in one of its stores, the Co-op decided to hold a fire damage sale. The date was fixed for Monday 5 May, which was the May Day public holiday. The USDAW committee was not happy that its employees might feel under obligation to work on a bank holiday and decided to withdraw membership from anyone who volunteered for work – which, because of the closed shop agreement, would mean they'd lose their jobs. As a result, those who had initially volunteered withdrew their offers to work.

At this time, Margaret Thatcher had been prime minister for almost exactly a year and the map of industrial relations in Britain was being redrawn. Trade union members were no longer patriotic workers who were seeking their just entitlements and asking to be part of the discourse in industry; they were soon to become 'the enemy within'. The Co-op, notwithstanding its history as a stanchion of the labour movement, was among the first organisations to take advantage of this changed landscape.

A week later, when Robinson finished his deliveries, a washing-machine remained on his van. He hadn't been able to deliver it; the customers weren't in and, as it was after five-thirty on a Saturday evening, the shop was closed. So, as normal, he parked the van in the Co-op compound with the washing-machine still inside, locking both the van and the outside gates.

When he returned to work after the weekend, he was told that the manager wanted to see him. The washing-machine had supposedly disappeared.

'I've got instructions from head office to suspend you', he was told.

Robinson was amazed.

'Do you really think I've pinched it, like?' he asked.

Clearly, the manager, whom Robinson knew well, didn't actually think that, but he reiterated, 'Well, I've just been told to suspend you'.

As chairman of the local branch, Robinson was allowed a union representative from regional head office. He told Robinson that all the committee members involved in the May Day bank holiday dispute were being targeted; all were being accused of a variety of offences that warranted instant dismissal.

The union rep asked Robinson whether, even though he had nothing to do with its disappearance, he would be prepared to pay the cost of the washing-machine. This would have been money that Robinson could ill afford, but he offered that.

'He didn't take it', the rep told the managers, 'but if it will save his job, he's prepared to pay for the cost of the washer, so the Co-op doesn't lose over it.'

'Their faces dropped. They weren't expecting this. They told us to wait outside. They called us back in and said, "No, we've discussed that, it's not satisfactory. We've decided to summarily dismiss you".'

So the Co-op managed to inflict serious damage on the union by ridding itself of the activists who'd tried to block their plans for a special sale on May Day bank holiday. In the event, Robinson was not summarily dismissed. He got full severance pay – a tacit acknowledgment that the grounds for his dismissal were bogus.

Nevertheless, this led to a wretched period for him. As well as losing his job, he and Sylvia lost their home. They'd always lived in rented accommodation but had been encouraged to buy in consequence of the right-to-buy policy that was another aspect of the Thatcher revolution. Unfortunately, they overstretched themselves and, with the combination of Robinson having lost his job, at a time of rising interest rates, could not meet their payments.

At the time, they were with Northern Rock, the building society that in 2008 would be held responsible for having triggered the banking crisis in the UK economy. Robinson feels nothing but gratitude towards them.

'They were very good, they tried all ways to help us', said Robinson. 'It was traumatic because we loved the house'.

The family moved back into rented accommodation, which is where they still are today.

Robinson worked at a centre for disabled people, at Hepscott Park, before being offered a job at The Mount, an old people's home on the outskirts of Morpeth run by Northumberland Council. For more than seven years he worked there as a care assistant, driver and handyman. He was then employed by Blyth Disabled Forum for a couple of years before, in 1999, taking a job with Phoenix Taxis.

2

Everything went smoothly until, in March 2002, he went to see his doctor. He had suffered dizzy spells and also was worried about his sexual potency. He was diagnosed as diabetic and treated for that. The doctor prescribed a medicinal cream to treat his erectile dysfunction, though it had no effect.

Robinson didn't usually work weekends, but had agreed to work that Saturday, the 16th of November, because of increased demand in the build-up towards Christmas. He was on the early shift. As he drove in to the offices at 6.00am, he saw a black cab parked outside.

'What's 101 doing outside?' he asked.

'Mark's phoned in sick', replied the office manager.

The company only had four black cabs altogether, and this one was available because of a colleague's illness. Robinson took it instead of his own vehicle.

'It was more spacious and had a wide door', he said, 'you can fit buggies in, you're going to make more money.

'That's how fate dealt its hand. If Mark hadn't been sick, he'd have been in his cab and I'd have been in my own car.'

It was just before 2.00pm that Robinson received the call to pick up Hayley Fearney. As he was aware, she was in a wheelchair and suffered from a serious illness. The Robinsons knew of the woman. Susan, their eldest child, recalled helping her older sister to bath Hayley when she was a young child. Robinson said he had carried her three or four times before in his cab. Although Fearney would dispute this, her mother also thought that Hayley had been picked up by him before.

He went round to her house, and picked her up at 2.06.

This is his account of what happened:

'She had her vanity bag. I remember her Mam said, "Don't drop that" – I forget what it was but there was something breakable in it – I made some remark, like, "I'll see to that for you". I pushed her round, lowered the ramp and put her in the taxi. Fitting the wheelchair in was not easy. When I put her in the taxi, she was facing the offside, though I put the wheelchair in at a slight angle, diagonally, just for stability.

'I put the brake on the right-hand side, leaned over and put the brake on the left-hand side. I took her bag and put it on the floor. As I came up, my eye caught the sight of the hair across the mouth, stuck there with saliva. I said, "Lass, you've got some hair stuck there", and I just wiped it away for her. I backed out of the taxi.

'With all the exertion of arranging her in the wheelchair in the back, my underwear had ridden up on us. It's unpleasant, I know, but I had on elasticated trousers and I just pushed my hand down and adjusted my underwear to make myself comfortable for driving. I got in and drove off.'

He took her the way all other taxi-drivers would have taken her. This was not the most direct route. Adding a small loop was standard professional practice. After all, Robinson's return from this would be only £2.65p. If he was going to make any less, it was uneconomic to do the job at all.

She was not wearing a car seat-belt. She held on to the strap by the door in the car. However, she was held in to her wheelchair by a lap-strap. Along the way, she complained more than once that the end of this had become trapped in the wheels of the wheelchair. So Robinson stopped the cab and went into the back and disentangled it for her.

When they arrived at her boyfriend's, he went round to the back passenger door and wheeled her out. Her boyfriend came out of the house. Robinson stopped the meter at 2.27pm. The fare came to £5.30p. The boyfriend gave Robinson £6.00 and told him to keep the change.

'That's it', Robinson said. 'That's what happened.'

He then took another call and drove a woman home from the Co-op supermarket. After that, he received a 10-3 over his intercom: that means return to base straight away.

WHEN HE GOT BACK, the manager, Michael McPake, was standing outside. He walked straight up to Robinson.

'We've had a complaint against you', he said.

The complaint at this point was the original one: that Robinson had asked Hayley to lift her top up. It was the first that McPake had ever received about Robinson, whom he described as 'flabbergasted'. Robinson's instinctive reaction was to imagine there had been some misunderstanding. He drove back to the boyfriend's house and knocked on the door. There was no reply. (In fact, by then they had all gone back to Hayley's own house.)

Robinson was bewildered and upset. He had no idea what to do, so he signed off work. He divided the day's takings between himself and Phoenix and returned home. Just as he did every day when he got back from work, he had a bath. He then settled down uneasily on the sofa to watch the Saturday afternoon sport on television.

At about 6.15, Malcolm Robinson received a call from the police asking for his father's address. He gave it, and at 6.30 the police arrived at the family home. They took Robinson upstairs and asked for the clothes he'd been wearing during the day. He picked them out of the laundry basket for them and handed them over.

At Bedlingham Police Station, he was told to strip completely. He was physically examined, and intimate samples were taken, except for fingernail scrapings. The doctor looked at Robinson's bitten-down nails.

'Oh, I'm wasting my time there,' he commented.

Robinson was put in a cell and left alone. After a couple of hours, by which time the duty solicitor had arrived, the police interviewed him about what had happened. The solicitor appeared impressed with his client.

'You did OK there', he said approvingly.

Robinson was rather taken aback. 'Well, it's the truth', he said.

He spent an uncomfortable night in the cell and the next morning demanded to have a shower. The police even found a very old razor for him so Robinson shaved, using a piece of plastic as a mirror. He was given nothing to eat all day. Towards evening, he was taken out of his cell, but the relief was short-lived. The prosecution lawyers had given the go-ahead for him to be charged with rape. He was taken back to his cell.

A while later, the solicitor came down and lifted the flap on the cell.

'Any chance of bail?' Robinson asked him.

'George, it's a serious charge', replied the lawyer. 'Getting bail is somewhere between very difficult and impossible.'

By now, Robinson was thoroughly exasperated. 'Tell that custody sergeant that I'm not spending another night in this cell', he said.

Fifteen minutes later, the solicitor came back. He'd arranged bail, though Robinson couldn't stay in Blyth; the scale of the danger he represented to society can be gauged from the fact that he was ordered to stay at his sister-in-law's in Shiremoor, which was all of eight miles away.

Three days later, Robinson appeared at the magistrates' court. He couldn't believe the case would be proceeded with, and was still mainly preoccupied with getting back home.

'Can you not get me back home with Sylvia?' he asked. 'This is ridiculous.'

So his barrister put it to the magistrates. They asked the views of the prosecution team, who just shrugged their shoulders. Robinson was given bail to his home address.

THE TRIAL OPENED at Newcastle Crown Court on 29 July 2003. The Crown case was that Robinson stopped the cab during the journey, and then went into the back of the car through the nearside passenger door. He took Hayley's clothes off and raped her. Hayley gave evidence by video link. This is the kernel of her account:

A: I went in the car and he drove for a bit ... After we drove away from my estate, that's when he started to [say] like, 'Why don't I take you somewhere?' ... and then he says, 'Do you want sex?', and I said, 'No', but then he stopped the car ... I was in my wheelchair. He picked us up, two arms, and I telt him, 'No'. He says, 'Can you get on the floor?' and I told him, 'No', and he dragged us on the floor. You know I tried to defend myself. I was there for about a couple of hours because he stopped the car ... Well, five hours at the most ... He asked, could he do it? He asked again, could he do it? and I said, 'No', and he basically forced it in ... We were there for like five seconds.

Q: What happened after he put it in?
A: Well, I felt it. It feels awful once it goes in, I felt as though he was never going to get it back out. When he actually put it in, I felt it going in.
Q: How did you get your clothes back on?
A: He put them on us. I'm useless with buttons.
Q: Had there been any problem with the wheelchair?
A: The belt got stuck and I said, 'Can you please help us get this belt on?, and stuff. It was stuck in the spokes. This was before I got back in. It was before I got, he put me back into the wheelchair.
Q: When he re-dressed you and put you back in the chair, that's when you say the belt got stuck?
A: Yeah, but on the way from getting to, into the taxi it was stuck anyway.

This was her evidence. She also said that, at the end of the journey, she was dropped off 'in the middle of nowhere'.

Under cross-examination, she gave these replies:

Q: If he did it, why is it that you could not remember when you spoke to [the woman police officer]?
A: Yeah, well, he, I'll be quite frank with you, he never.
Q: He never what?
A: He did try and put it in, but he said he was wetting his hands and I didn't ask him like what …
Q: Isn't that right, he didn't actually put it in any hole at all?
A: Well, no, he didn't.

Hayley had suffered some mental impairment and had no concept of time. Nor was she capable of giving a fully coherent account of the journey.

Beside Hayley's testimony, the Crown relied on four key pieces of evidence: an internal examination of Hayley revealed the presence of sperm in her vagina; scientists also detected a partial profile of Hayley's DNA on Robinson's underwear; there were scratches on her body; and her shoelaces were tied differently, the prosecution asserted, to how her mother had tied them earlier.

The vaginal swab had showed the presence of three sperm heads. The judge pointed out that exactly when Hayley last had sex was of 'some importance', because the presence of the sperm heads when she was medically examined indicated that she must have had sex at some time during (at most) the last ten days. That was the maximum period the sperm heads could have survived.

Asked about her sexual history, Hayley said she had had sexual intercourse with her boyfriend and that had led to a pregnancy, which was terminated just over a year earlier. That was, she said, the only time she had had sex with him. She testified that she had not had sex since the abortion.

Her account was, in fact, contradicted by her boyfriend, who said that they had had sex 'ten or more times'. He couldn't remember the last time. It was probably during that calendar year, but was 'quite a while ago'. There was a second key difference between them, because the boyfriend testified that they had been going out for three years and had never broken up and from time to time shared a bedroom; Hayley said they always had separate bedrooms.

The evidence of the sperm heads, together with the evidence of Hayley's DNA on Robinson's underwear, must have been hugely persuasive. That is precisely the kind of valuable base evidence that criminal cases of this kind need: reciprocal evidence of him on her and her on him. In addition to this, there was the mother's evidence about the shoelaces being tied differently; and the further evidence of the scratches on Hayley's body, which appeared to indicate that she had been subject to rough treatment.

Of these factors, the shoelace evidence disappeared during the trial. The mother's story about noticing the differently-tied shoelaces was contradicted by Hayley's sister, who said that she had taken Hayley's clothes off immediately afterwards (and had noticed no problems with her clothing or shoes.)

Although the scratches could have suggested that an assailant had found difficulty in re-dressing her afterwards, one of the scratched areas were parallel marks scratches, a sign that they were caused by fingernails. Yet Robinson's nails were bitten down to the quick and so the defence pointed out that he could not have been responsible for any scratches.

Overall, the defence was based primarily on Robinson's own unblemished conduct; he was, said the judge, 'a man of proper good character'. Nor was there enough time for the offence to have been committed. Robinson also suffered erectile dysfunction. He had not even had sex with his wife for the previous ten years, and would not have been capable of committing such an offence.

The jury deliberated for some time and so the judge gave a majority direction. Then the jurors came back to say that they had found Robinson guilty of rape by a 10-2 majority. The judge, His Honour Judge Milford QC, sentenced Robinson to nine years' imprisonment and ordered that he should sign the sex offenders register for the rest of his life.

AS A RULE, IT WOULD be expected for the families of sex offenders to suffer community retribution, perhaps by having their houses vandalised. Smashed windows and graffitied walls would certainly be anticipated.

This did not happen in Blyth. On the contrary, there was shock and bewilderment that a well-thought-of local man had been found guilty of such a crime and given a lengthy prison sentence. There was deep sympathy and concern for him and his family. One of those who acted with particular generosity was their landlord who told them that, in these distressing circumstances, they should forget about the rent. Ronnie Campbell, the local MP whom Robinson had known for many years, also lent unstinting support.

Though they had few enough resources of their own, the family were desperate to pursue the case. They managed to raise £5,000 for legal costs and to commission fresh reports in the case. One of the areas of the case they wanted to develop was Robinson's erectile dysfunction. At trial, they felt, his legal team had erred in not substantiating this point; Robinson himself and Sylvia had given evidence, but the defence lawyer had not called the doctor to give evidence, but merely submitted a written report. Nor had the lawyers asked an expert in this field for his views. Robinson said he was incapable of achieving an erection; was that genuinely the case? If that point could be strengthened, the family felt, there was a strong possibility that Robinson would be able to win his appeal.

And so the case papers, with Robinson's complete medical records, were sent to Dr A. R. Markos, who was consultant at mid-Staffordshire hospitals in genito-urinary medicine and sexual health.

Dr Markos looked through the papers. The more he studied them, the more concerned he became. It was not, however, Robinson's virility, or the lack of it, that bothered him. What bothered him were those three sperm heads in the complainant's vagina. This alone told him that Robinson could not have committed the offence. He could see from the medical records that Robinson was incapable of producing sperm. He had had a vasectomy in 1975.

3

It is extraordinary that the case should have gone to trial without anyone having been aware of this. However, Robinson had been completely focused on his erectile dysfunction for two obvious reasons: he believed it provided the complete explanation of why he could not have committed this crime; and it was, in any event, a matter of ongoing concern to him at the time. In these circumstances, he did not pause to consider whether there was an even stronger reason why he did not commit the crime.

Nevertheless, the fact that the trial had gone ahead with everyone in complete ignorance about this indicated incompetence on every level of the legal process. Obviously, Robinson's own lawyers should have taken his point about erectile dysfunction far more seriously and sought authoritative supporting evidence – in which case the evidence should then have come to light. 'Many a competent solicitor', the appeal court judges would later say, 'would have at least asked for the GP records and might then have noticed [the] vasectomy'.

However, this was not a matter for the defence alone. Prosecutors too are under a broad duty to undertake enquiries which might exculpate as well as incriminate the suspect.

Dr Markos also drew attention to matters which any disinterested observer could have raised. He pointed out that there was no forensic evidence whatever of Robinson on the complainant. He also wondered why there had been no DNA analysis of the sperm heads, and why there were so few.

In fact, there had been DNA analysis of the sperm heads – but, strangely, it hadn't yielded a result. Further, routine ejaculation would have produced a far greater number of spermatozoa. Together, these factors strongly suggested that there had been no sexual assault just a few hours earlier, but rather that intercourse had occurred some days earlier. This should have been linked to Dr Markos's other point. In view of the complete absence of forensic evidence of Robinson on the complainant, it was virtually inconceivable that the alleged assault had happened.

Dr Markos also pointed out that there was always a theoretical possibility that a vasectomy could spontaneously reverse itself. Accordingly, Robinson, who had by this point instructed fresh lawyers, was tested.

In the sombre surroundings of Frankland Prison he spent an embarrassing couple of hours striving to produce a semen sample. Finally, he managed it. The specimen was sent off for analysis. The results were conclusive: no spermatozoa were present. To his complete delight Robinson learned that, twenty-nine years after he'd had the operation, his vasectomy was still intact.

The case went to appeal in July 2005. Not surprisingly, in view of the new evidence, Robinson's conviction was quashed. However, the judges sent the case back for retrial. This has become standard procedure in recent years, although whether or not a retrial takes place is a matter for Crown Prosecution Service, whose lawyers must decide whether it is in the public interest to seek a fresh indictment for a fresh trial. In this instance, astonishingly, the decision was taken to go ahead.

The second trial took place, again at Newcastle Crown Court, in November 2005. Again, the complainant gave her evidence by videolink. By this stage, it was known not only that Robinson had nothing to do with the semen, but that he had nothing to do with the scratches. To supplement the lack-of-sharp-fingernails point, it had belatedly been acknowledged that the scratches were at least two days old. As the prosecution now accepted this, the defence expert did not even need to give evidence; the judge apologised to her for her wasted trip.

The judge directed that there should be no mention of the fact that this was a retrial. The reason for this is obscure (it could even have been a misguided attempt to assist Robinson), but in practice it proved calamitous. During cross-examination, Robinson had to say in response to one question that he couldn't answer without straying into areas which the judge had instructed him to avoid. Although the judge then told Robinson that he must answer in whatever way he wished, the damage had been done. The barrister didn't put the question again but moved on to a fresh one. The jury would have been left with an uneasy feeling that there was more to the case than they were privy to.

Whether or not that explains it, the outcome was still an immense shock. Robinson was found guilty again. He had been convicted originally by a 10-2 majority verdict; the jury verdict now, with most of the original evidence having been discredited, was unanimous. If ever one needed an encapsulation of the occasional absurdities of the criminal justice process, here it was.

Robinson went back to prison, this time for eight years (having, of course, already served one year).

THE CASE HAD by now reached a surreal point. If the allegation had been true, there would have been three main areas of evidence: forensic evidence of the suspect on the complainant; and of the complainant on the suspect; and from the scene, especially as the supposed crime scene was a closely confined space – one that was therefore readily conducive to providing forensic scientists with vital information.

From two of these three areas, there was no evidence: none whatever from the scene; and none whatever of the suspect on the complainant. These factors by themselves should have told prosecutors that the incident was extremely unlikely to have happened.

To these areas of non-existent evidence may be added the evidence of the scratches and the shoelaces. By the time of the retrial, both points had, in terms of being Crown evidence, fallen by the wayside. So they disappeared into a kind of evidential black hole. But that was not how they should have been regarded. Clearly, both areas of evidence were now compelling arguments for the defence.

Hayley was incapable of dressing herself and had to be dressed by her family. It is hard to imagine that an assailant would have been able to take off her clothes, and then dress her again afterwards, doing up all the buttons, zips, and other fasteners correctly. This is the context in which the mother's evidence that only the shoe-laces were wrongly tied should be set. (In any event the mother's evidence was contradicted by the sister, who said that it was she who had tended to Hayley afterwards and she had noticed nothing amiss.) To this point must be added the obvious one that he would have had to have done all that *hurriedly* and *without leaving any forensic evidence of himself whatever on her clothing.*

The evidence of the scratches was of similar importance. At the first trial, the prosecution claimed that these demonstrated that Hayley had suffered some rough treatment. In fact, this evidence was untrue. Being at least two days old, the scratches could have had nothing to do with events that Saturday lunchtime. So, again, the evidence was actually important for the opposite reason. The notion that Robinson would have been able to strip her of her clothes and then rape her without leaving any physical marks on her body – and also without her having attempted to defend her-self in any way – is inconceivable.

All these evidential points related to the interaction of the com-plainant and the alleged assailant, and showed that there was no evidence where one would have expected a great deal. In addition, there were several other reasons why the alleged attack had not taken place.

If Robinson committed this crime, what had happened to the wheelchair? According to Hayley's account, it stayed in position, in the back of the taxi. But neither of them was small; both were over medium height. How could he have put her on the floor of the cab and then got on top of her? There wasn't room.

Nor was there enough time. The entire journey took twenty-one minutes and cost £5.30p. Taxi meters are slightly complicated mechanisms, since they charge at one rate while the vehicle is in normal motion and a different rate when it is moving below ten miles per hour or is stationary. This is uniform practice; given the exigencies of running a taxi business, there could be no other system. If charges were based just on the distance travelled, then taxis being stuck in traffic much of the time would render the business not economically viable.

Evidence was given at trial by Jeff Harris, who understood the taxi-metering system. He drove the route and calculated that there was twelve minutes of waiting time on the journey. Six or seven minutes of this could be explained by natural hold-ups at traffic lights, intersections and roundabouts. That left only a maximum of five or six minutes when the cab could have been stopped. The prosecution script could not have been performed in this time. The defence argued that the few minutes available could be fully accounted for by stopping the vehicle to allow Robinson to disentangle the end of the lap-strap from the wheelchair.

The jury seems to have been told that the area where the taxi stopped was 'relatively secluded'. If they were told that, it was untrue. The place was on a well-used road, with an expanse of open ground on each side which, especially on a Saturday afternoon, was used by children and dog-walkers, and for ball games and other activities. There were houses – local council housing, or former council housing – both behind and in front. There would have been a constant stream of traffic, buses included, moving past the parked cab.

Hayley did not say in her account whether or not the rear nearside door was closed, but it is immaterial. Had there been anything untoward occurring in the back of the cab that Saturday afternoon, then it is bound to have attracted attention. Yet no one – no car driver, no bus passenger, no one out and about – saw anything. Again, there is a complete absence of evidence where one would naturally have expected a number of witnesses.

At some point, Hayley suggested the cab might have been taken somewhere quiet where 'all you could see was trees'. However, this was clearly not the case. Although Robinson knew the entire locality like the back of his hand, and so could have taken the cab somewhere quiet, both the limited time available and the taxi-meter evidence proved that he had not driven off his route. In any case, this was another part of her story that was contradicted by others. Her boyfriend gave evidence that she told him they stopped 'around some houses'.

Another giveaway sign that the complaint was untrue is that it changed. Originally, the complaint was that Robinson had asked her to lift her top up; a couple of hours later, it was a rape allegation.

Hayley used Phoenix Taxis on two separate occasions on Sunday evening. Of course, the idea that a victim of a rape ordeal by a taxi-driver would order a taxi from the same company the following day and risk a further assault is simply unthinkable.

Hayley's testimony contained other indications that it was not true. There was nothing in it to suggest that she was describing a real event. Even making allowances for her mental state, the descriptions were just too vague and superficial, particularly bearing in mind that the event was supposed to have just happened. She agreed that the strap had got caught in the wheels – thereby bearing out Robinson's account of why he had needed to stop the cab in the first place; and also agreed that Robinson had wiped her hair off her face at the start of the journey.

The DNA evidence was the only potentially viable evidence left, and yet no Crown scientist could tell whether the material on Robinson's underwear was saliva or vaginal fluid. Further, the complainant herself had fully endorsed the defence explanation of what had occurred. That was a full and sufficient explanation of the evidence. It was only given added credence by Robinson's background as a carer. It was familiar territory for him.

Then there is the major evidence of the sperm heads, which proves that the complainant had misled the court at the first trial about her sexual history.

At the original trial, Hayley twice appeared to retract her evidence and admit that it wasn't true. ('Isn't that right, he didn't actually put it in any hole at all?' '*Well, no, he didn't*').

One imagines that she could have been put up to fabricating the allegation with the aim of a claim for criminal compensation.

Two other matters could have told those familiar with criminal justice procedures that this prosecution was flawed. The first was a bogus reconstruction – frequently a factor in flawed criminal trials. If a journey is going to be reproduced in order to time it, it must replicate as closely as possible the original conditions; if that is not achieved, then it is a waste of time and money. In this instance, the original journey took place at a busy Saturday lunchtime; the police reconstruction was done on a quiet Tuesday morning.

Then there was the key missing evidence. Telephone calls into Phoenix Taxis were routinely recorded. The tapes of those calls were vital evidence. Indeed, that would have been the first piece of documentary evidence in the case. Those all-important tapes were collected that Saturday. Afterwards, when they should have been available to bear out the defence case, they went missing.

There is one final, hardly insignificant, matter. Had Robinson been a rapist, then he would have had ample time to cover his tracks. He was warned by his office manager that there had been a complaint. He had three hours' notice of his impending arrest. So what did he do in the intervening period? He did nothing. When the police arrived and asked for his clothing, he looked into the laundry basket and gave them what he'd been wearing. Had he committed the offence, then he could easily have substituted other clothing. The whole irony of the case is that the CPS could only prosecute George Robinson for rape because he obviously wasn't a rapist.

If the jury was not to be misled at retrial, then it was important that the prosecution explained to them that the defence explanation of the complainant's DNA on the accused's underwear was a sufficient explanation and there was nothing to contradict it; and that the complainant had lied about her sexual history at the previous trial. Further, she had lied about the matter that was the core of the case. Of course, this would have made the retrial a nonsense, but that is precisely the point. The only way the retrial could take place at all was by withholding key information from the jury.

Taking the case to retrial at all had placed Robinson in enormous jeopardy. At the original trial, the judge had said, in view of the woman's mental and physical disabilities, that 'the very allegation is bound to raise in any right-thinking person feelings of shock, revulsion and sympathy'.

That is precisely the problem. The trial was bound to throw the jurors into emotional turmoil; it would be hard for them to remain dispassionate. In the circumstances, it was vital that the CPS examined the case papers with especial diligence. The idea that in effect it should abdicate its duties and let the jury resolve it is absurd. A guilty verdict at the end of the day does not vindicate the decision to prosecute but may merely underline, as it did here, the folly and irresponsibility of having taken the case to trial.

Chapter 8

'Oh, goody!'

Rob Giannetto's story

1

On 12 September 1994, at 8.30 in the morning, Julia Giannetto telephoned her husband, Rob. She needed him to look after their son that morning instead of in the afternoon, as previously arranged.

Julia and Rob had been together since 1980 and had married in 1987 as a last-ditch attempt to patch up problems in their relationship. Almost inevitably, the difficulties continued and, in December 1992, Julia left Rob to go and live with her widowed father in London.

She then found out that she was pregnant, and so they resolved to make a fresh start. Jonathan was born in September 1993. However, relations again deteriorated and in May 1994 they separated again, with Rob going back to live with his parents while Julia remained in their flat. They started legal proceedings over custody of their son. In August Julia was awarded custody, with Rob allowed access for two-hour periods three times a week.

However, once these matters are before the courts and in an adversarial process, with lawyers involved, they can sometimes become more polarised than they need be. Julia claimed that Rob was threatening her, and subsequently got an order prohibiting him from setting foot in the flat which they had shared until three months earlier and which had been bought for them by his parents. Nevertheless, the access arrangements for Jonathan were unchanged.

On that day, 12 September, she wanted to make the last-minute change because there was a children's party that afternoon; she'd be able to take Jonathan. The change was quickly agreed. At 10.30, Julia dropped the child off at Rob's parents' house.

When she did not arrive to pick him up, he became anxious. Usually she was punctual. Witnesses saw him holding the child, looking out of the front window. He was in a quandary. Bearing in mind the court restriction, he could not simply go round to the flat. At 2.00pm, he phoned his solicitor. They agreed that he should

285

go out to get some lunchtime food for the child. Throughout the afternoon, he continued phoning both Julia and the police, asking if there had been reports of an accident.

Because of the court order, his solicitor strongly advised him not to go to the house alone. So at about 6.00, when he needed to collect night clothes and other items for the child, he telephoned the police and it was arranged that he should go to the flat accompanied by an officer. They let themselves in at about 6.45.

Julia's body lay partly in the hallway and partly in the living-room. She had been bludgeoned about the head, stabbed several times and her throat was cut.

Of course, Giannetto was the immediate suspect, despite the alibi evidence. In November the following year he was put on trial and convicted of – but that's the strange thing. No one's ever been sure precisely what he's been convicted of. It might be one thing or it might be, well, another. Even though it's a riddle no one has ever been able to answer, he was sentenced to life imprisonment.

GIANNETTO'S FATHER, Carmelo, came from Santa Theresa di Riva, a village just south of Messina on the north-east coast of Sicily. With little work available, he went to Rome and trained to be a tailor, and then settled in Turin. During the Second World War, he fought with the partisans against Mussolini's fascists, while his sister helped Jewish families escape from Italy across the Alps into southern France.

When the war was over, he met and married his wife, Maria. Their eldest son, Paul was born in Turin in 1953, by which time they were planning to leave. In 1954, they moved to England and settled in Bristol, where Rob was born in 1955.

Carmelo continued as a tailor; Maria worked as a cleaner. As is often the case with immigrant families, they put in long hours to try to get a foothold in their adopted country. However, the child care arrangements turned out to be less than satisfactory; Paul got pneumonia after the childminder left him in his pram outside in the snow. So, the children were sent back to be looked after by Maria's mother in Turin. They stayed there for two years.

The Giannettos' hard work began to pay dividends. They got a mortgage and bought a house. A few years later, a compulsory purchase order was placed on it, as the site was needed for the expansion of the Bristol Royal Infirmary, so they were paid a full market price for it. The family – there was by now a daughter, Danila – then decided to move again, this time to the US, to Waterbury, Connecticut. Family cousins were already established there.

Carmelo made bespoke suits and Maria worked in the local shoe factory, but the children were unhappy. 'My parents were working so hard', Danila said, 'I didn't see my mother at all during the week'.

After three years, they returned to England and Judy, the fourth child, was born in 1968. By now, Carmelo and Maria had saved enough money to buy three five-storey houses in Bristol and Bath – although all were in need of complete renovation. Gradually, the family did the houses up. The boys did their share; they'd arrive home from school to knock down walls and do other labouring jobs, working evenings and weekends.

The family rarely took summer holidays in Italy (there were only two, in 1963 and 1972) and their links with the Italian community were not strong, even though it was well established in Bristol. Carmelo and Maria didn't do much socialising; they concentrated on work and raising their family.

In 1970, Giannetto was expelled from school because he wouldn't cut his hair. This led to considerable tension at home. There was the same generational friction in homes throughout Europe and the United States between parents who'd survived the war years and post-war children who were by now part of the Woodstock generation. For a while, Giannetto simply dropped out and enjoyed himself listening to music – Led Zeppelin, Pink Floyd, Jimi Hendrix and the Rolling Stones. 'It was my first taste of freedom from my family', he said, 'and I grabbed it.'

He was gregarious and open and, somewhat unusually, integrated himself into the social networks of both hippies and bikers. He loved travelling and began making regular long-distance jaunts across Europe, either by car or motorcycle.

From his early teenage years, Giannetto developed a passion for motorcycles – particularly British bikes like BSAs and Triumphs. 'He was so young but so into bikes', recalled Danila. 'Eventually, our father gave in and bought him a bike to renovate. Jim, a member of the local Hell's Angels chapter, would come round for tea and afterwards he'd help Rob work on the bike.'

Carmelo decided to return on his own to the US, realising that there was more money to be made there. He stayed there for five more years. By the time he returned, he'd saved enough money to enable the family to buy another house. They did that one up too, and begun to make money in the property business. They became landlords, renting out rooms to students.

Carmelo's brother had taken over a pizzeria, but when he became too ill to run it, the Giannettos stepped in to help. The family business was spiralling, but it was all work, work, work. Carmelo even tried farming. Some days, he would be working at the pizzeria until 2.00am, only to get up three hours later, at 5.00, to go and feed his cows.

They started a guest-house, with Danila helping out in the kitchen. 'By the time I was fourteen', she recalled, 'I would be getting up at five to help my mother cook the breakfasts – and then go to school. When I came home, if a member of staff at the restaurant hadn't turned up, then I'd get a call and have to go down and be working 'til midnight, washing dishes.'

Then the pizza chef left. Rob offered to stand in.

'You?' his Dad retorted. 'You've never made a pizza in your life.'

'I've been watching', he replied.

'Go on then, make me one'.

So Giannetto did. His father tasted it, and approved.

'OK', he said. 'You're the pizza chef'.

It was the summer of 1976. Giannetto remembers it, when he was the pizza chef and Britain enjoyed blissfully hot weather, as one of the happiest periods of his life.

Even after they shut down the restaurant, there was still plenty to do. Giannetto was collecting rents, working in the guest-house, doing repairs. What spare time he had in those days was almost exclusively devoted to the world of motorcycles. In his early twenties he got his first Harley-Davidson. He began rebuilding bikes and so his passionate interest provided him with some income.

'Everything seemed to take off just through word of mouth', he said. 'People would say, "I've heard you can rebuild a Harley gearbox". So I was going round the country, doing work for other people on their bikes, and getting well paid for it.'

He started bringing bikes over from the US. He travelled extensively through the mid-West states like Minnesota, Iowa, Illinois, Missouri and Arkansas.

'They were the cheaper states to find Harleys', he explained. 'Sometimes you'd find them in barns, still in their original condition. I bought them and put them on a plane to England. You'd freight them up over there and get a truck to take them to the airport. So you'd pay around £6,000 in the first place, plus freight costs would be about £500. Then you could sell it for eleven or twelve thousand.

'I paid £1,900 for one, an ex-South Africa police bike. It was freighted through Northern Ireland and, in doing so, it picked up the registration number OIA 8. Of course, eight is a lucky number for the Chinese, so I sold the number plate alone for £1,400 to someone for whom that particular registration was obviously special. I then restored the bike and sold it for £9,500.

'It wasn't just the bikes themselves. People were interested in all kinds of artefacts associated with bikes. I was dealing in literature and memorabilia. I bought brochures and booklets. Over there, you'd see original tins of paint from the '50s with the label still intact – so you could pick them up for £5 and they were worth £80 in the UK. You could go to America and pick up stacks of stuff.

'Because I knew the ropes, I was sometimes asked to go down to customs and help others with the paperwork. I'd have the pick of stuff. I'd know what other people were looking for and what sort of profit there was in it. So it had started off as my hobby but became a very good way to make some money.'

By this stage, Giannetto had picked up two minor convictions, the first for possession of cannabis in 1976 and the second for driving while over the alcohol limit in 1979. Partly as a result of that, he decided to give up drink and has been teetotal since 1982.

In 1979, one of his former girlfriends, Annie Lacey, had a baby. Giannetto went round to see the baby and offer his congratulations. There he met one of Annie's friends, Julia Palmer, who'd been present at the birth. He and Julia hit it off straightaway. A languages student, Julia had a passion for reading and learning, but was a bit of a Bohemian herself and had just dropped out of Bristol University. They got a flat together.

Julia took up Giannetto's passion for motorcycles. He was conscious that some of his associates in the motorcycle world would treat women patronisingly. 'But they were never like that with Julia', he said. 'She commanded a hell of a lot of respect; she'd argue and discuss things with them. She fitted in and got to know all my friends really well.'

They would go on riding holidays together and travelled round Europe several times, striking up many friendships. Giannetto, of course, could speak Italian and Julia was fluent in French. 'We had a great time', he said.

It was his own fault that the good times ended. He had an affair with a woman who was then just embarking on her career as a BBC television presenter. She had a flat in one of his father's houses. He went round to collect the rent and one thing soon led to another. He could probably have kept the affair quiet, but her flat-mate deliberately brought Julia round to the house at a time when she knew that Rob and the woman would be in bed together – purely, it seems, out of spite.

'That was a weird one, wasn't it?' reflected Giannetto.

'Julia took it really badly. Obviously, we split up. She started drinking heavily. I felt really bad about it. We got back together, but it was never the same again. We actually did get married in 1987, when we'd been together for seven years. It was a low-key wedding, just a few friends.'

His parents bought them a two-bedroom flat at 12a Oakfield Road, a short walk from where they lived in Beaufort Road.

'For a while, everything got back to normal – we were going abroad, riding our bikes', he said. 'But then things would suddenly explode. Sometimes Julia would turn on the TV and see the woman I was with, so it would bring it all back to her.

'Then her mother died of cancer, and she never really recovered from that. She started having nightmares: nightmares about my affair; nightmares about her mother.'

In 1992 Giannetto, who had acquired computer skills, was hired to do emergency work for the BOC Group (formerly British Oxygen Company) which, following a fire at its Bristol base, needed its entire computer system sorted out quickly. He found himself working a ninety-hour week.

This led to fresh marital problems and precipitated the break-up, when Julia went to live in London. Her subsequent discovery that she was pregnant led to an unsatisfactory reconciliation. Within a few months of Jonathan's birth, they had drifted apart again.

After the discovery of Julia's body on 12 September, Giannetto was taken to the police station. As he was detained overnight, Jonathan was being looked after by his grandparents. At 3.00am the following morning, social services arrived to wake up everyone and take the child from them.

'My mother begged them to wait until he'd woken up', said Danila. 'His mother had just been murdered, and she didn't want him to have to wake up in a different place surrounded by strangers. But they didn't think about Jonathan at all. They ignored my mother and seized him then, at three in the morning.'

2

Two days after being taken in for questioning, Giannetto was released. In October he voluntarily returned for further questioning and was then charged with soliciting murder. He was remanded in custody.

In March 1995, his legal team applied for bail. They were quite confident; after all, in five months the prosecution hadn't been able to come up with any substantive evidence. Then, however, Giannetto was charged with murder. He believed at the time that this was merely a ploy to prevent him getting bail. By the time that the case went to trial, however, murder was the sole charge. The indictment, dated 24 March 1995, read as follows:

Robert Vincent Giannetto is charged as follows:

Statement of Offence

Murder

Particulars of Offence

Robert Vincent Giannetto on the 12th day of September 1994 murdered Julia Ann Giannetto

It's not usually necessary to point out the actual wording on the indictment but in this instance, as in others, the case would prove exceptional.

The trial was at Bristol Crown Court. The judge was Mr Justice Rougier, who was the son of the leading romantic novelist, Georgette Heyer.

The prosecution case was that, after all the bitterness of the divorce and the child custody battle, Giannetto had wanted her dead. Julia's solicitors spoke of her 'anxious and fearful' demeanour. Her diaries contained references of acts of violence by Giannetto – punches, kicking, throwing things, threats to her life and to take the child away to Sicily. There was one particular reference to Giannetto running his finger across his throat.

When she was murdered, her throat was indeed cut, but that was not the cause of her death. She would have died from the blows to her head. She had also suffered many other injuries, and was stabbed ten times in the chest. The judge described all this to the jurors in highly-charged language that would not have been out of place in one of his mother's books:

Twelve blows to her head shattered her skull and the brain within it … The knife plunged deeper, again and again, as if searching for the vital organs … It must have struck all of us that for a young mother to be butchered like this in her own home is an outrage …

The timing of Julia's death could be fixed with some precision. She was seen alive at 12.05 and she would have started out to pick up Jonathan at about 12.25. She must have been murdered in that short period.

The prosecution assembled its points of evidence. Giannetto had tried, but failed, to get his son put on his passport – indicating, they claimed, that he had been preparing to take him out of the country. A scene-of-crime officer testified that the scene of disturbance inside the flat had been artificially created; it was not a genuine burglary. The police also said that they had found no clothing at Giannetto's home. This led them to believe that he must have another flat nearby where his clothing was and where he would have been able to hide a weapon and bloodstained clothing.

Giannetto was also betrayed, the prosecution argued, by the fact that when he first saw Julia's body, he was not visibly upset and held himself in check. The prosecution asserted that this detached demeanour at the scene was evidence of guilt.

The main thrust of its case, however, revolved around a character named William Welch. He had engaged Giannetto in conversation on 8 June when the latter went to the Passport Office in Newport. Welch acknowledged that he had waylaid Giannetto, 'for the specific purpose of getting money from him'. They met on this and three subsequent occasions.

Three months later, after he saw the news of Julia's death on television, Welch went, firstly, to a local priest, and then to the police. He said that Giannetto had given him money to have Julia killed. According to Welch, Giannetto had said at their very first meeting, 'I'm going to have to do her in'. He then straightaway offered Welch, who suggested running her down in a car, £5,000 to arrange the murder.

The prosecution claimed there was support for Welch's story in that he'd gone originally not to the police but to a priest, which suggested a man with a troubled conscience. There was also evidence that he had bought a wallet, indicating he'd come into money.

The problem for the prosecution was that Welch's evidence did not in any way fit in with the circumstances of the case. After all, Julia had not been run down by a car; Welch said he'd had nothing to do with her death; and, in any event, there was no evidence that he and Giannetto had been in any contact in the months before her death. With a prosecution scenario as vague as this one, the

Crown felt it expedient to draw up an outline of what its case actually was.

This was the key part which prosecutors wrote out and handed to the jury:

> The Crown contends that it is clear that the accused was criminally involved in his wife's death, and seeks to demonstrate that fact by four questions.
>
> [1] What is the likelihood that the accused, wishing his wife dead, should have the good fortune to find that a stranger has stepped in and done the deed uninvited?
>
> [2] And during one of those three two-hour periods in a week when the child was not in her company?
>
> [3] And after the accused has unsuccessfully paid money only two months before to have the deed done?
>
> [4] And to find that this unsolicited stranger has chosen to inflict upon the body the very injury which the accused had threatened?
>
> The chances that someone unsolicited by the accused happened to murder the wife he wanted dead, when the child was not in her company, and then to inflict upon her body the injury the accused had threatened, are fanciful. The inference of guilt is inevitable.

After the judge's summing-up, the jurors were sent out on 30 October 1995. They returned five hours later. They had written down the following question:

> How much of an involvement in the murder does the defendant need to have in order to convict him of the murder? i.e. (i) planning, (ii) paying for, (iii) knew of and did not prevent.

The jury's third alternative – that Giannetto knew of, but did not prevent the murder – was the most bewildering. This was because it had not in any respect formed part of the prosecution case. 'It is not very easy to determine', said the judge, 'what scenarios the jury have created in their minds.'

During discussions between the judge and counsel, in the absence of the jury, Paul Chadd QC, for the prosecution, said, 'On the facts as we know them, I find it difficult to envisage anything that encompasses (iii)'. Mr Justice Rougier agreed: 'So do I, and I am bound to say that I propose to make that comment to the jury'.

So he should have done. Unfortunately, he didn't. What he did say to the jury about (iii) was this:

> … has given us all a bit of a headache because it is rather difficult to deduce the scenario you have in mind … Supposing somebody came up to you and said, 'I'm going to kill your wife'. If he played any part, either in encouragement, as little as patting him on the back, nodding, saying, 'Oh, goody!', that would be sufficient to involve him in the murder, to make him guilty, because he is encouraging the murder.

The judge concluded by saying:

> The situation … is a rather difficult one on the facts that have been presented to you and the case which has been put by counsel. If you think it is a possibility, of course, you will consider it.

The jury retired again. They returned and convicted Giannetto. He was sentenced to life imprisonment.

Even though this is a case unlike any other in recent history, the two questions at the heart of it are exactly the same as those that should be at the heart of every case: did the defendant commit the crime? And, did he have a fair trial and so was correctly convicted according to criminal justice procedure?

3

William Welch said that on Tuesday 13 September he watched the local evening news at 6.30. He was in Bed-and-Breakfast accommodation, where he had been housed by social services after his release from prison. Alone in his room, he saw the report about Julia's death. It said that there was 'a man in custody over the incident'. Welch was intrigued but, for the moment, bided his time.

The following evening he watched the news again with keen interest. 'They said the man had been released', he said, 'and the police were baffled.' Leaving aside the fact that it is unlikely the report had said that, Welch then acted.

He went to see a pastor with the Bristol Christian Fellowship, Alistair McSorley, a man whose kindness he had intermittently prevailed upon for the last ten years. Welch told him that he was conscience-stricken because he knew something about the murder. McSorley had been unaware of the crime, but he advised him to go to the police. He said that if Welch had any qualms, he would accompany him in the morning. Welch, though, had no hesitation. He went straight away to Southmead Road Police Station.

'I just can't live with it', he told police, 'I couldn't live with this, I didn't think it was gonna, he was gonna do what he's done …'

So, at 9.20pm, the police interviewed him. The entire dialogue was recorded and transcribed.

Welch, who was from Manchester, was then thirty-five years old. He was practised at playing the state benefits system. He had arrived in Cardiff that summer. 'I went to see a doctor', he said, 'told him I was an alcoholic and he issued a sick note to this effect. I duly registered as unfit to work at the Cardiff social security office … I used to just walk in, tell 'em I was there, they'd call me out at half-past-ten, I'd give 'em a National Insurance number and then they'd just hand over my Giro [benefits payment].'

Having picked up his money, he went to have a few beers. How many, exactly?

''Bout forty-five pounds' worth'.

So he immediately spent all his social security money on booze. For the rest of the week, he survived by begging or 'rabbing'. He admitted to being 'an accomplished liar when I am seeking to obtain money'.

Welch preyed on charitable and well-meaning strangers, duping them with a variety of hard-luck stories. 'I come out with some sort of sob story', he explained. He claimed, amongst other things, to be a former Australian soldier who had been a mercenary in south-east Asia. 'I spent nine years in Australia and New Guinea and have perfected an antipodean accent. I claim to have only just arrived in this country and ... not qualifying for dole. Generally, I am successful in this.'

In order to elicit extra sympathy, he would tell people that his wife and child had died in an accident.

He acknowledged in court that he had thirty-five criminal convictions, both in this country and Australia. These included convictions for dishonesty. He had also stolen from and physically attacked people who gave him money. Murder apart, said Mr Justice Rougier, it was almost impossible to 'find a sin that Welch would not admit to'.

One Monday in June, according to his account, he picked up his money at Cardiff, spent it all on drink as usual and caught a bus to Newport. He was sleeping rough and the next morning was woken up by a police officer. He still had a couple of cans left, and drank those and took a few drugs ('cannabis and amphetamine'). Asked if he was still drunk from the previous day, he agreed that he was, but qualified it by saying: 'I wasn't falling over drunk, I wasn't completely sober ... it was probably the combination of the effects of the drugs and the alcohol'.

He noticed Giannetto, who was waiting for the Passport Office to open, and started chatting to him. Welch then waited outside while Giannetto went in. Afterwards, Giannetto bought him a couple of beers. Welch said that Giannetto told him his name was 'Peter'. According to Welch, the conversation came round to the idea that Giannetto 'was gonna do his wife in'.

This surprised the interviewing police officer. 'And this is the first time you met him?' he asked.

Indeed it was. Welch continued: 'he said he was gonna bump her off, strangle her, and make it look like a sexual assault, and I said ... well, if I was gonna kill somebody I'd have a couple of pints of beer and then run 'em over in a car ...

'He said to me he would give me five thousand pounds if I'd run his wife over. At the time I was taking quite a lot of drugs and the only thing that actually came into my mind was money ...'

At this point, the police officer pointed out again, Welch had only been in Giannetto's company for two hours

'He's told you he's having trouble with his wife', said the officer. 'Lots of people have trouble with their wives. It doesn't necessarily make them want to say to a complete stranger, I'm gonna kill her and I'm gonna make it look like a sexual assault … What particularly made him talk like that [to you]?'

That was an astute and pertinent question. Welch couldn't answer it.

Resuming his narrative, he said that, in the course of their conversation, Giannetto had mentioned that the Passport Office had asked him to return in seven days' time. So, the following week, Welch did what he'd done the week before. He picked up his money, spent it all on beer and drugs, went to sleep and then caught a bus to Newport. He was hoping Giannetto would be there: 'I wanted to see if I could get some more beer out of the guy'.

This time, Welch accompanied Giannetto into the Passport Office. As it turned out, Giannetto was not able to pick up his passport, so he'd had a fruitless journey. He left, with Welch doggedly following. To Welch's dismay, Giannetto said he hadn't got any cash with him, so he had to settle for a lift into Bristol. He remembered Giannetto playing Ry Cooder music on the car stereo.

In Bristol, he managed to get his booze after all, as Giannetto used his credit card at an off-licence. They went and sat in Kingswood Park ('It's quite a comfy park, I've slept in there before') and talked. When Giannetto got up to leave, Welch said he'd see him again in the park.

'What was he going to see you there for?' said the officer.

'I assume it was 'cos he thought I was gonna run his missus over'.

'Even though you hadn't spoken about it?'

The cracks in Welch's story were already visible, though the particular reason he wished to skate over the details of what had happened would shortly become clear.

A few days later, Giannetto turned up, he said, with a photograph and gave him the address where his wife lived. However, there still seemed to be no conversation about the murder itself. Again the police found this baffling.

'[He's saying] here's a photograph of her, I want her run over, she lives in this house', the police said to him. 'Did he tell you when she's likely to be walking along the street, or which way she walks to the shops?'

'No'.

Giannetto and Welch parted. Welch said he gave him a phone number (Alistair McSorley's, in fact), saying that somebody there would always know how to get hold of him.

Again, the police pressed him. Was Giannetto going to be getting any money? Welch said that Giannetto was going to be making some money by selling a Harley-Davidson motorcycle.

'Did you mention how much money you wanted up front?'

'Yeah, he asked me how much I wanted up front, I said five hundred pounds'.

Welch said that, about two weeks later, Giannetto phoned to arrange another meeting. By this time Welch was in different accommodation and so he wanted to meet somewhere more convenient. He suggested nearby Eastville Park. It was there, he said, that Giannetto gave him £500.

'What did you do with the money?' asked the police.

'I stuck it in my pocket'.

'You've got five hundred pounds in your back pocket?'

'Yeah.'

According to Welch, he said he would go to Manchester, buy a car, drive it back down to Cardiff, and then they would meet again the following Monday; but none of that happened. He said that Giannetto dropped him off in the High Street and 'that's the last I've seen of him'.

'What did you do with the £500?' the police wanted to know.

He said he spent it on drink and drugs.

The police asked other questions.

'Are you here with the thought of reward?'

'No.'

'Are you aware that there is a reward being offered?'

'No'.

There were further questions. The police asked him to explain the blood marks on his jeans; Welch said that was a result of having injected himself. The police then pointed out that a photograph of the murdered woman was shown on television.

'Did you recognise it?', they asked.

'Never seen her before', he replied, forgetting that just fifteen minutes earlier he claimed to have been shown a photograph of her.

A statement was taken from Alistair McSorley, the pastor. Welch seemed to have said broadly the same things to him. In the key passage, McSorley explained: 'Bill said he asked for some money up front and was given £500, he then said that he took the money and ran'.

GIANNETTO WAS QUESTIONED about all this. He had never imagined that his fleeting contact with Welch would become any part of his life-story, let alone a major component.

His account was very different. He said that on Tuesday 8 June, he went to the Passport Office in Newport. He arrived early and, while waiting for it to open, bought a motorcycle magazine. Welch then approached him, speaking in an Australian accent which, given Giannetto's passion for travelling, drew his attention. A conversation developed around their shared interest in motorcycles. Giannetto offered to buy him a coffee. Welch said he'd much prefer a beer but, at that early hour, his hopes were inevitably dashed.

Welch did not immediately seem a down-and-out. He was wearing a short tan leather coat with a bag slung over his shoulder. He said he'd been involved in an accident as a result of which his wife, who was riding pillion, had died. He was travelling the world to try to come to terms with her death, something for which he blamed himself. It was certainly a story eliciting sympathy. Like the rest of us, probably, Giannetto had never before met anyone who would make up something like that.

Giannetto went into the office and asked about adding his son to his passport. When he came out, Welch was still there. Beer could now be purchased so Giannetto stood him a few drinks. They chatted on a bench in the sunshine while Welch spoke about his travels and Giannetto talked a little about his separation from his wife. When he said he thought Julia was giving him a hard time, Welch responded that she sounded, 'a right nutter who needed topping'. That was the only time that the possibility of any harm coming to Julia was ever mentioned. Giannetto then left, and mentioned that he would be back the next day to collect the passport.

That afternoon, the Passport Office telephoned Giannetto at home to tell him that, as there were custody proceedings, his son could not be added to his passport. So he returned the next day to retrieve it. Welch was there again. This time he went in with Giannetto. Afterwards, Giannetto bought Welch a sandwich and a coffee and they had a few games of pool with some locals. As Giannetto started to say his goodbyes, Welch asked for a lift into Bristol, saying he had friends there. During the drive, Welch was able to look at a photograph of Jonathan with his aunt, Danila, Giannetto's sister.

By the time they got to Kingswood Park in Bristol, Welch was anxious: what if he wasn't able to contact his friends? So Giannetto agreed to return later that day; he would be passing that way anyway, to visit friends of his own. If Welch hadn't found his contacts, he would drive him back into Wales. Welch looked concerned, but Giannetto assured him that he would keep his word.

So, later in the day, Giannetto passed by Kingswood Park. He didn't expect to see Welch, but there he was. Moreover, he'd injured his shoulder and was in pain. So Giannetto drove him to casualty at Frenchay Hospital. Welch gave an address in Brisbane, he noticed. The initial diagnosis was that Welch may have fractured his collarbone and would need an x-ray.

Welch now began to get difficult, both with Giannetto and the hospital staff. (At the time, Giannetto thought it must have been because of the pain he was in.) Welch said he was concerned about getting back to Wales and didn't even want to wait for the x-ray. Giannetto stayed with him for a while, trying to comfort him. He agreed that in two days' time, on Friday, he would drive by Eastville Park, which was not far from the hospital; if Welch was there and still hadn't found his friends in Bristol, Giannetto would give him a lift back to Wales. Then he left for his own social engagements.

On Friday, Giannetto drove past the park. Welch was indeed there. He appeared still to be in pain. He said he didn't want to go back to Wales; he wanted to try again to find his friends, so Giannetto drove him back to Kingswood Park. Welch tried to get Giannetto to go for a drink with him. Giannetto, whose good-will had by now been stretched far enough, reminded him that he didn't drink. He gave Welch a few pound coins and drove off, believing that he'd never see him again.

Those were the two accounts of the meetings.

BY THE TIME Welch came to give his evidence at trial, his account had changed from what he'd originally told police officers in three highly significant respects.

Firstly, he now mentioned that on the second occasion he did have a shoulder injury and that Giannetto had taken him to Frenchay hospital and stayed with him for two or three hours. There was an obvious reason why Welch had not originally mentioned the trip to Frenchay hospital; the fact that Giannetto had behaved with kindness and solicitude hardly squared with the kind of character portrait that Welch needed to paint. However, the visit could be confirmed from hospital records so, of course, his account needed to be changed.

Secondly, Welch now said he'd had *two* payments from Giannetto. He said that at the third meeting, he received £200 in four fifty pound notes which he spent on 'taxis and drinking'. Clearly, the purpose of this change in his evidence was to try to bolster its low plausibility rating. According to Welch's original version, Giannetto had in effect recruited him with lightning speed at Meeting 1 but then done nothing further until Meeting 4. This didn't provide a coherent and credible narrative so in the revised version an inter-vening, additional payment was added to the story.

The problem surrounding this new element in his story was that Welch had given the original version both to the police and to the pastor. He told them all about it, or so he said, because he was conscience-stricken. So if that had been true, then there would have been no problem in saying that he'd received £700 rather than £500. Yet £500 was the sum, the only sum, he mentioned when giving those original accounts.

Thirdly, he said that he had bought a wallet: 'I also remember that when Peter gave me the £500, I went to the leather shop … I bought a wallet to put the money in'.

Had Welch suddenly come into hundreds of pounds, then it is likely that the police would have been able to find some form of corroborating evidence. Yet there was nothing, absolutely nothing. In fact, all that could be found was a statement from a shop-owner about someone purchasing a leather wallet. So that explains this third change. Welch had to fit it in to his evidence because, by way of corroboration, it was all there was.

The transcript of Welch's police interview runs to ninety-eight pages. Additionally, he made a twenty-one page statement. In those 119 pages there is no mention whatever of him buying a wallet. And what had happened to this supposed wallet? Welch couldn't even be bothered to invent a story. 'I haven't got the wallet any more', he said.

In fact, the 'wallet' merely highlights the absence of genuine evidence – as there surely would have been if a vagrant like Welch had suddenly started throwing money around.

The mere idea that he bought a wallet is absurd. Why would Welch waste good drink-and-drugs money on a wallet? He would have stuffed the money in his pocket. Not only was this his over-whelmingly likely reaction, but *it is precisely what he told the police he'd done.* If he wasn't being believed about this, why was he believed about anything at all?

Whichever version of Welch's evidence one chooses to adopt, original or revised, there are many other problems with it. Most obviously, there is the timetable. According to Giannetto, the meetings all occurred within one week. Welch had, however, put forward a disjointed and protracted time frame, according to which the second meeting took place not the day after the first, but a week later.

The dates could obviously be checked from Passport Office records. It would have been clear from those that it was Giannetto's recollection that was accurate. So what happened at trial? In trying to explain away this yawning credibility gap in Welch's account, the judge said this to the jury about the second meeting:

> Originally, Welch thought it was the next week — he was hopeless about the dates. When he was shown other evidence, he agreed it must have been the next day.

The judge makes it seem as if Welch, being the sort of person he was, could not be expected to provide an accurate timetable. Yet when Welch was originally interviewed by police, he hadn't simply confused 'the next day' with 'the next week'. We know this because he gave them an account of what he had done during the week between the meetings:

> Welch: I just carried on as normal for the next three or four days ... I just hitchhiked all over the place ... From Newport I went up the M6, I didn't come straight back into Bristol, I went up the M6 to Manchester, managed to get a few quid going up there and then I came back down the M6 ...
> Q: So you didn't actually come back to Bristol then?
> A: Not that week, no.
> [Welch explained that you only needed to be there once a week to sign for your dole money.]
> Q: Once a week?
> A: ... once a week.
> Q: So the following Monday then you've been all over the country?
> A: Got me Giro.

From just this one part of the story, it is clear that Welch's story was invented. On the other hand, Giannetto's was confirmed by documentary records; it was accurate. This information would have been all the jury required in order to be able to gauge Welch's credibility; yet they were kept in the dark about it. Mr Justice Rougier compounded the deceit (accidentally, perhaps, but none-theless crucially) by making it seem as though Welch's inability to recall dates was just an excusable foible.

It is hardly necessary to add anything else, but there are many more reasons why Welch was obviously lying. If he was coming into this sort of money as easily as he maintained, what was to prevent him carrying on? Why stop when he did? If there was any truth in what Welch said, he could have met Giannetto again, told him he'd bought a car, and then got a further and much greater advance payment out of him.

Let us suppose, though, that Giannetto had made a payment to Welch. Wouldn't he have wanted to know what had happened to his money? If he was so unscrupulous that he was prepared to hire someone to kill his wife, you would have expected him to go looking for Welch when he failed to honour his side of the agreement.

Although Welch had rudimentary information to create a story that he knew would interest the police, he had no knowledge of Giannetto's actual circumstances. Welch said that Giannetto was 'staying with various friends in different places, he said he spent a couple of nights with one friend and a couple of nights with a different friend … he wasn't living in the family home at the time'. In fact, that was precisely where Giannetto was: in the family home. He had moved back in after his separation from Julia. When specific information was required, Welch couldn't produce it, as the police should have realised.

Similarly, Welch said that Giannetto had said to call him 'Peter'. The prosecution held that this indicated that he was trying to hide his identity and that it was effectively a *nom du crime*. 'Is this a name', the judge asked the jury, 'that he uses when he does not want to be traced or when he wants to remain anonymous?'

Remain anonymous? If Giannetto was recruiting Welch to murder his wife, then Welch certainly needed to know who his potential victim was. Indeed, according to Welch, he did know who she was and where she lived, and that was why he recognised the name when he heard it on television and so was able to go to the police in the first place. If Giannetto had been asking Welch to murder his wife, then logically Welch must have known who Giannetto was.

Welch was there at the Passport Office when Giannetto was getting his passport. He would have probably heard and seen Giannetto's name. He could also have seen letters and documents in the car (on the journey from Newport to Bristol) bearing Giannetto's name and address. What may have happened is that

Welch could vaguely remember the address and the surname, but not the Christian name. He took a chance on Peter; it was wrong.

Welch said he asked Giannetto for a photograph of Julia, and the prosecution argued that this was important evidence, bearing in mind that Julia had recorded in her diary that he had asked her for a photo. Yet the defence was able to show that Welch must have been shown a photograph some days *before* Julia recorded that she had been asked for one. Even apart from that, there are obvious flaws with the evidence. If Giannetto had wanted to hand someone a photograph of Julia, he hardly needed to ask her for one; he'd got hundreds already. Secondly, Welch was completely unable to describe Julia and, when he made a vague attempt to say what she looked like, it was clear that the photograph he must have seen was not of Julia but of Danila.

But why had Giannetto assisted Welch at all?

From his late teenage years, Giannetto had travelled widely in Europe and the US. On many occasions, he had himself been the recipient of spontaneous generosity as total strangers went out of their way to assist him.

This squares with experiences of my own. I well remember, as a student, travelling with a friend in Germany. We were walking by the roadside when we were caught in a sudden rainstorm that drenched us within moments.

Then a good Samaritan drew up in his extremely plush BMW. A German businessman who spoke no English, he drove us to the nearest town. We were so bedraggled and short of funds that the first small hotel refused to take us in. He persisted and found us accommodation that we could afford. As we walked out into clear blue skies the following morning, he came by again and dropped us back on our original route. He hadn't wanted anything other than to help us.

Naturally, Giannetto himself tried to behave with the generosity that others had displayed towards him.

It is not difficult to piece together what might have happened. Welch would have seen the news broadcasts about Julia's death, and considered the financial possibilities. He concocted the outline of a story and seized the moment.

Evidently, staff at the Crown Prosecution Service had not read George Orwell's *Down and Out in Paris and London*, otherwise they would have understood the short-termism of the needy.

'The great redeeming feature of poverty', wrote Orwell, 'is that it annihilates the future. When you have only three francs, you are quite indifferent; for three francs will feed you till tomorrow, and you cannot think further than that.'

Orwell needed merely food to keep himself alive; Welch's needs, after a lifetime of dependency on drink and drugs, were no less imperative but far more costly. He did whatever was necessary to score his next fix. He was, as Orwell had said, indifferent to all else. Those in Welch's position do not suffer debilitating pricks of conscience.

He may have lacked scruples, but Welch did retain vestiges of natural intelligence. It was clever of him to go to see McSorley first. He would afterwards be able to claim that he'd gone to the police only after being advised by a pastor. It would help to instil the impression that he was wrestling with his conscience. It would also give him a tiny amount of wriggle-room should he be taunted as an informer. He didn't need to think even momentarily about McSorley's advice, much less to sleep on it; he went straight to the police.

It emerged that Welch already knew one of the officers at Southmead Road Police Station, so this could suggest that he was an occasional police informer. He would certainly have been as adept at playing this system as the benefits system.

The advantages for him were colossal. His circumstances would be dramatically transformed. For the foreseeable future he would have all he needed by way of finances and even a get-out-of-jail-free card.

Once he had placed himself at the heart of the prosecution case he had to be accommodated – in every sense – as he well knew. At the time that he approached the police, he was on a waiting list in his B-and-B accommodation; almost straightaway he got income support and housing benefit and the police found new accom-modation for him. However he rarely stayed in one place for long. Usually he would be asked to leave because of drunkenness or other unacceptable behaviour. The police admitted to finding him fresh accommodation on 'approximately' ten occasions.

They also arranged for him to go to a dry-out farm in Dorset. He acknowledged at trial that a police officer had been 'looking after' him and giving him sums of money from time to time.

On one occasion, the Social Security office refused to make a payment for him; so Welch contacted the police, who telephoned the office and ensured that he got his money. A pair of his jeans was sent for forensic examination and returned damaged. Welch created a fuss, saying they had been very expensive and demanding to be compensated. Even though the police disbelieved his story that the jeans were expensive, they paid him the £42 he wanted (which would have been a top price for jeans at the time).

During this period, Welch was able to commit further crimes with impunity. He was convicted of shoplifting and arrested four times for being drunk and disorderly – and each time was released. Given his lengthy criminal record, such leniency can only be explained by his involvement in this case. On one occasion, he was fined £50 for an offence known as 'bilking'(making off without payment). A few days later, the police gave him most of the money to pay the fine.

Yet even that was not all; there was the reward too. Welch said that he didn't know that a reward was being offered. That may have been true but, whether or not he *knew* of a reward is immaterial; as someone familiar with the system, he would certainly have anticipated a reward.

The judge made two references to the advantages that Welch accrued from giving evidence. He told the jurors that the police had 'no policy whatsoever with regard to treating Welch with a less heavy hand that they had before. In other words, no deals'.

He further invited them to believe that there was insufficient reason for Welch to have invented it all. 'To put it at its most blunt', he said, 'is Welch not only a rogue and a vagabond, but so evil that he is prepared to tell this lying story, with all its possible consequences to a man who befriended him, merely to get himself a few beers and a doss-house?'

And so Mr Justice Rougier flagrantly misled the jury. Of course, there didn't need to be a particular 'policy' or 'deal' in place for events to have unfolded as they did, just as Welch would have envisaged. He would have understood precisely how to wheedle out of his handlers whatever benefits he wished. During the trial, he admitted that he had tried a little blackmail on the officers 'looking after' him. He told them that if he wasn't given money, he would have to commit further crimes and the prosecution would lose its star witness. He had 'seven birth certificates, and could disappear if he wanted to', he warned them.

For the judge to suggest to the jury that all Welch had gained during the year the case was being prepared was 'a few beers and a doss-house' – that was an unbelievable distortion of the reality. *(see Notes, page 469)*

4

The prosecution had other evidence. They pointed to references in Julia's diaries that Giannetto had physically assaulted her. There was also the entry, made on 1 July 1994, according to which he made a slitting sign across the throat with his finger.

The defence argued that, although Julia had kept a diary for some years, the passages picked out by the prosecution were written at a time when she was having consultations with her lawyer. The passages would have been very helpful as evidence in the matrimonial dispute; they had been written for a specific purpose. There was no corroborating evidence for any of the allegations and no physical signs that Julia was attacked prior to her murder.

Giannetto, who had never intruded on Julia's privacy by looking through her diaries, did not know what was in them; but the defence believed that if they had been able to see them all (there were several that the prosecution did not disclose), then they would have benefited him. The house, of course, belonged to the Giannetto family and, until 18 August, Giannetto had unrestricted access. If Julia had been genuinely afraid of him, it is likely that she would have needed to conceal the diaries; yet there was never any suggestion that she had to keep them hidden.

The prosecution asserted that Giannetto's attempts to have his son put on his passport indicated that he was preparing to flee overseas with him. Giannetto explained that all he had wanted was some continuing recognition that his son was a part of his life. He had made no plans to go abroad. He did not attempt to deceive the passport authorities. After his visit, he was telephoned and informed that checks had been made; with custody proceedings in progress, it was not possible for him to have his son put on the passport. Giannetto accepted the situation. If he had had any intention of taking his son out of the country, then it would have been straightforward for him to get Jonathan put on his Italian passport.

The prosecution also relied on evidence that Giannetto withdrew £4,000 from his bank account on a day he met Welch; but the reason for the withdrawal, he explained, was to build up the cash float he kept for buying bikes and spare parts.

Another part of the prosecution case concerned Giannetto's reportedly restrained behaviour when he went to the flat and found the body. The judge summarised this prosecution point as follows:

> By his behaviour at the scene, the defendant betrayed the fact that he knew very well what they would find ... Any husband, say the prosecution, who loved his wife would have instinctively rushed forward and the fastest sprinter in the world would not have overtaken him before he got to the body.

Such evidence, regarding a suspect's reaction on first seeing the body of a loved one, frequently becomes Crown evidence in criminal trials, though the frequency of its use is no guide to its merit.

If the bereaved person, the suspect, has some kind of hysterical reaction and breaks out in floods of tears, the Crown can deem such conduct to be suspicious because the suspect is being histrionic and putting on a show; if there are no tears and emotions are held in check, the Crown can deem such conduct to be suspicious because the suspect is detached and uncaring.

The truth is that no one can envisage how they themselves or anyone else might behave when confronted by the awful reality of the savage murder of someone close.

Moreover, there is an additional point to be made here. Had Giannetto been involved in the murder, there was no need for him to have 'found' the body. He could have used the obvious excuse (that he wasn't allowed into the flat) to ensure that someone else 'found' it.

A senior scene-of-crime officer gave evidence at trial. He said in his statement:

> This room [the bedroom] had the appearance of being ransacked as the drawers of a pine wood chest had been pulled out and tipped over on top of each other. On seeing this scene, *my immediate reaction* was to think that it was staged. (italics added)

This statement was made on 29 September 1995, more than a year after Julia's death and his visit to the crime scene. It was served on the defence on 19 October, two weeks after the trial had started. The officer appeared as a witness the same day. The judge explained the thrust of his evidence:

> To the experienced eye of the experienced scene-of-crime officer, this did not look like any professional burglary. The method was wrong, everything seemed to be done in the wrong order, things were still there which you would have expected a burglar to take. To him, it looked rather more like somebody had tried to make it look like a burglary.

The belated tendering of his evidence had handicapped the defence in two respects: lawyers did not have time to assimilate the statement properly and research the background to it; and were unable to seek evidence of their own on this point. In legal terms, it was a case of the prosecution ambushing the defence.

Nevertheless, during cross-examination, the defence did make some headway. The officer said that he had made contemporaneous notes that it appeared 'not a realistic burglary scene'. The defence asked to see these notes. When they were produced, the officer had to concede that they contained no such comment.

So the defence continued the cross-examination:

Q: How many statements did you make in relation to this?
A: In relation to the state of the room?
Q: Yes.
A: Sorry, in what way do you mean?
Q: Witness statements.
A: The witness statement that is produced before the Court is the only statement I have made in respect of that room, my Lord.

It was only after the trial had finished that the defence found out that this wasn't true. That wasn't the officer's one and only statement; there was an important earlier one. This first one, about which the Crown had said nothing at all, had been made on 7 December 1994. In this statement, the officer said that he'd attended the scene on 12 September. 'The rear main bedroom showed signs of disturbance', he said, 'as the contents from a pine chest had been tipped out onto the bedroom floor.'

The original statement contained nothing that suggested that the scene had been staged. Indeed, it was apparent from this statement that he'd been to the flat four times between 12 and 15 September. He was there for six hours on the first occasion and another six hours the fourth time. So not only was the 'staged burglary' idea not his 'immediate reaction', it hadn't even been his reaction after four visits, two of which were lengthy.

It is regrettable that the CPS put him forward as a witness of truth when they knew the evidence he was going to give was contradicted by his original statement; and, to make matters worse, they deliberately deprived the defence of the opportunity to examine the evidence in its full context.

But it wasn't a faked burglary anyway. There was an actual burglary. One of Julia's most precious pieces of jewellery, a ruby bracelet which had belonged to her mother and which she would never have sold or given to anyone, was missing. Her jewellery box had been searched and a camera was also missing.

Not only was the evidence of this scene-of-crime officer false but, at the very end of his court appearance, its dishonesty was compounded – again unintentionally, one presumes – by the judge:

Mr Justice Rougier: You apparently have investigated many burglaries?
A: Yes, my Lord.
Rougier: In your experience, is it common for the burglar, on being surprised by the householders, to beat their brains out, stab them repeatedly in the chest and slit their throats from ear to ear?
A: No, my Lord.

So the jury, having been incorrectly informed that this 'immediately' appeared to be a faked burglary, now learned that this kind of savage assault would not have happened in what might be termed a natural burglary. In fact, this too was untrue. It may have been uncommon for a burglar to behave with such violence; it was certainly not unknown (and indeed there are some well-publicised cases in which, plainly, this is what has occurred).

The strongest points for the defence were Giannetto's complete lack of opportunity and the absence of forensic evidence. He had extremely good alibi evidence – both from his parents, who said he was at home all morning, and also from two labourers who were working at an adjoining house. They saw him holding his son in the front window of his house. One put the time at 12.45; the other at 12.50. '[Giannetto] waved to us', one of them remarked. Both were questioned again about the time and made supplementary statements confirming how they could be sure (they had checked the time as it was just before their lunch-break).

These vital statements, which meant that it was virtually impossible for Giannetto himself to have murdered Julia, were collected by the police. The defence knew nothing about them until they were handed over by the prosecution as part of the unused material just before the start of the trial.

The murder occurred on a morning when Julia herself had made, in fact, two last-minute changes to the baby care arrangements. (She had telephoned to ask Rob to have him at 10.00, but then rung back to change the time to 10.30.) So, if he was supposed to have had an accomplice, how would he have contacted him to alert him? There was no evidence of suspicious telephone calls from the Giannettos' house. There was virtually no evidence that Giannetto himself went out of the house that morning or that his car left the driveway.

There was no forensic evidence to link him with the crime; and nor was there forensic evidence in the car. The Crown forensic scientist, John Owen, accepted that the murderer would have left some traces somewhere – on his clothing, perhaps, or in his car.

How did the Crown attempt to deal with this vacuum in its case? They said that none of Giannetto's clothing could be found at the Beaufort Road address except, curiously, for three socks. So, as the judge put it, 'the prosecution suggest that there was another address somewhere that they have never found and is probably still there and there might be some bloodstained clothing [there]'.

The Crown was implying that Giannetto had murdered his wife, gone to a secret location to change his clothing and destroy all forensic evidence, and then returned home. But there was no evidence whatever to support that. All this occurred around midday and there is no evidence that Giannetto was out, either on foot or in his car, at a time of day when somebody might have seen him

And where was the hideaway? Had it existed then, given the time-scale, it must have been very close. Finding it should not have presented unusual problems. Yet nothing was ever found. There was simply no evidence of any other accommodation or any hide-away. Having failed to find evidence, the prosecution resorted to inventing it.

In any event, the suggestion underlying all this was untrue; Giannetto's clothing was at his house where one would have expected to find it. Here, just as with the evidence of the 'staged' burglary, there was a strange absence of documentation. The officer who claimed not have found any of Giannetto's clothing at Giannetto's home (with the exception of those three socks) had not made any contemporaneous notes to record what would have been this extraordinary non-discovery.

5

On 3 October 1994, three weeks after Julia was murdered, Graham Chapman telephoned the police. He owned the Stage Coach Inn, a public house and restaurant in Berkeley, Gloucestershire, north of Bristol. He told them that he thought one of his employees, Giuseppe Vincini, could well have killed Julia.

'I just feel he may be capable of murder', commented Chapman, 'as he is a very strange individual.'

That very same day, by an astonishing coincidence, Margaret MacDonald called at the police incident kiosk to say that she saw a man going down the steps to the basement flat at 12a Oakfield Road on the day of the murder.

Two days later, she contacted police again, wondering why no one had followed up her information. A statement was then taken from her. She said that she saw the man just after 12.00 noon, and that she knew the house, as a former occupant of the second-floor flat was a friend of hers. At this stage, no information regarding the time of the crime had been publicly released.

Margaret McDonald described the man as white, of continental appearance, about 5'10", of powerful build, and with long grey greasy hair pulled back in a ponytail with a thick rubber band.

She further said that on the previous Monday, 5 September, she had seen this man, talking with another man in a foreign language in the Café Premiere. She also noted that they were talking to a woman who, from the description, could have been Julia Giannetto and who, said MacDonald, 'looked frail and vulnerable. I had the impression it was an intimidating atmosphere'. She also said that she saw the two men again on Friday 9 September.

It quickly became clear that MacDonald and Chapman had referred to the same man. Vincini was fifty-four years old, and had recently come to live in the Bristol area. He had arrived from San Diego, California, which he left in a hurry after his marriage failed. He walked out, taking all of his wife's savings.

When he arrived in Bristol, he tried to find a job and contacted Giovanni Fucci, owner of the Numero Uno pizzeria. Fucci needed no staff at the time, but recommended Vincini to Graham Chapman, who took him on. According to Chapman, Vincini was a 'very experienced chef who was good at his trade'. Chapman added that he would sometimes wear his hair in a ponytail.

However, Vincini's kitchen skills were let down by his interpersonal ones. Chapman described him as overbearing towards other people, particularly women. He said his English was poor, and he was rude to other staff and customers alike. After a few short weeks, five members of staff had left because of conflicts with him. On 2 October, Chapman decided to let Vincini go.

Chapman had further interesting information. 'Vincini always had Mondays off', he said. 'I was aware that on these days he would always go to Bristol and, because he is Italian, associate with the Italian fraternity in the Whiteladies Road area of Bristol.'

On Monday 5 September, Vincini went to the Numero Uno pizzeria with Chapman's son and met Fucci, with whom he had struck up a friendship. There then follows an important piece of information: the three of them went to Giuseppe Galli's hair salon. Galli said he gave him a trim: 'I tidied [Vincini's] hair up, but left the length as it was'.

Monday 12 September was, of course, when the murder happened. Vincini again went to the Numero Uno pizzeria at about 11.00am. He asked after Fucci who, however, did not go to work that early in the day, and Vincini left. He returned later, and when Fucci did arrive at about 1.30–1.45, Vincini was already there.

Then, at about 3.00, according to Fucci, 'Vincini said he was going to [Galli's] salon to have his hair permed. It was the first that I had heard of this.' Galli himself arrived at his salon just before 5.00 and was surprised to see Vincini there. 'I did not expect to see him in the salon', he said, 'and it was not by appointment'.

So just a week after having visited his hairdresser's, Vincini made what seems to have been an emergency return visit. He now asked to have his ponytail cut off and for his hair to be restyled and permed. The perm was done by Renata Luchette (who, as it happened, gave up her job and returned to Italy at the end of that week).

Nor was that all. When Vincini was seen in the morning, he was wearing a short jacket; in the afternoon, he was wearing a long black coat – a surprising choice, given that it was a hot summer's day.

So we know where Vincini was that afternoon. But where was he during the critical 12.00 to 1.00 period? No one knew. None of his associates could account for his whereabouts.

Further, although they seemed to be some of his closest companions, even they had not warmed to him. Fucci said their relationship was soured because he found out that Vincini would turn up at the restaurant when he, Fucci wasn't there, order an expensive meal and wine and leave without paying. 'I cannot make this man out', he said. 'I have the impression that there is something more to this man, but I cannot say exactly what it is'. Galli arrived at a similar conclusion: 'I formed the impression that he was not a nice man'.

Once they had statements from MacDonald and Chapman, the police made enquiries in the United States. They then discovered that Vincini had signed on in Edmonton, north London, on 6 October and took him back to Bristol for questioning.

The police interviewed him on 1 and 2 November. Vincini gave garbled and incoherent answers. He tried to deny that he had ever worn his hair long and in a ponytail. He originally said he didn't know where Oakfield Road was, and then had to admit he had stayed in a hotel there. He said he'd never had a US passport. In fact, not only did he have one but he must have had more than one. Graham Chapman said that he saw Vincini ripping up an American passport; yet the police were able to establish that, after Chapman sacked him, he was still using a US passport to book into hotels. In his first interview, he said he went to Numero Uno at 11 o'clock; in the second interview, he said he went there at 12 o'clock. During the key period, when the murder was committed, he says he had been shopping for shoes; but he had bought none, and was unable to give the name of a single shop where he had looked.

On 2 November he was put on an identity parade. MacDonald picked him out without difficulty as the man she had seen going into the basement flat at Oakfield Road. She added that he had had his hair cut since she saw him then.

Yet the Vincini trail was abandoned. The police decided that MacDonald was not a reliable witness. She said she had been on her way to pay money into her building society when she saw Vincini at Julia's flat; yet the branch records showed that the time of her transaction was actually 2.06pm. Further, the report of her first visit to police gave the time that she saw the man as 4.00pm.

She was to argue that they had recorded it incorrectly. Certainly, the visit to the building society at 2.06 appears not to undermine her evidence but rather to strengthen it; she was certainly out during the lunchtime period. After her evidence was brusquely rejected by police, she put in a complaint about how officiously she had been treated.

When Julia's body was found, her key-ring was in her right hand, and a small Swiss army knife was open. Perhaps she had been trying to defend herself. The most straightforward explanation is that she disturbed a burglar, perhaps after letting herself in. The back door was usually left unlocked and there was an unknown footprint in the garden. Still to this day, no one knows who killed her or why.

However, the points of evidence against Vincini are cumulatively highly persuasive. MacDonald and Chapman had independently reported him to police as a possible suspect on the same day. MacDonald pinpointed three occasions when she saw him. Her identifications for 5 and 12 September appear to have been spot on. They were Mondays, which was Vincini's day off work, and it is clear from other evidence that he was in the area. She did say she saw him going down the steps to the basement flat at the time of the murder. She certainly knew the house. She was also particularly confident in her identification.

Then, in interview, Vincini gave incoherent and untruthful answers, regularly taking refuge in his poor command of the English language. He had no alibi for the time of the murder, and acted guiltily in its aftermath, trying to alter his appearance significantly.

So it is bewildering that he was eliminated from enquiries so prematurely. As far as one can judge from the records, the officers who interviewed Vincini seemed taken aback when told to release him. There are theories that he may have been an informer who could rely on police protection. However, he had not long been in the country. Another possibility is that he was an informer for US police agencies, who asked their British counterparts to lay off him.

The jurors were unaware of all this information. All they were told was that Vincini was one of those arrested in connection with the investigation. The defence, too, was unaware of it. It was not until nearly two years later, after the trial and the failure of his appeal, that Giannetto obtained the documents from which this analysis of Vincini's potential involvement in the murder has been gleaned.

6

Hilary Rittner, an antiquarian bookseller in London, began a correspondence with Giannetto during his imprisonment, as he searched for particular out-of-print titles. She became sure that he was innocent and that the case was extraordinary.

The fact that sets the case apart is that no one understands what Giannetto has been convicted of. He was entitled to know precisely the charges, the case and the evidence that he had to answer. To this day, he does not – and cannot – understand the legal and evidential basis on which he was convicted. As he has been shuttled from prison to prison over the past two decades, he has derived grim amusement from disabusing the reception warders of their assumptions.

'Giannetto WB1699,' they'd say, 'You've been convicted of the murder of your wife'.

'No, I haven't', he'd respond.

They would naturally assume he was being contrary, so Giannetto would give them the paperwork to examine.

'Blimey', they'd say (or something stronger). 'No, you haven't'.

IN 1861 THE LIBERAL GOVERNMENT of Viscount Palmerston consolidated the criminal statutes which were, in those days, few enough anyway. First-hand murder was covered by the Offences Against the Person Act; and procurement of murder was covered in the Accessories and Abettors Act. So these were then, and have been ever since, offences covered by different criminal acts which were passed in the same year. There can be no doubt that the government regarded them as separate offences.

The charge on the indictment was, plainly and simply, 'murder'. Obviously, a defendant must know what the charge against him is so that he has a proper opportunity to defend himself. It is axiomatic that he should not be charged with one crime and convicted of a different one. So the Crown should not have been allowed to put forward a case for the procurement of Julia's murder.

In any event, when an accused faces a charge of procurement of murder, he is referred to as the secondary party. In order to reach this stage, the Crown should have satisfied two pre-conditions: if Giannetto was being regarded as the secondary party, then there must be a principal party, and there must be an evidential link between them. Neither of these two preconditions was satisfied.

Further, those charged with investigating the offence are legally required to put the prosecution case to the suspect in interview. Over five days of interview, never once did the police ask Giannetto whom he had recruited to murder his wife; or how much money was agreed between them; or how the plan was hatched between them – something of particular importance in view of Julia's own switch in the normal arrangements for baby care on the day she was murdered. None of these questions was even asked. Just as the procurement charge was never put on the indictment, nor was it put to Giannetto in interview.

It must be emphasised that there was no evidence of any link between Giannetto and Vincini. In interview, Vincini was asked if he knew the Giannetto family. He said he did not. Giannetto was shown a photograph of Vincini. He said he had never seen or heard of him. There were no further questions. The police would not tell Giannetto who Vincini was or why he was asked about him.

The prosecution had tried to shore up its case with the four-point clarification *(see page 294)* and its concluding suggestion that 'the inference of guilt is inevitable'.

But there were solid objections to this 'clarification'. According to the first point, Giannetto 'wished his wife dead'. The evidence for this is non-existent. The second point (that all this happened during a time when the child was not with Julia) turned reality inside out, since it was Julia herself, not Giannetto, who had made a late change in the baby-care arrangements. Accordingly, any advance plans Giannetto may have made for someone to commit the murder were likely to have been dashed. The third point was that he'd already paid money for someone to commit the murder. There is no basis for this other than Welch's highly suspect testimony.

The fourth point (that the murder happened in the way that Giannetto had threatened) was particularly economical with the truth. The prosecution case was that the purported Welch plan was a genuine attempt to hire a hitman; but, of course, there was no similarity at all between what was planned and what was effected. The method of killing which Welch described was dissimilar to that which actually happened. So the prosecution can scarcely claim the means of murder as an indicator of Giannetto's involvement when they'd discounted the same point themselves. Nor, in fact, was Julia killed by having her throat cut. She was murdered by being bludgeoned and beaten and stabbed.

At what is termed the halfway point in the trial, after the prosecution had completed its case, the defence made a submission of no case to answer. 'There is not one jot of proof, direct or indirect, so far as this man's involvement in the causation of this woman's death is concerned', argued Charles Barton QC. 'On that basis, and on that basis alone, this ought not to be allowed to go to the jury.'

Barton felt he was on solid ground and knew that he could cite in his support one of the most famous of appeal court axioms. In the classic case, *R v Wallace* (1932) (which was the first occasion on which the appeal court had quashed a conviction for murder), Lord Chief Justice Hewart said, 'A court is not concerned with suspicion, however grave, or with theories, however ingenious'. Wallace was set free to be engulfed by cheering crowds outside the Royal Courts.

Nevertheless, Mr Justice Rougier declined to stop Giannetto's trial.

Legal argument then moved on to a different area. Barton stressed that the prosecution should have to prove one of their allegations, whichever one they chose, and that they should do so based on evidence. At this point, Paul Chadd QC, the Crown barrister, broadly conceded that there was insufficient evidence to press either charge. 'A procurement and an actual participation in the wielding of the weapon', he said, 'One could not possibly have the two counts; upon each it would be arguable that there was no evidence.'

So here was the prosecution admitting that there was not actually sufficient evidence for its case.

Nevertheless, Rougier turned down this submission also. 'It has long been settled law that if the evidence does not permit the prosecution to choose between direct participation and abetting or procuring', he said, 'then they may advance their case to the jury (as has been done here) on the alternative basis.'

However, this completely missed the point. There are cases where the prosecution is unable to choose between particular charges. The case generally referred to as having set the precedent was the case of *R v Thatcher*, which was heard in the Supreme Court of Canada. However, this case is not the equivalent of the Giannetto case; it is the exact opposite of it. The point about *R v Thatcher*, as the justices said, was 'the overwhelming mass of the evidence against the appellant' – and that abundance of evidence was consistent with either charge. In this case, it was the absence of evidence (as the prosecution fairly conceded) that was the key distinguishing point.

So there was uncertainty about just what the jury was deciding. Yet there was legal precedent that the matter under consideration had to be absolutely clear. In a previous case (*R v Brown 1984*), the Court of Appeal had declared:

> ... where there are two routes by which a murder may have been committed, and those two routes comprise completely different acts happening at different times, the jury must be unanimous on which act leads them to a decision to convict. In such a case, the judge shall direct the jury that they must agree on the basis of the defendant's guilt before they can convict him.

This had not happened here. It raised the possibility that some jurors may have thought they were convicting him of one purported action, while others thought they were convicting him on a different one.

However, the jurors then returned into court to ask their remarkable question:

> How much of an involvement in the murder does the defendant need to have in order to convict him of the murder? i.e. planning, paying for, knew of and did not prevent.

A reasonable inference from the way the jurors phrased their question would be that they had excluded the possibility that Giannetto had killed Julia himself. They were therefore examining the possibility that he had procured or encouraged someone to do it for him.

In answer to the first part of the question – planning – the judge, Mr Justice Rougier, explained:

> He would not be guilty, of course, if he made a plan which fizzled out, came to nothing and left it there ... Supposing you come to the conclusion that there was a genuine attempt to recruit Welch, but it fizzled out, if you stop the clock there, nothing has happened. There has been a plan, but she is still alive. What you have to be sure of is that her death, when it occurred, took place as a result of a plan, that is another plan, made by this defendant.

There was no evidence whatever of this plan – *another plan* – to kill Julia; nor was there any evidence of Giannetto having handed over money and commissioned someone to kill her for him. No evidence regarding this was put before the court. So from this point on the trial became shrouded in a fog of speculation. Matters quickly became even worse. In answer to their third point, the judge said:

> ... has given us all a bit of a headache because it is rather difficult to deduce the scenario you have in mind ... Supposing somebody came up to you and said, 'I'm going to kill your wife'. If he played any part, either in encouragement, as little as patting him on the back, nodding, saying, 'Oh, goody!', that would be sufficient to involve him in the murder, to make him guilty, because he is encouraging the murder.

So this is the 'Oh, goody!' moment.

The judge had already said that he was worried about the scenarios the jury had 'created in their minds'. Now he compounded the problem by feeding them a scenario he had created in *his* mind.

If the jury convicted on the 'Oh, goody!' premise – and they may well have done – then they convicted Giannetto on the basis of a suggestion that even the prosecution had disowned. It was something that he was not charged with and was not on the indictment; that had never been mentioned in evidence; and against which he had had no opportunity to defend himself.

Mr Justice Rougier wrote a report on the case to the Home Secretary. In this he said:

> Nor is it possible to be certain whether it was the work of the defendant himself, or some other hitman that he had hired for the purpose; my preference would be for the former.

For four separate reasons, these thirty-four words are astonishing. Firstly, they appear to make it crystal-clear that it was impossible even for the judge to understand what Giannetto had been convicted of. Secondly, he alludes to 'the defendant himself, or some other hitman'. *Other* hitman? So he must have believed that Giannetto himself was a 'hitman'? But there was no evidence whatever of this. The prosecution had never suggested it. Thirdly, the total ignorance of the identity of what the law would call 'a principle party' is underlined by the vagueness of that reference to 'some other hitman'.

Fourthly, Rougier's preference is *'for the former'*. He had conducted this trial and concluded at the end of it that Julia's murder was more likely to have been 'the work of the defendant himself'. How had he managed to reach a view that contradicted what the jury appeared to believe about the case? Had he listened to the alibi evidence? Hadn't he noticed the complete absence of forensic evidence in circumstances where one would have expected a great deal? Had he been following the evidence at all?

7

From the start, Giannetto and his family were treated by the authorities with particular hostility – largely, it seemed, because they came from Italy, but specifically because Giannetto's father came from Sicily. The Giannettos were instantly assumed to be a dangerous family.

Soon after Julia's murder, Giannetto drove his parents to Heathrow as they were catching a flight to Italy. They were subjected not just to the normal airport security; each was thoroughly searched. They later learned that the police believed they may have been taking money out of the country in order to pay a Mafia hitman.

And so the Mafia theme became a key component of the unreal background to the case. When Giannetto was allowed to see his son during those few weeks before he was charged there were, astonishingly, always armed guards present. It was as if all the Avon services dealing with the case had become collectively seized by this Mafia fantasy.

They held firm to this fantasy despite the fact that there was no basis for it other than their own overworked imaginations. UK police went over to Turin and broke down the door of the Giannettos' flat. They found nothing. Then they went to the family home in Sicily. Perhaps they had expected a secluded villa behind high walls with an entry intercom, marble floors and ornate furnishings. They found only the rustic peasant cottage where Carmelo was born seventy years earlier.

After being convicted, Giannetto went for a first meeting with his probation officer. The latter instantly assumed that the wrong man had come in. He'd been led to believe that he was dealing with a Mafia heavy. The small and inoffensive man standing before him didn't fit the picture.

Giannetto was allowed just two final meetings with his son. The last time, social services wanted him to tell Jonathan that he would never see him again. Giannetto refused. 'I made it just like an ordinary day', he said. 'Of course, after they'd taken him I broke down, but while he was there I managed to smile and held it together.'

Not surprisingly, Giannetto suffered incalculable grief after being told that he would never see his son again – something that social services appeared not to understand.

'You'd have thought that professionals would be able to assess the situation', commented Anita Bromley, his current solicitor.

One of the professional people who could assess the situation was Tim Rose, Giannetto's trial solicitor, whose longstanding commitment to his former client is remarkable.

'This was a wholly different situation to that of other criminal trials in which it is impossible to prove every last detail', he commented. 'In this case, no one knew what happened, as is amply illustrated by the judge's stated preference for what was in fact the least likely scenario.

'There was nothing to show that Julia had not been murdered by another hand altogether. Not one fact advanced by the prosecution excluded this possibility.'

William Welch died an inevitable death, even if the actual circumstances were a little strange. He died of a drugs overdose in a Manchester park in 2002. Bizarrely, a wedding party was nearby at the moment he expired. The bride had some training in first-aid and rushed forward in her wedding-dress to try to revive him.

So consistently ill-informed has the treatment of Giannetto been that social services now suggested that he may have had some hand in Welch's death. Yet there was nothing suspicious about it. In fact, this was just another example of social services' irrationality. Giannetto would have been fully justified in despising Welch for what he had done, but he certainly needed him alive. Deathbed confessions rarely occur outside fiction but while there's life, there's hope. Once Welch was dead, the guttering flame of hope was extinguished.

Then, in September 2009, fourteen years after the trial, the family discovered an important document. The police had taken stacks of material from the flat including, apparently, all of Julia's personal effects. After the trial, the detritus was gathered up in boxes, taken to Giannetto's parents' house and left to gather dust. No one believed there was anything valuable there.

However, they then found what seemed to be the draft of a

letter from Julia. It must have been important for her to have made a draft beforehand, in which there were crossings-out and alterations. Obviously, this document was something the police had missed.

The letter was a bombshell. Julia was writing to someone, perhaps called Jason, with whom she must have had a secret affair. In her script, dated 14 April 1992, she wrote:

> For myself, life continues on a semi-even keel, since Rob is again working twelve hours a day, which leaves little time for anything apart from eating and sleeping when he gets home ... I am beginning to consider the possibilities of life beyond my present situation and, although somewhat constrained by practicalities on the whither, when and how front (which will probably take some time to resolve) it is an enormous relief in itself to be able to think positively on my own account again.
>
> I do want to thank you, Jas, for the contribution you have made towards this and hope that you do not feel compromised in any way by your involvement in 'la cosa nostra'. I realise that any such feelings could only arise from the way that I took advantage of your kindness and sympathy ... Any regrets in the matter should be mine – I assure you I have none.
>
> I also want to assure you that any anxieties you might have with regard to future repercussions from your involvement are completely groundless. I know I appear to shoot my mouth off on occasions but even in extremis (or under the influence) there are some things which never escape my lips – your name or anything leading to it is one of them; you have my word on this.

Julia had indeed kept her secrets.

The letter immediately threw fresh light on the whole case in two crucial respects. Clearly, there was a secret side to Julia's life of which Giannetto had been unaware. The family had always believed that the murder happened as a result of a burglary-gone-wrong; in view of this letter there could perhaps have been another explanation. Perhaps there were other references to this side of her life in her other writings; perhaps these held the clue to her murder.

The important reference to 'la cosa nostra' was presumably Julia's mocking way of referring to Rob and his family when matters between them were strained. What is extraordinary is that the police and social services should have been so naive as to take it at face value – and that this became the factor that determined their approach from then on.

'From very early on, the Sicilian card was played', explained Judy Giannetto, Rob's younger sister, who today works in publishing in Chicago. 'The ignorance and racism appalled me. I remember at a custody hearing for Jonathan, a social worker saying, "If one's a murderer, they all are". It's that mentality that I fear.'

Sometimes his family wondered whether the authorities understood the embarrassment that the case represents – the criminal justice process exists, among other things, to combat dishonesty and racism, yet here was a prosecution deeply infused with dishonesty and racism – and so, in order to save face, made sure that Giannetto himself was buried alive. The Criminal Cases Review Commission also turned down the case.

'When the CCRC was set up, it seemed as though it was giving us real hope', commented Giannetto, 'but it turned out to be just another wall.'

The final twist in this journey of madness occurred when some social services personnel declared themselves discretionary victims in this matter, and therefore their feelings and sensitivities needed to be accommodated. The social services are able to get away with extraordinary conduct because they are not subject to outside scrutiny; all their dealings can take place under the safety of a media blackout. So no one was able to report that this gave them a clear conflict of interest, as professionals in other fields would instantly have acknowledged.

In an effort to try to understand why the authorities were being quite so oppressive, Giannetto succeeded in obtaining some of the documents in his prison file. These included the 'Summary of Offence' drawn up by the Offender Management Unit of the Ministry of Justice. This contained the following passages:

Oh, goody!

Although [Welch] was a drug addict, alcoholic and confidence trick-
ster, *everything he said was corroborated by witnesses or documents* ...

In interview *[Giannetto] agreed everything [Welch] had said*, other than
paying him money and asking him to kill Julia ...

Giannetto [had] an alibi by his parents but *independent witnesses showed
this to be weak and flawed* ...

On 30 October, at Bristol Crown Court, *Giannetto pleaded guilty* to
murder ...

The italicised parts are not merely inaccurate; they are nonsense.
From this material, one derives the impression that because those
working for both NOMS (National Offender Management
Service) and social services have the reassurance that their work
will never be subject to public scrutiny, they are able to operate
with impunity at a level of staggering incompetence. Such incompetence, of course, costs the country hundreds of millions of pounds
– and perpetuates the ruin of the lives of those, like Giannetto, who
have the misfortune to be ensnared.

'THE ABSURDITY OF the case angers me', said Judy Giannetto.
'This is a tragedy of grand proportions – for both families.

'Although our relationship had faltered after her break-up with
Rob, Julia's loss remains very much alive to me. This person, who
had been so pivotal in my adolescent life, who had taken such an
interest in me and my happiness and who had shared so much time
with me, was suddenly gone.'

One cannot tell, of course, what perceptions Jonathan will
develop about all that has happened, both to his parents and to him.

'As a family, we've had a son, nephew and grandson taken from
us', Judy reflected. 'Jonathan is now approaching adulthood. If, one
day, he has questions, he will be free to seek out any of us for
answers. One might presume that, so far, he knows only what he
has been told.

'I suspect, though, that he deserves more credit than that. He is,
after all, the son of two fiercely defiant, free-thinking people, both
of whom have met with ends they do not deserve.'

Chapter 9

Changing the indictment

Jonathan King's story

1

On 23 November 2000, at eight o'clock in the morning, there was a loud knock at the blue door of Jonathan King's house in Bayswater, central London. He looked out of an upstairs window. The visitors told him they were Surrey police and needed to speak to him on an important matter. Fearing it concerned his elderly mother, King hurtled down the stairs and opened the door.

It didn't concern his mother. Instead, he was told that 'certain allegations' had been made against him. As he was driven away to be questioned at Staines Police Station, a number of officers remained behind to search his house.

King was interviewed and then charged with indecently assaulting three boys during the late '70s/early '80s period. Having surrendered his passport, he was given police bail and allowed to leave at 8.00pm. His solicitor drove him back to his house. The police had told him they would not allow the day's events to reach the national media, but he knew that was a hollow promise. He was up very early the following morning and had left the house by the time the photographers began to congregate outside it.

Predictably, news of his arrest was the front-page headline of the *Sun* newspaper, and this, equally predictably, generated a barrage of deeply wounding publicity. In due course, the complaints with which King was originally charged were abandoned by the prosecution. He stood trial at the Old Bailey in 2001 solely on the basis of complaints from people who came forward in the aftermath of the publicity storm instigated by the *Sun*.

The judge grouped the charges, and ordered that there should be two trials. At the end of the first trial, King was found guilty by eleven members of the jury, although a reporting blackout was imposed pending the outcome of the second trial. In the event, the remaining charges were dropped so there was no second trial. However, King was sentenced to seven years' imprisonment on the basis of the guilty verdicts from the first trial. The jubilation of the British press was unconfined.

TOWARDS THE END of the Second World War, on 6 December 1944, Jonathan was born Kenneth George King in an expensive private clinic in the West End of London. The cost of this nursing home was, unfortunately, no guarantee of its competence. A botched forceps delivery meant that the baby's mouth was wrenched out of position and King was given a lopsided grin that became an unwanted trademark throughout his life.

By that time, his father, Jimmy King, was a prisoner of war. He had been born in New Jersey, on the eastern seaboard of the United States. On moving to Britain with his family in the 1930s, he retained his US passport and, when war broke out, enlisted with the American Field Service. He was captured in France, and so Ailsa, Jonathan's mother, went to flirt with Joe Kennedy, patriarch of the Kennedy family and then the US ambassador in London, to try to get assistance for him. In the event, Jimmy took matters into his own hands by escaping.

After the war, he became managing director of a leading men's clothing company, Tootal Ties and Shirts. The family – Jonathan by then had two younger brothers, James and Andy – moved to an extensive eighteenth-century cottage in Ewhurst, Surrey. In August 1954, Jonathan, then aged nine, and seven-year-old James returned home from a cycling trip to be confronted by a huddle of people in the front garden. They were quickly ushered to their bedroom. The next morning Ailsa told the boys that their father had died; aged forty-two, he had suffered a fatal heart attack while mowing the lawn.

Despite being widowed in her thirties, Ailsa managed the family income to ensure that her children continued to receive a good education. King went to Charterhouse, which would certainly have been in the Top 10 of English public schools. By the time he got there, however, he was already obsessed with Top 10s of a different kind: the pop charts.

'I would write down the charts from Radio Luxembourg', he recalled, 'and predict – usually fairly accurately – where the records would be the next week.'

On his 12th birthday, King got his first 45rpm record. He can still remember making his mother drive round record shops in search

of *Singing the Blues*. Not the British cover version by Tommy Steele
– every shop had that; Jonathan wanted the original American
version by Guy Mitchell. 'Even at that age', he pointed out, 'I could
tell the difference between an original and a copy.'

His passion for pop music became more and more intense. When
Buddy Holly produced his string of hits, King started wearing
Buddy Holly glasses.

In the autumn of 1963, he passed the entrance exam for Trinity
College, Cambridge. He would read English literature, and was
due to take up his place at the start of the next academic year in
October 1964.

In those days, gap years were not *de rigueur* for students but
King's mother was far-sighted. She told him he'd never again in his
life have the opportunity to spend several months doing exactly
as he pleased. To make sure it was an opportunity that he seized,
she gave him a round-the-world air ticket together with £1 a day
living expenses. Exciting as this was, King had no wish to miss
out on developments in the exploding pop music scene in the
UK. His mother solved that difficulty, too, by promising to air-mail
each week's copy of *New Musical Express*, the indispensable weekly
music paper, to the nearest Thomas Cook.

As he set out, though, King's overriding objective was to estab-
lish some first-rate contacts in the music business. He flew to
Athens, where he picked up the first of his weekly *NMEs* from
Thomas Cook's, and then made his way through Europe and
Asia to Australia. He planned to catch the Beatles' world tour in
Melbourne.

By using YMCAs and cheap hostels, King had managed to
save enough from his daily allowance to be able to book into the
Southern Cross, the hotel where the Beatles and their entourage
were staying. What King wanted was an introduction to Brian
Epstein, the Beatles' manager and the man rightly regarded as the
Svengali of the pop music business. Once in his room that was (by
anyone's standards, but especially a student's) absolute luxury, he
picked up the phone and asked to be put through to Epstein.

'I'm sorry', the telephonist informed him, 'Mr Epstein checked
out a few days ago.'

His well-laid plans in disarray, King was momentarily crestfallen. However, the helpful hotel telephonist said she'd put him through instead to Epstein's deputy, Derek Taylor. King introduced himself and said he'd been desperately hoping to meet Epstein.

'Brian has gone off for a holiday', explained Taylor. 'He's gone to Hawaii. Are you planning to go to Hawaii?'

Hawaii hadn't been on King's itinerary before, but it was now.

'He's staying at the Royal Hawaiian Hotel on Waikiki Beach', added Taylor. 'This is his room number. Contact him there and tell him you've spoken to me.'

King flew off to Hawaii and checked into the YMCA. 'The first thing I did was to telephone Brian', recalled King. 'He said, "I'll be on the beach, come round and see me".'

King rushed over. Happily, a branch of Thomas Cook was en route.

'Brian was sitting at a table at the back of the beach', explained King. 'I introduced myself and his first words were, "Oh, God, is that the new *NME*? Brilliant". He read it from cover to cover, and then said, "That's the best thing that's happened in weeks, I haven't been able to keep up with what's been going on".

'We spent about two hours together. He couldn't have been nicer.'

'Of course, those things don't happen anymore', he reflected, 'at least not outside the movies. But I've never forgotten the spontaneous kindness of Derek and Brian, and I've always been a great believer in giving the time of day to people who need advice. In fact, it was one of the reasons I found myself standing in the dock at the Old Bailey.'

KING CONTINUED WITH HIS worldwide trip and arrived in San Francisco in the middle of July 1964, just in time for the Republican Convention at the Cow Palace.

He already had excellent US contacts through his father's cousins, the Elliotts. Among the family were Jock Elliott, the chairman of Ogilvy and Mather, one of the world's largest advertising agencies; and his brother Osborn, the distinguished journalist who was then editor of *Newsweek* magazine and who would become deputy mayor of New York under Abraham Beam. Their mother was Jonathan's godmother.

Osborn ensured that the nineteen-year-old King was well looked after. He not only provided him with a special pass to the convention, at which Barry Goldwater was selected as the candidate to fight the incumbent president, Lyndon Johnson, in that year's presidential election, but also arranged for him to be introduced to Goldwater. King was then asked to courier the *Newsweek* photographs for the next edition back to New York – a huge responsibility which naturally necessitated an upgrade to first-class for the flight.

Back in England, King went up to Cambridge to start university life. However, the allure of pop music remained strong and he wrote to a number of leading figures in the industry. He received just the one reply.

Tony Hall, of Decca Records, invited him to his office in Great Marlborough Street, just behind Oxford Street. King found himself waiting to speak to Hall alongside two other equally callow youths. All three were desperate to pick up whatever advice they could. The others were Andrew Lloyd Webber and Tim Rice.

The former has now been ennobled and the latter knighted but, of the three, it was King whose career achieved lift-off first. He'd written *Everyone's Gone to the Moon*, which was released in June 1965. King decided that neither 'Kenneth' nor 'George' were viable names for a pop singer, so he decided to call himself Jonathan. The decision seems to have been a good one, as the record instantly became an enormous hit in the UK, the US, and worldwide.

Straight away, King, who still resembled the geeky undergraduate he actually was, found himself in a rarefied milieu, at the apex of what would shortly be characterised by *Time* magazine as the 'Swinging London' scene. He was one of the fashionable pop stars of the day – along with the Beatles, the Rolling Stones, the Animals, the Who, Manfred Mann, Marianne Faithfull and Sandie Shaw.

Nevertheless, he had no wish to embark on the standard career path of the '60s music star.

'I was offered a £1,000 a night to do a 60-night tour as second on the bill to Gene Pitney, whom I worshipped. I'd have got £60,000 – an absolute fortune in 1965. But I didn't even think before turning it down. People thought I was mad, but I said, "Hold on, I didn't want to be a pop star – I've always wanted to do other things". I wasn't a very good singer anyway. I could sing in tune but I had a weak, pathetic little voice.'

Instead, King wrote and produced a huge hit, *It's Good News Week*, for Hedgehopper's Anonymous, a group formed of air force personnel. In any case, he was still at Cambridge.

'I was 20, I had a bit of money and could afford a car and a flat in London', he recalled. 'So I was often whizzing up and down, attending lectures in Cambridge and then joining my new friends in London.'

One factor that set King apart from his contemporaries was that he didn't take drugs.

'At the time, I was smack in the middle of the two big drug cultures – in the universities and the music scene. But I made the decision not to do drugs. I wanted to be in control of my life. I didn't smoke either, and I didn't drink.'

Eric Burdon, lead singer of the Animals, dubbed him 'King Loon' – on the grounds that King, being simply high on life, was higher than the rest of them put together. As the evenings in the clubs wore on into the small hours, King could frequently be found sitting and chatting with Cynthia Lennon and Jane Asher. They, too, didn't do drugs.

'John Lennon and the others did like having me around', reflected King, 'because they knew I'd look after them. I was straight and together, but in a tolerant way. I was the guide for LSD trips, when that became the drug of choice. I remember once guiding John through an LSD trip at my apartment in Dorset Street.

'He was really out of it, saying, "I've gotta have a pee, JK, come and help me have a pee". I had to take him along to the toilet, remove his underwear and point his penis in the right direction. As he was standing there gazing at it, he said, "Oh man, look at the colours in my pee, they're fantastic".

'I said, "John, that's exactly why I don't do drugs. It's because you're entranced by your own urine".'

King may have eschewed the drugs but was not otherwise abstemious. He discovered that he was bisexual.

At a time of sexual liberation, he was as liberated as the rest. He quickly found out that a surprisingly high proportion of this exclusive set was gay. He was able to renew his acquaintance with Brian Epstein – a highly promiscuous gay man – on a much less unequal footing. 'I was in a club with him, everyone was dancing around, and I'd taken my shirt off. I slumped back down next to him. He was very stoned, and it was four in the morning. He looked at me, and said, "Jonathan, you have probably the best body of anyone in the music business".

'He then paused and said, "Pity about the face".

'I laughed, and he immediately said, "Oh God, I don't believe I said that. That's so rude, it's so awful".

'I said, "No, Brian, don't worry, it means we're never going to have any problems on that level" – and we never did.'

King met Jimi Hendrix the very first night that he arrived in London. Chas Chandler, the bass player with the Animals, brought Hendrix to Britain from Seattle and became his manager.

'Chas picked him up from the airport. Jimi had nowhere to stay, so I put him up in my apartment a couple of nights. He was a very sweet guy, we got on very well, but he was very naïve and had two huge problems. One was that he used to do every known drug, and the other was that he'd screw the most unsuitable groupie girls.'

King graduated from Cambridge in the summer of 1967 and was immediately given his own prime-time television show. A weekly show, it ran for six months, and went out on ITV on Saturday evenings at 6.30. That was not quite the triumph it may have seemed; trying to get an audience on ITV in that slot was next to impossible. In ratings terms, the BBC's early evening schedule – with *Doctor Who*; the chat-and-music show, *Dee Time*, hosted by Simon Dee; and *The Monkees* – was unbeatable.

By now, King was having lunch every Thursday with Brian Epstein in the King's Road, Chelsea, another epicentre of the

Swinging London scene. Their last such lunch took place on 24 August.

'The Bank Holiday weekend was coming up. He begged me to go down with him to his country house in Sussex. He said, "It's so boring, and I'm so lonely" – we used to have very queeny conversations, as you do, when you know someone that well. I was busy, so I couldn't go. But I didn't get the slightest feeling that he was depressed. I would have sussed if it had been serious.

'That was the weekend he was found dead. He hadn't gone to the country, he'd stayed at his house in Belgravia.

'It was far and away the most affecting death of my life. When my father had died, I was much too young to understand really what it meant. When Brian died, we were very close, he was a lovely guy. I'm sure that what happened was just an accident, and of course I knew that if I had gone down with him, it would never have happened.'

BY THIS STAGE, King already knew Sir Edward Lewis, the founder and head of Decca, the highly reputable British company that had developed radar towards the end of the Second World War. As the '60s progressed, however, its once-formidable record division went from bad to worse. Having become notorious as the company that had turned down the Beatles, Decca had also signed up, but then prematurely let go, artists like Rod Stewart and Joe Cocker.

King told Sir Edward that the record division was 'completely falling apart'. He was able to speak so bluntly for one simple reason: Lewis was also an alumnus of Trinity College, Cambridge, and so King had become like a favoured son. Lewis now asked him to run the company. King was just 23.

He began to turn things around, but there remained a major problem with the one significant act the company did have on its books – the Rolling Stones. The group was seriously disenchanted with the company, there had been a major falling-out with Sir Edward and they hadn't delivered any product for over a year.

'I asked Mick to come to a meeting', explained King. 'Just him and me. We hadn't known each other that well socially, but I understood his strengths. The reason the Stones have gone on and on is because Mick is the great business-brain behind it all.'

'We must have a single', King told Jagger. 'I know I'm working for Decca so it's in my interests that you remain big; but it's also in your interests to keep the momentum going. The Stones are going cold.'

'OK, I'll do it under one condition', responded Jagger. 'You have to give me your guarantee that you will put the record at No.1 in the charts.'

'Absolutely no problem', said King, 'I will guarantee it.'

Knowing full well that he was in no position to give any such guarantee, he could feel his stomach somersaulting as he said it.

A few weeks went by. King returned to his office in Great Marlborough Street one day to find a tape and a note from Jagger:

JK: I've done better than give you a hit single. I've given you two (the A-side and the B-side). But you still have to get them both to No.1. Love Mick.

'I thought, fucking hell', recalled King. It was with some trepidation that he played the tape.

The songs were *Honky Tonk Women* and *You Can't Always Get What You Want*. 'I sat down a very relieved man. I thought, I'll have no difficulty putting this to No.1 all over the world.'

One day, when King was invited to revisit his old school, Charterhouse, a student pressed a cassette into his hand. He listened to the tape by an unnamed group. The first thing that impressed him was the voice of the singer, Peter Gabriel.

'During the school holidays, they all came up to town [London]', recalled King. 'They stayed in my apartment and we recorded an album. I wanted to call them Genesis and the album was *From Genesis To Revelation*.

'When they were all leaving school, I had a meeting with them – the band then was Gabriel, Mike Rutherford, Tony Banks, Anthony Phillips and Chris Stewart – and their families. Their parents wanted them to study to be lawyers or accountants, and not to go into something as precarious as the music industry.'

'Can you really advise them to do this?' the parents asked.

'Normally, I'd say "No" to anyone who asked', responded King, 'because the chances of success are minuscule. But I do think they have great performing and songwriting talent and, yes, I do think you should let them go ahead.'

Genesis, by then with Phil Collins in their line-up, went on to become one of the biggest groups in the world.

KING LEFT DECCA and started to concentrate on producing hits in his own right. Most songs were released as singles and attributed to non-existent groups for which he invented ad hoc names. For example, he recorded a violin arrangement of the Four Tops' hit, *It's the Same Old Song*. On that occasion, Phil Ochs, the radical folksinger whom King had got to know in Los Angeles, came up with a name: the Weathermen. This was the name of a group of political revolutionaries who had just, rather pompously, declared a state of war against the US government; Ochs felt like pricking their pretensions.

Another name that King used for an ad hoc group was 53rd and 3rd. This was the location of the notorious gay pick-up area in Manhattan. At this time homosexuality was still a subject not talked about openly. So while most of New York, and everyone on the gay scene, would have understood the allusion, almost no one in Britain, where the record became a small hit, was aware of its significance.

In 1972, he set up his own record label, UK Records, and almost immediately signed up an act which became one of the most commercially successful of the '70s. For some time King had known Eric Stewart and Graham Gouldman, who had been together in Wayne Fontana and the Mindbenders. 'When I formed UK, I called them up and said, "Have you got anything?" They said, "We've got this song that everyone's turned down". It was *Donna*. I heard it and said, "I think it's a smash".'

So *Donna* became the first of a string of hits, that also included *The Dean and I*, *Rubber Bullets*, *The Wall Street Shuffle* and *I'm Not In Love*, for the group that King named 10cc.

Jack Tinker, the *Daily Mail* theatre critic, mentioned to King that he'd just spent his most enjoyable opening night at the theatre in a long time. On his recommendation, King went to the next performance at the Royal Court's Theatre Upstairs. At the end, he was so excited that he went backstage to meet the cast. The show was *The Rocky Horror Show*, and King was one of those who made sure that it became a sensation.

'There and then, I bought the rights to do a soundtrack album. That weekend, when they had their day off, I took the entire cast plus the band into a studio and recorded it all. I wouldn't let them leave until it had all been voiced and mixed; they were all sleeping on the floor. The album became a great success. Tim Curry had only sung his part on stage six times, it was so fresh. To this day, the album has got that wonderful made-in-24-hours sound.'

AFTER 10cc LEFT HIS LABEL to sign for one of the major industry companies, King became disillusioned with the British music scene and decided to live in New York. His saddest moment there occurred on 8 December 1980 when he heard there had been a shooting outside the Dakota Building on 72nd Street on the Upper West Side. Instantly appreciating what had happened, he alerted his friend, Tom Brook, the BBC's man in New York, thereby allowing Brook to be among the first to deliver the awful news that John Lennon had been shot dead. King and Lennon had arranged to have lunch the following week.

As a British voice in the US, who was knowledgeable and opinionated about most things, King quickly found himself guesting on various radio shows. Before long, he was offered his own daily show. He was attracted by the idea because the station was WMCA, the self-styled 'home of the good guys'. He'd loved it in the '60s, as the best rock music station in the city, and it was now the last major city station in the US in private hands. It was owned by Peter and Ellen Strauss – 'a lovely couple, they were both terrific'.

Peter and Ellen offered King the 10.00-12.00 mid-morning slot and he agreed to do it for a year. One of his first guests was the then junior Wimbledon champion, Ivan Lendl.

'He was about eighteen', said King. 'He was gorgeous. I think all the women at the station almost passed out with excitement because of how dishy this guy was. The figure he cut as a tennis player was that he was terribly serious and rather moody. But from the moment you met him, you knew he had a great sense of humour, was a lovely man, and was highly intelligent. I instantly became the all-time Ivan Lendl fan.'

He couldn't have realised it then, but the high regard in which he held Lendl was to prove remarkably significant.

After leaving WMCA, King developed an idea for a BBC TV programme, *Entertainment USA*. This was a weekly show about the US music scene which King presented. It notched up huge ratings and ran for some years during the '80s.

By then, King was writing his weekly column from the US for the *Sun* newspaper. He also developed a kind of counterpoint show to *Entertainment USA* to run alongside it. It was called *No Limits*. Whereas *Entertainment USA* was about established rock acts in the US, *No Limits* looked at up-and-coming acts in Britain. It was presented not by King himself (though he did appear in the programme), but by newcomers Anthony Baker and Jenny Powell, whom King had recruited specifically to give the programme freshness.

During the 1990s, King helped to promote the Irish band the Corrs, and Eva Cassidy, the Washington D.C. singer whose enormous success in Europe was sadly posthumous following her death from cancer in 1996. On the other hand, he also helped to ensure the success of the brashest and most bombastic of music industry events, like *The Brits* awards and the *Record of the Year* gala.

He had produced *The Brits* in 1990 and, in order to publicise it, persuaded the Prime Minister, Margaret Thatcher, to croon her favourite record. To national amazement, this turned out to be *How Much Is That Doggie in the Window?*

In 1995, the BBC gave him carte blanche to reinvigorate Britain's long-frustrated efforts to win the Eurovision Song Contest. At the third time of asking, he duly obliged. Having found strong performers (Katrina and the Waves) and a hit song (*Love Shine a Light*), he gave the country its only victory since 1981. As a result, he was named Man of the Year by the music industry in 1997. On that occasion, one of those offering his congratulations was the new prime minister, Tony Blair. Another, via a live link from Las Vegas, was Guy Mitchell. Like all those whose lives and careers have been shaped by music, King had never forgotten his very first record.

There was, in the 1990s, time for just one last piece of business. King heard another song which he thought had huge commercial potential: *Who Let the Dogs Out?*

'I was convinced it was a hit', he said, 'It drew very strong reactions from whoever heard it. But I couldn't get anyone to release it. I was trying for a couple of years.'

Then, he took it to a good friend, Steve Greenberg, who was then head of A&R at Mercury. 'I used to take him out to dinner in New York, take him back to my apartment and play him the tape. Eventually, after about eight dinners, he said, "I agree it could be a hit".'

Greenberg then recorded the song with one of his own acts, the Baha Men.

'Sure enough, it exploded', King recalled, 'and was a huge hit. It became, as I knew it would, something that everyone would yell out in sports stadiums.'

In 2001, the song won a Grammy for best dance recording. As Greenberg collected his award he knew that, over in England, the man who had brought him the song was now facing serious criminal charges.

2

The chain of events that led to Surrey police pounding on King's front door had begun when a 46-year-old man went to see Max Clifford. The only UK publicist who was a household name,

Clifford was in a league of his own with, as Simon Hattenstone wrote, 'a prurient finger in every pie'.

Clifford told the man that he wasn't interested in his allegations, because the person he'd mentioned was not high-profile enough. A few days later, the 46-year-old returned and mentioned a different name: Jonathan King. Now, Clifford *was* interested. However, he told the man that, in view of what he was alleging, he must instead go to the police. So it was that King's name was given to Surrey police in connection with allegations of historic sexual abuse, and this then led to his arrest on 23 November 2000.

He was taken to Staines Police Station and interviewed throughout the day. At eight o'clock in the evening he was charged with offences of abuse, given police bail and allowed to leave. An hour later, his solicitor dropped him back at home. In just a few hours, the *Sun* was reporting news of his arrest with the headline: JONATHAN KING HELD OVER CHILD SEX CLAIM. The report began:

> Pop mogul Jonathan King was dramatically arrested yesterday over paedophile claims.

How the *Sun* could have obtained the story that quickly is a matter that has never been resolved; but it is of continuing interest and considerable significance. It clearly suggests channels of communication between the police and Max Clifford and News International newspapers.

According to the report:

> His arrest came after months of research and information-gathering by the Serious Sex Offences Unit of the National Criminal Intelligence Service ... Millionaire King was seized after a string of men told police of sex attacks they claim they endured when they were underage ...
>
> Detectives searched [King's] flat in trendy Bayswater, west London, and took away computer equipment and videos for analysis.

The news was immediately picked up by all other media outlets. The *Mirror* reported that:

King was held after a nine-month probe by Surrey police and the Serious Sex Offences Unit ... bachelor King [has now been charged with] an indecent sex act, one attempted indecent sex act and indecent assault ... King has never married, saying he does not want to be 'tied down' by a permanent relationship

The *Daily Mail*, although saying that King 'emphatically denied that he was guilty of paedophile offences', provided what he would have regarded as a worrying update:

The *Mail* has learned that the 55-year-old bachelor may face further charges. At least two men are believed to have contacted police yesterday following news of King's arrest, claiming they too were victims.

The quaint use of the word 'bachelor', which occurred in nearly all the reports, illustrated the homophobia underpinning the press reports. 'Bachelor' was tabloidese for homosexual and therefore, in the context of alleged paedophile offences, guilty.

There were other coded signals in the reports; the *Sun* told its readers that King had a 'flat' in 'trendy' Bayswater, no doubt the better to put across the suggestion of sordid liaisons. But King didn't have a flat, he owned a house; and Bayswater, as the *Sun* well knew, had not been trendy for about thirty years.

King could respond to the storm of adverse publicity only by defiantly stating, 'I have great faith in the British legal system', which showed just how misinformed a millionaire pop mogul could be.

The instant demonization by the media is naturally going to make it harder in every respect for defendants to prepare for cases. For example, King now needed to find two people, in addition to himself, to put up substantial sums for unconditional bail. An A&R man whom King had known for twenty years said he would do anything to help. King rang him.

'Yes', he replied, 'you don't have to ask, yes'.

The man was Simon Cowell.

'That was a superb thing for a friend to do', reflected King. 'His integrity and generosity do not necessarily square with the image that people have had of him.'

The case was set down for trial at the Old Bailey. As a result of the publicity, a number of complainants had come forward and, on the basis of their accounts, there were a number of charges against King. However, the man who had gone to see Max Clifford, and so started the ball rolling, was not involved; the prosecution had decided not to take his complaint any further.

The judge, His Honour Judge Paget QC, divided the charges and said they would be heard at two separate trials. Because he felt that adverse publicity could affect the fairness of the latter trial, he imposed a blackout on media coverage of the first.

This was immediately challenged. UK media groups instructed highly reputable barristers to attend the court to argue that this was a fundamental breach of the media's right to report court proceedings and that it was overwhelmingly in the public interest that the trial should be fully and properly reported.

Paget rejected the arguments. The media blackout stood.

The first trial then started. It was to consist of six charges, concerning allegations of sexual assault – including one of buggery and another of attempted buggery – from five complainants.

As if the entire process wasn't already problematic enough, the trial began on 10 September 2001, the day before 9/11. So throughout the three-week duration of the trial, many of those in court were understandably preoccupied with events in the US.

THE FIRST COMPLAINANT, Fred Southall, said he had first met King when he was 'thirteen or fourteen' with his parents and sister. Afterwards, he had gone to King's house with a friend. He said he had been masturbated by King. He came forward, he said, as a result of seeing the publicity surrounding the arrest. At no time did his friend make any complaint.

Andrew Ellison was born in Zimbabwe in August 1971. His family came to England when he was fifteen and, to begin with, stayed in a hotel in Bayswater. One day, sometime between January and March 1987, King spoke to them on the Bayswater Road. Later that evening, he telephoned their hotel and invited Ellison and his mother to his house. The next day, Ellison went on his own.

'Andrew was excited', his mother explained, 'and didn't want me to go'.

He said that King took him upstairs, unzipped his trousers, and masturbated him. Afterwards, he left and never returned.

Jeremy Croft said that during a family holiday in London in the summer of 1984, he and his parents saw King in a shop in Bayswater. Croft, recognising him from the TV programme *No Limits*, asked for his autograph. Subsequently Croft was invited to his house – 'my parents were thrilled' – and he went there on a few occasions. The first time, King unzipped his trousers and grabbed his penis, and afterwards they masturbated together.

Croft, who confirmed that both his sister and the police had mentioned criminal injuries compensation to him, said that on one occasion, 'He asked me to pretend I was a girl and he would have sex with me … He tried to do it, but I clenched my buttocks and wouldn't let him'.

That was the evidence on the charge of attempted buggery.

Croft claimed to have been thirteen when he met King. Both he and his sister gave evidence that they remembered this because they regularly watched *No Limits*. However, the defence then pointed out that *No Limits* did not begin transmission until 30 July 1985. On being informed of this, Croft suddenly told the court that his account could be corroborated because his mother had recently found a diary in which she had recorded details of his contact with King.

'[She] kept a log of every time he phoned me', he testified, 'every time – the times I went there as well.'

No one involved in the case had known of the existence of this diary and, at the request of the judge, the police immediately made a 300-mile round-trip to retrieve it. The mother's diary was then taken to court the following day. According to this, the teenager had met King not in 1984, as he said, but in 1985; and he would then have been fifteen.

Peter Frecklington had a remarkable story. He said that one day in the summer of 1983, when he was fourteen, King had approached him in a record shop in Soho and immediately taken him into an adult sex show, where they had masturbated together.

This was, attested Frecklington, some seven minutes after King had introduced himself.

He said that on a number of occasions subsequently he went to King's house. 'Every time', claimed Frecklington, 'he got me in the mood, and it led to buggery.'

Asked why, if he was being consistently assaulted, he regularly went back for more, Frecklington responded, 'I thought he was my friend and I must admit I liked the aura.'

A friend gave evidence that he and Frecklington had been to King's house together. Again, the friend had made no complaint. There was a Christmas card that King had sent them in December 1985 wishing them "a happy 1986". In March of that year, Frecklington would have been seventeen.

In the wake of the publicity over King's arrest, Frecklington did not go to the police. He went to the *News of the World*. They declined to publish anything, so he went to the *Sun*. They then referred the matter to the police. Asked why he had approached the papers, he said he wanted 'to sell my story'. A heroin-user, he admitted that he owed money to drug-dealers and feared for his safety. He was adamant that he was entitled to compensation.

'I think he is the beginning of what ruined my life', he said, 'and that is why I think I deserve compensation.'

Ian Dodds, the final complainant to give evidence, was born in May 1974. He grew up in Gillingham and went to see King with his elder brother when he was 'twelve or thirteen'. He said that King 'touched me on the outside of my trousers'. Dodds didn't like it. He said that he 'took some records and left and never went back again'. He contacted police after reading of King's arrest.

He denied that he had come forward merely in the hope of gaining compensation. He admitted that he had had credit card debts. There was a county court judgment against him, but he told the court that that concerned someone else of the same name. (This point should have been properly pursued; if the witness was lying about this, then that significantly weakened his credibility. It is typical of the lax standards in English courtrooms that it wasn't. However, the prosecution naturally has no interest in undermining its own witnesses.)

Dodds suggested that he had documentary evidence to support his testimony. He testified that King had given him photographs of King himself with Samantha Fox, the model and singer, whose career in music King had helped to launch.

King always denied even knowing Dodds. It was, in any event, hard to understand why he should have given Dodds personal photographs such as these.

Yet, however Dodds had acquired them, their evidential value was not what he thought. Fox's personal assistant gave evidence that they could not have been taken before May 1989. Therefore, even if the photograph had instantly been given to Dodds, he could have been not 'thirteen or fourteen', as he claimed in his evidence, but at least fifteen. King's explanation of how Dodds acquired the photograph is that it was taken from his house, presumably by police, after his arrest and then given to Dodds.

The prosecution had to concede that King was a man of good character who had never been in trouble for anything. However, the prosecuting barrister told the jury that the allegations were interdependent: 'you could use the evidence of one of these young men to support the evidence of the others'.

It was part of the original prosecution case that King had given the teenagers 'seduction packs'. Though the press had eagerly seized upon this point, the prosecution had subsequently downplayed it – not surprisingly as, on closer inspection, these 'packs' turned out to be Concorde souvenir wallets. King made transatlantic flights so regularly he accumulated a small harvest of them.

When King went into the witness box to give evidence on his own behalf, he saw that the press benches were empty. He agreed that he had known four of the men as youths but insisted that he believed in giving youngsters the time of day. He knew how much, as a teenager himself, he had benefited from professional advice and encouragement. Those giving evidence in court against him had, he said, all lied, but he would like to think he had shown 'nothing but kindness' to the four he agreed he had known.

He explained that some of the evidence lacked any credibility. 'It is absurd to suggest that I took [Frecklington] into a peep show', he pointed out. 'It would have been a terrible risk if someone had recognised me and contacted the press or the police.'

King underlined his central point, which was that he had always regarded it as important to ask young people their views about music. That was one of the ways in which he kept his ear to the ground and sharpened his own intuition. 'Success comes from talking to people', King explained, 'listening to what they have to say, and thinking about their attitudes – and not getting the information second-hand, whether through the media or a research company.'

'If that was such a good idea', the Crown barrister asked rhetorically in his closing speech, 'why wasn't everyone doing it?'

Sitting in the dock, and condemned to silence, King reflected to himself that this was the clearest affront to common sense. One has only to transpose the context ('If founding Facebook was such a good idea, Mr Zuckerberg, why wasn't everyone doing it?') to see how absurd it was. The same point might as easily have been put to anyone in any area of business, commerce or the arts who was imaginative or resourceful enough to forge ahead of competitors.

In the poisonous atmosphere created by the media, anyone sticking their head above the parapet on King's behalf risked obloquy, but fortunately there were those – like Sir Tim Rice and the broadcaster Simon Bates – who had the moral courage to do so. They went to court to appear as character witnesses for King. Another who did so was Anthony Baker, one of the original presenters of *No Limits*. What made his contribution especially remarkable was that in the intervening period he had left the television industry. By a curious quirk of fate, he was now a prison officer. He had the strength of character to resist the pressure placed on him not to attend court on King's behalf.

Others could have been called on his behalf and would have had no hesitation in speaking up for him. One of the youths King had known, and whose life was clearly not ruined by association with him, was Keith McNally. He was appearing in the West End in London in Alan Bennett's play *40 Years On* when, as an 18-year-old, he met King.

'I got on particularly well with Jonathan', McNally told me.

'He was articulate, witty, unconventional, and a terrific deflater of pretensions, his own included. Of course, to the public he was seen as arrogant and opinionated, as he was to an extent, but I saw that more as a shield, a way of keeping people at bay.

'Though it was clear that he had gay predilections and I didn't, and that must have been dispiriting for him, I felt close to him and enjoyed being with him. I was over at his house now and then – talking, looking through his records, that sort of thing. I didn't drink or take drugs and neither did he. Jonathan knew I wasn't gay and never once tried to impose himself.'

Subsequently McNally became one of England's most successful exports to the United States, creating a group of New York's most fashionable restaurants, before returning to London to open Balthazar in Covent Garden in February 2013.

THE KEY ISSUE at trial concerned the ages of the complainants at the time they met King. In 2001, they were all men in their mid-30s; in the 1980s, relationships between consenting homosexuals between the ages of sixteen and twenty-one were still illegal but a complaint needed to be made within twelve months – otherwise the 'offences' were retrospectively legalised. Consequently, if King could show that the complainants had been sixteen or over at the time (and setting to one side the fact that he denied their accounts anyway), then he could not be found guilty.

This meant that the dates when the offences had allegedly occurred were of critical significance.

By the time all the evidence had been heard, however, the defence had made significant progress in disproving the complainants' accounts.

It was at this point that the prosecutor applied to the judge to alter the indictment and to change the stipulated periods in four of the six counts – those concerning Southall, Croft and Dodds. The judge acceded to this last-ditch request. The dates on the indictment were changed. According to the revised charges, the complainants were still under sixteen, just, but *in all cases* they were older than when the prosecution had put its case to the jury.

King had naturally prepared his defence on the basis that he had to answer the specific charges on the original indictment. Now, he suddenly found himself facing revised charges to which he was not allowed to put a defence.

King wanted to make a vigorous protest but had no one to make it for him. Neither his solicitor nor barrister was in court at the time. His solicitor was out of the country, skiing in Switzerland; meanwhile the clerks at his QC's chambers had double-booked him, and so before King's trial finished he was in a different court-room, representing one of the parties in the Victoria Climbié inquiry.

The indictment having been altered, the judge summed up. Ironically – in view of what would later come to light – he indicated that the defendant should not be condemned merely because of his inability to provide alibi evidence for specific time-periods. However, he did impress upon the jury that the mother's diary had allowed them to fix some points of time:

> In due course, we obtained the diary and we do therefore *know the dates* and you have it, of course ... [Croft] did agree that it was possible that he did not meet King until 1985 and *the diary confirms that this is so.* [italics added]

The jury was sent out to consider its verdicts. The discussions were protracted. After a couple of days, King bumped into one juror by the Old Bailey elevators. She was one of those in whom he had set great store. Now, she just looked at him and raised her eyebrows. To his consternation, he realised she was walking out of the jury.

The remaining eleven found him guilty of the six charges. He was sentenced to seven years' imprisonment.

Six weeks later, he was due to face a second trial with different complainants. The judge stopped this from going ahead, and directed that King was not guilty of all charges. There were a few residual charges; the judge advised the prosecution to abandon them.

In the reports which then appeared, the newspapers gave lurid and sensational accounts of the crimes that King was supposed to have committed. The newspapers neglected to mention that so many charges had failed evidential tests and that a second trial had led to a complete acquittal. They also failed to report the extraordinary development of the indictment being changed after the defence case had closed.

3

There is a general problem with historic allegations: how can they be adequately assessed in the courtroom? This is a problem that the UK criminal justice system has never addressed, let alone resolved.

Despite the high-minded principle of innocent-until-proven-guilty, a defendant is compromised merely by being the defendant, the one in the dock – and he is massively compromised when the case concerns sexual allegations. When the primary – or, sometimes, only – prosecution evidence is the testimony of the complainant, putting up a credible defence becomes extremely difficult. Because of the passage of time, and the complete lack of adequate research resources, rebutting evidence is unlikely to be available.

Many historic allegations will, of course, be true; but there is a variety of reasons why some might not be, and why witnesses might not be reliable. Some may find the thought that something awful had happened to them years ago a deeply seductive and comforting idea – it may provide the explanation of a troubled or unfulfilled life; some may imagine that the suspect really is a dangerous offender, and thus find self-respect and a sense of purpose in helping to nail him; some may be compliant or suggestible and easily induced to acquiesce with the thrust of police questioning. Some may be genuinely deluded. They may have come to believe that the matters they allege actually did happen. This is a point of particular relevance when the object of those allegations is well known. People may well have entirely innocuously (at least until the criminal justice processes are engaged) imagined interactions with celebrities or prominent personalities.

Whatever the precise psychological background, many undoubt-

355

edly believe that assaults happened, whether or not they actually did. Accordingly, the vehemence of their courtroom testimony will not necessarily be a reliable guide to the accuracy of their perceptions.

The allegations against King related to events that had supposedly taken place between fifteen and twenty years earlier. There were no contemporaneous complaints. In fact, there were no complaints of any kind until the approach to Max Clifford.

There are, though, key litmus tests that do allow the veracity or otherwise of the complainants to be gauged. Firstly, a trial of this kind can only be fair if the jury is given the opportunity to understand the totality of the complaints.

For example, the judge pointed out to the jury that two complainants had mentioned that King was circumcised (as, indeed, he was), and wondered how they could have known that:

> One of the points, obviously, the prosecution make is, if nothing happened, how do these complainants know that he was circumcised?

Considered superficially, this appears a telling prosecution argument; but when the complainants who may have suggested otherwise have been weeded out in advance, the point is clearly worthless.

The Crown alleged that a pattern of behaviour could be discerned in King's activities with these youths. The judge said:

> Another matter, which again is of importance, is whether the allegations reveal a pattern of behaviour ... The prosecution suggest that there is such a pattern ... If you come to the conclusion that there is a pattern, that the allegations of each are similar, it may be important because it gives rise to the question: have all of these complainants independently of each other made up false allegations? There is no suggestion that any of the five know each other, or could have put their heads together.

This is in any event disingenuous. The Crown had brought to court five men whose complaints ranged from the least significant (having a hand put on one's clothing) to the most significant (being buggered again and again). By no stretch of the imagination is that a pattern of behaviour.

Far more importantly, however, in an inquiry of this kind, the pattern-of-behaviour idea can only be assessed properly if the jury is given an opportunity to assess all the allegations that have been forthcoming and gauge their overall worth. After all, all the complaints have been generated by the same investigative process.

The problem is that by the time the case reaches court, the prosecution will have cherry-picked those allegations that are likely to pass muster in the courtroom. There has already been a culling of the unconvincing. The prosecution will have rejected those that, for example, are either intrinsically unbelievable or that do not fit in with whatever 'pattern of behaviour' it is striving to represent.

No one would expect to pass an opinion on a book from examining just a few pages, especially when it was realised that those few pages were not even representative of the whole because only the best pages had been pre-selected.

In the wake of a bank robbery, eye-witnesses may make a number of observations about the fleeing robbers. The prosecution will then separate the reliable witnesses from the unreliable, and use only the former at trial. That is an entirely legitimate exercise. In a targeted inquiry of this kind, the situation is completely different. These will not be potentially fallible statements from those who caught a fleeting glance of something. These are people who are giving first-hand testimony that a specific and identified person behaved in a specific way towards them. The jury need to have some appreciation of those complaints so that they can assess the flavour of the whole investigation, in order to establish the reliability of the proportion that is brought to court.

The fact that the prosecution may wish to put forward a pattern-of-behaviour point, if valid, is certainly understood; but the defence may well wish to argue the countervailing point: that there is a pattern of unreliability running through the allegations. As a rule, they cannot do so, because the prosecution is withholding the testimony of complainants who have fallen by the wayside – and so is concealing important evidence.

Another factor that will assist in the interpretation of historic allegations is the availability of supporting evidence. Usually, when the case reaches court, there isn't any; although, despite the passage of time, there is often the possibility of something (as this case would demonstrate), if only the investigation had been pursued diligently.

Croft had told the court he had supporting evidence available in the form of his mother's diary; yet, when it was recovered, that did not bear out his recollection of events. But there was another significant problem with his evidence: the colour of King's front door.

During his evidence, he referred to having particularly remembered the blue door at King's Bayswater home. The defence then brought forward undisputed evidence proving that the door had been white from the time that King bought the house in 1967, until July 1999 when it was painted blue for the first time. How then could Crofts have had a particular memory of a blue door?

A decade later, in 2010, *Eyewitness*, a BBC TV documentary series, investigated how witnesses gathered and recalled information. Amongst other things, it specifically examined the serious problem of memory contamination.

'The way the police gathered information in the past', reflected one senior police officer, 'was liable to contamination at all stages. Questions easily turned into leading questions. The police had beliefs about how they wanted to elicit the information and they had beliefs about where they wanted to end up.'

One expert in memory explained that, 'A memory is fragmentary and it is often difficult for people to know whether what they're remembering is actually a memory and not an unconscious inference that they've made' – after, for example, it had been suggested to them during interview.

It is an obvious possibility that the police, who knew which colour the door was when they arrived in November 2000, may, inadvertently or otherwise, have dropped hints which Croft had picked up about the blueness of the door. It was a telling indication that his evidence was not all his own work.

In this case, key features of the supporting evidence were clearly unreliable. With regard to two of its main witnesses, Croft and

Dodds, the Crown had anchored its case to particular exhibits – respectively the Samantha Fox photograph and the mother's diary – neither of which did bear out its argument, just as the blue door was also shown to be wrong.

Finally, it should be pointed out that there is a financial inducement for people to come forward with complaints because they can anticipate monetary settlements from the Criminal Injuries Compensation Authority. Those alleging sexual abuse are guaranteed anonymity, so accusations may be made with impunity. Moreover, for those tempted to fabricate allegations, this is one fruit machine that always pays out; even if the suspect is acquitted, compensation will still be due.

So a vital test in evaluating allegations of this kind is to understand the circumstances in which the original complaint arose and how the trail of suspicion started. In this case, the jury were deprived of the opportunity to perform this test also because the prosecution did not bring into court the original complainant. (In fact, his allegation was held back and, ultimately, the judge advised the prosecution not to proceed with it.) It was astonishing that the jury was deprived of the opportunity to assess the credibility of the man who triggered the investigation and the circumstances in which he approached Max Clifford.

Of course, Clifford knew all about celebrities – and ordinary members of the public who could attain flash-in-a-pan celebrity status – and what papers paid for their stories. If a story could be sold to the media, then the seller went to Clifford; he would get the highest amount possible, because he knew what had been paid for every other story of its kind. He was especially proud of his role in initiating the investigation into King and boasted that he had framed and hung on his office wall a letter from Surrey police thanking him for his assistance.

4

By March 2005, King had served exactly half of his seven-year sentence. Fifty per cent remission for good behaviour is available for those prisoners who pose no risk to the community, although it is frequently denied to those who continue to challenge their convictions. King's protestations of innocence notwithstanding, he was released from prison. He determined to try to piece together whatever information he could find in order to construct the defence he would have presented to the revised charges, had he been allowed to present a defence.

It was the count relating to the charge of the attempted buggery of Jeremy Croft that became the most fascinating. The charge on the original indictment sheet was:

> Kenneth George King, on a day between 1 October 1984 and 8 February 1985, attempted to commit buggery with …

However, Croft had stressed in his evidence that his account could be supported by his mother's diary. When this was produced in court, however, it did not bear out his account. Instead, it purported to show that it was on 8 September 1985 that her son spent the day with King at his house. As a result of the diary entry, therefore, the dates on the indictment were changed.

The prosecution gave themselves some leeway by ensuring that the new charge embraced not just the Sunday but the whole weekend period:

> … on a day between the 6th and the 9th of September 1985, attempted to commit buggery with …

King was convicted and sentenced to six years' imprisonment on this count.

While in prison, he was obviously in no position to research his own history. Even after being released, it was difficult to do so. Many personal effects were in his flat in Manhattan – and, under the terms of his release on parole, he was not able to leave the country, although, as a convicted sex offender, he would not have been able to return to the US in any event. Consequently, he had to ask friends to go there and bring back cases full of documentation.

It took months for all the material to be brought from New York and taken to his house in London, and then for him to go through it all.

Finally, he found what he was looking for. He discovered documents proving much of what he did in that period, and particularly on all the days 'between the 6th and the 9th of September 1985'.

On 22 August 1985, he flew to JFK airport, New York, at the BBC's expense, to prepare a new series of *Entertainment USA*. On Sunday 1 September, he attended a Bruce Springsteen concert at the Giants Stadium in New Jersey. On Friday 6th, he had lunch with his US accountant, and wrote a letter to the president of CBS records, thanking him for the Springsteen tickets. On Saturday 7th, he took Ursula Kenny, who worked for the BBC in New York, to see the newly-opened film *Back to the Future*, starring Michael J. Fox.

On Sunday 8th, he went to the US Open Tennis men's final between Ivan Lendl and John McEnroe. While there, he bumped into an old friend, Paul Marshall, an attorney who was admitted to the US Bar in 1952.

On Monday 9th, King did some shopping before flying from JFK later that day. He arrived back at Heathrow airport on the morning of Tuesday 10th. He had returned merely to get his visa renewed. He collected the new visa on the 11th, and flew straight back to New York on the 12th. He attended the MTV awards at Radio City Music Hall on the 13th and began filming the new BBC series on the 16th.

There are passport and visa details, bank receipts, American Express slips and other documentation to prove all this. He also wrote about many of these events at the time in his weekly column for the *Sun* newspaper.

King was convicted of two charges in relation to Jeremy Croft. But, that weekend, he was not committing attempted buggery at his home in Bayswater, London; he was watching Ivan Lendl, of whom he was such a great fan, win the first of his three US Open titles.

At the time this 'offence' occurred, he and his 'victim' were on opposite sides of the Atlantic.

ON 31 MARCH 2006, staff at the Criminal Cases Review Commission interviewed Mrs Croft. These are the key parts of the interview:

> Q: Can you tell us when you would generally make entries in your diary?
> A: Most likely that day, later in the day, or possibly the next day. It would depend on the circumstances, it could be when I got around to it ...
> Q: *(Shown diary entry for Sunday 8 September 1985)*. Does that mean that this entry definitely relates to that day?
> A: I am very confident it was a Sunday ...

The question was then asked again.

> Q: Can you be sure that [this] entry relating to Jeremy's visit to Jonathan King is accurate?
> A: It is reliable.
> Q: Is there any way that you could have got the date wrong?
> A: No.

There is accordingly a clear conflict of evidence between that given by the Croft family and that given by, for example, Paul Marshall, the highly-respected US attorney who provided a witness statement in which he recalled having met King at the US Open on 8 September 1985.

By this stage, Croft had been proved wrong about the colour of the door. He was wrong about the television programme. He was wrong in saying that his mother's diary would support his account. He had told the jury that "[She] kept a log of every time he phoned me". This was not true. Nor was it true that the diary supported his account of when he had met King. In fact, the diary placed Croft's meeting with King on a different day of the week in a different year. And the diary couldn't have been right anyway.

When they saw the family, the CCRC also took the opportunity of checking the diary of Croft's sister. She was the one who, at the outset, had suggested that Croft should go to the police and had also mentioned the possibility of compensation to him. But her diary didn't support Croft's account either. Nor did it correspond with her mother's.

The family's evidence was not internally coherent, and it was contradicted by other evidence. So what the judge had told the jury about all this was wrong. He took it as read that the diary was accurate. Yet it could not have been. Nor was any explanation forthcoming as to why not. There was only a denial of the possibility of inaccuracy. So had the jury known that not only were the dates first given by the family wrong, but so also were the revised ones, then they would have been entitled to view the evidence with the deepest scepticism.

The judge also told the jury that King would not be able to prove his whereabouts on a stipulated date many years earlier:

> He cannot, for instance, say, 'Well, that cannot be right because on that particular day or that particular week I was in America'.

Again, the jury was misled: Despite what would have seemed colossal difficulties, King managed to prove exactly that: on that particular week, sixteen years earlier, he was in America.

However the key complainant at trial, the only one who had alleged buggery, was Peter Frecklington.

Investigating this part of the case, I had a breakthrough. Someone contacted me saying that he had information about the King case. He was living about 50 miles outside London. I went to see him.

He was Stuart Williams. He explained that, after an industrial accident, he had become addicted to painkillers and then drugs. He had met Frecklington at a counselling service for drug addicts. Williams described him as a 'professional drug addict and small-time dealer'.

Williams knew from the local paper that someone in the area had been a witness in the King case but, although he'd known Frecklington for two or three years, he hadn't realised it was him. One evening, Frecklington told him what had happened.

'We were smoking pot and having a couple of drinks', recalled Williams. 'He came out with it. "You know, I was the one [in the case]".

'He said King never buggered him, he said it wasn't like he'd said in court. What he said had happened, hadn't happened. He said, "I said he'd done stuff he hadn't done – but I thought everyone was doing that." Those were his words, exactly. "I thought everyone was saying that, so I said it."

'His way of justifying it was to say, well, he must have done something wrong, so I wasn't worried about it.

'By then, he felt bad about doing what he had done. He said, "I feel terribly guilty". But he did it so that he could cash in on it. He sold his story, not once but twice, and even thought about doing it again. He got £45,000 the first time.

'Then, he got another £5,000 from another tabloid – I think, when King was released and it became newsworthy again. Him and another guy were just sitting around and they rang up on the off-chance. So they got another story out of it – how King had wrecked his life. Then they tried it again, but the papers said they weren't interested.

'With the £45,000 he bought a maisonette. I don't know what he did with the £5,000 – almost certainly, it went on drugs.'

There was one key aspect of all this that really bemused Williams. 'I'm surprised the Courts took him seriously as a witness', he said to me. 'He's making £50,000 out of it, he's a junkie, and a liar by nature.'

Williams, an ordinary citizen, could plainly see this essential absurdity. Unfortunately, those administering the criminal justice process could not. They were not disconcerted by the fact that King should be convicted and sent to prison and his life ruined on the word of someone who was not only being paid handsomely for his testimony but who was in any event a habitual liar.

The changing of the dates on the indictment is extraordinary. For example, let's suppose there was genuine uncertainty among the witnesses with regard to when these events had occurred; in that case, one would have anticipated that, logically, some estimates would be nearer and some further back in time. If there had been genuine uncertainty, that is what would have happened. But that is not what happened here. At King's trial the Crown had – *in every single instance* – understated the complainant's age. That in itself suggests that the entire case was bogus.

The changing of the indictment not only prevented King from answering the new charges, but it had also compromised the defence he had already made to the previous charges. For example, the defence QC had to cross-examine the adult witnesses on the basis that they were twelve or thirteen at the time of the alleged events. Had it been known that they were older than this, then their evidence that (for example) they knew nothing about top-shelf magazines or, indeed, sexual matters in general would have been implausible and would have fatally undermined their credibility.

The unfairness in not allowing him to defend himself has only been compounded by the passage of time. Had he known the scope of the charges he had to answer, he would, for example, have called the BBC's Ursula Kenny as an alibi witness. Sadly, he could no longer do so; she died in 2003.

The core matter was: had the original charges not been changed, would the jury have brought in guilty verdicts? Even the Crown had recognised that its evidence in support of them had become untenable.

5

The King case is another in which the outcome is attributable not just to the failure of the criminal justice process alone, but also to the UK media and the creation of a backdrop which undermined the possibility of a fair trial. Not only did the publicity in this case infringe the Contempt of Court Act 1981, but there are grounds for believing that it was *intended* to infringe the act.

The Act states that once the 'initial steps of criminal proceedings' have been taken, there should be no publicity concerning it that creates 'a substantial risk that the course of justice will be seriously impeded or prejudiced'.

There is no more damaging pre-publicity than that concerning sexual improprieties against children. Because of deep-seated public fears, such reports will automatically be given credence, even if only on the 'no smoke without fire' basis. They will be read and remembered, not necessarily accurately, and passed on as tittle-tattle. Whether or not they are true in the first place becomes irrelevant as the publicly-smeared person is buried under an avalanche of innuendo.

At the outset, the news of what had happened was instantly passed to the paper that was guaranteed to carry the most seriously prejudicial reports. In its 'exclusive' report, the *Sun* prominently displayed the terms 'child sex' and 'paedophile'. The prosecution could be assured that the scales of justice were decisively tipped against him from the outset.

'I have always believed', King said, 'that, were it not for the UK media, there would have been no investigation, no charges, no prosecution and no convictions.'

The fact that King himself had been, some years earlier, a *Sun* columnist did not benefit him. He had been a named contributor, not a staff member and, in any event, a demonising opportunity was rarely resisted by the tabloids.

At all stages of the case, the role of the media was crucial. The first complainant was not originally thinking in terms of a police investigation. His primary concern was to attract media attention and secure a financial windfall. The start of King's trial was then delayed by a legal dispute concerning publicity. The judge imposed blanket reporting restrictions. The press argued that they should be allowed to report the trial, but their arguments failed. At the end of the case, accordingly, the media had the chance to rectify the situation and provide comprehensive reports.

This did not happen. No media outlet carried adequate reports of the trial. For a start, it was impossible for them to report King's defence arguments; they hadn't bothered to go to court to find out what they were. Similarly, they failed to report the events at the end of the trial when, with many of the allegations having been undermined, the Crown changed the indictment after the evidence had been heard.

In failing to fulfil their journalistic obligations, the papers betrayed the hypocrisy of their objections to reporting restrictions. They had never had any intentions of reporting the case accurately, fully and fairly.

Having ensured through prejudicial publicity that the trial is heard in a wholly unsympathetic atmosphere, the press will always get their man. Then, after conviction, their target no longer has a reputation or any public credibility. The previous misreporting is retrospectively sanctioned. Henceforward the papers can say whatever they like.

One afternoon, not long after his release he was sitting on a deck chair by the Serpentine in Hyde Park, making calls on his mobile phone. The following Sunday, he was surprised to see a prominent report in the *News of the World* headlined: PERVERT IN THE PARK.

The report accompanying the photograph of King in his deck chair said that he was 'ogling an innocent child'. The photograph appeared to bear out that he was doing just that.

However, it wasn't just the fact that this was another made-up story that concerned King; after all, he expected press reports about him to be false. It was the fact that, in order to give their story even a veneer of plausibility, the *News of the World* staff had doctored their photograph.

King had been sitting looking out towards the Serpentine. In the *News of the World* picture, the lake was edited out and replaced by a wooded area with a path, along which a family with a child was walking. The depths of the *News of the World's* cynicism can be gauged by the fact that the child's face was pixillated – in order to create the impression that the paper was being scrupulous in its report, whereas it was actually being utterly unscrupulous.

King complained about the report to the Press Complaints Commission. His complaint was rejected, though that was not wholly surprising; evidence against him was given by the editor of the *News of the World*, Andy Coulson, and the chairman of the PCC was Les Hinton, executive chairman of News International.

The *News of the World* has since been closed down. In a series of *mea culpas*, former staff have apologised for a number of professional aberrations – though not yet for this one – and have sought to argue that they acted at all times in the public interest. But where was the public interest in fabricating a story and then fabricating the evidence to support it?

It does, though, suggest a continuing campaign, the purpose of which was to prevent the truth from emerging. Through its reports, the *Sun* had inhibited the chances of King receiving a fair trial; the paper then went on to try to sabotage his appeal; and its companion Sunday paper then undermined whatever faint chance King may have had, on his release, of restoring his credibility.

Even in the context of all that had happened, the 'Pervert in the Park' story was unconscionable. After all, had the authorities taken the story seriously, then King's supposed actions could well have been interpreted as breaching the terms of his licence, in which case he would have been returned to prison to serve out the remaining three-and-a-half years of his sentence.

THESE DAYS, King is, publicly at least, virtually a non-person. His achievements have been airbrushed from the annals of popular music. The website of MITS (Music Industry Trusts Awards) has been redesigned to remove the roll of honour of winners of their prestigious Man of the Year Award; and so, conveniently, King's name need not be listed.

The BBC and other broadcasting organisations no longer play his music on radio or television. This means, of course, that he is on a daily basis deprived of income that he could in normal circumstances expect to earn from his past material.

In October 2011, Mark Thompson, then Director-General of the BBC, apologised to King for having removed his performances from BBC programmes. Nevertheless, it continued to happen. A documentary, *Genesis Together and Apart* (October 2014), did feature contributions from King, but the BBC was clearly very nervous about how this would be received. So the next time a documentary was made about a band to whose success he had been crucial – *I'm Not In Love: The Story of 10cc* (December 2015) – pusillanimity prevailed. King was not interviewed and was mentioned as briefly as possible.

Keith McNally summed it all up. 'The case seems to me to be about the misuse of authority and the victimization of celebrity', he said, 'about the media and those in power pandering to the public's basest fears and, crucially, how innocent people in Britain do not get a fair hearing.'

And what is all this costing the country? At the time of his arrest, King was about to be invited to become chief executive of EMI. He may well have been able to rescue it, instead of which the company was finally sold off in November 2011. Along with Decca, EMI had once formed the apex of the UK record industry. The tale of how the company with the once-for-all worldwide advantage of having signed up The Beatles had squandered its fortune could be a parable illustrating the decline of Britain.

Chapter 10

The accident on the M25

Karl Watson's story

1

On Sunday 15 December 1991, at 1.15 in the afternoon, Karl Watson was driving his Mercedes in the outside lane of the M25 motorway when there was a blow-out in the front offside tyre. As he tried to hold on to the steering wheel, the car veered towards the hard shoulder and then, as the alloy wheel collapsed and dug into the road surface, ricocheted back across the motorway. It slammed boot first into the central reservation and came to a shuddering rest facing the oncoming traffic.

Watson became conscious of the screams of his children, eight-year-old Charlotte and three-year-old James, in the rear seats. He forced his way out – the panels had concertinaed together – and wrenched open one of the back doors. James was sobbing, pointing to the footwell and saying, 'I dropped my money' – which came as an almighty relief. They were safe.

He then looked back and saw an amazing sight. The traffic had stopped, headlights now blazing, across all three lanes. Watson managed to drive the car over to the hard shoulder. He removed the larger pieces of detritus from the road. The traffic re-started and moved past, with drivers tooting their horns in recognition of the drama and its providential outcome.

It turned out that three cars on the opposite carriageway were damaged by flying debris and afterwards twelve sections of the central reservation needed replacing. The Mercedes was a write-off; every part had suffered damage, though the car's excellent safety features and the fact that everyone was wearing a seat-belt ensured that they all came through unscathed. Even so, it had been a near-miraculous escape.

The police were on the scene by 1.40. They called Watson's wife, Heidi, who arrived to take her shaken family home. At 2.35 they were called away to attend another accident. Watson was in the car business and owned a trailer himself, so they left the recovery of the car to him.

That, surely, was enough drama for one day. The Crown Prosecution Service, however, reckoned otherwise. They put Watson on trial on the basis that, after suffering the accident, he went home with his wife and children but then immediately went out again in order to murder John Shippey, a businessman who was his mother's partner. Watson was convicted and has been in prison ever since.

KARL WATSON, the eldest of three sons, was born in Streatham, south London, on 22 May 1964 in the same house where all Watson children had been born since before the Second World War. His parents were Doug and Jo. Doug's two brothers also had houses in the same street, so Karl grew up with close family ties around him. Altogether, it was a blissful childhood.

'I thought everyone had an upbringing like mine', said Watson, 'until I ended up in prison. Hearing some of the horror stories of other people's childhoods, I can say hand on heart that we had it really good.'

He started school with his cousins at the same school his father and uncles had attended. Doug's mother, known as Nanny May, was the matriarch around whom everything revolved.

'My Nan was a craftswoman in her own right', Watson recalled. 'She could bake for England. Me and my cousins would run home from school because we knew there would be cakes and, the real bonus, the chance to lick out the big brown bowl and the sweet gooey mix.'

Granddad Fred, her husband, had been in the Eighth Army in North Africa during the Desert campaign of 1940-43. The war had left him both emotionally and physically scarred. The blood flow in one of his legs had been interrupted and infection set in; he developed gangrene and lost the leg.

Doug became a printer in Fleet Street – one of the sought-after occupations of the time. In those days, Australia was seeking to build up its labour force. Those with in-demand skills were able to emigrate for just £10. Printers were needed and so Doug decided to take his family there. Karl's middle brother, Adam, was born in

Christchurch, New Zealand in 1965. Watson remembers it as being idyllic, but Jo was homesick and so she returned with the children, back to the same home in the south London street, leaving Doug behind to work out his contract.

Back in Streatham, life slipped back into the same carefree mode, even if Jo, who had started working, wasn't around as much. Her side of the family was also closely-bonded. Watson's grandfather, Jim, a Romany, kept all manner of living things. Watson would ride miles from his home in Streatham to visit him and his menagerie: rabbits, two ponds full of fish, frogs and newts, an aviary with canaries and British finches of all kinds, a large loft for racing pigeons and in the front room – the room that was hardly ever used – the mynah bird that was always covered as soon as visitors arrived.

Jim was 'Lucky' Jim – an inevitable nickname, perhaps, which he'd acquired in dramatic circumstances. Digging a hole in the road with a pneumatic jackhammer, he struck a power cable. The blast blew him out of the hole and over the road onto the opposite pavement. Colleagues saw just a pile of charred clothing. No one thought he'd pull through, but he did. At the end of his life, though, it was 'Lucky' Jim no longer. His body was riddled with cancer – the long-term result, the family thought, of electrocution.

One day a stranger arrived at Karl's house. Everyone was thrilled to see him. They were calling him 'Doug'. It took a while for Karl to realise that this was his Dad. From that moment on, his father became a strong influence in his life. He taught him to play chess and got him interested in fishing. He adhered to a strong moral code and would never swear. Nor would he allow his children to swear.

He was able to get back his privileged job in Fleet Street, and soon the funds were flowing in. Every so often, the Watson clan would gather to see Doug's latest car, to admire the gorgeous wooden dashboards and lovely leather seats while the children clambered all over, fighting to be the one sitting in the driver's seat. In those days, there may have been only about ten cars for every hundred houses, which seems strange by today's standards; stranger still, all the cars were made in England.

One day, Karl was taken to Figges Marsh, near Tooting railway station, to see a large Bedford lorry, a decommissioned Royal Navy vehicle. His Dad had become a haulage contractor. In this business, too, he prospered, so much so that the family moved to a new home, a mock-Tudor house with oak beams and leadlight windows. Jo, who had social aspirations, enrolled Karl and Adam in a Prep school, not entirely with their father's blessing ('What's wrong with state schools, they were good enough for me?'). But it didn't work out for them. They were made to feel common, working-class boys who'd climbed above their natural station, although Karl found he excelled at maths and also developed a passion for rugby.

After their parents split up, Karl went with Doug and Adam with Jo; their younger half-brother went with his own mother. A close father-son bond developed between Doug and Karl, who later realised that his father's determination to make sure that his children did not suffer emotionally from the break-up meant that he gave them too much time and his business too little. The haulage company collapsed. Doug became a black-cab taxi driver.

In the family's reduced financial circumstances, the children were taken out of private school and sent to a state school, where they felt just as much fish out of water as they had at private school. Karl, however, continued with his rugby. Doug always went to see Karl playing for the school. They'd always watch England's international games together. Whenever England were taking a penalty, Doug would have to leave the room until after the kick, believing that it would bring bad luck to his country if he were to watch.

The extended Watson family circle was broken for ever when Nanny May died. Karl said that his father was devastated and just sat in his armchair and sobbed. Granddad Fred had died two years earlier. He developed the same complaint in his remaining leg and was told it would have to be amputated. He refused amputation and died. Afterwards Nanny May just pined away; they said she died of a broken heart. She was buried in Streatham Vale cemetery, underneath a large marble angel originally commissioned by her own grandmother.

'I would write her notes and leave them under a stone for her to read', recalled Watson. 'That's how I announced the births of my children to her.'

IN ORDER TO PLEASE his father, Watson took the civil service entrance examination. He passed, but knew a job in the Home Office wasn't for him. He already had a Saturday job, helping out in a garage. He'd discovered he was rather good at taking engines apart and putting them back together. During his last school holiday he bought a cheap Honda 250 motorcycle, a non-runner, stripped it down and reassembled it. He made a decent profit when he sold it.

Watson would scour *Motorcycle News* to pick up bikes cheaply, looking for anything he thought would bring a profit. As a school-boy business, it was ideal because he didn't need any more space than the shed at the bottom of the garden. But it was essentially a hobby. His father was still trying to get him into white-collar employment, and got him an interview with the Legal & General assurance company. He was offered the job; the money was good enough and it made his Dad happy, so he took it.

He began to use the telephone in his office to conduct his embryonic motorcycle salvage business. 'You get the bike, then you have to source the spare parts', he explained. 'You might purchase a bike with some damage at the front, and then find one with rear-end damage. So you fit together one perfect bike, but you'll have a quantity of spares left over. Selling the bike and the left-over spares produces the profit.'

He picked up the business smoothly and naturally. He learned how to gauge the market and to react quickly when he spotted bargains. Although it was dependent on finding the right motor-cycles at the right price, the business did well. But when his managers found out that his telephone was being used for outside business, he was asked to leave.

However, while working there he met Heidi, who worked for Reed Stenhouse (now Aon Reed Stenhouse), the insurance brokers.

'I used to go to his house quite a lot', she said, 'He lived with just his dad at the time, his Mum had left. I lived in Purley and he used to take me home about eleven o'clock on the bus and then get a bus back. I admired him for that.'

In 1983, when he was eighteen and Heidi a year older, they got married at St Swithun's church in Purley. 'It was a full family affair', said Heidi. 'His Mum and his Dad came, even though they weren't on speaking terms. In the photographs, they're at opposite ends.'

Over the coming years, they would have four children: Charlotte, Melissa, James and Bobby.

Although Watson took a full-time job as a plasterer, he was increasingly engaged in his motorcycle trade. When he found a likely model advertised through salvage contacts, he was advertising the spares for sale even before he'd taken possession of the bike. His original objective had been merely to fund the purchase of his ideal bike, a Yamaha RD250LC (liquid cooled). It was not long before he was walking into a showroom to buy a brand new one. Not only was he the envy of his friends, but he hadn't done it through parental assistance, he'd earned all the money himself.

He started up Croydon Bike Spares. He rented several garages, and advertised regularly in the spares section of *MCN*. The sideline also helped pay for his first home which he and Heidi moved into in Croydon. He was able to trade up to the larger Yamaha, the RD350LC, and he also bought a Ford Escort XR3i from a friend of his mother's, John Shippey.

While Watson enjoyed a very close relationship with his father, he saw his mother only infrequently. 'If it was someone's birthday or Christmas, she'd drop presents in the drive', remembered Heidi. 'But children want to see their grandparents; I don't remember her ever playing with them.'

His mother and Shippey had just taken possession of a new house in Ightham in Kent but had yet to move in when, on 16 October 1987, much of southern England was struck by a hurricane, the most serious in living memory. The next morning, Watson responded to his mother's call for assistance and went down to help clear fallen trees. He took with him Ernie Bullimore, who'd worked for him for some time. Another man, Bruce Cousins, who was nineteen years old, also turned up to help. Cousins had helped Adam Watson repair and spray a car, which was how Karl knew him. He would become a key figure in this story.

One day, two bikers turned up at Karl's house to purchase a frame and log book for a Suzuki GS550E. Weeks later, they returned. Watson noticed that one was now riding a Suzuki bearing the registration of the log book he had sold them. The bike had been ringed; its identity had been swapped with another bike to disguise the fact that it was stolen.

The bikers invited him to go with them to the Chelsea Cruise, which took place late at night at weekends, at Chelsea Bridge, near the top of the King's Road at Sloane Square. Large numbers of motorbike riders and custom car drivers would gather in a wonderfully gregarious atmosphere: they would meet people, watch the stunts and admire each other's cars and bikes. He and Heidi would drive up on his Kawasaki GPZ. 'It was a happy atmosphere', recalled Heidi, 'everyone was very friendly. Then we used to meet bikers at Thornton Heath pond on the way back. There was a bakers' there that opened at four in the morning, so we'd have a roll or a pasty and then go home.'

Some of the people they were introduced to were in the motorcycle business. A well-known champion racer was there, as well as people working for a firm that is now a highly-respected dealership – and all of them, Watson included, were trading spare parts, some of which were undoubtedly stolen.

At one stage, he did come to the attention of the police and was questioned about stolen bike parts. It seemed the only reason for their interest was that he'd been able to buy his own house and car at such an early age. He was released.

Soon, however, the police were back. He was taken to Norbury police station, where he was interviewed by officers from Scotland Yard's stolen vehicles squad. They were interested in a couple of parts that Watson thought had probably been stolen (although he noticed they also had a statement from someone identifying as stolen a part that he knew was legitimate). He was charged with handling stolen goods and bailed. He elected to go for trial at crown court.

The episode completely unnerved him. No one in his family

had a criminal record or had ever been in any kind of trouble with the police. By the time the case went to trial, Watson had disposed of Croydon Bike Spares and got a job as a financial adviser.

The evidence in the case having been heard, Watson was invited to have a private word with the judge in his chambers. The judge told him that he recognised that Watson had discontinued his spares business, and was a happily married man with a steady job. He said that if Watson pleaded guilty to two specimen charges, he'd impose a suspended sentence, but that all his stock – now in police hands – would be confiscated. So that was what happened. Watson got a minor criminal record but was free to go.

Watson was now selling pensions, savings plans and mortgages for which, in those heady days of Thatcherite consumerism, there was a rising demand. Margaret Thatcher preached the virtues of owner-occupation, made council housing stock available for purchase and tenants quickly got caught up in the rush to buy their own home. Through his contacts, Watson was able to arrange mortgages for people who could not obtain them through conventional channels. In other words, he worked in what would now be termed the sub-prime market. Opportunities would arise, for example, when a financial institution dumped large quantities of cash on to the housing market – usually if they had excess funds and wanted to avoid tax payments at the end of the fiscal year.

Meanwhile, Watson relaxed through fishing, and his friends got him playing rugby again. He played for Raynes Park, a club side, all over England and sometimes abroad. Watson was only thirteen stone, but he was fast and strong. It greatly heartened his Dad, who would watch him regularly. An added benefit was that Watson would get tickets for England games at Twickenham, which father and son were able to watch together, though Doug still couldn't bear to look when England took penalty kicks.

While strengthening family ties in that respect, Watson was seriously damaging them in another. He met another woman, Linda Mountain, and embarked on a second relationship. He arranged with Ernie Bullimore for her to rent a room at his house in Limes Road, west Croydon. Watson began dividing his time between his home address and Linda's.

In the early '90s, Margaret Thatcher was ousted from power and the financial markets crashed. Watson's business dried up. Friends who had once been grateful for his assistance in getting loans now wanted help to prevent their homes being repossessed.

Once more, he turned to the salvage business, this time in cars. He started buying from auctions, doing up cars and selling them. He began to specialise in a car he'd always had a passion for, the Porsche 911. He paid cash for genuine undamaged parts and 911 salvage, did them up and sold them on. He got premises, a garage in Link Lane, and worked hard; the more damaged the parts, the better – because the profit margin was greater. He paid someone a small fortune to get him *Exchange and Mart* magazine a day early – just as the first copies had come from the printers and before it went into the shops. That gave him a huge advantage over his rivals. He would buy cars so badly damaged they were classed as scrap and turn them around. His phone didn't stop ringing.

From time to time he would bump into John Shippey at his mother's house. Generally, he would be arriving as Shippey was leaving. Once he had dinner at Ightham when Shippey was there; on two occasions Shippey helped arrange finance for Watson's customers who were buying cars.

Because it was important to turn cars round quickly for resale, Watson asked Bruce Cousins to do occasional jobs for him. Cousins did these in his own time in the workshop which was owned by his employer. Then, in July 1991 Watson rented Unit C in Woodside Green, Croydon for Cousins. The arrangement was that Cousins would work there on Watson's stock, but that if he had nothing on, he could do his own work but would pay Watson rent.

At the end of the year, Watson was suddenly hit by serious problems. One of the friends he had secured a mortgage for had his home repossessed, leaving him and his wife and children homeless over the Christmas period. There was the accident on the M25. Then, on Saturday 21 December 1991, Watson arrived home to find a business card on the porch floor. There was a handwritten message and a phone number which he was asked to ring. The number was the murder incident room for the local police. The voice at the other end told him John Shippey had been found dead.

Watson was stunned. He told the officer he'd have to ring him back, and started ringing round to find his Mum to see if she was all right. Having tracked her down, she told him she was frightened but safe.

He then phoned the police station back. Watson said the officer was welcome to come and speak to him, and arranged for him to come round the following morning.

In the morning, however, five or six policemen arrived.

'I just let them in as if it was nothing', remembered Heidi, 'and asked, "Do you want a drink of tea or coffee?" They said, "Yes, please". So, I went out to the kitchen. Karl didn't show any sign of nervousness or anxiety. He just went in and sat down with them. I was just bringing the drinks in when one of them stood up and said, "Karl Watson, I'm arresting you for the murder of John Shippey". I dropped the tray and fainted.'

2

When he died, John Shippey was forty-eight years old and was under investigation for serious fraud offences. Jo Watson was his partner – or rather, since his personal relationships would turn out to be as tangled as his business affairs, one of his partners.

He had been finance director of the Dove group, whose companies were involved in the motor trade and financial services. Janet Davenport, the personnel manager, stated that Shippey looked after two of Dove's subsidiary companies, Translease and Denby House Finance. He was a long-serving employee but there had been growing concerns about him. He was clearly getting huge sums of money from somewhere in addition to his income. After all, he earned about £36,000 per annum. This could hardly have explained the houses, one of which was a villa in Spain, the cars – the Porsche alone cost twice his annual salary – and the boat.

Auditors at Dove had lately noticed that a debt owing to Denby had been paid into the account of JB Services, a company that Shippey had set up with a partner, John Bacon, in 1982. Bacon, however, believed that this company had ceased trading two years later in 1984. Asked what would be his reaction if he was told that now, in 1991, there was £400,000 in the JBS account, he said, 'I'd be absolutely staggered'.

By the time of his death, Shippey's activities were being urgently monitored inside the company. He had previously been able to sign cheques for any amount; now, the amount was drastically reduced and a second company signature was required. Meanwhile, from 6 December 1991 – just nine days before his death – his company Jaguar car was replaced by a Ford Sierra Sapphire.

Shippey and Jo Watson regularly socialised with Joe and Sue Kavanagh. The four of them frequently met at Osman's, a restaurant in Croydon, and also the Cricketers, a pub in nearby Selhurst. They had also been on three holidays to Spain together.

'When I first knew them, [Shippey] was living at Ightham with Jo three or four days a week' explained Kavanagh. He explained that the relationship was a fraught one. 'They communicated by using barbed comments to each other', he said. '"Happy" is not a word you would have applied to their relationship'.

'They just bitch at each other', agreed Sue Kavanagh. 'You were always on your guard. One would say something and the other would automatically say something against it.'

They both recalled one incident earlier that year when Shippey purchased a new Porsche. Jo drove it and scraped the wheels. Shippey, they said, went 'absolutely crazy'.

In recent months, the social engagements had become fewer. 'We saw less of him in the period leading up to Christmas', Kavanagh acknowledged, 'and his visits to the pub became less frequent.'

This wasn't surprising. Shippey clearly had many demands upon his time. He was married to Valerie, who lived in the family home in Farnborough Park with their (then) eight-year-old daughter. Shippey enjoyed a third long-term relationship with Sue Hipperson, with whom he shared a home in Caterham. From the summer of 1991 he began a fourth relationship with Christine, a barmaid at the Cricketers, who seems to have been, by the time of his death, his preferred squeeze.

Karl's brother Adam who, unlike Karl, was very close to his

mother, had begun to dislike Shippey. 'We did not see eye-to-eye on certain things, like the way he talked about my mother', he explained.

'About eighteen months ago I was having a drink with him in the Cricketers. During the conversation, I suddenly found out that he was married and that he had a daughter. I can only recall my reaction as being totally devastated by this news. The sudden shock hurt me very much. Since that time, I have had very little or nothing to do with him.'

Adam's distaste for Shippey only intensified after he found out that he had physically struck his mother in front of friends when they were in Spain together.

Shippey carried two briefcases around with him. 'He was like a gypsy', said Adam Watson. 'Everything went round with him in these cases'. He had two floppy disks which may have contained details of devious financial dealings. One of the rumours was that the company needed these disks, but that Shippey was demanding £250,000 for them.

Shippey must have been in serious trouble. Auditors subsequently found out that he had defrauded his company by more than £800,000 and lawyers believe he was involved with organised crime.

He appeared to have been trying to rationalise his personal life, though not because of moral qualms – merely to raise funds. He admitted to Sue Hipperson that he desperately needed to raise money and was thinking of selling his three English homes. He wanted to force Jo out of Ightham and was trying to sell the house behind her back. She had caught him forging her signature and reported the matter to the Land Registry. Some thought that he was on the point of bolting to Spain, possibly to set up home there with Christine.

Almost nothing is known about his final days. Valerie, his wife, said that she last saw him on Thursday 12 December. There is no evidence about where he was after that until 7.30 on the Saturday evening, when he and Jo arrived at Osman's for their meal with the Kavanaghs. Joe Kavanagh described the atmosphere between them as 'reasonable – a few barbed comments, but they were good company'. They ate well and Shippey told Kavanagh about another girl in the company that he fancied.

Unusually, he was not drinking alcohol. 'He implied he had a business meeting the following day [Sunday]', said Kavanagh. 'He didn't say where or with whom.' At 1.00am he and Jo drove off in the Sierra, heading south towards Ightham.

It was reported that Shippey had threatened to take others down with him, should anything happen to him – which, it seemed, it was about to. That Sunday morning, police arrived at Dove premises to arrest him, though this presumably wasn't the business meeting that he had had in mind. However, he couldn't be found so that was how he became a missing person.

Three days later, at about 10.50 on the evening of Wednesday 18 December, John Boyce, his daughter Sarah, and her boyfriend, Steven Dale, were on their way to pick up his wife from Nutfield Priory Hotel. As they were driving south down Hilltop Lane towards Warwick Wold, not far from the village of Merstham, they noticed two cars, probably a Ford Cortina and a Ford Sierra, parked at their side of the road. Boyce had to pull out to avoid them.

This only became significant when, ten minutes later, they returned along the road and noticed that one of the cars they'd seen, the Sierra, was now on fire. Boyce, who happened to be an off-duty fire brigade officer, radioed immediately for assistance. Because of that chance occurrence, the fire service quickly arrived to douse the flames. There was a body in the car's boot.

The car, with the body still inside, was moved to Reigate police station. It was lunchtime when Dr Iain West carried out the post-mortem at the East Surrey Hospital in Redhill.

Shippey was identified from his dental records. The postmortem revealed that he had died of stab wounds. West discerned two sets of two stab wounds to the chest, one set coming from a left direction and one from the right, both sets angled downwards. Those from the right, he said, had passed through the breast-bone. These would have been fatal and must have been administered with considerable force. One of the blows from the left had severed the coronary artery and would also have been fatal.

There was also a facial injury, a downward slash across the cheek, from the outer corner of the eye to the tip of the nose, which may well have been made with the same knife. He said that, because the blood vessels there were close to the skin, the wound would have bled profusely.

He also noticed that the tongue was clenched between the teeth, a result of convulsion during the process of dying. There was also bruising to the face and jaw, which West described as blunt force trauma, and was possibly the result of punches to the face. More importantly, West observed that two pieces of cartilage at the back of the neck had snapped off. He said the Adam's apple had been crushed against the spine, and explained that this was as a consequence of either a martial-arts type blow or a military-style stranglehold. Quite a lot of force, he said, would have been used for quite a short period.

His considered view was that someone stood behind Shippey and had placed his arm so that the elbow choked the windpipe. The armlock round Shippey's neck caused him to be bent backwards in a slight arc. That would account for the downward trajectory of the stab wounds. The two sets of stab wounds from distinctly different directions, from the left and the right, could well indicate two assailants attacking from the front while the third held him forcefully from behind in the armlock. So, according to his analysis, there may well have been three assailants altogether.

AFTER WATSON'S ARREST, there was considerable local publicity. He was questioned at Reigate Police Station on Sunday and Monday, 22 and 23 December, and went into detail about his movements during the period that Shippey had been missing. Obviously, it was all fresh in his mind.

On Saturday evening, he was at home with Heidi and the children. Her father was in a diabetic coma in King's College Hospital and was near to death. Heidi had been spending most of her time with him but returned on the Saturday night, emotionally and physically exhausted. He tried to console her, and they cuddled on the sofa together.

On Sunday morning, Watson was up by 7.30 and, with the family still in bed, drove over to West Croydon to see Linda. He arrived just after 8.00 and woke her up. He was supposed to have taken her out the previous night so, not surprisingly, she wasn't happy, but before they had a chance to talk the telephone rang. It was Karl's mother, who had tracked him down. She asked if he could go round and fix a broken window. It seems that she and Shippey had had another row when they'd arrived home – in the course of which she'd locked him out and he'd smashed a window to get in.

Watson usually took the children out after Sunday school, so he needed to rush. Without telling Linda where they were going, he persuaded her to follow him in his car. He thought it would be a good idea for Linda and his mother to meet; perhaps they would get on – after all, Heidi wouldn't have anything to do with her. But he needed Linda to take her own car so that he wouldn't need to take her back home before collecting the children.

They drove off. Just before the village of Seal, he pulled in and she stopped behind him. He walked back to tell her they were just popping in to his mother's. She was much angrier than he'd anticipated. She turned round and drove to her own parents' house.

It was about 9.30 when Watson arrived at his mother's. He attempted to fix the window, but she had no proper tools. He was simply dislodging the remaining pieces of shattered glass when he cut his thumb. Not only did his mother have no tools, she didn't have basic first-aid either. He wrapped some kitchen-roll paper round his hand and drove off, telling her he'd return with the proper tools and a pane of glass.

He went to Croydon to get tools from his garage and arrived home about midday. He took two of the children with him and drove back to his mother's. That was where they were going when the front tyre blew. Charlotte Watson clearly remembers the accident.

'The car was in really bad shape', she said. 'If Dad hadn't strapped us in, we'd have been killed. I was sitting behind the passenger seat and James was behind Dad. He was holding a handful of coins.

'After the car came to a stop, he was screaming, really screaming.

Dad was struggling to get out of the car and then to open the back door. He was saying to James, "What's happened? Are you all right?" and James was crying. Then he said, "I've dropped my money".

'So now, looking back on it, you can see the funny side. But at the time I was petrified.'

Watson's call to the emergency services was timed at 1.16pm. The police arrived at 1.40 and contacted his wife. The children were shivering with cold and shock. Heidi arrived with Melissa in their blue Renault and at 2.35, the police left to attend another road traffic accident.

Heidi drove off, following the M25 round to the Orpington turn-off. They saw a phone box and Watson asked her to pull over. He made two calls: the first to his mother, to explain what had happened and emphasise that they were all safe; the second was to Linda. He asked her to phone Bruce Cousins and say that Watson needed him to pick up the Mitsubishi van from Limes Road and then meet him at his home in Selsdon, in order to hitch up the trailer and go to retrieve the Mercedes.

Heidi and Watson arrived home and spent some time comforting the children. Cousins did not turn up. Watson drove to Limes Road in his silver RS Turbo. The van was still there. He picked up the keys from inside the house and drove back to Selsdon where he hitched up the trailer himself.

He set off again, stopping for petrol on the way. He drove back to the M25 but the Mercedes was no longer there. He made another call from the same emergency phone box and was told that a different police force had picked up the car and he would have to pay for its recovery.

Understandably, he complained vehemently. The upshot was that the operator spoke to her manager and they agreed to waive the fee. They then gave him directions to the location in Oxsted where they said the car had been taken. These calls were timed from 5.15 until 5.40.

By now night was closing in. So was the fog. It was difficult to see anything, and it was also bitterly cold. Watson had to go further along the M25 before reaching a slip-road where he could exit, turn round and drive back. He followed the directions, but they were not accurate and in those conditions it was hopeless. He had to call it a day and drove back to Selsdon where he unhooked the trailer.

His mother's natural concern had only deepened when she drove round the M25 and saw the smashed car on the motorway verge. She called at Linda's – so, in these circumstances, they did meet – and waited a couple of hours but had gone by the time Watson arrived back at about 8.00pm. He had a bath and something to eat and spent the night there. The next morning, in daylight, he did manage to find his car. He hitched it up. He bought a pane of glass, drove over to Ightham and fixed his mother's window.

On Tuesday he saw Cousins. Watson wanted to know why he hadn't bothered to help out on the Sunday. Cousins made a few feeble excuses. Then, Watson and Linda went horse-riding.

Wednesday was Linda's birthday, so at lunchtime he went shopping with her and bought her a gold locket. Heidi was at the hospital again, so he returned home to pick up the children from school. Heidi got back about 6.00pm, about two hours later than expected, and he went out again.

He returned to Linda and spent a couple of hours with her and her parents. Then he returned home. Heidi suggested a Chinese takeaway, so he picked one up on the way. He arrived back at about 8.30. They had the meal, and watched a film together.

When Heidi went to bed, at about 11.00, he drove back to West Croydon to apologise to Linda for not having been there for much of her birthday. He tried to explain about the seriousness of Heidi's father's condition but Linda, not surprisingly, was upset with him. So he returned home and got in just after midnight.

That was Watson's account of his movements during the relevant period, from Saturday 14 to Wednesday 18 December. Because it was a lengthy period, the alibi was necessarily a meandering one. However, it was given within a few days and, in key respects, it was substantiated. There was a recording of the original call on the M25, and police were satisfied that it was Watson's voice. The crash and the times of the other calls and the purchase of the glass were all checked and confirmed.

Watson was released on police bail and asked to return in six weeks' time. When he did so, in early February, no one was interested in seeing him.

3

In August 1992, nine months after Watson's crash and the murder of Shippey, Bruce Cousins, who was then twenty-four, was arrested and charged with seventeen counts of car-ringing and false documentation. In fact, Watson had found out four months earlier that Cousins was using the Unit C garage to ring cars. So he had given up the garage and taken another, at Avon Path, this time making sure that Cousins did not have keys. *(see Notes, page 470)*

When Cousins was arrested, his flat was searched. The police found some kind of pistol (it is described as a 'starting-pistol' in some court documents and as a 'gun' in others), a knife, a can of ammonia and duct tape. They also found some puzzling pages of script concerning the still-unsolved Shippey murder. According to these, Cousins appeared to be saying that he had helped Watson to carry out the murder. The pages were drafted not by Cousins himself ('I can't write or read that good'), but by his fifteen-year-old girlfriend, Lucy Richards, who said she 'altered some of [his] words to make it sound right'.

On 9 September, Cousins was charged with the murder. Initially, when questioned, he said he didn't know the name 'John Shippey'. At a second interview, when police revealed they had the pages of writing, he said he'd been present but that the murder was committed by Watson.

At this time, Watson was on a late-summer holiday with his family at a friend's holiday home in Jersey. During one of his periodic calls home to check how business was going, he learned that there were fresh reports in the press that he was about to be questioned again over Shippey's murder.

He was utterly dismayed. After talking it through with Heidi he resolved to go straight back to get it sorted out. He didn't want local gossip to spread any further. He also had the children to think of. His father had taught him to be honest with children, and that was what he ardently believed. He didn't want them to think that he was not prepared to face situations. 'If they think that you are lying to them,' he explained, 'how are they ever to trust you?'

So, the next day, they got the ferry back to England. When they docked, he phoned his solicitor, Colin Furness, and asked him to contact the police to let them know that he was in the country and available for questioning. Later, his solicitor phoned back to say that the police had no interest in talking to him about the Shippey murder.

The holiday had been ruined for nothing.

ON 5 APRIL 1993, COUSINS appeared in the dock at the Old Bailey and said that he had been involved in the murder of Shippey, although Watson had been responsible for it. Cousins pleaded guilty to false imprisonment and assisting in the disposal of a body. Sentencing was postponed and, having agreed to testify against Watson, Cousins was given bail.

Again, Watson was out of the country, this time on a rugby tour; again, he found out what happened in a telephone call home. He was due to fly back the next day anyway but, this time, the circumstances were very different. At the airport, one of his colleagues noticed that Watson's name was written in biro on the hands of one the check-in staff. When Watson went to the toilet, he felt he may as well have been at the head of a conga line as four men – obviously plain clothes officers – followed him in. Back in England, at Gatwick, he could hear the armed police talking into the microphones of their headsets as he walked through.

He went home. Heidi told him not to worry: hadn't his alibi already been substantiated? But early the next morning, 7 April, he was arrested. All Watson could think was that it was his Dad's birthday and how upset he'd be. He was charged with murder and was remanded to High Down Prison. Doug visited him.

'You said you could look after yourself', he said sadly.

Almost instantly, ill-feeling arose between investigating officers and potential defence witnesses. The police asked Doug if he thought his son was capable of murder. Mistakenly believing that honesty was required, Doug replied that he supposed anyone could be capable of murder in the right circumstances. The police then wrote up their notes of this conversation, according to which Doug had said that Karl was capable of the murder. He complained angrily that his words had been twisted. But the pressure was sustained. He was told that Karl was under psychiatric care and was having injections to keep him calm. 'Your son thinks he is clever because he leaves no evidence', the police said to him, 'but we know he did it.'

Linda was questioned. She was intimidated. There were threats to remand her to Holloway, the women's prison. When her father found out, he went to Reigate police station to remonstrate with the officers.

He received an apology from a senior officer, who told him that Watson had a lengthy history of violence. He did not believe any of it, but came to understand how straightforward it is for police to initiate character assassinations on their suspects and thus to induce unsuspecting witnesses to provide accommodating statements.

WATSON WAS PUT ON TRIAL for the murder of John Shippey at the Old Bailey on 1 November 1993 before Her Honour Judge Nina Lowry. By this stage, there were thousands of prosecution documents. This enormous edifice of a case had been founded on the testimony of Bruce Cousins. The proceedings lasted five weeks, and it was Cousins' account that dominated them.

Remarkably, there were only two sources of independent evidence about what had befallen Shippey: the pathologist, Dr Iain West; and the Boyce family, who noticed the burning car containing the body.

John Boyce was driving, so the evidence of the others in the car was perhaps more important. Steven Dale said the first car was a Ford Cortina Mark 5. He thought there was someone in the front passenger seat. The other car was a Ford Sierra. Sarah Boyce, his girlfriend, agreed that the first car was a dark blue Cortina. She recognised the model because her mother also owned a Cortina. She thought there may have been two people in the front seats of the car. More importantly, she noticed someone leaning into the rear offside door of the Sierra 'as if they were doing something inside the car'. This man, she added, was wearing wellington boots. When they returned about ten minutes later, the Sierra was on fire. All three of them felt sure it was the same car they had just seen.

A forensic examiner gave evidence that the fire was started with petrol and explained that 'petrol fires tend to be very fierce for a relatively short time'. In the car there were also three gas canisters, which had ruptured, and this naturally added to the ferocity of the fire. The body may have been completely consumed had it not been for the extraordinary fact that the one passing motorist happened to be a fire officer himself, and so could summon especially rapid assistance.

The prosecution told the jury that there was evidence to corroborate Cousins' account. Police had searched Watson's house in Croydon in January 1992 and found bonfire remains in the garden. When the debris was eventually analysed, it revealed the remains of seven studs from the fastenings from a Dannimac coat. There are also fragments of material that may have come from a Dannimac – the company employee called to give evidence was unable to identify them with certainty. There was some evidence that Shippey wore a Dannimac and, indeed, kept one in his car.

One such coat was exhibited in court. A witness commented, 'I'd almost stake my life on it being I believe owned by John'. But the court Dannimac was just a sample coat. The Crown didn't have the actual coat, they didn't even have its buttons, they had only those burnt-out studs found in the ashes. Additionally, Sue Hipperson described Shippey's coat as maroon, but the man from Dannimac Ltd. said they weren't manufactured in that colour; and Shippey's wife said she wasn't aware that he had a Dannimac of any colour.

Watson pointed out that he dealt in scrapped and salvaged cars. Nine times out of ten, these contained abandoned personal effects. Watson would simply clear them out and throw away the rubbish.

Old clothing would sometimes be used as bedding for his dogs before being burnt.

Nor did this area of evidence even make sense. The suggestion was that Shippey kept his Dannimac in the boot of the car; if he needed it at the end of a drive, it would be there. So, irrespective of who murdered him, why remove it from the car? The killers' objective must have been that the body, and with it pieces of incriminating evidence, would be consumed in the Sierra fire. What would have been the point of taking out the coat in order to burn it on a different fire?

Then there was the briefcase. On 18 September 1992, the Avon Path garage was searched. Police found a briefcase on top of fishing tackle. Its locks had been forced. The case was full of Watson's papers: for example, cheque books, paying-in books and his fishing licence. Watson had bought the briefcase from the Whitgift Centre in Croydon. It was manufactured in Germany in 1987 and was not expensive. The importers said they had brought in 45,000 and that it was a good-selling line. The prosecution tried to argue that this was actually Shippey's briefcase, and thus was a factor capable of corroborating Cousins's account.

However, Shippey's briefcase was more expensive and much older. It was made by Antler, the long-established UK luggage company. His wife said he had it for at least two years before they moved house in 1987. His secretary, Janet Davenport, said he had had it 'for as long as I can remember'. He also had a second brief-case made by Samsonite, the leading US luggage manufacturer.

So there should have been no confusion; but there was con-fusion partly because, as with the coat, police introduced a newly-purchased sample briefcase, made by Franzen. When one or two witnesses said, 'that's the one police showed me', it wasn't clear which they were referring to. Adam Watson had made a statement supposedly 'identifying' Shippey's case as a Franzen, but when this was put to him at trial he asserted, as the judge pointed out, that 'he had never in fact said that'.

In fact, the only marginally incriminating aspect of the brief-case found in Watson's garage was that the locks had been forced. Watson said he was no wiser than anyone else about how that had happened. During the trial, however, Heidi, his wife, said that she had forced them when she needed to refer to some papers. Cross-examined on this point by a sceptical Crown barrister, she simply took the sample briefcase and demonstrated how she had done it. *(see Notes, page 470)*

The Crown also argued that, when he was first arrested in December 1991, Watson concealed information about the Unit C garage and another one in New Addington.

The police asked if there were any other places, apart from the Link Lane garage, where he would be able to keep a car.

'No', answered Watson.

The police argued that this was a lie because at the time Watson had those other premises. The Crown made out that it was significant that Watson wanted to dissociate himself from them. If they had been made aware of them at the time, they argued, they might have found traces of evidence relating to Shippey or his car.

Watson's explanation was that the Unit C garage was sub-let to Cousins who paid the rent and did his maintenance work there. In fact, as he already suspected that Cousins was using it to ring cars, he was likely to be circumspect in drawing police attention to it. In any event, the garage was always full, as was a small second garage at New Addington which was only taken on a temporary basis (Cousins used it to store a BMW shell). The police carried out a demonstration merely to see if a Sierra could fit into it.

Electrical cable ties were found in the Link Lane garage – about a thousand of them. The prosecution tried to make out that these might have been used to restrain Shippey; but they were only cable ties, used to tidy loose or unsafe cables. A witness called by the defence said he'd got them in the course of his work for British Telecom and had given them to Watson.

One witness, Trevor Sillett, testified that Watson admitted to him that he'd burned Shippey's body. Unsupported confessional evidence of this kind is always highly suspect – with good reason.

The history of Sillett and Watson's relationship was a brief but telling one. Watson had invested some money in a night-club venture started by Sillett's brother but withdrew his backing after discovering the extent of drug-taking there. The club closed and this led to some ill-feeling between the families. It also emerged that Sillett had worked for a company linked to Shippey. In the fall-out from the financial scandals that broke after Shippey's murder, this company collapsed and Sillett lost his job.

A source confided to Watson that Sillett was subsequently arrested for possession of drugs. He was told that he should go to a police station, ostensibly on his own initiative, to make a state-ment that could be used against Watson; the charge would then be dropped. Of course, unattributable as it is, this is easily dismissed as baseless gossip. Nevertheless, the bald proposition – that Watson would confess to someone he had little time for, while maintaining his complete innocence to family and friends – is strikingly lacking in plausibility.

Probably the main disquieting feature of the case was the com-plete absence of what should have been core evidence. There was no evidence that Watson had ever harmed anyone or was violent in any way. Nor was there any history of animosity between Watson and Shippey, or any motive for Watson to murder him. On the other hand, unused material for the murder trial revealed the iden-tities of gangland figures, several of whom would have had the motive, and certainly the wherewithal, to bring about his demise.

There was also the alibi evidence to support Watson's account of his movements on the Saturday, Sunday and Wednesday. The overall alibi fits in with all the available evidence, especially that concerning the car accident on the Sunday afternoon. The police investigated his movements immediately afterwards and, at the time, were satisfied with his account. However, the prosecution set no store by the evidence, on the grounds that it was provided by his wife and girlfriend. Yet in these circumstances, Watson could not have taken their support for granted. His infidelities, once out in the open, would hardly have endeared him to either woman.

So everything depended on Cousins. Clearly, a prosecution founded on his testimony needed to be even more punctilious than usual. The Crown conceded that he was hardly the most morally upright of witnesses. Nevertheless, they emphasised to the defence that all material in respect of him had been disclosed. Whatever misgivings there might be about such a disreputable key witness, they said, the core of his story was accurate. As the Lord Chief Justice, who later considered the case, emphasised, 'the Crown put the case on the basis that Mr Cousins as a witness could be relied upon'.

4

Cousins was in no position to expect people to take his word on trust. He had been in trouble all his adult life. A range of previous convictions included stealing from cars, taking and driving away, and indecent exposure. He was then found guilty of an assault charge in 1987 and, in 1989, of possessing an offensive weapon for which he received an eight month prison sentence. When arrested on car-ringing charges, he could have expected a substantial prison sentence.

From the start of September 1992 until the following April, he was held in custody. He spent those months in the prison hospital. He was first remanded to Lewes Prison, where he tried to hang himself but was cut down in time. He went to High Down, but was transferred to Brixton where he self-harmed again. His solicitor wrote to the Crown Prosecution Service, arguing that he feared for his client's wellbeing, and so Cousins was moved to Belmarsh, hardly an appropriate environment in these circumstances. Later he was returned to Brixton.

He originally said the account that Lucy wrote for him was prepared by them in August 1992 – about two weeks before he was arrested. When giving evidence at trial, however, he testified that they had drawn up the account immediately after the events it purported to describe – that is, in December 1991.

During Watson's trial, Cousins, remarkably, had three spells in the witness-box. His first lasted from Wednesday 3 until Friday 5 November. This is the account he gave then:

Three or four months before the murder, Watson said that a man owed him money and he had a plan to murder him. An abortive attempt to kidnap him then followed. Watson asked Cousins to wait in his car and follow a Jaguar car when it pulled out of the car-park at Osman's restaurant. Cousins tried to tail the car but soon lost it and nothing happened.

On the morning of Sunday 15 December, at about 7.30, Watson came over to his flat and yelled up to his top-floor flat to get him out of bed. He then asked Cousins to 'babysit' a man whom he was holding at his Unit C garage.

When Cousins arrived, there was a man sitting in the front passenger seat of a Ford Sierra. The man was bound with plastic ties holding his hands behind his back, and gagged with sticky brown parcel tape over his mouth. His feet were also bound. Cousins had no idea how the man had got there and said he did not know and had never heard of Shippey: 'I never knew the man's name at that time, I learnt it afterwards'.

The man was able to roll the tape back from around his mouth, and 'I had some conversation with him'. The man said that he was cold, so Cousins went home to fetch a fan heater. When he got back, the man was now sitting in the middle of the back seat. Cousins opened the rear offside door and directed the fan heater towards the man's feet.

Watson arrived back about 9.00am. Cousins said he had to see someone about some work and so Watson allowed him to go. Cousins returned to the garage at about 10.30, when Watson said he had to leave but would return in half-an-hour. Cousins was told to stay watching over the man.

Watson didn't return in half-an-hour. Cousins got fed up with waiting and, at about 2.30, he went to his girlfriend's house in Mitcham. While he was there, he received a call from Linda asking him to pick up the van and then to meet Watson back at the unit where they would hitch up the trailer.

Cousins did as he was asked. When he got back, he saw Watson's blue Renault outside. Inside the garage, Watson was sitting in the rear seat of the Sierra behind the driver's seat. Shippey was now in the front passenger seat again. They were having an argument. Watson told Cousins to go and hitch up the trailer.

'After I had attached the trailer', said Cousins, 'I thought we were going to go and pick up the Mercedes and bring it back and that Karl was going to release the man.'

But he said the argument was still going on. Watson was shouting that Shippey should have paid the money; Shippey was saying, 'I'll pay, I'll pay'. Shippey then succeeded in breaking the ties that bound his hands. This enraged Watson.

Cousins said he was standing at the rear offside door as he saw what happened next.

In a rage, Watson reached over and placed his hands under the armpits of Shippey and dragged him through to the back seat where he lay diagonally across Watson's chest. His feet were fully in the rear of the car and his head was on Watson's right shoulder facing the roof.

Asked how Watson could have accomplished this, Cousins said, 'It seemed quite easy, it seemed like he got strength out of nowhere, he was berserk when he was doing this, he seemed like a man possessed.'

Cousins said that Watson then seemed to accept that the man was going to pay the money and calmed right down. However, he asked Cousins to get the knife that was on the roof of the car.

'I thought Karl was going to cut the cable ties and then release him', Cousins said.

Instead, Watson told him to stab Shippey. Cousins refused and handed the knife over to Watson, who then stabbed Shippey himself. The two of them were in the same position, with Watson effectively underneath his victim.

'While Karl was doing the stabbing', Cousins stated, 'he went absolutely berserk again.'

Cousins dragged Shippey out of the rear door and on to the floor of the unit. Shippey was lying on the floor, moaning that he was in pain. Watson told Cousins to put a wet towel over his mouth to smother him. So Cousins sat on Shippey's chest and pressed down on his mouth until he stopped breathing.

Then they left the unit to go and retrieve Watson's crashed car. Cousins was driving the van and trailer. When they couldn't find the car, they returned to the unit. They cut the plastic ties and tapes off the body, removed his jumper and watch, and placed all those items in a plastic bin-liner with the knife. They then put Shippey's body in the boot of the Ford Sierra. Watson drove it out of the garage and told Cousins to follow in his [Watson's] Renault. They took the car to the lock-up garage in New Addington.

Cousins drove Watson back and then went to his girlfriend's house, at the end of what must have been a memorable few hours. 'I said things to her', he explained, 'about the events of that day'.

The next day, Monday, Watson phoned to check that he was OK.

Two days later, Watson asked him to buy gas canisters and two cans of petrol, saying he was going fishing at the weekend. Cousins said he only got one can of petrol. He then met him at about 8.00-8.30pm outside a pub in Mitcham. Cousins was in his Ford Fiesta;Watson was driving his RS Turbo Escort.

They drove off in Watson's car to find a place to bury Shippey's body. They went to Box Hill, a well-known local beauty spot. Watson walked into the middle of a field, and said he was going to bury the body there. Then, on their way back to pick up the body, they saw a burnt-out car at the side of the road. So Watson decided to burn it instead. They went back to the pub in Mitcham and collected Cousins' car and drove to his girlfriend's house, where they collected the gas canisters he'd bought. Cousins left his car and its keys with his girlfriend and they continued in Watson's car. They got more petrol and then went to the New Addington lock-up.

Watson drove out the Sierra; Cousins, driving Watson's Escort Turbo, followed. They then returned to the roadway where they had seen the burnt-out car. Watson asked Cousins for the gas and petrol. He opened the offside rear door of the Sierra and leaned in. As he did so, a car went past.

Watson then parked up the Sierra nearby. He set it alight and ran back to where Cousins was waiting at a safe distance with the Turbo. On the way, Watson threw his trainers out of the window. They returned to Cousins' girlfriend's house and Watson then drove off in his own car.

Just after Christmas, Watson gave up Unit C. Before giving up the garage, Watson changed the tyres on the RS Turbo because he was worried about tyre tracks at the scene of the fire. When Cousins last saw the garage, he noticed that the floor had been painted red and assumed that Watson had done it.

Cousins continued to work for Watson at the Avon Path garage. Watson also had another unit. He asked Cousins to pick up two briefcases from this and store them in Cousins' own garage. Cousins said that before doing so, he took the briefcases to his girlfriend's house and looked at them there. One contained Shippey's paperwork. The other was full of Watson's documents.

Cousins said that over the ensuing months he became increasingly anxious. He phoned Watson from his girlfriend's house and told him that he'd have to go to the police because, 'I could not cope with what had happened'.

He said that Watson came 'racing round'. Cousins added, 'He told me not to panic and said he'd sort something out for me. He threatened to kill me as well if I went to the police.'

After that, Cousins said he decided to write down a record of what had happened.

Altogether, he had to give his account on a number of occasions. Whenever he did so, it changed. At trial, Watson's QC caught him out a number of times. Cousins argued that the murder itself had happened after Shippey broke the ties that bound his wrists. Then, when asked what he'd thought when Watson had asked him for the knife, Cousins replied, 'I thought Karl was going to cut the cable ties and then release him'. Clearly, he'd instantly forgotten that, according to him, the ties were already severed.

The defence QC invited him to explain the contradiction, Cousins said, 'I said in my statement that he broke free, but I wasn't 100% sure. I put in bits that I knew actually happened as well as bits which happened at the time.'

That was what he actually said. It suggests someone struggling to construct sentences, let alone any kind of a narrative – someone completely out of his depth.

The impression is that he was tailoring what he said to fit in with the available evidence – which was, in essence, Watson's accident on the M25 and subsequent attempts to retrieve the vehicle; Linda's telephone call to him; and, on the Wednesday, the observations of the Boyce family. But while the account does (in a very crude sense) fit in with those aspects, it is otherwise marked by the absence of either corroborative material or convincing detail. It is never supported by independent information and, indeed, is frequently inconsistent with other evidence.

For instance, Cousins said that, on the Wednesday, he and Watson set out to find somewhere to bury the body. He recalled Watson walking into the middle of a field. It was only when he (Watson) saw another burnt-out car that he decided to set the Sierra on fire.

At trial, Cousins was cross-examined about when he had obtained the petrol and gas canisters. He replied that he'd bought the petrol earlier in the day and had taken the gas canisters from his girlfriend's father's garage. So, the barrister asked, if the plan was to set light to the car, why did they drive round looking for somewhere to bury the body? It was a logical and indeed predictable question; and, equally predictably, it stumped Cousins. He couldn't answer it.

He related that Watson was leaning in through the rear offside door when a car drove past. However, he had no idea why Watson would have been doing that. One suspects he was unable to think of a reason, but the detail had to appear in his account because he needed to incorporate details that matched the evidence from the Boyce family.

The family said that the two suspect cars were a Ford Sierra and a Ford Cortina. According to Cousins, however, the cars were a Sierra and Watson's RS Turbo Escort. So here was another inconsistency. Obviously, there was no dispute about the Sierra; what mattered was the model of the other car. In an attempt to reconcile this evidence, the prosecution made some attempt to suggest that Cousins was lying and that perhaps they'd used his mother's car, which was a Cortina.

This attempt, it has to be said, was demonstrably hypocritical, because if the Crown thought that Cousins was unreliable about something as straightforward as that then they should never have been putting him forward as a witness of truth. However, the attempt failed anyway. Cousins' mother worked in the evenings, she drove to work in her car, and she was at work that evening.

Where there is reliable evidence, Cousins' account does not withstand comparison with it. In other areas, his account cannot be compared with bona fide evidence because there is none. One suspects that he deliberately kept details to a bare minimum lest evidence emerge to contradict them. Even when, at some point in Cousins' story, there may have been a slim chance of witnesses, inevitably there are none. There were no witnesses, for example, to Watson's supposed early morning visit to Cousins' flat.

While the account lacks external support, it is also bereft of internal logic. The villainy began, so Cousins suggests, with Watson saying that Shippey owed him money and therefore he had decided to murder him. According to the account, Shippey was offering to pay the money anyway, so there would have been even less reason for him to be killed.

As the account is examined, other contradictions stack up. Shippey apparently said he was cold, which was why Cousins left to fetch the fan heater. Cousins said specifically that Shippey was able to talk to him and yet he was unable to recall any snatches of conversation between them. He even claimed not to know who the man was until he read it in news reports afterwards; yet if they had been talking together, one imagines that the natural first question might have been something along the lines of, 'Who are you?'

In one account, Cousins said that Shippey was able to roll down the tape from his mouth himself; in another, Cousins said that he himself removed it. Then, in court, he said he couldn't remember whether he'd done that or not.

He had to retreat into uncertainty because even he must have been aware of how illogical it was all becoming. If Shippey was not gagged when Cousins left for the heater, wouldn't he have been screaming for help? Wouldn't he have yelled and yelled as if his life depended on it (which, according to the circumstances as outlined by Cousins, it certainly did)? This was not some remote part of the United Kingdom; this was Croydon, south London. Nevertheless, under cross-examination, Cousins contradicted himself again, and agreed that he had removed the gag and did not re-tape Shippey's mouth before going out.

Asked about the heater, Cousins said he got it because it was cold. He then added that he directed it towards Shippey, and blew hot air in through the offside rear door. He'd clearly forgotten having earlier stated that at this moment Shippey was in the front nearside seat, in the opposite side of the car.

In fact, Shippey is, according to Cousins' account, sometimes in the front and sometimes in the rear seats. This is the kind of basic detail that suggests that he was not capable of getting his story straight. When he tried to correct himself during the trial, he simply dug himself into a deeper hole. According to his account, Shippey needed to be in the back seat (where he said he directed the heater) and also in the front seat (in order for Watson to pull him through to the back).

Cousins was asked about his account, and specifically about Shippey being pulled into the back of the car. How could that have happened? Cousins said he did not know, and that Watson seemed to get the strength from nowhere.

He was asked how Watson had managed to stab Shippey on both the right and the left sides. Could he demonstrate what he said he had seen? Cousins said he did not know how it was done, but it was done.

In the first supposed kidnap attempt, Cousins said he had to follow a Jaguar car; later, he said it was a Porsche. Someone who worked in the motor trade should have had little difficulty remembering which it was.

In one of his interviews with police, Cousins had said that Watson had stabbed him. In court, he agreed that was untrue, and amended his account by saying that Watson had lunged at him with a knife. Again, whether or not Watson stabbed him is not something that he could have misremembered.

That Sunday, Watson had cut his hand on the broken window-pane at his mother's house. The prosecution tried to suggest that this solitary injury had been caused during a struggle when Shippey was abducted. It was one of the straws they clutched at. Nor could Cousins assist them. He managed to give three different explanations of how Watson had cut his thumb. The judge told the jury:

> As to the cut on the defendant's hand, Cousins gave various accounts … he told you that he is not sure which was the accurate account.

The judge's comment may well have misled the jury because of its implication that *one of the three versions was accurate*. In fact, all will have been untrue. The variations suggested that Cousins was making things up as he went along and was unable to remember his previous version.

Cousins had received a call from Linda asking him to pick up Watson's van. That was accepted by everyone and there was no dispute about it. What was disputed was what happened next. According to Watson, nothing at all happened – Cousins didn't bother to help and so Watson had to go on his own; according to Cousins, he did as he'd been asked. In that case, it was put to him in cross-examination, where did he get the keys for the van? Cousins couldn't answer that question either. In fact, he would have needed to knock at the house for them. Linda gave evidence that he had not done that. Cousins also said he hitched up the trailer at Unit C, which he couldn't have done because the trailer was kept at Watson's house – as neighbours confirmed. (In fact, they had complained because he kept it outside.)

There may well have been more evidence to discredit Cousins. After Watson hitched up the trailer to his van, he called in for petrol. He has always believed that there would have been a fore-court CCTV to establish that he was there on his own at the time and, therefore, that Cousins' account was untrue. However, as this CCTV was not disclosed, the defence never found out what it did show.

Sometime in January 1992 the floor at Unit C was painted red. Watson said that Cousins did it himself because he was irritated by the dust from the floor blown up by the compressed air when he was spraying. Only about half the floor was actually painted.

This area of evidence was highly informative, albeit in the oppo-site way to that suggested by the Crown. Scientists had peeled back that paint four inches at a time, testing for blood as they went. Any liquid on the concrete floor would seep down and stay there. So, had there been blood on the floor that was covered up by the paint, they would have found it. (In fact, there were several patches of blood – not surprisingly, as it was a garage – but none was a match for Shippey.)

So the argument advanced by the prosecution was not merely wrong; bearing in mind Dr West's evidence that Shippey would have bled profusely, this evidence by itself showed that Cousins' account was untrue.

There are glaring gaps in the account. There is no information about where and how Shippey was taken, nor of how Watson could have accomplished the abduction of a taller and heavier man on his own. The murder weapon was never recovered. The motive concocted by Cousins does not hold water. He was incapable of conceptualising one that fitted in with the background about Shippey so far as it is known – his embezzlement of hundreds of thousands of pounds from his company, his possible involvement with other fraudsters, and the fact that he disappeared only a few hours before the police were going to arrest him. Logically, all of that cannot be irrelevant to his murder – yet, according to Cousins' scenario, it was.

Indeed, there is a character missing in Cousins' account – and that is Shippey himself. Despite his size and build, he seemed passively to acquiesce in everything that happened to him. Wouldn't he have put up a struggle or at least tried to talk his way out of trouble? Yet, in Cousins' narrative, he says and does virtually nothing. It's as if he wasn't there at all: precisely what the defence believed.

So Cousins' account reeks of implausibility; but it becomes even less credible when one takes into account the context of that particular day. At the moment when, according to Cousins, the murder occurred, Watson and two of his children had just narrowly survived what could easily have been a fatal car crash. Was it likely that Watson could put the shock and trauma of the accident aside and turn straightaway to the cold-blooded murder of his mother's partner?

Although Cousins changed his story several times, he still failed to relate any special features of the murder or to harmonise his account with the mechanics of the murder itself. The latter were identified by the pathologist, Dr Iain West. He sadly died in 2001 but at this time was widely regarded as the country's leading pathologist. He was highly sceptical of Cousins' account of the murder.

The first aspect that concerned him was Cousins' suggestion that Watson had pulled Shippey through to the back of the car. That meant pulling him through the front seats, which had head-rests, over the gear-stick and into the back seats, so that he was lying on top of Watson. Shippey was 6'2" and weighed sixteen stone. Even if he had been entirely passive, it is impossible to understand how Watson could have accomplished that; and Shippey is hardly likely to have been passive.

How could Watson have stabbed Shippey as Cousins related? West pointed out that with them both together on the back seat, the confined space would leave very little room for wielding the knife. The assailant would be able to generate very little force, let alone the force required to split the sternum.

West described the sternum as the armour-plating for the heart. The knife wounds had split the sternum not just once but four times and had penetrated the heart. In West's opinion, it would have been almost impossible for the wounds to have been inflicted as described by Cousins. He said that in his view the assailant would have had to be standing in front of Shippey to generate the force needed to pass through the sternum.

There were two further points. West said in his experience the 'north to south' direction of the stab wounds indicated a forward stabbing motion – and not a stabbing from behind while trying to swing from the side (which was Cousins' description). Also, of course, the wounds were inflicted from two directions – from left and right – and Cousins' account could not begin to explain that.

Then West pointed out that Cousins spoke of Shippey moaning and asking for help. West pointed out that, having been stabbed through the sternum and the heart, Shippey would have gone into shock and not been able to speak.

Cousins said he placed a towel over Shippey's face and pressed down on it. That was remarkable evidence. It came close to suggesting that it was Cousins himself who was actually responsible for Shippey's death – except, of course, that cannot be true, because we know that Shippey did not die like that. Shippey had suffered serious and very obvious facial wounds, including a large slash down his face. Not only was there nothing in Cousins' testimony that could have explained these wounds but, as part of his account included kneeling over Shippey as he was dying, he apparently did not even notice them when he was staring down at his face.

This was one case where the defence did not instruct their own pathologist. They did not need to. At one point during the case preparation, Watson naturally became anxious and asked his lawyers how it was that the defence did not have its own post-mortem evidence. They pointed out to him that not only was West the best pathologist in the country, but that his evidence could not get any better from the defence point of view.

Indeed, West's evidence brought about an unusual hiatus at trial. Having heard his testimony, the judge adjourned the court. She asked for a full transcript of Cousins' evidence.

When proceedings resumed, West returned to the witness-box. The judge then asked him whether it might have been possible for the knife to have been wielded from the far left of the car. She asked, could this not provide the necessary momentum? West pointed out that Watson was not left-handed.

From this juncture, the whole trial went awry. The judge recalled that Cousins, in making his claims about Watson, had said, 'I don't know how it was done, but it was done'. She then asked West if the body was capable of uncharacteristic bouts of performance and strength. He explained that adrenalin is released into the blood-stream and will boost short-term performance levels.

West was then asked two hypothetical questions to which, as a courteous man, he responded. Even though it had already been established that what Cousins claimed to have witnessed was virtually impossible for Watson (or, indeed, anyone) to have done, the judge asked:

'If we include the adrenalin surge, would that be a method by which these injuries could be caused?'

'It is a method', responded West, 'but a difficult method, particularly to do it twice'.

The problem with the question – '*if we include the adrenalin surge*' – was that a huge speculative leap had suddenly been made. It was suddenly being assumed that, like a superhero, Watson was capable of extraordinary levels of performance. Of course, that wasn't established at all; it was just wild theorising.

The mistake was, however, compounded by a further question. West was asked whether 'leaving aside the car issue' there was a possibility of the assailant going 'berserk' and inflicting the first two wounds and then the second two; West again replied courteously, saying that that was possible. Suddenly, the prosecution was ploughing a different furrow, and now suggesting that the murder might not have taken place in the car.

'*Leaving aside the car issue*': in other words, ignoring the entire thrust of Cousins' narrative, was this possible? But this approach was futile at best and dishonest at worst. Evidence cannot be examined piecemeal, setting aside the inconvenient bits. It has to be examined in its entirety. Cousins' evidence was what he claimed he saw *in the car* – that was the case for the prosecution, that was its evidence. The evidence having failed, a new case should not have been invented.

Cousins was then recalled for his second spell in the witness-box. Taking his cue from this new scenario, the prosecution counsel put it to Cousins that from where he had been standing, and with the roof line, he might not have been able to see clearly.

Initially Cousins stuck to his story. The prosecution kept on. The defence then objected to 'the blatant leading questions' that the Crown were putting. The judge told the barrister to be more careful. However, the damage had been done. The penny had dropped for Cousins. Now, he said possibly you couldn't see into the car and perhaps he was wrong about some of his earlier testimony.

He was able to re-assert his new evidence when he was recalled again, on 24 November, and gave evidence for a third time. In her summing-up, the judge underlined Cousins' acquiescence with the prosecuting barrister's suggestions by saying:

> This is all agreeing with suggestions put … this is really the words of counsel which he adopts.

There is, however, something else to which Dr West drew attention. There were no stomach contents in the body. That was vital evidence. The restaurant owner gave evidence that Shippey ate a substantial meal on the Saturday evening. He was, after all, in the restaurant from 7.30pm until 1.00am.

The processing of stomach contents will be delayed by a number of factors – among them, if the body is cold, and if it is under some kind of stress. These factors suggest that Shippey's stomach contents would not have been processed in the body at a normal rate. That makes it unlikely that he was killed on the Sunday afternoon. Otherwise, there would still have been some remaining stomach contents in the body. It makes it likely that he was killed on one of the subsequent days.

It is extraordinary that the CPS espoused Cousins, knowing that his story could only be believed if one disbelieved the evidence of the only available witnesses: the Boyce family and Dr Iain West. The latter was a man of complete probity and the highest professional standards and someone on whom the CPS relied absolutely in hundreds of other cases. He thought that there could well have been three people involved (not two, as Cousins asserted) and this view chimed with the evidence of, in particular, Sarah Boyce who thought there were three people at the scene when the car and the body were torched. The family were consistent in saying that the second car involved was a Ford Cortina. They would have *known* because their own family car was a Cortina. This was the very best kind of evidence because it came from the very best kind of witnesses; they were entirely disinterested.

If such evidence is simply brushed under the carpet because it is inconvenient for the Crown, then the court process is simply supplanting good evidence with bad – and setting out along the road to injustice.

Doug Watson sat through every day of the trial in increasing disbelief. He didn't understand the judicial system. Didn't there have to be solid evidence, he asked himself, for someone to be taken to trial for anything at all, let alone murder?

The remaining eleven members of the jury (one had been discharged) were sent out on Monday 6 December. Watson, confident that he would be acquitted, took a last look at his cell and got ready to resume his life.

However, the jurors had asked a question during closing speeches: where was Jo Watson? Why hadn't they heard from her? The judge gave the standard response, which is that the jury must examine the case on the evidence they have heard and not speculate about evidence that they haven't heard.

No doubt we all share the jurors' curiosity, but unfortunately there seems to be little information. On that Sunday morning, Jo and John Shippey returned to Ightham; they had another argument, and Jo locked him out, so Shippey broke a window to get in; the argument continued, he got in his car and left. That was that.

The next morning, she asked Watson to fix the window for her.

'The first time Karl got arrested', recalled Heidi, 'she came round, saying, "oh, there's nothing to worry about, I know Karl didn't do it". We never saw her again.

'What mother would leave their child in his hour of need? But she did. She didn't seem to have what I would call feelings. She never showed any emotion. She was always very materialistic. Maybe she got what she could and then ran off. If she did a runner with some of Shippey's money, then perhaps whoever got him has got her as well.

'I'm never gonna forgive her, but I wish I could see her again.'

The most persistent of the rumours is that she went to the United States.

The prosecution has access to official information (including passport and visa details). If they so wished, they would have had a realistic chance of establishing her whereabouts. But it would not have been in the Crown's interests to find her. Had her evidence been along the lines suggested above, then Watson was almost bound to have been acquitted; but if she didn't give evidence, then the jury would have been bound to construe her non-appearance as damaging to Watson. It would have seemed telling that even his mother did not come to speak up for him; the jurors would not realise that the defence team, in the ferment of trial preparation and without access to official information, would have no hope of getting in touch with her.

When they retired, the jurors were out for longer than antici-pated. Doug Watson was outside, driving round and round the Old Bailey in his taxi. Sometimes he stopped to ask if the jury had returned. As with watching England take penalty kicks in rugby, he couldn't bear to witness the critical moment and was super-stitious that it would bring bad luck if he did.

On Tuesday 7 December, however, the jury returned. They convicted Watson of murder and false imprisonment. Colin Furness, Watson's solicitor, went down to see him in the cells below. Furness broke down in tears, so Watson had to comfort him.

'Then I had to phone my father', recalled Karl. 'I had to listen to him sobbing. He kept saying, "Whatever did I do for you to deserve this?"'

'The whole thing seemed a set-up', Heidi stated. 'Some of the police were nice, just doing their job, but several weren't. I'd say out of six of them, four were nice and two were nasty. Probably it's like

that in all jobs, but in other jobs you can't take people's lives away
by putting them in prison for evermore.'

ON 18 FEBRUARY 1994, the crime which the English criminal
justice process had committed against Watson was completed when
Cousins appeared at the Old Bailey. In return for becoming the
main witness against Watson, he was given a suspended sentence of
two years. He was free to go.

On the other hand, Her Honour Judge Nina Lowry had sentenced Watson to life imprisonment with a minimum sentence of
twenty years. Her comments as she handed down sentence are
revealing:

> The reason for the killing is shrouded in mystery. It is tempting to
> speculate that it had to do with [Watson's] mother and money, but
> in my view there must have been other factors. There was evidence
> to suggest that [Watson] may have believed he could turn Shippey's
> ledger books and computer discs which were kept in a briefcase and
> later recovered from a third garage rented by [Watson] to his financial
> advantage by collecting monies owed to John Shippey and keeping
> them for himself.

Judges must always tell juries that they should never speculate,
so it is striking that a judge herself should admit, '*It is tempting
to speculate*'. However, there is no alternative to speculation here
because there isn't any evidence.

It seems from this that she was under the misapprehension that
Shippey's ledger books and computer discs were recovered from a
briefcase found in Watson's garage. That certainly wasn't true. What
was recovered was a briefcase that was Watson's own. The vague
comment, '*there was evidence …*' refers only to the intensely disputed testimony of Trevor Sillett; that aside, there was no evidence.
(see Notes, page 471)

In fact, these comments of the judge lay bare the lack of any
foundations to this case. The murder was not investigated in any
proper sense; all that had happened was that, by hook or by crook,

a conviction had been secured. At the end of the trial process, no one was any the wiser about any of the events that had led to Shippey's death. Essentially, the murder case remained, and remains, unsolved.

Although Cousins had placed himself at the centre of events, one is inclined to be sceptical about whether any of his story is true. In other words, even his own involvement was entirely invented; after all, if he had been there, he'd have been able to provide at least some convincing detail.

His motive in concocting false evidence is all too clear. Sometime in August 1992 he was warned by a colleague in the profitable car-ringing sideline about his impending arrest. He would have been thinking of a ruse to evade those charges. Convincing police that he could help them with the Shippey murder case may well have been a strategy that appealed to him. He would have known that Watson had been arrested earlier in connection with it and the burnt-out Sierra had actually been stored at the salvage yard in Caterham where he was working. The crime was accordingly at the forefront of his mind, and indeed he seemed to have a morbid obsession with it.

His problem was that he didn't actually have any information about the murder. Nor was he capable of constructing a persuasive account. It seemed that his only source material was the reconstruction of the crime as provided by the BBC's *Crimewatch* programme – that and other snatches of information he had gleaned from media reports. So the obvious explanation of why he had written it down (or, rather, his girlfriend had written it down for him) is that, in order to get his story straight, he needed some kind of script. It is hugely significant that the CPS did not call Lucy Richards to give evidence.

If the prosecution case was well-founded, one would have expected the Crown to call her, as she would have been able to substantiate Cousins' account of how his script had been drawn up. So legal observers would feel it was instructive that she was not called.

All we really know is that she made three statements in September 1992. There were three because she had to admit that

413

what she had said in her first statement was untrue, and that she had lied about the circumstances in which the script was drawn up, and even when it had been. With this background of unreliability, the defence would have been understandably wary of calling her.

So the background to Cousins' evidence is murky in the extreme, but the fact that sentencing for his own crimes was postponed until after the Watson trial was quite an inducement for him, when giving Crown evidence, to stick to his story – or as much of it as he was capable of remembering.

The overall result of all this was that an innocent man received a life sentence in prison, a weak, immoral and odious man was given what amounted to a State pardon, and the murderers of John Shippey escaped with impunity.

5

Doug Watson remained Karl's link with the outside world, and spent years driving halfway round the country to visit his son. Rugby remained their shared passion. Though separated, they ensured they'd always watch the England games together. Doug would call him at half-time and again at the end of the game to discuss the team's performance.

In other ways too, their relationship did not change. 'One day in the visiting room, in the middle of a heated discussion, I let slip a swear word', recalled Watson. 'I thought Dad had missed it and carried on talking. But when I'd finished his finger was wagging at me again, "If I ever hear you swear again, you'll get a clip round the ear". It was extraordinary to hear that, considering we were in a maximum security prison.'

Watson struggled to continue his fight, but the odds were heavily stacked against him. In January 1996, his case was heard at appeal by a court headed by Lord Taylor, the Lord Chief Justice. Four witnesses, prisoners themselves, gave evidence about Cousins' unreliability.

However, the appeal was rejected. In what seemed an unfortunate lapse from Lord Taylor's normally impeccable judicial standards, he declared that 'we do not find the accounts [of the new witnesses] credible'. He went on to allude to the fact that all of them, at the time they had spoken to Cousins, were in a prison hospital. Taylor said, 'this does not always give the greatest encouragement to the view that they will be reliable witnesses'.

This was an extraordinary comment, both in its general application (the courts have frequently relied on evidence of conversations from prison hospitals) but more specifically in the context of this case, which was founded entirely on the evidence of Cousins – a man who was himself in the prison hospital throughout his time in prison (which is precisely why he was in contact with these witnesses).

Later that year, on 8 September, Cousins complained to the police that he was being threatened by 'his wife's father and brother'. According to the report, Cousins 'believes trouble will occur and wanted [police] protection but [was] unwilling to make allegations' against anyone. It is not known whether the 'wife' was Lucy, the girlfriend who had helped with his account, or someone else.

Years later, Cousins would deny, notwithstanding the police records, that any of this had happened. Of course, one explanation of his diffidence in this – of why he wanted protection but would not make specific allegations, and why he would later deny all knowledge of it – is that he was being threatened because others were aware that his testimony had led to the imprisonment of an innocent man.

DESPITE THE DISHEARTENING setback of losing his appeal, Watson continued to do all he could to discover fresh information about his case. There were questions about Cousins' mental capacity; this had been one area on which the defence wanted to shed fresh light. However, the CPS had always assured the defence that all relevant material had been disclosed for the trial. After the conviction, Furness tried again. In a letter dated 23 February 1994, the CPS reassured him that 'with regard to psychiatric reports ... in the case of Cousins, we do not have such a report'.

That seemed to be that. Indeed it was – until November 1998, when the defence finally succeeded in getting hold of vital documents. One of these was a letter to the CPS from Dr Katrina O'Neill-Byrne, a psychiatrist at HMP Belmarsh, written on 3 February 1993. She wrote that Cousins' intelligence was 'very low' and added that 'he may be easily led in terms of statements'. She emphasised, although it scarcely needed emphasis, that this would have a 'major bearing' on court proceedings.

Accordingly, she asked that a 'comprehensive psychiatric report' on Cousins should be prepared. 'If the Crown Prosecution Service is agreeable', she wrote, she would ensure that one were prepared by Dr Jackie Craissati, principal clinical psychologist at Guy's and Bexley Hospitals.

So Dr Craissati then produced her report, which is headed: This report is prepared for the Crown Prosecution Service. It contained much enlightening information. She had conducted tests in line with the suggestibility scale devised by Professor Gisli Gudjonsson.

Her conclusions were that Cousins was 'abnormally susceptible to leading questions'. She added that 'his anxiety in response to negative feedback is such that he will change nearly all his answers, regardless of his memory for the facts'.

Craissati's report was apparently delivered to the CPS on 17 March 1993. Yet even though the authorities had all that information and knew that Cousins was 'easily led', and about his 'anxiety' under questioning, and the fact that he was likely to 'change nearly all his answers' to suit what he thought the questioners wanted to hear, the police nevertheless conducted extensive interview sessions with him soon afterwards. They interviewed him over two days in Belmarsh Prison (30 and 31 March) and again in Brixton (24 June).

Altogether, the CPS had nine months from receiving O'Neill-Byrne's letter and Craissati's report until Watson's trial to assess the situation. Yet despite what they knew about Cousins, they still put him on the stand as a witness of truth.

No one who had read the psychiatric report would have been surprised that his testimony at trial would finish with the judge making comments such as:

This is all agreeing with suggestions put ... this is really the words of counsel which he adopts.

It was predictable that he would behave in that way. It was exactly as Dr Craissati had said.

The account that Cousins gave in court would not have been regarded as credible in any other professional arena in Britain – but, astonishingly, it was credible enough for the Crown Prosecution Service.

This thoroughly appalling situation was in due course supplemented by another.

6

In March 2004, the CPS took Watson back to the Old Bailey. He was to stand trial again for a new, entirely unconnected offence.

A year earlier, on 13 March 2003, there was an attempted robbery of a Securicor van in south London. Two men in a BMW car followed the van to Effra Road, Brixton where, at 4.30 in the afternoon, it stopped to make a pick-up at a bank. The passenger in the car, who was wearing a Securicor uniform, got out and ran to the van. He succeeded in pulling open the door. That activated the alarm, so he ran back to the car.

The whole operation was doubly misguided. Not only was it fruitless anyway, but it was also under surveillance by armed officers of the Metropolitan Police's Flying Squad. Although the men drove off, they were quickly cornered on a nearby industrial estate. The passenger, Clifford Hobbs, gave himself up straightaway. The driver, Noel Cunningham, made a run for it. He scaled a fence, but was then arrested.

In the car there was a black shoulder bag containing five new large laundry bags, and a bottle of ammonia. The consignment in the van was significant: £900,000 in cash and £100,000 in cheques. It would have made an impressive haul. But as the Flying Squad was covering their every move, Hobbs and Cunningham had no chance of accomplishing anything other than to help swell police performance figures.

Yet they did not meekly accept their fate. Three months later, on 10 June, they were dramatically sprung from custody. The prison van in which they were being taken to Inner London Crown Court for an interim hearing, was attacked by two gunmen disguised as postmen. One of the attackers shot a guard in the leg; a second bludgeoned another guard with the butt of his pistol. Hobbs and Cunningham both escaped (as did a third man, who handed himself in to police a few hours later). It is the only armed escape from a prison van in British history.

Hobbs and Cunningham made good their getaway. Separately, each made his way to the continent.

What makes all this truly extraordinary is that when the robbery case went to trial the following year, the men standing in the dock were Ian Hellens, one of the guards in the Securicor van, and Karl Watson.

The Crown case was that Hellens was the inside contact and Watson had organised it. It is almost unbelievable that this was ever taken to court; why did no one smell a rat? Hellens' inside info can't have been very comprehensive if he'd failed to mention that when the door was opened, the alarm would go off; and just how was Watson, who had been in prison for the previous decade, supposed to have organised anything?

Yet the trial did indeed take place, at the UK's premier trial venue, the Old Bailey. Its scanty pretext was that Hobbs had visited Watson in prison.

In fact, Watson knew Hobbs' brother, Terry, from years earlier. In February 2003, Terry and Clifford Hobbs had visited him together. Their mother had lately died. She and Watson had often spoken on the phone; she told him of her own day-to-day life and listened to him sounding off. Watson was very grateful to her. When she died, he sent flowers and arranged for someone to go to the funeral on his behalf. The sons' prison visit was arranged as a consequence. It was the only time he ever met Clifford Hobbs. He has never met Cunningham.

A number of factors make it clear that Watson was being fitted up. The BMW car used in the aborted robbery was stolen from an investment banker in south London on 30 October 2002. It was then fitted with false number-plates so that it matched exactly a car used by City of London police as an undercover police vehicle. So the car was stolen to order before the raid – and some time before Watson and Hobbs had any contact.

When the attempted robbery took place, Flying Squad officers were waiting in numbers to ambush the raiders. Clearly, they had advance warning. Wherever that advance information came from, it was not from Watson. As a convicted prisoner, his mail, telephone calls and visits were all subject to the closest scrutiny. Yet no evidence was produced to suggest that information of any kind was relayed either to or from Watson.

There had also been police surveillance of the raiders beforehand. (It was codenamed Operation Pudsey.) We know this because in one of the documents there is a reference to a third man, 'John', who had slipped the police net. Both Hobbs and Cunningham were questioned about him.

Despite the thorough surveillance, however, there was no evidence to link Watson either with a robbery plan or with Hobbs or Cunningham.

The prosecution tried to maintain that Hobbs visited Watson in prison on two occasions. He hadn't. After a visit had been booked, Clifford Hobbs pulled out; he couldn't make it that day. The visit was re-booked. So there was just one visit. When asked by the defence to produce the evidence that two visits had indeed taken place, the prosecution responded that documentation had been lost or destroyed. Such information is usually retained for many years. How strange that it should go missing in this instance, just as it was going to bear out the defence explanation of events.

Nor is that all that went missing. The log-book detailing the movements of the Securicor van also disappeared. This harmed Hellens' case as he could not rely on it to bear out his own account.

So the Crown had no evidence; but what they did have by the lorry-load was all the prejudice that could be brought to bear on a man already serving a life sentence.

Just before trial, Watson's inmate status was changed from Category B to Category A. He was then transferred under armed guard to the special secure unit at Belmarsh. Category A prisoners are those who theoretically pose the greatest danger to the public. By changing Watson's categorisation, the authorities could ensure that he was taken to trial each day in a bullet-proof van with warders wearing bullet-proof vests and escorted by armed police.

While pointless in terms of public security, this was an essential part of the trial charade. Watson arrived in court double-cuffed at his wrists and also handcuffed to a security guard. A performance was usually made of the uncuffing, just to make sure that the court got the message that this man was a hardened criminal.

Nor was this Watson's only complaint. He maintained that his pre-trial legal visits in Belmarsh were being monitored. They should have been privileged so this, if it happened, was illegal. One day, he gave his solicitor a bundle of Christmas cards and asked him to post them. As the solicitor was leaving the prison, he was stopped by security and searched. The Christmas cards were confiscated. How could prison staff have known to stop and search him unless the visit was being monitored?

At trial, the prosecution case focused on Hobbs and Cunningham, even though both were conspicuous by their absence. The jury were clearly persuaded that it was enough to be involved with villains like that. On 24 March 2004, despite the remarkable absence of evidence, Watson and Hellens were both convicted.

Hellens (who, bearing in mind the absence of evidence, also appears to have been innocent) received six years. Watson's sentence was the same. Immediately afterwards, with the pantomime having served its purpose, Watson's status was restored to Category B.

Whatever the full explanation of the attempted robbery and the subsequent escape, it is clear that here was a major criminal undertaking. Hobbs and Cunningham knew that the van had a valuable load. They had a Securicor uniform. Both this raid and the subsequent escape took place with apparent unconcern on busy London streets in broad daylight with no anxieties about, for example, CCTV cameras or the security devices that would be placed around a Crown Court.

Major criminals will often have close relationships with particular police officers, and these events bring to mind such considerations.

Hobbs and Cunningham knew precisely the details of an under-cover London police car – information that should have been very secret. Having been arrested after the raid, they were then, strangely, put together in the same cell in Brixton, which conveniently gave them the opportunity to plan their escape. The gang who engineered that escape have not only never been caught, but little interest has been displayed in capturing them, despite the fact that, given their ill-treatment of the guards, they would normally have been regarded as highly dangerous offenders.

The third man, 'John' who, despite the ongoing surveillance, had somehow not been apprehended, turned out to be John Witherow, an armed robber of significant ill-repute. Later, in May 2010, he was arrested for an armed robbery in West Wickham, Sussex. While being held on remand in Brixton prison, he committed suicide.

By that time, Hobbs had been arrested in 2007. He was found in the so-called millionaires' playground of Puerto Banus near Marbella in Spain, on what some newspapers call the 'Costa del Crime'.

And Cunningham? He was arrested in Amsterdam in September 2009 after the *News of the World* tracked his girlfriend to Holland and then alerted police.

At the time, that sentence should have given pause for thought. It would have seemed strange that the *News of the World* – out of an enhanced sense of civic duty, perhaps? – was spending money and resources to perform the functions that should have been the concern only of the police. However, in the light of the phone-hacking scandal that had been bubbling gently since 2006 but which erupted spectacularly in July 2011 and led to the setting-up of the Leveson Inquiry, the episode will be regarded differently.

The relationship between the owners of the *News of the World*, Rupert Murdoch's News International, and the Metropolitan Police then came under close scrutiny, after the arrests of several journalists and the resignations of top police officers. The relationship was a two-way street, in which the police provided the newspaper with information and turned a blind eye to its frequently illegal activities, but the paper would also use those same methods to generate information about criminal activities that the police gratefully received. Obviously, it would have been professionally improper in many instances (and illegal in others) for the police to employ those methods themselves.

Having been recaptured, Hobbs and Cunningham were brought back to Belmarsh Prison and, in turn, put on trial at the adjacent Woolwich Crown Court – Hobbs in February 2008 and Cunningham in June 2010. They could not now stand trial for robbery, the charge they should have faced, because the Crown had already prosecuted Watson and Hellens on a different charge – conspiracy to steal. This carries a maximum seven-year sentence; whereas robbery, given Hobbs' and Cunningham's criminal records, would have led to life sentences. So Hobbs and Cunningham had no difficulty in pleading guilty to conspiracy to steal. For the benefit of the Court, Hobbs even reiterated the prosecution case as it was advanced at the earlier trial.

There were, though, other charges relating to the escape. The upshot was that Hobbs was given life with a minimum eight-year sentence, and Cunningham received eighteen years, as the judge imposed consecutive sentences on a number of counts. Probably, under the terms of the extradition agreement with the Netherlands, where life terms are disapproved of, the court was unable to impose a life sentence in his case.

At the end of Hobbs' trial, the judge told him sternly that, 'It took a lot of public resources to bring you to justice'. Perhaps, but it took considerably greater public resources to ensnare Karl Watson in a second miscarriage of justice.

'My solicitor told me there was no evidence against me, so I would not be charged', he said, 'but I was.

'I was then told the case would be thrown out before trial, but it wasn't. My name was hardly mentioned at trial and I was told the Crown case was so weak it would be thrown out at the halfway point; but it wasn't. I was told that a jury could not possibly convict on the evidence; but I was convicted.'

The moral of this incidental story is that it is child's play to fit up someone who is already serving a long prison sentence.

7

Still concentrating on the original objective – quashing the murder conviction – Watson had instructed a new lawyer to take his case to the European Court of Human Rights, on the basis that, because the material relating to Cousins had not been disclosed, he had not had a fair trial. His lawyer promised to do that. Over the coming months, whenever Watson enquired about the progress of his case, he was fobbed off with some excuse or other.

It finally emerged that his case was not at the ECHR, and never had been. Even though Watson had prepared the material for the lawyer, the papers were never submitted. Further, the case could no longer be submitted because appeals to the ECHR need to be lodged within six months of the conclusion of the criminal process (which is held to be trial and appeal). By now, it was completely out of time. This was another cruel setback for Watson.

Ever resourceful, he then took a civil action for negligence against the legal practice. This action finally reached trial before Mr Justice Owen in May 2008. The judge noted that it was a key requirement of both human rights law and English statute law that 'the prosecuting authorities disclose to the defence all material evidence in their possession'. Clearly, that was not done on this occasion.

The CPS tried to suggest that it had never had the disputed material, but the letter from Dr O'Neill-Byrne bore not just one but *two* stamped imprints indicating that it had been received by the CPS. So, at last, they admitted that they had had this document. On 18 November 2005, Harriet Harman QC, then minister of state at the Department of Constitutional Affairs, responded to Watson's MP, Richard Ottaway, acknowledging not only that this document had been in the possession of the CPS, but that 'a conscious decision' (as Mr Justice Owen described it) was taken to withhold it from the defence.

Mr Justice Owen therefore found, on the civil court test (the balance of probabilities) that if the application to the ECHR had gone ahead as it should have done, then the ECHR 'would have found there to have been a breach of Article 6' – in other words, that Watson had not received a fair trial. Watson won his action against the legal practice. After fifteen years, it was his first taste of victory in the courts. The judge further asked that a transcript of his judgement should be drawn up 'at public expense' as he recognised that it was something which Watson would wish to utilise in his continuing fight for justice. He complimented Watson's barrister, Mark Tempest, on having represented Watson for the hearing *pro bono*, adding that such work was 'terribly important'.

Mr Justice Owen clearly appreciated that the innocent should not be in prison in the first place, let alone remain there through administrative inaction. Tragically, however, all that is just what has happened. On 11 February 2014, after they had been intermittently considering the case for more than sixteen years, the Criminal Cases Review Commission dismissed Watson's application to take it back to the Court of Appeal. *(see Notes, pp 472–4)*

'I HAVE BEEN KEPT in the most violent high security prisons in the country', said Watson. 'I have been lied to and lied about. It has all affected me more than anyone will ever realise. I wonder if anyone knows, really knows, what it is like to have to spend years listening to your children crying.'

As he was close to his father, so he remained especially close to his eldest daughter, Charlotte. During the early years all the children, like the three in Edith Nesbit's *The Railway Children*, believed that their father would be returned to them. 'We just thought they'd realise it was a mistake', Charlotte remembered. 'All the time we used to think that.'

Throughout the long years apart, father and daughter corresponded constantly.

'I would go to my bedroom in the loft and sit on the window-ledge and write him letters', she said. 'When I came home from school, it was my absolute priority. We'd write in exercise books. I'd write my letter in the book, and send it to him and he'd write in his reply. So we sent it backwards and forwards to each other. There's quite a few exercise books that we've filled.

'I know that my friends had all that time with their Dads and

I've missed out on all that with mine. Though it will be wonderful when he's out, the sadness of all the times he hasn't been there will never go away.'

For more than fourteen years, Watson and his father exchanged views and ideas about not only how to remedy the injustice, but how to deal with accumulating everyday problems.

'We discussed the ongoing threat from the Prison Service that if I did not say I was guilty, then I would never be released', said Watson. 'I told him I would never kowtow to pressure and let my children down by pleading guilty to something I hadn't done. If I did that, I would just be lying – how could you ever teach your children the difference between right and wrong if you succumbed to that pressure?'

But Watson spent years with the knowledge that his father was sinking into despair and was grief-stricken with the realisation that he would never again spend time with his son.

'When we were beginning to prove not only that I had not committed the crime but that the crime had been done to me', Watson recollected, 'then he hugged me and said, "I'm proud of you, son".' But the admission from Harriet Harman came just weeks after he died of despair and a broken heart.

'I still have his ashes. The first thing I'll do when I'm free is to take him to join his beloved mother.'

'He went in when his children were babies', reflected Heidi. 'He missed them growing up, now he's missing his grandchildren growing up.

'The people who've done this to him, who have taken his life away – and not just his life, because this affects all of us – they're not going to get punished.

'That's not a justice system.'

Chapter 11

Casualties of justice

The ideal of justice has always been carefully cultivated in Britain. At the UK Supreme Court, one notices almost straightaway Richard Kindersley's beautifully-designed inscription: 'injustice anywhere is a threat to justice everywhere'. The notion that Britain has a perfectly-conceived judicial system, the best in the world, has endured through the centuries. Given this widespread perception, and the country's central place in the development of judicial traditions, the level of expectation has always been especially high. It was widely assumed that England would deliver, as if from emporia in Bond Street or Knightsbridge, only the finest quality of justice.

The fundamental framework gave the system its integrity and authority: habeas corpus; the double jeopardy provision; and the right to silence. There was what judges and lawyers recognised as a core virtue – the 'equality of arms' between prosecution and defence. The overarching principle was the presumption of innocence in the defendant's favour. The burden of proof was borne by the prosecution who needed to persuade a jury of disinterested citizenry that its case was proven beyond all reasonable doubt.

But what if there was a once-in-a-blue-moon problem? What if something went awry?

Judges and leading figures in the judicial system privately took the view that there were bound to be, as it were, casualties of justice. No entirely perfect system could be devised. So the occasional error was the price paid by some unfortunate, in order that the integrity of the system could be maintained. Indeed, Lord Denning publicly articulated that viewpoint in the 1980s:

Denning: After a decision by judge and jury, the media must not go round trying to get what they call fresh evidence in order to show, if they can, the decision was wrong. That is undermining our system of justice altogether.

Q: Are you saying that the integrity of the system is more important than the fate of individuals?

Denning: Certainly. The integrity of our system of justice and upholding it is one of the foundations of society.

Denning was fond of courting controversy, and in any event had
the excuse that by then he was nearly ninety years old. But his
viewpoint, albeit normally unstated, was probably widely held
in the past. Judges might have been forgiven for looking unsym-
pathetically on those who asked for retrospective justice. Their
unspoken reaction may have been: stop whingeing and get on with
your life. If someone was wrongly convicted and imprisoned, he
would serve his sentence but then regain his freedom and be able
to resume his life; wrongful convictions were unfortunate, certainly,
but (with the obvious exception of capital punishment cases) not
lastingly detrimental.

If such sentiments were still to be held by anyone in judicial
authority, they would be wholly hypocritical. A defendant in a
criminal trial today has far more than his immediate welfare in
jeopardy; the consequences of being convicted today are far greater
than they have ever been. Today, it is not merely a question of a
finite prison sentence. While conviction and imprisonment may
not be the end of life, they represent the end of livelihood and
living; for all too many, rehabilitation is no longer feasible.

To begin with, the sentences are now much longer. The abolition of capital punishment in the 1960s had created an anomaly.
Those convicted of murder were instead given a sentence of life
imprisonment. But, in penal terms, 'life' was a malleable concept.
In practice, the length of the prison term could well be interpreted
generously. Some of those convicted of murder could anticipate
release after as little as six or seven years' imprisonment.

This lit a fuse of public concern about the terms of imprisonment that those convicted of serious crimes actually served – albeit
a slow-burning fuse. Finally, the Labour administration that came
to power in 1997 was receptive to growing demands from victims'
organisations and sections of the press for less lenient terms of
imprisonment.

Now, life sentences are accompanied by specific terms, which
tend to be upwards of twenty years. These much longer sentences

have also had an effect in ratcheting up terms of imprisonment for other serious, albeit non-fatal, offences. We have seen how Geoff Hyde received a twenty-two year sentence, which would have been a harsh punishment for the offence even if he had been guilty of it.

Another factor that transformed the landscape was the change in both personal experience and general perception of routine crime. From the 1970s onwards, perhaps instigated by the media's tireless coverage of the subject, the concerns of ordinary people about the prospect of becoming victims of crime increasingly took hold. By the '80s and '90s, much quotidian crime was either mindless vandalism, or theft or violence carried out either under the influence of various drugs or because of the need to pay for them. This type of criminal activity was only going to alienate the general public. Although the fear of crime has been out of all proportion to actual crime, the crime has nevertheless been real enough. People demanded stiffer punishments for those who wrecked their lives, their homes or just their peace of mind.

More aspects of behaviour were criminalised. It was reckoned that the Labour government of 1997-2010 created over 4,300 new offences. Much that had previously been swept under the carpet was now pulled out into the open.

Sexual offences, particularly against children, were reviled by the public and regarded with increased opprobrium. Demands were made for the greater protection of children. The sex offenders register was introduced. Those convicted of sexual offences and imprisoned for thirty months or longer would be required to sign the register for the rest of their lives: a lifelong punishment.

In former times, once a prisoner had served his sentence then, if he was not a career criminal, there was at least some opportunity for him to start afresh, reintegrate into society and rebuild his life. The past really was a foreign country; whatever had happened there was not necessarily going to impinge on this new start.

Once a criminal case was concluded and sentences had been handed down, newspaper editors would consider it closed. It was deemed etiquette not to refer to it again. That code of honour was shattered after Rupert Murdoch bought the *News of the World* in 1969. Needing sensationalist material to boost circulation, he re-published the saga of the 1963-65 Moors Murders, for which Ian Brady and Myra Hindley were sentenced to life imprisonment.

At the time, this was viewed by the rest of Fleet Street as in very bad taste. However, it changed the landscape totally. Ever since, major criminal cases have continued to remain newsworthy despite the fact that logically – because there are no new developments – they should not be newsworthy at all.

The Murdoch papers also coarsened the language and the rhetoric; those convicted were described as, 'thugs', 'perverts' or 'monsters'. It was stylistically a long way from the decorum of the pre-Murdoch *Times* which, in its rare reports about prisoners, had always referred to inmates as 'Mr'.

So, those convicted now have irredeemably ruined reputations and, consequently, wrecked life chances. Those working for charities seeking to rehabilitate prisoners are swimming against an increasingly strong tide.

Further, the internet now ensures that life histories are available to all. If you have committed an offence that has been publicised then, within the average Google search time of less than a second, it will arrive on screen; and whereas detrimental past publicity may once have applied only in one's one country, it now applies world-wide. Those trying to bury their criminal past will find they are ostracised at home; but neither will an overseas retreat necessarily provide a solution.

In Britain in the eighteenth century, those found guilty of certain offences might be branded with an iron so that they carried their criminal record with them forever; in the twenty-first century, the branding is metaphorical but just as indelible.

NONE OF THIS, of course, necessarily provides cause for concern – it is merely the imposition of the punishment that some sections of society are demanding – *providing that the criminal justice system is getting it right*. But if it is getting it wrong, it means that the injustice is now far, far greater.

In Alexandre Dumas's *The Count of Monte Cristo*, Edmond Dantès is wrongly imprisoned for exactly fourteen years; in Charles

Dickens's *A Tale of Two Cities*, Dr Manette is 'recalled to life' from wrongful imprisonment after eighteen years. In each case, the author makes it clear that this represents an inconceivable, almost unsurvivable, term of incarceration. Those are, of course, fictional examples. Yet – not in fiction, but in real life – Karl Watson has already served a longer term of wrongful imprisonment; and so have others in the UK prison system.

The serving of a prison sentence and – even when finally released – one's subsequent status as a former prisoner, is far more serious for the innocent than for the guilty. The guilty can accept it as the consequence of their activities. It will be much more psychologically damaging for the innocent, and will impact on their re-adjustment to the outside world far more.

In 1979, William Whitelaw, the Home Secretary, freed from prison two men, Michael McMahon and David Cooper, who had been wrongly convicted of the 1969 Luton post-office murder. Like the angel of the Lord freeing St Peter from prison in Jerusalem, Whitelaw let them walk out. They were free to resume their lives. The public considered the matter finished; it was no longer a tantalising *cause célèbre*. Sales of *Wicked Beyond Belief*, Ludovic Kennedy's book about the case, plummeted.

However, the Home Secretary had acted precisely because the judges had failed to do so. The convictions stood. So the men were released but not rehabilitated; neither their reputations nor their mental well-being were restored. Their subsequent lives were very difficult. It was only because of the pertinacity of their solicitor, Gareth Peirce, that their convictions were finally quashed in 2003. By then, however, the justice was not merely belated, it was posthumous: Cooper died in September 1993 and McMahon on his fifty-fifth birthday in June 1999. In the wake of Cooper's death, Peirce wrote:

> To our shame, all of us who had been motivated by desperation while they were in prison viewed their release as an alleviation of their suffering. This was not the case. I now know that doctors are at last equating the psychological damage done by wrongful imprisonment with that caused by irreversible physical injury.

That was true then, and it is truer still today. Some members of the judiciary would like to ignore cases that happened some time ago on the grounds that sentences have been served and there can't possibly be any public interest in reconsidering them. That approach is not just wrong but immoral. In the UK today, sentences for the innocent become life sentences. Those wrongly convicted and their families will still be enduring the adverse effects years and decades afterwards.

The innocent who do get swept up into the criminal justice system are disadvantaged precisely because they are innocent. They will be deceived by the ideology. Despite the recent history of the UK's criminal justice system, they imagine there will be a just outcome. They naively believe that the playing-field is a level one.

However, the system is by no means perfectly conceived. It contains a number of basic flaws. A fundamental problem is that the premise on which it is founded is no longer valid. Everyone giving evidence first of all takes the oath: to swear before almighty God that the evidence they give will be the truth, the whole truth and nothing but the truth. The conceit is that as a direct result of taking the oath, they will indeed feel compelled to tell the truth. The system was designed for a God-fearing people in God-fearing times – and for centuries, after a fashion, it worked.

Moreover, one of the beautifully-conceived fail-safe aspects of the system was that it frequently needed only one person to feel a moral or spiritual compulsion to tell the plain truth for the real nature of the case to be revealed.

It is superfluous to point out that religious sensitivities today are very different from what they once were. As a rule, people do not expect to be struck down from above if their evidence consists of something less than the whole truth, or even of outright lies.

The difficulties are only increased if those giving evidence have either come to an arrangement with the prosecution to settle for reduced sentences for crimes of their own, or to have them remitted altogether, in return for their evidence; or if the witnesses had little probity to start off with; or if innate human decency has been abraded by years of dependence on drink and drugs. Yet Crown witnesses in many trials will fit into one of these categories.

The philosopher Ludwig Wittgenstein posed a simple question: why should one tell the truth if it is in one's interests to lie? But, however simple, this question has never been addressed, let alone answered, by the UK criminal justice process. Bizarrely, there is no requirement at all for witnesses to make declarations of interest, and particularly of financial interest. One thinks of witnesses like William Welch in the Giannetto case. Have witnesses received, or can they expect to receive, any kind of remuneration or assistance as a consequence of their appearing in court and giving testimony? Such information should be available to the jury. Since declarations of interest are not currently made, however, this creates the anomaly that standards in the courtroom are actually *lower* than they are in other professional arenas in Britain.

One of the important aspects of the process, albeit a largely unrecognised one, is that conditions suit the dishonest witness better than the honest one. Imagine a situation where someone has been seen fleeing a bank after a robbery. Eyewitnesses will be asked in court, 'Is the man in the dock the one you saw running away?' The honest witness is likely to say, 'Yes, I'm almost sure of that, say, 98% sure'. Appreciating the frailties of human observation and recollection, our honest witness is likely to leave open some small window of possibility that he could be wrong. This gives the cross-examining barrister an opportunity he is unlikely to spurn.

'So you mean you're not 100% sure?' he'll say. 'There is some doubt in your mind?'

By contrast, there will be no equivalent difficulties for the dishonest witness, who will stick to his guns and say, 'Yes, he's the man I saw, no doubt about it, I'm 100% certain.'

There will be no area of uncertainty for the barrister to open up. Although, of course, matters are in the hands of the jurors, the mechanics of the courtroom tend to give dishonesty a natural advantage.

It is also an essentially theatrical arena, so that those who like a stage on which to perform will be able to rise to the histrionic opportunity; correspondingly, those who are naturally unforthcoming or nervous or introverted will find their diffidence more cruelly exposed in the courtroom.

However, jurors should never be put in the position of having to decide which is the more compelling of what may be acting performances; and, if ever they are, then logically they must acquit, as the prosecution cannot satisfy the fundamental judicial test.

And what is this test? What level of cogency must a prosecution case attain in order that the jury can consider it proven? The level, in fact, is not that which the general public believes, because a significant change in recent years was brought in without fanfare – or indeed any publicity at all. A case no longer needs to be proved 'beyond all reasonable doubt'. Judges have jettisoned that phrase. These days, they simply tell juries that they must be 'sure'.

The change is very important. The lack of publicity can be explained by the fact that, in a number of respects, it is verging on the dishonest. First, the official reason for the change is that juries found the phrase confusing. This is nonsense. Juries, having been weaned on the phrase through crime fiction and decades of television dramas, understood it perfectly. The genuine reason for its abandonment was to try to boost conviction rates.

Secondly, it is dishonest because, when asked to give a clearer definition, judges tend to be evasive – as well they might be. What I think the judiciary was trying to do in introducing the test of 'sure' was to come up with a pliable word or term that could be used in a vague way; because any attempt at a definition of 'sure' would quickly put the judges in deep water. In the Oxford English Dictionary, and Chambers Dictionary, and most reputable dictionaries, 'sure' and 'certain' are given as synonyms. There is a very resonant phrase, with which many jurors would be familiar, from the Anglican funeral service about 'the sure and certain hope of the resurrection'. It's a phrase that defies easy understanding (how can a 'hope' be 'certain'?) but the only aspect that matters here is whether 'sure and certain' is a tautologous phrase, with the adjectives used to reinforce each other. I believe it is. I believe it is not possible to ascribe differences in meaning to those words in that context.

So in introducing the 'sure' test, the judges have created myriad difficulties for themselves. The solution is simple. The time-honoured phrase 'beyond all reasonable doubt' is the one that the

British public expects, and naturally understands, and still serves infinitely better than any other. If judges really object to restoring it, then they had better come clean and start telling jurors that 'sure' and 'certain' are synonyms.

The criminal justice system is surprisingly fertile ground for misconceptions. This can be illustrated by reference to a US rape case in which the victim incorrectly identified her assailant. As a result, an innocent man was sentenced to life plus fifty years. He'd got through ten years of this appalling sentence by the time DNA scientific testing enabled the real offender to be identified. The victim of the rape, Jennifer Thompson, and the victim of the justice system, Ronald Cotton, subsequently formed a friendship and collaborated on a book about the case which bore the apt title, *Picking Cotton*.

Thompson explained what happened at the fateful identity parade:

> I wrote '5' [Cotton was number five] on the piece of paper in front of me, and slid it over to Detective Gauldin. He nodded and showed it to a few other men in the room. Then they led me back out into the hallway.
> 'We thought that might be the guy', said Gauldin.

This is how the double delusion takes hold: the officer believes the right suspect has been arrested because that is what the witness is telling him; and the witness is encouraged to believe in the correctness of his or her evidence as that is the signal he or she is getting from the police. As the case progresses towards trial, and indeed beyond it, this becomes a symbiotic process, with each being reinforced in their views by the increasing confidence of the other.

Other delusions may be deliberately created. There are cases in which witnesses have said that police deceived them about the strength of the prosecution position, and so encouraged them to give embellished or untrue testimony. The man who gave perjured evidence of buggery in the Jonathan King trial did so because he had been led to believe that he was one among many; he'd been told that several other men would be giving evidence along the same lines. Only too late did he discover that he was the only one.

The structure of a trial favours the Crown. After miscarriage-of-justice cases have been fully explained, members of the public generally react by saying, 'How on earth was he ever convicted in the first place?' But the key point is that cases are not necessarily put to the jury in a linear way; they are often presented in a jumbled form which inhibits a clear understanding, so that the jury are expected to deal with a confusing picture and fit together pieces of evidence for themselves.

An additional problem is the increasing length of trials. The longer a trial lasts, the more jurors are tempted into thinking, 'Surely this can't all be a mistake? Surely they wouldn't have gone to these lengths if there was any possibility of error?'

The defence team go second. They will never know how much work should be done. In Shakespeare's *Julius Caesar*, after the assassination of Caesar, Brutus makes the critical mistake of insisting that he should address the crowd first, thereby allowing Mark Anthony to go second and whip up public feeling against him and the conspirators. In theory, going second should give the defence an in-built advantage. However, a trial is not a question of two rivals briefly addressing a volatile crowd. It is generally a tedious legal process. Defence lawyers will be concerned that by the time they even start to put their case, most jury members will have had enough. To impose much further on their time, they feel, might be to alienate them altogether. The result is that dangerously truncated defence cases are regularly heard at court.

With the exception of the alteration of the judicial test (from 'beyond all reasonable doubt' to 'sure'), the key changes to the judicial system in recent years, virtually all of them detrimental, have been introduced by parliament. The judicial system has been almost completely remodelled. The process began under the Conservatives, even though they had in fact strengthened the essential elements of the system by passing the Police and Criminal Evidence Act 1984, which provided for the taping of police interviews of suspects.

With the Criminal Justice and Public Order Act 1994, the government of John Major removed the historic right of silence. It was argued by proponents of the change that the existing protection was being exploited by professional criminals, whereas the genuinely innocent did not seek its protection. Opponents pointed out that its abolition would introduce an intellectual inconsistency; drawing adverse inferences from someone's uncommunicativeness was logically at odds with the presumption of innocence.

Inevitably, this helped to bring about injustice. In two especially notable cases, there were convictions of innocent people who did not go into the witness-box. Michael Stone was convicted in October 1998 at Maidstone Crown Court of the murders of Lin and Megan Russell in Chillenden, Kent. His conviction was quashed in February 2001 but a retrial was ordered.

The obvious venue for the retrial was the Old Bailey, but prosecutors are wary of that court, since metropolitan jurors are reckoned to be attuned to potential police malpractice. So, the retrial took place in Nottingham, one of the UK's most crime-ridden areas, and those engaged in the proceedings travelled from Kent, through London, to reach the East Midlands. Stone was then re-convicted by a 10-2 majority – putting him, along with George Robinson, in that particularly unfortunate group of people who have been wrongly convicted twice.

Barry George was wrongly convicted in July 2001 of the murder of television presenter Jill Dando. His conviction was quashed in November 2007 and again a retrial was ordered. This time it did take place at the Old Bailey, and George was acquitted in August 2008.

The Major government also legislated to drop the stringent requirement for corroborative evidence in cases of alleged sexual assault. From now on, prosecutions could be brought on the word of a complainant alone. This allowed inquiries to be conducted with a little less than rigour; if people are given the opportunity to work less than they did before, then that is what they will do. The legislative change allows investigators not to bother to try to seek out supporting evidence. The diligent work that should be put into investigating cases is frequently never carried out. But without evidence, there is anarchy. Not surprisingly, what have ensued from this change are complaints from some that there are too few convictions; and complaints from others that too many of the convictions are wrongful.

Then there was the Criminal Procedure and Investigations Act (CPIA) 1996. As was explained in the Emma Bates chapter, the act introduced a formal procedure into the exchange of papers before trial. The prosecution would set out the framework of its case to the defence; the defence would then pass to the prosecution the material showing what its case was; after this defence bundle had been received by the Crown, then the CPS would pass across the material in its possession that was relevant to the defence. What tends to have happened as a result is that material is frequently handed over to the defence as late as possible. It will often be a large body of material that the defence has neither the time nor the resources to assimilate. So, this Act allows the prosecution to ambush the defence. It now happens routinely.

The CPIA also allowed the Crown Prosecution Service to choose what material to release to the defence. The Court of Appeal had always cautioned: 'when the prosecution acted as judge in their own case … they committed a significant number of errors which affected the fairness of the proceedings'. Yet, in passing the Act, parliament blithely ignored the wise words of the judiciary. Because senior judges are sometimes wrongly blamed for failings in the system, it is helpful to remember that in 1992 the judges laid down a valuable and essentially incontestable principle about disclosure in order to ensure 'the fairness of the proceedings'. It was politicians who tore it up.

The other iniquitous aspect of the CPIA was its objective of preventing proper reporting of cases by withholding documents from journalists. As a result incompetence, negligence and malpractice has been withheld from public attention and a huge swathe of injustice has been created.

Yet it was the Labour administration, first elected in 1997 and re-elected in 2001 and 2005, that really took the wrecking ball to England's criminal justice traditions. Tony Blair, the prime minister under whose aegis most of this happened, was himself a lawyer. In 2002, he famously stated that, 'It is perhaps the biggest miscarriage of justice in today's system when the guilty walk away unpunished'.

Leaving aside the semantics (that may well be a failure to achieve justice, but it certainly isn't a miscarriage of justice), such a viewpoint represents a total misperception of the functions of the criminal justice system. Helena Kennedy QC quickly and forcefully rebuked him, pointing out that his idiosyncratic view represented 'a complete reversal of the approach to justice that every mature democracy in the world respects'.

Nevertheless this 'complete reversal' continues to disable the criminal justice process. If a society concentrates on getting convictions any which way, then the approach becomes counterproductive, because a less rigorous process merely increases the possibility of the guilty thwarting justice.

Many of the Labour government's new measures were contained within the mammoth Criminal Justice Act 2003, which tipped the scales against the defendant and destroyed the concept of fair trials in England and Wales. Under this Act, previous convictions could now be put before the jury. Also, bad character evidence could be used at trial. Hitherto, the rule had been that a person's past conduct, however disreputable, could not form part of the proceedings unless the defendant himself brought the issue of character into the trial by, for example, attacking the character of prosecution witnesses.

For the first time ever, hearsay evidence would be allowed. There had always been a strict rule against the use of hearsay, primarily because it could never pass standard tests of evidence. Anonymous witness evidence was allowed. Objective legal observers were dismayed; this was a new nadir in the history of British justice. How could witnesses be cross-examined if the defence didn't know who they were? How can this be compatible in any way with a fair trial?

A further change of the Criminal Justice Act 2003 was to allow those working in the legal professions and the police to become eligible for jury service. Finally, there was provision, in certain cases, for juries to be dispensed with altogether and cases heard by judge alone. A disturbing precedent for judge-alone cases had been set in Scotland with the bizarre Lockerbie trial, when judges brought in an incoherent verdict – acquitting one defendant and convicting the other, even though the evidence against each was identical.

There has so far been only one judge-only trial in England, when four men were charged with armed robbery at Heathrow Airport in February 2004. Not surprisingly, the men were convicted; equally unsurprisingly, the case remains controversial.

Then matters got even worse. In June 2006, Allan Chapelow, a retired journalist who was an authority on the playwright George Bernard Shaw, was murdered in his house in Hampstead, north London. He lived alone and by the time the body was found, it was badly decomposed; so it is uncertain when the murder occurred. Wang Yam, a dissident who had fled China after the Tiananmen Square protests and was granted refugee status in the UK in 1992, was charged with the murder.

In December 2007, the Home Secretary, Jacqui Smith, signed a Public Interest Immunity (PII) certificate allowing much of the trial to be heard *in camera* on the grounds, or so the press were told, of national security and in order to protect witnesses. So the prosecution went ahead under what was effectively a total media blackout. 'It is thought to be the first time a murder trial has been held under such circumstances', the *Daily Telegraph* commented.

At the start of the trial, Mr Justice Ouseley instructed journalists that they were not even to speculate about the reasons for the secrecy and Smith's extraordinary decision.

The jury could not reach even a majority verdict on the murder charge, so the case went to a second trial in 2009. Wang Yam was convicted and given a life sentence. It would be strange indeed if justice could be achieved in such conditions, and it certainly appears as if it wasn't; Wang Yam continues strenuously to assert his innocence, even though no one is currently permitted to reveal on what grounds.

This case merely brings into sharp focus the spiralling provisions for secrecy in the judicial processes. There are various ways in which judges are now able to inhibit the reporting of cases before them. The restrictions may even continue after the end of the trial. Just as Nelson's fleets were handicapped by the need to sail at the speed of the slowest ship, so the British press has been frustrated by the lack of principles of the sleaziest paper.

The police and prosecution can always use the anticipated

misconduct of the most irresponsible as the excuse for imposing restraints on all. Geoffrey Robertson and Andrew Nicol wrote, as long ago as 1984, 'It is regrettable that so much of media law should impinge upon public interest reporting and so little of it work to eradicate discreditable press practices. The blind Goddess of Justice seems to raise her sword against investigative journalism while her other hand fondles the Sunday muckraker.' That has proved prescient. So, on the pretext of curbing the malicious excesses of the sensationalist press, the authorities have drawn the teeth of responsible journalism.

All these legislative changes and judicial developments mean that the core principles of English justice – that defendants were to be tried by a jury of their peers in open court with the press and public present, and convictions could be obtained solely on the basis of direct evidence bearing upon the crime itself – were destroyed.

FIVE FACTORS compounded the irresponsibility of all these sweeping changes. The first is that these legislative changes were put in place at a time when it was already known that Britain had a significant problem with miscarriages of justice. What, following the Birmingham Six case and many others, was done to prevent a recurrence of similar judicial errors? The answer was, of course, nothing at all.

The second is that they were being brought in at the precise moment when there should have been no need for them at all. By the start of the twenty-first century, far-reaching technological change had swept through the country. Personal computers are now in most homes and a high proportion of people have at least one mobile phone. (Mobiles are reckoned to have 124% penetration in the population, as many possess more than one.) Cell-site analysis means that it is possible to determine the locations in which calls are made and received. If the caller tries to conceal his whereabouts by switching off his phone, that position will be recorded too. Anyone who is arrested today for a serious offence can expect to have their computer and mobile phone seized, thereby allowing police to put together a record of their recent movements and activities.

If suspects have been out and about, police will still be able to track their movements. Satnavs will record details of where a car has been. Almost all urban areas and retail sites, and even some residential roads, will have a filmed record of a day's events. The UK, with one surveillance camera for every thirty-two people, now has more CCTV per head of population than any other country in the world.

On top of all that there is DNA technology, which has taken forensic science to new and entirely unforeseen levels and almost guarantees that some record of a criminal's presence will be left at the scene; just sneezing could be enough to lead to his capture. In September 2011, it was reported that poachers could be identified through DNA traces on animal carcasses.

Investigators in previous decades could only have dreamed of the availability of such extraordinary investigative tools. For politicians to dilute the criminal justice system to tilt the scales still further to the advantage of the Crown at a time when prosecutors already have all these advantages coming on stream – that is unforgivable.

The third is the routine collusion between the prosecution and the press. As the media has been emasculated in recent years – largely through its lack of resources to pursue intensive and time-consuming investigations – it has increasingly toed the prosecution line. The police and prosecution are able to use the media as an extra limb in their strategy of creating a backdrop of public prejudice and so helping to secure a conviction.

The basic contempt of court rules which prevent media discussion of cases before trial mean that *sub judice* applies from the time of charge. This freezes the publicity process at the point of maximum disadvantage for the defendant. Those who will become jurors then learn nothing more about the case from the media until they come out of court and see the newspaper placards and the reports of the Crown opening. If it is not a high-profile case then, in all likelihood, they will see nothing more before they deliver their verdict.

This would not occur if the trial was being reported properly, but there has been no proper reporting of criminal trials in Britain for many years. In recent years local newspapers, which historically provided excellent coverage, have taken their lead from the more scurrilous tabloids and chosen to report the Crown case in the most fawning terms and the defence case not at all.

Even for the very few high-profile trials of national interest, journalists do not attend regularly so they can hardly report them adequately. Often, they turn up for the Crown opening and the verdict and do not know what goes on in between. Indeed, the journalistic desertion of the courtroom helps to put into context controversies about the holding of occasional secret trials. For all practical purposes, the overwhelming majority of criminal trials in the UK are already held in secret, simply because the media no longer report or even attend them.

Just one of the aspects of unfairness is that the media may report individual verdicts as soon as the jury has delivered them. This means, in some instances, the creation of highly prejudicial publicity while the jury may still be deliberating on further charges in the same case, and prior to the judge handing down sentence.

This is clearly wrong; there should not be press comment on an ongoing trial until the jury has delivered all the verdicts and sentence has been imposed. The premature media reports serve only to put pressure, in the first instance, on the jury to convict on the remaining charges; and, in the second, on the judge to impose a harsher sentence than he otherwise would have done.

Afterwards, in cases where there are growing doubts about the safety of the conviction, the papers are reluctant to become involved; after all, that could perhaps alert readers to their own poor journalistic standards. Having contributed to the creation of miscarriages of justice either directly (through prejudicial reports) or indirectly (by doing nothing to help to prevent them), they are disinclined to assist when the focus has shifted, and the relatively straightforward task of railroading someone into prison is replaced by the infinitely more exacting one of getting them out.

The fourth factor is the arrival of the internet which, notwithstanding its huge benefits, has not proved helpful so far as the administration of justice is concerned. Charles Spurgeon, the nineteenth century Baptist preacher, was apparently the first to assert that a lie can travel the world while truth is putting on her boots. In the internet age, that observation becomes more meaningful than ever. What was needed, with the risk of prejudice swelling so precipitately, was some reinforcement of safeguards, not a diminution of them.

The fifth factor underlying the irresponsibility of the legislative changes to make convictions easier, is that, as they were being brought in, the government was simultaneously acting to reduce significantly the amount of money available to lawyers through legal aid. The inevitable result is that many leading solicitors' practices believe that it is now impossible to defend clients facing serious charges on a legal aid budget.

In April 2014, Nigel Evans, former Deputy Speaker of the House of Commons, was acquitted of a series of charges of sexual assault. He had resigned his position after being charged in May the previous year. In the wake of his acquittal Evans demanded, entirely understandably, that the CPS, having wrongly prosecuted him, should now reimburse his legal costs of £130,000.

It did seem fitting that a senior Member of Parliament now had first-hand experience both of the CPS's capricious approach to prosecutions and of the tremendous costs involved in defending oneself. The overwhelming majority of those who face criminal charges would have no means of raising sums like £130,000 to mount a proper defence. They would just have to assume that, however threadbare the evidence against them, their conviction was a foregone conclusion.

With the defence undermined, convictions could be obtained even in circumstances where searching questions should have been asked about prosecution procedures (for example, the 'loss' of the entire missing person's inquiry of 1976, one of the factors leading to the wrongful conviction of Gordon Park). Parliament had overlooked the reality that the criminal justice process exists to combat dishonesty, fraud, malpractice, racism, *et cetera*; but whenever it achieves convictions by means of dishonesty, fraud, malpractice, racism, *et cetera*, it is intrinsically worthless.

AFTER THE TRIAL, there is the appeal. Unfortunately, this too offers those forced to rely on it only empty promises of justice. If anyone has been wrongly convicted, their attempts to challenge their conviction are likely to be frustrated at every turn. Legal teams who have stressed their loyalty during the trial will become distant and uncommunicative; though, in fairness to them, the available funding for a team for appeal is likely to be minuscule. There will inevitably be problems getting hold of all the correct paperwork. The trial should have been recorded, but core documents like the judge's summing-up will take ages to arrive. Tapes will frequently be lost. Sometimes prisoners complain that their efforts are deliberately blocked. Their cells will be spun – that is, searched – and afterwards important documents may be missing.

When the promised land of the appeal court is finally reached, the wrongly-convicted will discover that the jury verdict is regarded as all but inviolable – as indeed it should be, were the system capable of living up to its mythology in the first place. The appeal will be mainly concerned with the management of the trial and the appeal court judges will only intervene if there has been some glaringly improper aspect.

A better qualified and more distinguished forensic expert than the one used at trial may have now been instructed. He may perhaps have provided an illuminating fresh opinion, but his evidence may not be accepted. The Court doesn't allow the defence merely to substitute one expert for another. Nor are defendants and their legal teams able to try Plan A at trial and, when that has failed, deploy Plan B at post-trial hearings.

The judges will tend to dismiss oversights or even glaring errors, arguing that they were not significant enough to have influenced the jury's decision – even though they themselves have no knowledge at all of what did influence the jury's decision. The Court of Appeal still hasn't taken on board the iron rule of the courtroom: if juries are given the wrong information, they will reach the wrong verdict.

There is some basis for the contention that appeal court judges refuse to confront reality when considering the performance of the trial legal team and occasional charges of incompetence. Lord Justice Dyson, himself an appeal court judge, forthrightly acknowledged that, 'sadly, such incompetence is far from rare'.

Nevertheless, what is certainly rare is the prospect of a conviction being quashed because of failings at trial by defence lawyers. It's no use an appellant arguing that he wasn't adequately represented first time; the Court of Appeal will almost never accede to the argument that defence counsel may have been incompetent, or even have put in a slightly below-par performance, at the original trial. All trial lawyers, it seems, are perfect.

This is a curious doctrine to uphold. Imagine if it were to be transferred elsewhere; imagine returning a purchase to Marks & Spencer or John Lewis and being refused an exchange or refund on the grounds that, 'We're sorry, but there can't have been a fault – our staff do not make mistakes'. That would not just be unthinkable; ironically, it would also be illegal.

Nevertheless, the Court of Appeal persists in maintaining that trial lawyers put the case to the jury as well as it could possibly be put. As this is not always the case, it means that there are hundreds of people in prison today because their legal team failed to perform on the day, or made flawed decisions, or simply wasn't up to much in the first place.

Following sustained public criticism of the performance of the Court of Appeal, the Major government set up the Criminal Cases Review Commission (CCRC) to sift those cases which had gone awry at trial and appeal. However, despite the well-known mantra that 'justice delayed is justice denied', the CCRC is glacially slow. Further, even after deliberations spanning not months but years, it will, perplexingly, fail to refer to appeal even outstandingly meritorious cases. It routinely emasculates itself by consulting trial lawyers whose priority (not for all of them, but for far too many of them) will be to protect their own interests, rather than those of their erstwhile client. Crucially, the CCRC must defer to the Court of Appeal's agenda, and so can never be the corrective body that the public thought it was going to get.

The concept underpinning it is absurd. The justice system has a defective criminal trials process; and a defective criminal appeals process; and then abdicates its responsibility for the failings by expecting an extra-judicial body to make good the deficiencies.

Having created a new criminal justice structure, making it far more likely that there would be wrongful convictions, the Labour government then legislated to make life as difficult as possible for anyone who was somehow able to emerge from all that adversity with a quashed conviction.

First they changed the rules for providing compensation payments to those wrongly imprisoned. When Labour took office, there were two separate compensation schemes in place: a statutory scheme enshrined in the Criminal Justice Act 1988; and an ex gratia scheme, which had been in place since Douglas Hurd, as Home Secretary, had announced it in parliament in 1985. Overnight in 2006 the government ended the ex gratia scheme.

The government also set about reducing the application of the statutory provisions in three ways: firstly, by capping the amounts of compensation payable; and, secondly, by withholding a percentage of sums that were awarded on the grounds that the prison service should be reimbursed for providing full board and lodgings. If Terry Waite and John McCarthy had been obliged to pay for their food and shelter while chained to radiators by their Lebanese captors between 1986 and 1991, there would have been seething administrative anger in the UK. Yet it was precisely this principle that the Labour government introduced.

Thirdly, the statute was deliberately interpreted ever more narrowly. Claims that would have been waved through in the administration's early years were now rejected. The civil servants would just refuse to pay and let disappointed applicants challenge them in the courts. The courts, taking their lead from what appeared to be the political will, were not inclined to be sympathetic.

In the *Criminal Law Review*, John Spencer QC, Professor of Law at Cambridge University and the President of the European Criminal Law Association, wrote:

> The current rules [for] compensation to victims of miscarriages of justice in England are as bad as it is possible to make them ... They are harsh and arbitrary and devoid of intellectual justification.

The Labour government also brought in legislation to prevent those convicted of criminal offences from writing memoirs. The passage of the measure through parliament was deliberately low-key; indeed, it was smuggled in under the cloak of the Coroners and Justice Act 2009. The government was reminded, during its passage, of some of the great works of literature that may never have appeared had this legislation been in place, but ignored the warnings. The measure was clearly unnecessary, both because there were already sanctions in place to prevent sordid and gratuitous accounts of criminality being published in newspapers or elsewhere; and also because the overwhelming likelihood is that the financial reward for anyone writing their memoirs will be meagre.

The important points of principle were swept aside. There are authors who, though convicted of a crime, wish to set out the case for their innocence. One thinks of Alfie Hinds' *Contempt of Court*, the valuable and atmospheric autobiography in which Hinds sought to persuade the reader of his innocence. He didn't convince me but at least he was able, in those unfettered days of 1966, to put forward his arguments free of government interference and in the knowledge that he'd receive the customary author's stipend for his work.

These arrangements to disallow compensation claims and to prevent first-hand accounts being written were the coping stones on a new edifice of injustice. Even so, in 2014, the Conservative-Liberal Democrat coalition government went still further, in seeking to legislate to make it virtually impossible for anyone to be able to claim any compensation for wrongful imprisonment from the State that had mistakenly – or even malevolently – prosecuted them.

ONE OF THE KEY mistakes made during the past quarter-century has been to focus on remedying the system by improving the appeals process. It hasn't worked but, even if it had, it would have been a mistaken strategy. Clearly, it is fundamental to reform the trial process itself. It's no use worrying about the post-trial situation; by then, the damage has been done. It is essential that the trial itself functions properly and that the available evidence is genuinely tested in court. Indeed, the ultimate objective should be to create a situation that as nearly as possible meets scientific standards so that however often the test is performed (that is, however often the case goes to trial), an identical result is achieved.

In the first place, there should be proper day-to-day transcripts of all jury trials. This can be achieved by embracing new technology. At present, whatever is said will be taped – but transcripts are only prepared in particular circumstances. Judges and lawyers will create their own records of proceedings by writing it down as they go along.

After a few years tapes will have been lost or destroyed, leaving no permanent record of what was said. When cases are being heard at appeal, perhaps years later, no one can really be sure what was said at the original trial.

With proper contemporaneous transcripts the judge and the lawyers, relieved of the obligation to create their own records, will be able to concentrate ever more closely on the trial and the evidence. Further, the existence of transcripts will aid in reducing perjury. Witnesses' awareness that what they say is being properly recorded and documented will provide a strong disincentive for those tempted to give dishonest testimony.

It is sometimes said, also, that judges are reluctant to embrace new technology but that has never seemed the case to me. I think the truth is that the judiciary, just as much as the rest of us, are thwarted by cumbersome bureaucratic machinery and the inertia in the system itself. His Honour Judge Simon Brown QC, in a letter to *The Times*, pointed out that countries such as the United States, Australia and Singapore had already achieved the transition to new technology.

'In the sphere of justice, they have now adapted so that almost all records are stored, sorted, produced and transmitted electronically', he wrote. 'Here in the UK, the situation is the converse: almost all evidence and court files are still in anachronistic, inefficient and expensive paper form.'

In fact, the standard argument against producing transcripts is the inhibiting cost; it is said they will be too expensive to prepare.

That is a bogus argument. In terms of vastly improving the efficiency of the entire process, proper transcripts will actually save the country millions of pounds.

Should the jurors have access to these transcripts? In my view, they should have access to them throughout the trial and during their deliberations.

Similarly, jurors are sometimes shown video interviews. It is remarkable that, while jurors are being forced to watch these videos, the lawyers and the judge, and sometimes the reporters too, are all following the interview by referring to the transcripts as the tapes or DVDs are being played. It is an aid that greatly increases comprehension. Yet jurors are not allowed to do this. In other words, everyone in court is able to gain an enhanced understanding of the recordings by following them through the transcripts – except the most important people of all, the jurors. So this is another perplexing feature of criminal trials.

It is illogical that everything must be verbalised, and jurors are expected to absorb everything through speech alone. If evidential material can be seen on the page as well as heard, then it is likely to be better understood and assimilated. Not only would most people acknowledge this, but the professionals who would most obviously recognise this are lawyers and judges; they above all are people who want to see everything written down.

So, it would be enormously beneficial for the management of trials if jurors were provided with day-by-day transcripts, and if they were provided with transcripts of any material they are expected to follow in video form. Further, if jurors ask for specific statements, I do not understand why these should not be provided to them. This is the material that – in studying the case – everyone else will focus on, including, if the case has gone wrong at trial, the Criminal Cases Review Commission in its subsequent considerations. So what is the point of allowing the CCRC to see it after the event but not the jury? If the jury were to see it to begin with, the trial need not go awry and the CCRC need not be involved because justice will not have been miscarried.

Regarding legal representation, one simple change would be welcomed: that prosecution and defence lawyers must never be appointed from within the same chambers. This continues to happen. The majority of lawyers see nothing wrong in it. It is just another example of how insulated the criminal Bar continues to be.

What tends to happen is that, after a case has gone to trial, the losing party and their family belatedly learn that both prosecution and defence came from the same address. They then immediately and understandably conclude that the trial process was a fix from start to finish. In fact, it hasn't been (frequently there is scant mutual respect among barristers from the same chambers), but this is another instance where what matters is not simply fairness but the appearance of fairness. It is certainly true that in some niche areas of the law barristers must necessarily come from the same chambers, as there are only a few specialists in the field; but for ordinary criminal work, prosecution and defence must not be perceived as being in bed together – which, given the general public's automatic understanding of the word 'chambers', tends to be the conclusion jumped to.

The situation at trial with regard to jurors is particularly odd. In order to function, this system uniquely needs to take people from other walks of life. It needs them to down tools and temporarily change their livelihood. This is a civic duty which most accept conscientiously. But these people, many of whom are no doubt skilled and dedicated in their own occupations, are drafted into this world as outsiders only to enter an arena where professional standards fall seriously short of those that they themselves would expect as routine.

Further, anyone taking steps to enlighten themselves had better watch out. Someone I knew who, even after a good few years, had better remain anonymous, told me about his own jury service. The case was a burglary. This juror had got on his bicycle and gone to the scene of the crime, thereby showing (in my view) particular diligence. He discovered that the scene was not as it had been described in court and, indeed, that the defendant could not have entered the property in the way that the Crown alleged. He returned, told the other jurors and the result was an acquittal.

If someone is sufficiently public-spirited and resourceful enough to do that, and to try to find out additional information, and indeed to replace the Court's misinformation with his own accurate information, well, isn't that splendid? Not according to the Courts; such initiatives are frowned upon – and even criminalised.

One juror's assiduity came to national attention. It happened at Newcastle Crown Court in August 2008 in the trial of Dale Patterson, a 17-year-old student, who was charged with the manslaughter of Raymond Quigley, a 72-year-old taxi driver. Quigley, who had been taking Patterson from Newcastle train station to Sunderland, died of a heart attack, seemingly after grappling with the youth in an argument over the fare. This particular juror, who was not identified, visited the crime scene, took photographs, studied the case on the internet, discussed his findings with the other jurors and came up with a list of thirty-seven questions about the circumstances of the incident.

After the extent of his investigations became clear, the judge, His Honour Judge David Hodson, stopped the trial. However, he did not order a fresh one. He pointed out that, 'It cannot be shown that the defendant did any unlawful acts that contributed to the death of Mr Quigley'. The prosecution then offered no evidence and 'not guilty' was entered on the indictment.

So it's possible that the juror may have helped to prevent a miscarriage of justice. Before the trial was abandoned, he was asked to explain his actions. He said, 'I wanted to ensure that I and my fellow jurors reached the right verdict'. So we can put his enterprise this way: in order to make sure that the objective was achieved, he was going the extra mile.

In all other professional arenas in the country, that would have been considered laudable. Once again, therefore, in seeking to ban such activities, the criminal justice system is setting itself *lower* professional standards than those we would expect elsewhere. If counsel for each side had performed brilliantly, and if all necessary information had been placed before the jury, then the juror's actions would have been, at worst, redundant. But, plainly, this was not the case. It was accepted in court that the juror had been trying to gather information 'that neither the prosecution nor defence had put before the jury'. Some of those thirty-seven questions showed insight into the case and needed answering. So the juror's application to his allotted task should, it seems to me, have been applauded.

In just a few years, the internet has changed our society and all our lives. Any business that ignored it would be derided as moribund. The public, too, can participate. There are already documented examples of illnesses that have confounded doctors but which those suffering from them or their family members have correctly diagnosed through the internet. The professionals can never have all the answers.

If I were ever a juror, I would certainly wish to read round the subject matter of the trial on the internet. It is what I would automatically do in all social or professional areas of my life, so there seems no reason why jury service should be any different. Indeed, it seems to me the responsible approach to take.

However, those administering the criminal justice system view such initiative very differently. In June 2011, and in January 2012, and again in July 2013 jurors were sentenced to terms of imprisonment for using the internet to research the background of cases they were hearing. Contempt of court proceedings in these cases were initiated by the Attorney General, Dominic Grieve.

'Jurors who use the internet to research a case undermine justice', commented Grieve. 'I take no pleasure in bringing such cases, but they send an important message.'

Unfortunately, all this exposes the judicial authorities at their most blinkered. Even in the context of all that has happened, this is one of the bleakest developments in British criminal justice. A system that purports to uphold freedom of expression should not be curtailing access to information. What are the courts afraid of? One suspects they're afraid that jurors will come across information that has been withheld from them. Of course, this could include details of previous convictions for the defendant; but these may now be revealed to the jury in any event. On the other hand, the internet could reveal details of previous malpractice by the police force involved. The arguments will cut both ways; but jurors should be trusted to be able to assimilate extraneous information and set it into the context of the case they are hearing.

The way to combat unprocessed comment, which may have congealed into a mass of prejudice, is not to pretend it doesn't exist but to allow jurors, if they wish, to consider it – in which case they will presumably recognise it as the nonsense that, usually, it is. Of course, it must be emphasised to jurors that anything they may pick up outside the courtroom is not evidence on which the case is being tried and that online reports are frequently wrong – but that if they have chanced upon important and relevant additional information, then they should be encouraged to raise it.

As we have seen, newspapers report what is essentially prosecution propaganda; they can be controlled. The internet cannot be. It represents a serious threat to the State's ability to administer criminal justice on its own terms. That, it seems to me, is the real reason why the authorities are so staunchly opposed to it.

Jurors should not be intimidated by the trial process; they should be encouraged to be more interventionist. Further, if they subsequently learn something about a case after the trial has finished, they should be able to say, 'Had this information been available at trial, then the jury discussions may have taken a different course'; and that case should then be referred to appeal.

However, some citizens are now becoming jurors who certainly should not be. Jurors should certainly be fully cognisant of all that is happening. Anyone who is illiterate, or whose literacy skills are in a language other than English, is obviously not suitable to be a juror. Bizarrely, HM Courts and Tribunals Service does not hold this view and sends out jury summonses in seven languages. When the *Daily Mail* understandably questioned the wisdom of this, HMCTS blithely responded that they were 'committed to encouraging the widest possible participation by the public'. They should instead be committed to ensuring a complement of jurors who can properly understand the matters before them.

As a result of the changes concerning jury selection, leading judges and lawyers and police officers have now been empanelled. Indeed, it already seems almost inevitable that someone associated with the police will be on a jury. This is perhaps not so surprising. While pressing commitments at work, or unsympathetic bosses, may cause those in other professions to try to defer jury service, police officers will always be ready and able to attend. There have been some remarkable jury decisions in recent years. Whether or not this has been because of this change to jury selection, one can, of course, only speculate.

The police and legal professions are barred in many jurisdictions round the world, and this is the approach that makes obvious sense. The whole point of the system should be that those within the criminal justice process are putting their cases to those outside it. Lord Bingham said that 'the integrity of the trial process hangs on the jury's integrity'. It was the fact that the arbiters were genuinely impartial that gave the system its unique authority. This measure, introduced by Home Secretary David Blunkett as part of the Criminal Justice Act 2003, fatally compromises the integrity of the system. The *status quo ante* must be restored, so that those who are professionally part of the system should be ineligible to arbitrate within it.

Meanwhile, those outside the system altogether – the general public – have always been able to comment on ongoing judicial proceedings with impunity, whether on the doorstep or in the workplace or over a pint in the pub. Now, with up-to-date technology, they have an opportunity, and some even appear to feel a compulsion, to make their views known to friends and colleagues through Twitter or other social media.

Unfortunately, these views are then picked up by a significantly wider audience and, even more unfortunately, they are in contempt of court. Such demotic initiatives are taken very seriously. The police and prosecution pursue them zealously; they are slam-dunk cases (the comments are obviously recorded) that can be processed with a minimum of effort. So the incautious Twitterers can quickly find themselves up before the judge and then, perhaps, in prison.

All of which highlights the system at its least creditable. However misinformed or offensive or disgusting the remarks, this smacks of bullying and an implacable resolve to punish the none-too-bright for their grievous offence of being none-too-bright.

Science in the courtroom is a genuine hazard. A scientist's word has become gospel. Cases now depend to such a large extent on forensic science evidence that it is critical that there should be no dispute about the validity of the work. Yet, sometimes, the sample analysed by the scientist will have been used up in the process, so the claimed results will be verifiable by no one at all. In Britain today there are many serving sentences of twenty-five years and more whose fate has effectively been sealed by the opinion of just one person.

It must be pointed out that whenever the Forensic Science Service released a public statement, it was nearly always emphasised that convictions should never be based on scientific evidence alone. However, this cautionary note is rarely heeded. Judges and juries tend to be befuddled by science and, perhaps, as a consequence of their collective incomprehension, place unquestioning faith in it; as a rule, the less they understand, the more readily they will accept it. The situation was then made even more problematic by the closing of the Forensic Science Service in March 2012, so that all scientific work for the UK criminal justice system is now handled by private companies.

There are generally two stages in scientific work for the courtroom: the results of the analysis of the specimen, and the interpretation of those results.

In DNA analysis, by far the most important area of forensic science, the DNA crime scene sample is routinely divided into three parts, or aliquots. The prosecution, or its laboratory, will test two of these. The third is kept in reserve and may be used later.

This, instead, is what should happen: the two aliquots to be tested should be sent to different laboratories and analysed independently of each other. The raw data resulting from the analysis should then be provided to the Court, where both Crown and defence will have access and be able to interpret the results. The analysis, and the scientific interpretation, should be done separately by different scientists.

The current system is flawed. One scientist will both perform the tests and analyse the results. By the time the defence becomes involved, the case may well be set for trial and the defence scientist may be able to do little more than rubber-stamp the Crown's interpretation. Too often the defence opinion is based merely on an assessment of the Crown scientist's report, not on an assessment of the original data.

The teenager Stephen Lawrence was murdered in April 1993. In January 2012, Gary Dobson and David Norris were convicted of his murder on the basis of scientific evidence, the significance of which was only realised more than fourteen years after the crime itself. Yet, because of the social and political ramifications of the murder, no case had ever been subject to more intensive scrutiny. This amply demonstrates the necessity of retaining exhibits. If vital evidence can be overlooked for fourteen years in the pre-eminent Lawrence case, there is every possibility that it will have been overlooked in every other criminal case.

However, there is an additional point. Perhaps the most significant aspect of the development of DNA evidence is not the science itself but the corollary: this means that we can never know today what evidential information exhibits may yield tomorrow. This is an even more important reason for preserving exhibits in adequate conditions. If, at the end of a trial, there is an acquittal, then the case may well be unsolved and so remains open; if there has been a conviction, then the system must ensure that it is a conviction of absolute integrity. Whichever it is, the evidential material must be collected and properly stored.

Arguments about whether the appeals machinery was ever especially well-oiled in the past are now irrelevant, because in recent years it appears to have seized up altogether. As the Court of Appeal has dismissed appeals in meritorious cases, so fewer cases have been referred to them.

The central problem is that cases develop organically as the years pass. Documents emerge; there may be new developments or new witnesses. Yet no single tribunal hears all the evidence, or the case in its totality. To clarify the position, I believe that parliament should order what I would call 'clean slate appeals'.

Whatever the previous legal history of the case, the slate would be wiped clean at appeal. Counsel would simply say: my client was wrongly convicted for the following reasons. The defence barrister would not, of course, be able simply to reiterate the case that was put at trial; but providing something has changed – if, for example, the prosecution or its witnesses misled the court at trial; or if there have been fresh developments and the thrust of the case is altered – then the case has become a different one to that heard by the jury. It should be irrelevant why arguments or lines of defence were not broached in the first place. They may well not have been deployed at the original trial because counsel either overlooked their significance or erred in some other way. If there are clean slate appeals, there will be no need to apportion blame.

An alternative solution is also available. At the House of Lords in 2001, Lord Bingham, the senior law lord, emphasised 'the central role of the jury in a trial [which] is an important and greatly-prized feature of our constitution'. He further clarified the position, adding: 'Trial by jury does not mean trial by jury in the first instance and trial by judges of the Court of Appeal in the second'. All that mattered, declared the Lords in their important judgment, was the view the jury would have taken of the case.

So today, in the present circumstances, when a case has been referred to appeal by the Criminal Cases Review Commission, why is the appeal court itself holding lengthy hearings about it? The CCRC has considered the case. Its case officers have seen far more evidence than the jury ever did; and they have concluded that there are serious doubts about the conviction. So the Court of Appeal's own view is constitutionally otiose; the matter of guilty or not-guilty is not theirs to consider. That's what the House of Lords said. Where the CCRC has referred a case back, the appeal court should simply have a formal ten-minute hearing in which to quash the conviction and send the case back for retrial.

One well understands the determination of the judiciary to ensure that there is finality in the trial process; it is in no one's interests for cases to be in an endless criminal justice loop. However, that is precisely what does happen far too often at present; cases which should have been efficiently and expeditiously dealt with remain in the judicial process for years and even decades. So producing an efficacious appeals process should be a secondary concern. The prime objective must be to put in place safeguards to ensure that the courts get it right first time. The malfunctioning of the criminal justice process is not only destroying thousands of lives quite unnecessarily, but is also costing the country hundreds of millions of pounds, equally unnecessarily.

It should always be remembered that the judicial system in England and Wales now pits a tiny, seriously underfunded and per-petually handicapped defence team against a prosecution which has all the powers of the State and is regularly augmented by all the powers of the established media.

Only in a country where judicial myths are as divorced from reality as they are in the UK could this be described as equality of arms.

Notes

Some names have been changed, sometimes to avoid the possibility of prejudicing potential future legal proceedings. Complainants and victims in sexual assault cases are legally entitled to anonymity, so those names too have been changed.

P43, para 3 The names of the guest-house owner and her partner have been changed.

P112, para 1 Neither Emma's trial solicitors nor her trial barrister responded to emails inviting them to comment about the case

P114, para 3 It is also significant that neighbours heard nothing, even though the houses are tightly-packed and people were still up at that hour (as was shown by their coming out onto the street when the police and ambulance arrived). Had there been an altercation between Wayne and Emma, there would have been raised voices.

P123, last line This final remark, 'standing in my living room' was communicated to the judge by the prosecution barrister (that is, 'He said, "I was standing in my living room"').

P126, line 26 The crux of the case is the claim by Westlake that he called Wayne at 02.27 on the morning of 12 April and that the call then stayed live for three minutes, so that he was able to overhear what happened when Wayne suffered the fatal knife wound. But did this call happen?

It is axiomatic that if A phones B, that will be verified by corresponding phone records – of A making the call, and B receiving it.

In this instance, there is no such documentary correspondence.

A month afterwards, West Midlands Police needed to clear up difficulties with Westlake's phone record regarding the call from Emma at 02.24. He had told police that he'd received it on his mobile – but there was no record of that call. In fact, Westlake's recollection was mistaken; Emma had phoned his girlfriend's phone. So, on 12 May, the police took fresh statements from both Westlake and his girlfriend. He then admitted to having made a mistake with regard to Emma's call. Having clarified that, the police then, on 13 May, drew up the *Chronology of Events leading up to the Death of Wayne Hill.* The key information appeared as follows:

02.17 Telephone call from Bates to Nicola Giles telling her Hill had taken the car
02.24 Telephone call from Bates to [Westlake's girlfriend]
02.29 999 call made by Bates
02.33 Police informed by ambulance control
02.34 Text message from Westlake to Wayne's mobile 'Im at the door'
02.41 Police and ambulance arrived at the scene

So the *Chronology* was clear: there was no call from Westlake to Wayne at 02.27.

Two factors – the inclusion of the text to Wayne at 02.34; and the fact that they had taken fresh statements regarding inconsistencies in the telephone records only the previous day – showed clearly that at this juncture the police had already examined Westlake's phone documentation.

Other pieces of evidence support the idea that there was no call from Westlake at this time. When he originally reported it to police, immediately after the incident, he indicated that he'd made the call while walking down the road; then he changed his account and said he'd made it from his home. Further, it is of interest that, although his girlfriend supports Westlake in saying that he did make the call from their living-room, she says tersely that '[he] phoned Wayne but I didn't hear what was said'. This is strange. If the call had been made, she would surely have heard at least Westlake's part in it. Moreover, during the call from Emma just moments before, she overheard not just what Westlake was saying, but some of what Emma said at the other end ('I could hear Emma's voice on the phone').

It may be that Westlake actually had tried to phone Wayne, but the number was engaged, because there is indeed a call to Wayne's phone at 02.27, but it was not from Westlake. We can be sure of this partly because it does not appear on Westlake's telephone records; and partly because, if it had been from him, it would have been recorded on Wayne's handset as being from DAN. The 'Im at the door' text that he did send does appear as from DAN, as do the other communications from him during the previous two-year period. We also know that Westlake was not using his girlfriend's phone, as she emphasised in her statement that the call she took from Emma was the 'only call' in these events that involved her phone, and that is borne out by the records.

West Midlands Police asked the police liaison manager at Virgin Media for the call data from Westlake's phone three times: on 30 April, 21 May and 30 June. On each occasion, it seems he provided the information, but that information – which is crucial in the context of the case – has never been disclosed to the defence.

It is also significant that in the documents handed over to the defence by West Midlands Police, no number is given for the incoming call at 02.27. Lastly, the phone records do show that Westlake received a call on his mobile at 03.00. Bearing in mind that social calls are not usually made at such times, it is highly likely that this call would have had some bearing on the case. Accordingly, the details should have been disclosed to the defence; they were not.

In November, with the trial approaching, documentation had to be handed over to the defence. The defence received the records of Westlake's calls in a scrambled form. Calls are listed in the following order: undated, 12 April, 22 March, 12 April, 22 March, 26 March, 12 April, 01 April, 12 April, 26 March, et cetera. No one would be able to tell at a glance that there was no record of a 02.27 call from Westlake to Wayne. Under the stress of last-minute trial preparation, no one was going to be able to go through the phone records comprehensively.

Further, the defence inferred that the confusion over the timing of phone calls could be attributed to the fact that Wayne had not altered his setting from Greenwich Mean Time to British Summer Time, when clocks had changed two weeks earlier. Leaving aside the fact that these telecommunications records were provided by major companies (Orange and Virgin Mobile) whose timings, just like those on all our computers and up-to-date technology, are instantly and automatically adjusted from GMT to BST, so there is no confusion whatever – leaving that aside, this was still a serious blunder.

It is crucial that Wayne's phone settings were out not by one hour, but by one hour *and one minute*. This is not surprising. It is difficult for anyone to adjust time settings to a specific minute.

One needs to re-examine that original *Chronology of Events* drawn up by police. The timing of the 'Im at the door' text is given as 02.34. The police were working from the information (from Westlake's phone data) that the text was sent from Westlake's to Wayne's phone at 02:35:10, and (from Wayne's phone handset) that it was received at 01:34:32. (Again, this emphasises the importance of corresponding records; the text was sent and received, and that is fully confirmed by the documentation.)

When the police incorporated that into the *Chronology* on 13 May, the timing was given as 02:34 – indicating that they had taken it from Wayne's records, which *they had adjusted for BST*; if they had taken it from Westlake's records, they would obviously have written in the time as 02:35.

This underlines that, six months before the case went to trial, the police were fully aware that Wayne's records had not been adjusted to BST. However, the defence were informed of this only at the last minute, just as the trial was starting, and so were duped into believing that the GMT/BST disparity was the explanation of the discrepancies in the phone records.

A document then appeared which purported to be a list of the outgoing calls and texts from Westlake. However, the document (numbered 639 in the court bundle) appears very strange. These records should all be computerised; there should be proper documentation. This purported list contained no official identifying marks. It contained several errors. It looked crude and inauthentic. Anyone could relatively easily have drawn up a similar document. In any event, this didn't remove the problem that according to the primary, original data there was no record of Westlake having made this call or of Wayne having received it.

Although the defence team at trial was out of its depth in dealing with these matters, it must be emphasised that there are hundreds of pages of telephone information. It can take weeks to analyse data in order to be able to unscramble it. Now that parliament has enacted a schedule that allows the prosecution to use ambush evidence at trial – as also happened with the pathologist's important statement, first shown to the defence on the morning that the trial started – there is no possibility that any defence team, however expert, however well-equipped, would be able to assimilate and react to the new information in time.

P130, line 8 Amongst other things, Emma told the CCRC that Wayne had threatened to kill her before, and that it was 'normal' for him to pin her against the wall as a 'warning', but the way he had pinned her against the stair spindles in those early hours of 12 April five years earlier, was 'not his normal grab'.

P151, para 8 Public Interest Immunity is a procedural device that allows the Crown to keep the defence in the dark regarding some areas of evidence, on the grounds, for example, that they do not wish to alert criminals to surveillance techniques (as would no doubt have been argued in this case).

P175 The actual text message read:
I HAVE FINISHE U AND U CAN TEL CARA IF I C HER I WIL SMASH HER FA2E IN U DICK I 3UCKING HATE U RO U CAN TEL HER WOT A PHYCO I AM U FUCKING FAIRY

P176 The actual text message read:
IVE JUST HAD SOME MAN SHOUT OUT FROM THE BUSHER
THAT I HAD BDTEQ COME IN THE BUSHER CAUSE HE HAD
A GUN POINTING AT MY HEAD GBDTI WAS SO SCARED I
GQANG U...
... UP BUT U CARED THAT MUCH U HAD LE3T THE PHONE
NF

P194, para 3 Lord Devlin: see note below

P196, para 1 Historically, identification evidence had been the bane of
the criminal justice process. The Adolf Beck case (1895-1904) brought
the issue of mistaken identification evidence to the forefront of public
attention and led directly to the setting-up of the Court of Appeal.

However, for the next three-quarters of a century, the problem was
allowed to fester. Finally, after a cluster of cases had again highlighted
the issue, an inquiry was set up under Lord Devlin. His report, delivered
in April 1976, recommended that prosecutions should not go ahead in
cases which depended solely on identification evidence: there needed to
be corroborative evidence, and judges must also give specific warnings to
juries about the problems inherent in identification evidence.

The recommendations were never put into law but were given
legal force later that year by the Court of Appeal in the leading case of
Turnbull and so became known as the Turnbull guidelines. However, this
deprived defendants of the strict protection against wrongful identification being enshrined in statute law, which was what Devlin had strongly
recommended.

Nevertheless, an issue which had bedevilled the system for decades
virtually disappeared overnight. In fact, protection for those accused of
sexual assault had already been provided through the Sexual Offences
Act 1956, which had emphasised the need for corroboration of witness
testimony. However, the Criminal Justice and Public Order Act 1994
repealed those passages of the act, removing the need for corroborative
evidence in cases of sexual assault and, at the same time, undermining the
legal framework that Devlin had drawn up.

P203, fourth para Malkinson's solicitor, who was then practising in
Oldham, pleaded guilty to fraud offences and was sentenced to twelve
months' imprisonment. He was struck off the solicitors' roll in December
1993. In 2002, he applied to be readmitted. Malkinson noted wryly that
his application was based in part on the fact that he had 'worked closely'
with the police and, indeed, his application was supported by the Chief
Constable of Greater Manchester.

Despite this, in March 2002, his application for readmission was rejected. Nevertheless, he went on to represent Malkinson at his trial in February 2004 and, of course, conveyed nothing of this to him.

P221, line 8 In May 2014, during a television interview given as part of a promotional tour for her new film, the actress Charlize Theron compared media intrusion into her private life with being raped. There was an ensuing controversy over whether that was a legitimate comparison. Of course, that is a huge subject. One would, however, make two observations: firstly, she did not give the impression that she was making the comparison gratuitously; and, secondly, anyone whose considerable income is derived from the sale of their work directly to the public must necessarily accept at least a degree of intrusion. The experience is bound to be of a different order for someone who has always been, and who has expected to remain, an entirely private person.

P235, line 6 Jailhouse snitches are routinely used by the prosecution in both the UK and the US. The suggestion will be made in court that a defendant has confessed in prison to a fellow inmate. Indeed, the opportunity to manufacture jailhouse snitch evidence is one particular reason why the prosecution is so interested in remanding suspects into custody. (The broader reason is that it will restrict the suspect's access to legal advice and will seriously compromise his ability to mount a defence case at trial.)

The chances of jailhouse snitch evidence being perjured are astronomically high. Prisoners are uniquely vulnerable, and may have a variety of reasons for wishing to ingratiate themselves with the authorities. Some, like Glen Banks, will be of very low intellectual calibre; others will be emotionally labile.

Jurors are advised not merely to disregard the testimony of jailhouse snitches, but seriously to consider throwing out *any* case in which such evidence is brought forward – on the logical basis that the mere use of jailhouse snitches is a sure sign of barrel-scraping by the prosecution.

P250, para 3 The Crown Prosecution Service was set up in October 1986 primarily to prevent what were thought of as 'police hunch' cases going to trial. Its objectives then, as itemised by the Director of Public Prosecutions, included 'to be, and to be seen to be, independent of the police'; 'to ensure that the general quality of decision-making and case preparation is of a high level'; 'to conduct cases vigorously and without delay' and 'to seek to improve the performance of the criminal justice system as a whole'. (see Joshua Rozenberg, *The Case for the Crown*, Equation Publishing, 1987).

In pursuing these objectives, the CPS has not distinguished itself. Its most conspicuous failure is never having been seen to be independent of the police. Its work appears solely directed towards increasing the number of convictions. Far from 'improving the performance of the criminal justice system', it has – as with the case of Gordon Park – helped to accelerate its decline.

P251, three lines from bottom Tony Benn died on 14 March 2014

P252, para 3 It was difficult to understand why the Gill Beckingham case was in the criminal justice process at all. At the end of the trial, she was found guilty of a charge under section 7 of the Health and Safety at Work Act 1974, but the jurors were unable to reach a verdict on the main charge of the manslaughter of seven people. Astonishingly, the prosecution then decided to take her to retrial. This time, with no police interference from the public gallery, she was acquitted.

P285, para 3 'Jonathan' is not the real name.

P309, para 2 The judge's comments were shocking because they were untrue and because they would certainly have misled the jury. However it is important to point out that *even if they had been accurate* they would still have misled the jury, as the quote from George Orwell, on the previous page, makes clear. Whether police informers are destitute, emotionally damaged, drug- or alcohol-dependent, or a combination of all, they are in no position to bargain – and the price of perjury, as we know from other cases, can be amazingly small.

P315, line 2 Giuseppe Vincini is not the real name.

P346, line 2 Simon Hattenstone, The Rise and Fall of the UK's King of Spin, the *Guardian*, 2 May 2014

P359, last para On 28 April 2014, Max Clifford was found guilty of eight indecent assaults on women whose ages ranged from fifteen to nineteen. He was sentenced to eight years' imprisonment. 'Live by the sleaze, die by the sleaze', wrote Hattenstone (see above).

P358, para 4 *Eyewitness*: see also page 195

P367, three lines from bottom Both Coulson and Hinton would later resign over the phone-hacking scandal. Coulson stood trial at the Old Bailey in October 2013. He was found guilty of conspiracy to intercept voicemails (messages left on telephone handsets) and, in July 2014, was sentenced to eighteen months' imprisonment.

P390, para 2 Car-ringing is a profitable business. A car will be stolen and its registration and other identifying features changed, usually to be replaced with those of a vehicle that has been written off. The car can then be sold on to an unsuspecting buyer. The headache for anyone buying a ringed car is that legally it won't belong to them; it will belong to the former owner or his insurance company.

P390, para 3 Lucy Richards' age is given as fifteen in some documents and sixteen in others. The name is not her real one.

P395, para 1 Documents that defence lawyers only saw for the first time in 2013 included an internal message of 20 February 1992 which reveals that police officers knew then that Shippey's briefcases were an Antler (made by a UK company) and a Samsonite (made by a US company). So the attempt at trial, twenty months later, to portray Watson's German-manufactured briefcase as one stolen from Shippey was highly misleading.

P397, four lines from bottom Cousins gave evidence in three sessions: from 4-5 November 1993; on 11 November; and on 25 November. He was to give evidence for a fourth time at Watson's appeal in January 1996.

P401, line 2 One of the slightly disquieting, but nevertheless inbuilt, features of the criminal justice system is that the process itself will frequently give testimony a greater coherence and credibility than it intrinsically possesses. This is because later in the trial the account will be reported back to the jury by the judge in the course of the summing-up. Because clarity of communication is paramount he or she will, merely through professional rigour, reshape the testimony into a comprehensible narrative. I need hardly add that this process is then continued if an author needs to relate what happened. Again, it all needs to be put as plainly as possible. The end result is that the description of Cousins' combined testimonies given here, while still containing non sequiturs and other illogicalities, is more coherent than the original account, or accounts, that he gave during his appearances in the witness-box.

P406, para 3 It should be added that, in addition to all the inconsistencies, ESDA (electrostatic document analysis) and oblique light analysis testing of Cousins' statement revealed further discrepancies, and suggested that he may well have given different details on pages which were then discarded.

P407, four lines from bottom In fact, many years later, Watson's defence lawyers did decide to consult their own expert. Dr Sacha Kolar, the Home Office pathologist, echoed Dr West's findings. In his report of 24

February 2011, he said, 'Like Dr West... I am uncomfortable that suffi-cient force could be generated to cause the penetration of the sternum in the restricted setting of the deceased resting upon the alleged assailant in the vehicle'.

P412, four lines from bottom In November 2013, Surrey Police finally acknowledged in a letter to Watson's solicitor that Shippey's briefcase containing the ledger and a computer disc had actually been taken by police from Shippey's home address, presumably in the days following the murder. It should be added that, according to Watson, these com-ments of the judge were used by the Prison Service for the next twenty years to discredit him – yet they are entirely inaccurate.

P415, para 4 The reports concerning Cousins' complaint to police were uncovered by the CCRC during their inquiries. They then asked Cousins about this matter in April 2012, with the upshot that he denied ever having made such a complaint. Watson's lawyers argued that, in their consideration of the case, the CCRC ought to have taken into account Cousins' conduct at this meeting. He attended with his lawyer, then tried to leave, then had a private consultation with the lawyer, and then left having denied all knowledge of his complaint, a matter that appeared to be properly documented in police records. All this, said Watson's legal team, should have cast further doubt on his openness and credibility.

P416 para 3 Gisli Gudjonsson, emeritus professor of forensic psychology at King's College, London, is world-renowned for his work on suggest-ibility, the vulnerability of suspects in police custody and false confessions. His books include *The Psychology of Interrogations and Confessions* (John Wiley, 2003).

P416, para 6 To this day, the CPS maintain that they never had sight of Dr Craissati's report before the trial. After Watson's conviction, his defence asked the CPS if they had been in possession of psychiatric or medical reports on Cousins prior to trial. On 21 September 1995, they responded:

> There is a duty upon the court to obtain and consider in all cases of murder, a psychiatric report before sentence... Neither the CPS nor prosecution counsel are allowed to see such a report which is in fact forwarded to the Court...
> The prosecution in accordance with normal practice requested a report... However the prosecution did not have sight of the report... This remained the case in fact up to March 1995 when the Craissati report [was] forwarded to the CPS by Cousins' solicitors.

William Clegg QC, who was acting for Watson at appeal, wrote that 'those instructing me have made extensive inquiries... We have unearthed no evidence that the CPS ever had a copy. The CPS themselves have issued a written denial'.

Nevertheless, the matter is very strange.

First of all, the CPS acknowledged the requirement 'in accordance with *normal practice*' to obtain 'a psychiatric report *before sentence*'. Of course, that itself is correct; but it didn't apply in this instance. The report was commissioned prior to trial – *not before sentence*. This was not *normal practice*. The first two sentences of the report are: *This report is prepared for the CPS. I understand that Mr Cousins is pleading not guilty to charges of murder, kidnapping and false imprisonment.* So the CPS response of 21 September 1995 is clearly disingenuous.

Secondly, the CPS say they only obtained the report from Cousins' own solicitors. Yet, if the report had been prepared for court proceedings, it would have been lodged with the court. Why had the CPS not obtained it from there? If defence solicitors had received a copy but not the CPS, that would have been exceptionally strange.

Thirdly, the report itself is headed: *This report is prepared for the Crown Prosecution Service.* As a matter of plain common sense, this should have been regarded as clinching proof that this was indeed a report for the CPS.

Dr Craissati would have been paid for her report. So who paid her? One imagines that it must have been the CPS.

It should also be pointed out that, although it turned out that Watson's lawyers had seen the Craissati report before appeal, Watson himself had always maintained that he was unaware of it until November 1998.

P422 line 4 On the close relationship between the Murdoch press and the UK authorities, see also pages 366–68.

P424, para 2 After the escalation of public concern about miscarriages of justice in the 1980s and early 1990s, parliament brought in the Criminal Appeal Act 1995. Curiously, this act did nothing whatever to try to stem the tide of miscarriages of justice. It did, however, establish the Criminal Cases Review Commission (CCRC), a body specifically set up to identify cases of wrongful conviction and then, when there was a 'real possibility' that the convictions would not be upheld on appeal, return them to the appeal court.

The CCRC started its work on 1 April 1997, and Watson applied to it that same year. The CCRC, however, turned down his case in September 2000. So Watson re-applied, and in September 2003 he suffered a second rejection. Undaunted, he applied again and was rejected in October 2007. So he then applied a fourth time, only to receive another thumbs-down in February 2014.

The 2014 rejection was the most telling demonstration to date of the failure of the 1995 Act to deal with the problem of miscarriages of justice; and, beyond that, it was also indicative of the UK's enduring administrative inability to put right what has gone seriously wrong.

Rather than examining the cumulative force of the evidence of wrongful conviction – which was overwhelming – the CCRC tackled the case in a piecemeal way. They argued that there was no ultimate unfairness as a consequence of the non-disclosure because 'it is established that disclosure post-trial and pre-appeal can cure unfairness' and, at appeal, Watson's lawyers had chosen not to use the psychiatric report.

At trial, the CCRC stated, the defence strategy was 'to paint Cousins as an outright villain in his own standing'. As such, the belatedly-disclosed psychiatric report would have conflicted with, rather than strengthened, their previous arguments.

However, the CCRC should have taken into consideration that the trial strategy was formulated at a time when important material was being improperly withheld. Colin Furness, Watson's trial solicitor, wrote in November 1999:

> It is obvious that if the report had been available, a different and perhaps more pressing style would have been adopted... the [defence] team's view of how to deal with Cousins was based on less than adequate information, as it turned out... Ultimately, if we had known what is [now] known about Cousins, [we] would have gone in harder [in cross-examination].

Mr Justice Owen confirmed that if defence lawyers had been provided with the information, as they should have been, then 'the defence [may have] been conducted on an *entirely different footing*' (italics added).

In 2001, Lord Woolf, the Lord Chief Justice, said: 'If a defendant has been denied a fair trial, it will almost be inevitable that the conviction will be regarded as unsafe'.

This seemed incontrovertible. The CCRC, however, seized on the use of the word 'almost' to assert that an unfair trial would not necessarily mean that a conviction was unsafe. They then deemed the Watson case to be one of those rare exceptions.

In two respects, the CCRC seem to have misinterpreted Lord Woolf's comment. Firstly, of course there were going to be rare exceptions, but those exceptions would be in cases where, as the Court of Appeal later emphasised, 'the appellant's conviction was *a foregone conclusion*' (italics added). Clearly, this could not apply to the Watson case, in which every single aspect is controversial.

Secondly, Woolf said what was 'almost inevitable' was the quashing of the conviction; but that was the second stage. The first stage, the only one with which the CCRC is concerned, is whether the 'real possibility' test has been passed. Lord Woolf might perhaps have expanded and clarified his comment by saying: 'If a defendant has been denied a fair trial, *it is inevitable that the case will be referred back to appeal by the CCRC* and almost inevitable that the conviction will *then* be regarded as unsafe'. We do not know; but we do know that it is a two-stage process, and the CCRC appeared to confuse the second with the first stage.

So they should have taken one of the four opportunities they were given to refer it to appeal; certainly, at the very latest, the case had passed the 'real possibility' test by 2008. By not referring it to appeal, they were guilty of extraordinary blunders: they were failing in their own responsibilities; they were usurping the functions of the Court of Appeal, the body constitutionally entrusted with resolving matters such as an unfair trial process; and, having encroached onto its territory and appropriated its decision-making powers, they then compounded the error by reaching the wrong decision.

Mr Justice Owen, who found in 2008 that Karl Watson had not had a fair trial, subsequently chaired the inquiry into the death of Alexander Litvinenko. His report concluded that Litvinenko, the Russian dissident who was granted asylum in the UK and became a British citizen, was murdered in an FSB (Federal Security Service) operation that was 'probably approved by Nikolai Patrushev, the then Director of the FSB, and also by [Russian] President Vladimir Putin'.

The inquiry report, published on 21 January 2016, was widely praised. In the *Observer*, Will Hutton described it as 'a classic of the genre – scrupulously evidence-based, impartial and judicious. It is what a rule-of-law society should produce'.

P430, line 2 See *Re-Trial by TV: The Rise and Fall of Rough Justice* (BBC4, 4 April 2011)

P432, para 6 Article 17 of the European Union's data protection directive grants citizens 'the right to be forgotten'. In May 2014 the Court of Justice (ECJ) upheld that principle, ordering Google to remove links that were deemed 'inadequate, irrelevant or *no longer relevant*' (my italics). Would the 'no longer relevant' provision apply to those with a criminal past (even assuming that the Court can ever ensure that it applies to those without one)? See Charlotte McDonald-Gibson, Google must delete 'irrelevant' links, rules top EU court, *The Independent*, 13 May 2014.

In June 2014, the Supreme Court ruled that 'some past cautions and convictions' should not be disclosed as part of criminal records checks on those seeking employment (Clive Coleman, BBC News, 18 June 2014).

P433, bottom of page *The Independent*, 18 September 1993

P434, para 1 Whenever hostages – for example, John McCarthy and Terry Waite, held by Islamic terrorists in the Lebanon; and Ingrid Betancourt, the Colombian politician held in the jungle by FARC (Revolutionary Armed Forces of Colombia) guerrillas – are freed from long periods of captivity (in all these cases, roughly five to six years), the media focuses intently on the long-term psychological damage of their confinement and how long it might take them to recover from their ordeal. While no one would wish to underestimate their suffering in any way, it should be pointed out that periods of confinement suffered by the wrongly convicted in the UK can be significantly greater. For example, Victor Nealon was released in December 2013, having been wrongly imprisoned for *seventeen* years. Further, by preventing him from attending his own appeal, the Ministry of Justice denied him even the momentary sunburst of publicity that, one would have thought, was the very least that the State owed him. (see Bob Woffinden, *Inside Time*, February 2014; also see note page 412).

P434 para 5 *Living with Difference: Community, Diversity and the Common Good*, a report published by The Woolf Institute (7 December 2015) highlighted trends in society that have 'revolutionised the landscape on which religion and belief in Britain meet and interact'. The most notable of these trends was that the proportion of the UK population describing themselves as non-religious had leapt in a thirty-year period (1983–2013) from less than a third to almost half.

Even though the Woolf Institute has been named in honour of the Rt Hon Lord Woolf, the former Lord Chief Justice, I could find no reference in the report to the repercussions of this finding for oath-taking in criminal trials.

While some witnesses may choose to affirm, police officers and other prosecution witnesses will almost invariably swear on the Bible. In many instances, they will be doing so hypocritically; plainly, the taking of the oath has become a PR exercise.

P435, line 1 Ray Monk *Ludwig Wittgenstein The Duty of Genius* (Vintage 1991)

P437, para 4 *Picking Cotton*, Jennifer Thompson-Cannino and Ronald Cotton, St Martin's Press, New York, 2009

P439, para 4 In April 2014 Nicholas Jacobs was acquitted of the murder of police officer Keith Blakelock who was killed during riots on the Broadwater Farm estate in Tottenham, north London, in October 1985. Jacobs, who was sixteen at the time of the murder, did not go into the witness-box in his own defence.

This case has an exceptional history. Previously, three men – Winston Silcott, Mark Braithwaite and Engin Raghip – had been convicted of the murder, although their convictions were overturned on appeal in November 1991. Three years later, the *Guardian* reported (9 August 1994) that there was concern in Whitehall over the prosecution of this particular case and others because of 'the way in which the police were securing convictions in high profile cases'.

Nevertheless, twenty years later, Jacobs was put on trial for this offence on the evidence of three men who were all addicted to alcohol or drugs, who all had a criminal history, who were all testifying anonymously and at least two of whom had been, in the words of the Crown QC, 'provided with financial assistance by the police'.

The fact that the case went to trial at all highlighted, specifically, the baleful effect of the legal provision to allow anonymous evidence in court; and, more generally, the deterioration in criminal justice over the past quarter-century. In the immediate aftermath of the murder, higher standards would have been applied. 'It is surprising that the charge was brought in the first place', commented Courtney Griffiths QC, Jacobs's barrister, 'because much of the evidence relied on *was available twenty-eight years ago and the prosecution decided not to proceed at that time.*'

P442, para 5 The author, the dissident and a trial held in secret: Duncan Campbell and Richard Norton-Taylor, the *Guardian*, 23 January 2014. See also note, page 407

P443, para 1 Geoffrey Robertson and Andrew G.L.Nicol, *Media Law*, Sage Publications, 1984

P443, para 3 In August 1975, six men – Paddy Hill, Gerry Hunter, Richard McIlkenny, Billy Power, John Walker and Hugh Callaghan – were convicted of bombings in Birmingham city centre that killed twenty-one people. They were sentenced to life imprisonment. Appeals in 1976 and again in 1987 failed, before the men finally succeeded at the appeal court and were released in March 1991. They had served seventeen years' wrongful imprisonment.

P444, para 5 UK authorities always seem intimidated by the Murdoch press. On 28 April 2014, in a particularly heartbreaking case, the schoolteacher Ann Maguire was stabbed to death in front of her class at Corpus Christi College in Leeds. One of her fifteen-year-old pupils was arrested. In such circumstances, the press and broadcasting organisations can nticipate that, as soon as charges are laid and the case reaches court, there will be an order prohibiting the naming of the youth. However, there is inevitably a hiatus between the incident itself and the start of the court case. During this period, the overwhelming majority of the media behaved in accordance with the widely-anticipated – indeed, virtually inevitable – ruling of the judge. The *Sun* newspaper, however, named the youth on its front page.

When the case did reach court, the judge did impose the expected reporting restrictions and gave a stern warning to those whom he termed social media users that there would be 'serious consequences' if these were breached. So: the man and woman in the street would face 'serious consequences'; but for the *Sun*, which had already defiantly let the cat out of the bag, there would be no 'consequences' at all.

P445, para 2 In June 2014, the Crown Prosecution Service applied to hold a terrorism trial entirely in secret, with even the names of the defendants being withheld. Mr Justice Nicol (the co-author, thirty years earlier, of *Media Law*, see page 443) acceded to the request.

This took the near-total secrecy provisions from the Wang Yam trial to their logical – or, as many would maintain, illogical – conclusion. The development was condemned by many national newspapers: 'Britain's First Secret Trial', *Daily Mail*; 'case to be first for centuries heard entirely in secret', the *Guardian* (5 June 2014). The CPS argued that if it was to be heard in public, 'there was a serious possibility that the trial may not be able to go ahead'.

The matter was then argued before the Court of Appeal. The judges brushed aside the CPS's fears and instead expressed 'grave concerns' about the 'cumulative effects' of a trial held in secret. Accordingly, they ordered that the defendants should be named – they were Erol Incedal and Mounir Rarmoul-Bouhadjar – and that parts of the trial should be held in open court and that a group of accredited journalists would be allowed to sit through the entire proceedings.

The CPS's desire for secrecy had proved counter-productive: they had now created such a high level of interest in the case that aspects of it would certainly be reported; had they just taken it to court in the normal way, it may well have slipped under the media radar.

P446, para 3 Nigel Evans faces ruin over £100,000 gay sex case bill: Frances Gibb, the *Times*, 12 April 2014. (The costs figure was subsequently estimated at £130,000.)

P450 para 2 The Coroners and Justice Act 2009 introduced an 'exploitation proceeds order' which would be taken out against those writing about serious offences of which they had been convicted. This would apply irrespective of the fact that the motivation of many would have been precisely to draw attention to their case and explain why their convictions were wrongful. They would then have been able to use any proceeds to fund further legal representations.

The Act was not restricted to memoirs, but covered any remuneration received 'by any means whatsoever'. So the Labour government of the time was not only wrongly convicting innocent people but also closing off possible avenues to retrospective justice.

P450, para 3 The Price of Injustice, Matt Foot and Paul May, *Inside Time*, March 2014. They wrote that the proposed change, introduced as a provision of the Anti-Social Behaviour, Crime and Policing Bill, would place 'an impossible burden' on miscarriage of justice victims who would need 'categorically to prove their innocence' (a concept with which, historically, the criminal justice process has never been concerned) in order to be granted compensation.

Victor Nealon, a 36-year-old Irishman, was at home decorating on the evening of 15 September 1996 when he was arrested by West Mercia police for an indecent assault six weeks earlier. On the basis of evidence that was either mistaken or dishonest, he was convicted of attempted rape and sentenced to seven years' imprisonment. Because he protested his innocence, he ended up serving seventeen years before, on 13 December 2013, the Court of Appeal quashed his conviction. On 17 June 2014, Chris Grayling, Justice Secretary, informed Mark Newby, Nealon's solicitor, that he would not pay his client any compensation for wrongful imprisonment.

P451, three lines from bottom *The Times*, 23 March 2011

P455, para 2 In May 2014, the UK charity Nesta (National Endowment for Science, Technology and the Arts) announced a £10 million Longitude prize for solving one of the scientific and environmental challenges that the world faces today. 'If you want to solve a problem', the charity's chief executive explained, 'one method is to go to top scientists. But over the years, and this was something pioneered by the original Longitude prize in the eighteenth century, it's often better to open it up to anyone.' Exactly the same principle – that the answer may lie not with the professionals but out there in the community – should apply in criminal justice. Jurors have already been recruited for their common sense and individual experiences. They should be encouraged to apply these fully, not to have them circumscribed by what are best described as fuddy-duddy rules.

P455, para 4 In January 2012, Dr Theodora Dallas, a psychology lecturer at the University of Bedfordshire, was sentenced to six months' imprisonment for conducting background research via the internet into a case she was hearing as a juror. In December 2013, she announced her intention of taking her conviction to the European Court of Human Rights. However, her appeal was not to be on the ground (as I would have ideally wanted it to be) that she was enhancing, rather than undermining, the administration of justice. Instead, her challenge was on the ground that, having been born in Greece, she was not a native English speaker and the judge's instructions had not been sufficiently clear.

P455, para 5 Dominic Grieve comments: see the *Guardian* 23 January 2012; and the *Independent* 30 July 2013.

P457, para 4 For an example of the police zealously pursuing such 'offences', there is the experience of Michael Abberton, an assessor for an examinations board, who was visited by two Cambridgeshire police officers after using his Twitter account to publish satirical material about UKIP, the political party. See: MP condemns police for sending two officers to home of Twitter user *Daily Mail* 13 May 2014.

P457, para 5 In June 2014 Leeds magistrates sentenced Jake Newsome, 21, to six weeks' imprisonment for posting a Facebook message about the murdered Leeds schoolteacher Ann Maguire. The message was certainly unpleasant. However, one feels that the matter could have been dealt with much less censoriously and that the remedy might instead lie – as schoolteachers would doubtless agree – in education.

P457, line 5 The government should probably start a public safety campaign: *Think before you tweet.* Frequently even the well-placed and highly intelligent are embarrassed by thoughtless tweets. But perhaps the whole point of Twitter is to eliminate proper thought processes.

P461, last line On 27 May 2014, a front-page headline in the *Daily Telegraph* read: If NHS [National Health Service] were an airline, 'planes would fall out of the sky all the time', says [leading] QC.

It was difficult to resist the thought that if a leading surgeon had been asked to examine the UK criminal justice system, he might well have reached a parallel conclusion: that if the criminal justice system were an airline, planes would be dropping out of the sky all the time.

Acknowledgements and sources

I owe an enormous debt of gratitude to those convicted of these crimes and their families and friends for taking the time to explain, at what may well have seemed to them tedious length, just who they are and what has befallen them. The text has been constructed largely from their accounts and reminiscences, as well as from the case documents.

In several instances, lawyers have been very helpful and I am especially grateful for their assistance. I would particularly like to thank Maslen Merchant of Hadgkiss Hughes and Beale, and also the barrister Arthur Blake.

David Godwin has been an enduring source of support and encouragement, as too has Heather Godwin. She also edited the manuscript brilliantly. Jane Roberts took on the difficult task of copyediting the book, and I am grateful for her enthusiasm and punctiliousness. I am also immensely grateful to Adam Speker, of 5RB in Gray's Inn Square, for his valuable advice and careful consideration of the manuscript.

Whenever difficulties need to be resolved, I have been fortunate in being able to turn to Steve Sinclair who has an astute understanding of all these issues. My former colleague Richard Webster tragically died in 2011, but his guiding spirit never seems far away. There are still moments when I realise that what I have just written would never have passed his exacting standards, and delete it immediately.

And thanks for everything, as ever, to Anne and Kate and Eddie.

Also available from Bojangles Books

Bad Show

The Quiz, the Cough, the Millionaire Major
by
Bob Woffinden and James Plaskett

On 10 September 2001, Major Charles Ingram won the
£1million prize on ITV's top-rated quiz show, *Who Wants To
Be A Millionaire?*

Glitter and confetti showered down on him and his wife,
Diana. He was feted as the programme's third million-pound
winner.

But within a week his triumph has turned to dust. Allegations
were made that he was cheating and that the coughing of a
fellow contestant had guided him to the correct answers.

ITV called in the Metropolitan Police.

In 2003, eighteen months after the programme recording,
Charles and Diana were both found guilty.

These developments became newsworthy on television and
radio bulletins across the world. More than half-a-million newspaper articles were written about the supposed 'coughing' plot.
ITV's documentary about its case was watched by over sixteen
million viewers in the UK and was sold throughout the world.

Ingram had to resign his commission in the army. He lost not
only the million-pound prize but also everything he already had.
He faced life as a ruined man.

But what really happened?

Bad Show tells the true story of the events of that night,
and what occurred during the months beforehand and what
happened afterwards.

It is a story that, for all the extraordinary levels of publicity
that the case has received, has never been told before.

ISBN: 978-0-9930755-2-0
eISBN: 978-0-9930755-3-7

Index

Note: asterisked names are not the actual names of the people concerned; their names have been changed either through legal requirements or for reasons of sensitivity.